Pr

Adobe
Premiere Pro CC
2019 release

CLASSROOM IN A BOOK®
The official training workbook from Adobe

Maxim Jago

Adobe Premiere Pro CC Classroom in a Book® (2019 release)

Writer: Maxim Jago
Adobe Press Executive Editor: Laura Norman
Development Editor: Victor Gavenda
Senior Production Editor: Tracey Croom
Technical Reviewer: Jarle Leirpoll
Keystroke Reviewer: David Van Ness
Copyeditor: Kim Wimpsett
Proofreader: Scout Festa
Compositor: Kim Scott, Bumpy Design
Indexer: James Minkin
Cover Designer: Eddie Yuen
Cover Illustration: Benoit Paillé, www.behance.net/Benoitp
Interior Designer: Mimi Heft

ISBN-13: 978-0-13-529889-3
ISBN-10:   0-13-52988-9

4 2019

WHAT'S ON THE DISC

Here is an overview of the contents of the Classroom in a Book disc.

The *Adobe Premiere Pro CC Classroom in a Book (2019 release)* disc includes the lesson files that you'll need to complete the exercises in this book. Each lesson has its own folder in the Lessons folder. In addition, there is an Assets folder containing files that are used for multiple lessons.

You will need to copy **the entire Lessons folder** to your hard drive before you can begin the lessons. This will require about 7 GB of storage, so make sure you have sufficient free space on your storage device before beginning. See the "Getting Started" section at the beginning of this book for more detailed instructions.

● **Note:** If you have purchased an ebook edition of this book, you'll need to download the lesson files from peachpit.com. You'll find instructions for doing so on the first page of the ebook, in the section "How to get your lesson files," and in "Online content" in "Getting Started."

Important!

The video clips and other media files provided with this book are practice files, provided for your personal use in these lessons only. You are not authorized to use these files commercially or to publish, share, or distribute them in any form without written permission from Adobe Systems, Inc., and the individual copyright holders of the various items. Do not share videos created with these lesson files publicly. This includes, but is not limited to, distribution via social media or online video services including YouTube and Vimeo. You will find a complete copyright statement on the copyright page at the beginning of this book.

Thanks to Patrick Cannell for the music "Ambient Heavens," Copyright © 2015 by Patrick Cannell.

Thanks to Patrick Cannell for the music "Cooking Montage," Copyright © 2015 by Patrick Cannell.

Footage from *Andrea Sweeney NYC*, Copyright © 2015 by Maxim Jago.

Footage from *Laura in the Snow*, Copyright © 2015 by Maxim Jago.

Footage from *Theft Unexpected*, Copyright © 2014 by Maxim Jago.

Footage from *She,* Copyright © 2017 by Maxim Jago.

ACKNOWLEDGMENTS

Producing effective learning materials for such an advanced technology is a team effort. Friends, colleagues, fellow filmmakers, and technology experts have all contributed to this book. There are too many names to mention, but let's say this: I have often joked that in Britain we don't say "awesome." Instead, we say "perfectly acceptable." On this occasion, "perfectly acceptable" isn't enough. Rather, I will have to say our British equivalent of "super awesome": Those people who make this world better by sharing, nurturing, caring, showing, telling, demonstrating, making, and helping are all "definitely more than acceptable."

Everything on these pages was inspected by a team of experienced editors who checked and corrected typos, spelling errors, naming errors, false attributions, suspect grammar, unhelpful phrasing, and inconsistent descriptions. This wonderful team didn't just highlight text that needed correcting. They offered positive alternatives that I could simply agree to, so in a literal sense, this book is the product of many people's contributions. I'd like to thank the teams at Peachpit and Adobe Press, who made it possible to produce such a beautifully finessed work.

As each draft lesson was completed, and with the helpful guidance of Laura Norman, the most amazing and highly experienced Victor Gavenda checked over the text to make sure it was ideally accessible for learners, and all references to the technology were run by the remarkable media technology expert Jarle Leirpoll, who has an incredible depth of knowledge of Premiere Pro.

An amount of the content of this book is derived from material written by Richard Harrington, five versions back. The original table of contents was worked out by the two of us, and though I have updated Richard's lessons, rephrased, and reworded them, a substantial amount remains unchanged or is significantly informed by his great original work.

Finally, let's not forget Adobe. The passion and enthusiasm demonstrated by those wonderful individuals, who are so committed to creatives like you and me, qualifies as "the most acceptable of all." They are, indeed, extraordinarily awesome!

—Maxim Jago

CONTENTS

GETTING STARTED

Adobe Premiere Pro CC, the essential editing application for professionals and video enthusiasts, is an incredibly scalable, efficient, and flexible video editing system. It supports a broad range of video, audio, and image formats. Premiere Pro lets you work faster and more creatively without converting your media. The complete set of powerful and exclusive tools lets you overcome any editorial, production, and workflow challenges to deliver the high-quality work you demand.

Importantly, Adobe has carefully developed a user experience that is intuitive, flexible, and efficient, with unified design elements that match across multiple applications, making it easier to explore and discover new workflows.

About Classroom in a Book

Adobe Premiere Pro CC Classroom in a Book (2019 release) is part of the official training series for Adobe graphics and publishing and creative video software. The lessons are designed so that you can learn at your own pace. If you're new to Premiere Pro, you'll learn the fundamental concepts and features you'll need to use the program. This book also teaches many advanced features, including tips and techniques for using the latest version of this software.

The lessons in this edition include opportunities for hands-on practice using features such as chromakeying, dynamic trimming, color correction, media management, audio and video effects, and audio mixing. You'll also learn how to create files for the web and mobile devices with Adobe Media Encoder. Premiere Pro CC is available for both Windows and macOS.

Prerequisites

Before beginning to use *Adobe Premiere Pro CC Classroom in a Book*, make sure your system is set up correctly and that you've installed the required software and hardware. You can view updated system requirements here:

helpx.adobe.com/premiere-pro/system-requirements.html

You should have a working knowledge of your computer and operating system. For example, you should know how to use the mouse and standard menus and commands and also how to open, save, and close files. If you need to review these techniques, see the documentation included with your Windows or macOS system.

It's not necessary to have a working knowledge of video concepts and terminology, but if you come across a term you're not familiar with, consult the glossary at the end of this book

Installing Premiere Pro CC

You must purchase an Adobe Creative Cloud subscription, or obtain a trial version, separately from this book. For system requirements and complete instructions on installing the software, visit www.adobe.com/support. You can purchase Adobe Creative Cloud by visiting www.adobe.com/creativecloud. Follow the on-screen instructions. In addition to Premiere Pro, you may want to install Adobe Photoshop CC, Adobe After Effects CC, Audition CC, Adobe Prelude CC, and Adobe Media Encoder CC, which are included with the full Adobe Creative Cloud license.

Optimizing performance

Editing video places high demands on your computer processor and memory. A fast processor and a lot of memory will make your editing experience faster and more efficient. This translates to a more fluid and enjoyable creative experience.

Premiere Pro CC takes advantage of multicore processors (CPUs) and multiprocessor systems. The faster the processors and the more CPU cores there are, the better the performance you'll experience.

The minimum system memory is 8 GB, and 16 GB or more is recommended for ultra-high-definition (UHD) media.

The speed of the storage drives you use for video playback is also a factor. A dedicated fast storage drive is recommended for your media. A RAID disk array or fast solid-state disk for your media files is strongly recommended, particularly if you're working with UHD or higher-resolution content. Storing your media files and program files on the same hard drive can affect performance. Keep your media files on a separate disk, if possible, for speed and media management.

The Premiere Pro Mercury Playback Engine can harness the power of your computer's graphics hardware, or *graphics processing unit* (GPU), to improve playback performance. GPU acceleration provides a significant performance improvement, and most video cards with at least 2 GB of dedicated memory will work. You will find information about hardware and software requirements on the Adobe website at helpx.adobe.com/premiere-pro/system-requirements.html.

Using the lesson files

The lessons in this book use supplied source files, including video clips, audio files, photos, and image files created in Photoshop and Illustrator. To complete the lessons in this book, you must copy all the lesson files to your computer's storage drive. Some lessons use files from other lessons, so you'll need to keep the entire collection of lesson assets on your storage drive as you work through the book. You will need about 7 GB of storage space for the lesson files.

If you have purchased an ebook edition of this book, you'll need to download the lesson files from peachpit.com. You'll find instructions for doing so on the first page of the ebook, in the section "How to get your lesson files," as well as later in this section, in "Online content."

If you've purchased the printed version, you can copy the lesson files from the *Adobe Premiere Pro CC Classroom in a Book* disc (inside the back cover of this book).

Here's how to copy those assets from the disc to your storage drive:

1   Open the *Adobe Premiere Pro CC Classroom in a Book* disc in the Finder (macOS) or in My Computer or Windows Explorer (Windows).

2   Right-click the folder called Lessons and choose Copy.

3   Navigate to the location you have chosen to store your Premiere Pro projects, right-click, and choose Paste.

If you do not have an optical drive capable of reading discs in DVD-ROM format connected to your computer, see the "Online content" section for more information about downloading the lesson files.

▶ **Tip:** If you don't have dedicated storage for your video files, placing the lesson files on your computer's desktop will make them easy to find and work with.

Relinking the lesson files

The Premiere Pro projects included with the lesson files have links to specific media files. Because you are copying the files to a new location, you may need to update those links when you open projects for the first time.

If you open a project and Premiere Pro is unable to find a linked media file, the Link Media dialog may open, inviting you to relink offline files. If this happens, select an offline clip on the list and click the Locate button. A browse panel will appear; use this to navigate to the file's location.

Locate the Lessons folder using the navigator on the left and click Search. Premiere Pro will locate the media file inside the Lessons folder. To hide all other files, making it easy to select the correct one, select the option to display only exact name matches.

● **Note:** If media files were originally stored in multiple locations, you may need to search more than once to relink all the media for a project.

The last known file path and file name and the currently selected file path and file name are displayed at the top of the panel for reference. Select the file and click OK.

The option to relink other files is enabled by default, so once you've located one file, the rest should reconnect automatically. For more information about relocating offline media files, see Lesson 18, "Managing Your Projects" (print customers, see "Bonus Material" later in this section).

How to use these lessons

The lessons in this book include step-by-step instructions. Each lesson stands alone, but most build on previous lessons. For this reason, the best way to learn from this book is to proceed through the lessons one after another.

The lessons teach you new skills in the order you might normally use them. The lessons begin with acquiring media files such as video, audio, and graphics, and they go on to creating a rough-cut sequence, adding effects, sweetening the audio, and ultimately exporting the project.

Many pages contain additional "sidebar" information boxes that explain a particular technology or offer alternative workflows. It's not necessary to read these additional boxes, or follow the workflows, to learn Premiere Pro, but you may find them interesting and helpful as they will deepen your understanding of post-production.

By the end of these lessons, you'll have a good understanding of the complete end-to-end video post-production workflow, with the specific skills you need to edit on your own.

As you explore the skills described in this book, you may find it helpful to review earlier lessons you have already completed and to practice the fundamental editing techniques regularly. The advanced workflows build on fundamental principles introduced early on, and taking a few moments to recap earlier lessons makes it easier to discover the common principles that apply. Ultimately this practice makes you better at training yourself.

Online content

Your purchase of this Classroom in a Book includes online materials provided by way of your Account page on peachpit.com (some of these materials duplicate items on the DVD-ROM provided with print editions of the book).

Lesson files

To work through the projects in this book, you will need to copy them from the disc (see "Using the lesson files") or download the lesson files from peachpit.com. You can download the files for individual lessons, or it may be possible to download them all in a single file.

Web Edition

The Web Edition is an online interactive version of the book providing an enhanced learning experience. Your Web Edition can be accessed from any device with a connection to the Internet, and it contains the following:

- The complete text of the book
- Hours of instructional video keyed to the text
- Interactive quizzes

In addition, the Web Edition may be updated when Adobe adds significant feature updates between major Creative Cloud releases. To accommodate the changes, sections of the online book may be updated or new sections may be added.

Accessing the lesson files and Web Edition

If you purchased an ebook from peachpit.com or adobepress.com, your Web Edition will automatically appear under the Digital Purchases tab on your Account page. Click the Launch link to access the product. Continue reading to learn how to register your product to get access to the lesson files.

If you purchased an ebook from a different vendor or you bought a print book, you must register your purchase on peachpit.com to access the online content:

1 Go to www.peachpit.com/register.

2 Sign in or create a new account.

3 Enter ISBN **9780135298893**.

4 Answer the questions as proof of purchase.

5 The Web Edition will appear on the Digital Purchases tab of your Account page. Click the Launch link to access the product.

The lesson files can be accessed through the Registered Products tab on your Account page. Click the Access Bonus Content link below the title of your product to proceed to the download page. Click the lesson file links to download them to your computer.

Bonus material

This book has so much great material that we couldn't fit it all in the printed pages, so we placed Lessons 17 and 18 on peachpit.com:

- Lesson 17: *Multicamera Editing*
- Lesson 18: *Managing your Projects*

You will find these on your account page (Lessons & Update Files tab) once you register your book, as described in "Accessing the lesson files and Web Edition."

Additional resources

Adobe Premiere Pro CC Classroom in a Book (2019 release) is not meant to replace documentation that comes with the program or to be a comprehensive reference for every feature. Only the commands and options used in the lessons are explained in this book. For comprehensive information about program features and tutorials, refer to the following resources, which you can reach by choosing commands from the Help menu. Some of these resources can also be reached by clicking the Learn button in the Home screen (described in Lesson 1) and following links on the Learn tab.

Adobe Premiere Pro CC Learn and Support: helpx.adobe.com/premiere-pro.html is where you can find and browse Help and Support content on Adobe.com. You can also reach that page by choosing Help > Adobe Premiere Pro Help or by pressing F1. On the Learn & Support page, click User Guide for documentation on individual features or visit helpx.adobe.com/premiere-pro/user-guide.html. On the User Guide page, click Premiere Pro CC manual (PDF) to download Help as a printable PDF document.

Adobe Premiere Pro CC tutorials: For a wide range of interactive tutorials on Adobe Premiere Pro CC features, choose Help > Adobe Premiere Pro Online Tutorials or visit helpx.adobe.com/premiere-pro/tutorials.html. You can also access the same tutorials from the Home screen by clicking Learn. A different set of tutorials is provided inside Premiere Pro on the Learn panel. To open it, choose either Help > Adobe Premiere Pro In-App Tutorials or Window > Workspaces > Learning.

Adobe Premiere Pro blog: theblog.adobe.com/creative-cloud/premiere-pro brings you tutorials, product news, and inspirational articles about using Adobe Premiere Pro CC.

Adobe Creative Cloud tutorials: For inspiration, key techniques, cross-product workflows, and updates on new features, go to the Creative Cloud tutorials page, helpx.adobe.com/creative-cloud/tutorials.html.

Adobe Forums: Tap into peer-to-peer discussions, questions, and answers on Adobe products at forums.adobe.com. Visit the Adobe Premiere Pro CC forum at forums.adobe.com/community/premiere.

Adobe Create: The online magazine *Create* offers thoughtful articles on design and design issues, a gallery showcasing the work of top-notch designers, tutorials, and more. Check it out at create.adobe.com.

Resources for educators: adobe.com/education and edex.adobe.com offer a treasure trove of information for instructors who teach classes on Adobe software. Find solutions for education at all levels, including free curricula that use an integrated approach to teaching Adobe software and that can be used to prepare for the Adobe Certified Associate exams.

Also, check out these useful sites:

Adobe Exchange: www.adobeexchange.com/creativecloud.html is a central resource for finding tools, services, extensions, code samples, and more to supplement and extend your Adobe products.

Adobe Premiere Pro CC product home page: adobe.com/products/premiere has more information about the product.

Adobe Authorized Training Centers

Adobe Authorized Training Centers offer instructor-led courses and training on Adobe products, employing only Adobe Certified Instructors. A directory of AATCs is available at training.adobe.com/trainingpartners.

1 TOURING ADOBE PREMIERE PRO CC

Lesson overview

In this lesson, you'll learn about the following:

- Performing nonlinear editing

- Exploring the standard digital video workflow

- Enhancing the workflow with high-level features

- Checking out the workspaces

- Customizing workspaces

- Setting keyboard shortcuts

 This lesson will take about 60 minutes to complete. Please log in to your account on peachpit.com to download the lesson files for this lesson, or go to the "Getting Started" section at the beginning of this book and follow the instructions under "Accessing the lesson files and Web Edition." Store the files on your computer in a convenient location.

Your Account page is also where you'll find any updates to the lesson files. Look on the Lesson & Update Files tab to access the most current content.

Adobe Premiere Pro is a video-editing system that supports the latest technology and cameras with powerful tools that are easy to use and that integrate perfectly with almost every video acquisition source.

Starting the lesson

There has never been greater demand for high-quality video content, and today's video producers and editors work in an ever-changing landscape of old and new technologies. Despite rapid change in camera systems and the distribution landscape, however, the goal of video editing is the same: You want to take your source footage and shape it, guided by your original vision, so that you can effectively communicate with your audience.

In Adobe Premiere Pro CC, you'll find a video-editing system that supports the latest technology and cameras with powerful tools that are easy to use. These tools integrate perfectly with almost every type of media, including immersive 360 Video, as well as a wide range of third-party plug-ins and other post-production tools.

You'll begin by reviewing the essential post-production workflow that most editors follow, and then you'll learn about the main components of the Premiere Pro interface and how to create custom workspaces.

Performing nonlinear editing in Premiere Pro

Premiere Pro is a *nonlinear editor* (NLE). Like a word processing application, Premiere Pro lets you place, replace, and move video, audio, and images anywhere you want in your final edited work. You don't need to make adjustments in a particular order; you can change any part of your editing project at any time—that's the nonlinear part of an NLE.

You'll combine multiple pieces of media, called *clips*, to create a sequence. You can edit any part of the sequence in any order and then change the contents or move clips so that they play earlier or later. You can blend layers of video together, change the image size, adjust the colors, add special effects, adjust the audio mix, and more.

You can combine multiple sequences and jump to any moment in a video clip without needing to fast-forward or rewind. Organizing the clips you're working with is like organizing files on your computer.

Premiere Pro supports both tape and tapeless media formats, including XDCAM EX, XDCAMHD 422, DPX, DVCProHD, QuickTime, AVCHD (including AVCCAM and NXCAM), AVC-Intra, DSLR video, and Canon XF. It even has native support for RAW video formats, including media from RED, ARRI, Sony, Canon, and Blackmagic cameras, as well as support for multiple 360 video formats.

● **Note:** The word *clip* comes from the days of celluloid film editing, where a section of film would be clipped to separate it from a reel.

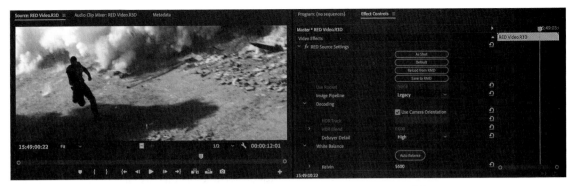

Premiere Pro features native support for RAW media from RED cameras, with settings to control the way the media is interpreted.

Using the standard digital video workflow

As you gain editing experience, you'll develop your own preferences for the order in which to work on the different aspects of your project. Each stage requires a particular kind of attention and different tools. Also, some projects call for more time spent on one stage than another.

Whether you skip through some stages with a quick mental check or spend hours (even days!) dedicated to perfecting an aspect of your project, you'll almost certainly go through the following steps:

1   **Acquire your media:** This can mean recording original footage, creating new animated content, or gathering a variety of assets for a project.

2   **Ingest the video to your storage drive:** With tapeless media, Premiere Pro can read the media files directly, usually with no need for conversion. If you're working with tapeless media, be sure to back up your files to a second location because storage drives sometimes fail unexpectedly. With tape-based formats, Premiere Pro (with the appropriate hardware) can convert the video into digital files. Use fast storage for smooth playback.

3   **Organize your clips:** Your project may have a lot of video content to choose from. Invest the time to organize clips into special folders (called *bins*) in your project. You can add color labels and other metadata (additional information about the clips) to help keep things organized.

4   **Create a sequence:** Combine the parts of the video and audio clips you want as a sequence in the Timeline panel.

5   **Add transitions:** Place special transition effects between clips, add video effects, and create combined visual effects by placing clips on multiple layers (called *tracks* in the Timeline panel).

6 **Create or import titles, graphics and captions:** Add them to your sequence along with your video clips.

7 **Adjust the audio mix:** Adjust the volume of your audio clips to get the mix just right, and use transitions and effects on your audio clips to improve the sound.

8 **Output:** Export your finished project to a file or a videotape.

Premiere Pro supports each of these steps with industry-leading tools. A large community of creative and technical professionals is waiting to share their experience and support your development as an editor.

Enhancing the workflow with Premiere Pro

Premiere Pro has easy-to-use tools for video editing. It also has advanced tools for manipulating, adjusting, and fine-tuning your projects.

You may not incorporate all of the following features in your first few video projects. However, as your experience and understanding of nonlinear editing grow, you'll want to expand your capabilities.

It's beyond the scope of one book to cover all of the deep creative tool sets and technical capabilities of Premiere Pro. Still, this book will enable you to fully post-produce professional projects and get you ready for further practice.

The following topics will be covered:

- **Advanced audio editing:** Premiere Pro provides audio effects and editing tools unequaled by any other nonlinear editor. As well as producing a soundtrack mix, you can clean up noisy audio, reduce reverb, make sample-level edits, apply multiple audio effects to audio clips or tracks, and use state-of-the-art plug-ins as well as third-party Virtual Studio Technology (VST) plug-ins.

- **Color correction and grading:** Correct and enhance the look of your footage with advanced color-correction filters, including Lumetri, a dedicated color correction and grading panel. You can make secondary color-correction selections that allow you to adjust isolated colors, adjust selected areas of an image to improve the composition, and automatically match the colors in two images.

- **Keyframe controls:** Premiere Pro gives you precise control over the timing of visual and motion effects without using a dedicated compositing or motion graphics application. Keyframes use a standard interface design; if you learn to use them in Premiere Pro, you'll know how to use them in all Adobe Creative Cloud products in which they're available.

- **Broad hardware support:** Choose from a wide range of dedicated input and output hardware to assemble a system that best fits your needs and budget. Premiere Pro system specifications extend from low-cost desktop computers and laptops for video editing up to high-performance workstations that can easily edit 3D stereoscopic, high-definition (HD), 4K, 8K, and 360 video for immersive experiences.

- **GPU acceleration:** The Mercury Playback Engine operates in two modes: software-only mode and graphics processing unit (GPU) acceleration for enhanced playback performance. GPU acceleration mode requires a graphics card that meets minimum specifications in your workstation. See http://helpx.adobe.com/premiere-pro/system-requirements.html for a list of tested graphics cards. Most modern cards with a minimum of 1GB of dedicated video memory will work.

- **Multicamera editing:** You can quickly and easily edit productions shot with multiple cameras. Premiere Pro displays multiple camera sources in a split-view display, and you can choose a camera view by clicking the appropriate screen or using shortcut keys. You can automatically sync multiple camera angles based on clip audio or timecode.

- **Project management:** Manage your media through a single dialog box. View, delete, move, search for, and reorganize clips and bins. Consolidate your projects by copying just the media used in sequences to a single location. Then reclaim storage space by deleting unused media files.

- **Metadata:** Premiere Pro supports Adobe XMP, which stores additional information about media as metadata that multiple applications can access. This metadata can be used to locate clips or communicate important information such as preferred takes or copyright notices.

- **Creative titles:** Create titles and graphics with the Essential Graphics panel. You can also use graphics created in almost any suitable software; Adobe Photoshop documents can be imported as flattened images or as separate layers that you can incorporate, combine, and animate selectively; Adobe After Effects motion graphics templates can be imported and adjusted directly in Premiere Pro.

- **Advanced trimming:** Use special "trimming" tools to make precise adjustments to the start and end of clips in sequences. Premiere Pro provides both quick, easy trimming keyboard shortcuts and advanced on-screen trimming tools, allowing you to make complex timing adjustments to multiple clips.

- **Media encoding:** Export your sequence to create a video and audio file that is perfect for your needs. Use the advanced features of Adobe Media Encoder to create copies of your finished sequence in multiple formats, based on presets or your own detailed preferences. Color adjustments and information overlays can be applied during export, and media files can be uploaded to social media platforms in a single step.

- **360 video for VR headsets:** Edit and post-produce stitched 360 video footage using a special VR Video display mode that lets you see specific regions of the picture, or view both your video *and* your edited clips via a VR headset, allowing a more natural and intuitive editing experience. Dedicated visual effects that meet the unique demands of 360 video are available.

Expanding the workflow

Although it's possible to work with Premiere Pro as a stand-alone application, it is also a team player. Premiere Pro is part of Adobe Creative Cloud, which means you have access to a number of other specialized tools, including After Effects, Audition, and Prelude. Understanding the way these software components work together will improve your efficiency and give you more creative freedom.

Including other applications in the editing workflow

Premiere Pro is a versatile video and audio post-production tool, but it's just one component of Adobe Creative Cloud—Adobe's complete print, web, and video environment that includes video-focused software for the following:

- High-end 3D motion effects creation
- Complex text animation generation
- Layered graphics production
- Vector artwork creation
- Audio production
- Media management

To incorporate one or more of these features into a production, you can use other components of Adobe Creative Cloud. The software set has everything you need to produce advanced, professionally finished videos.

Here's a brief description of the other components:

- **Premiere Rush:** Mobile and desktop editing tool that can produce projects compatible with Premiere Pro for advanced finishing.
- **Adobe After Effects CC:** The highly popular tool of choice for motion graphics, animation, and visual effects artists.
- **Adobe Character Animator CC:** A tool for creating advanced animation with natural movement for 2D puppets using your webcam for face tracking and keyboard shortcuts.
- **Adobe Photoshop CC:** The industry-standard image-editing and graphics creation product. You can work with photos, video, and 3D objects to prepare them for your project.
- **Adobe Audition CC:** A powerful tool for audio editing, audio cleanup and sweetening, music creation and adjustment, and multitrack mix creation.
- **Adobe Illustrator CC:** Professional vector graphics creation software for print, video, and the Web.

- **Adobe Dynamic Link CC:** A cross-product connection that allows you to work in real time with media, compositions, and sequences shared between After Effects, Audition, and Premiere Pro.

- **Adobe Prelude CC:** A tool that allows you to ingest, transcode, and add metadata, markers, and tags to file-based footage. Then create rough cuts you can share with Premiere Pro directly or with other NLEs.

- **Adobe Media Encoder CC:** A tool that allows you to process files to produce content for any screen directly from Premiere Pro, Adobe After Effects, and Audition.

Exploring the Adobe Creative Cloud video workflow

Your Premiere Pro and Creative Cloud workflow will vary depending on your production needs. Here are a few scenarios:

- Use Photoshop CC to touch up and apply effects to still images and layered image compositions from a digital camera, a scanner, or a video clip. Then use them as source media in Premiere Pro. Changes made in Photoshop update in Premiere Pro.

- Import and manage large numbers of media files with Prelude, adding valuable metadata, temporal comments, and tags. Create sequences from clips and sub-clips in Adobe Prelude and send them to Premiere Pro to continue editing them.

- Send clips directly from the Premiere Pro timeline to Adobe Audition for professional audio cleanup and sweetening.

- Send an entire Premiere Pro sequence to Adobe Audition to complete a professional audio mix, including compatible effects and level adjustments; the session can contain video so you can compose and adjust levels in Audition based on the action.

- Using Dynamic Link, open Premiere Pro video clips in After Effects. Apply special effects, add animation, and add visual elements; then view the results in Premiere Pro. You can play After Effects compositions in Premiere Pro without waiting to pre-export them.

- Use After Effects to create compositions containing advanced text animation, such as an opening or closing title sequence. Use those compositions in Premiere Pro directly thanks to Dynamic Link. Adjustments made in After Effects appear in Premiere Pro immediately.

- Use Adobe Media Encoder to export video projects in multiple resolutions and codecs for display on websites, via social media, or for archiving, using built-in presets and effects and integrated social media support.

Naturally, most of this book focuses on workflows involving only Premiere Pro. However, sidebars will explain ways to include Adobe Creative Cloud components in your workflows for powerful effects work and finishing.

Touring the Premiere Pro interface

It's helpful to begin by getting familiar with the editing interface so you can recognize the tools as you work with them in the following lessons. To make it easier to configure the user interface, Premiere Pro offers *workspaces*. Workspaces quickly configure the various panels and tools on-screen in ways that are helpful for particular activities, such as editing, special effects work, or audio mixing.

You'll begin by taking a brief tour of the Editing workspace. In an exercise, you'll use a Premiere Pro project from this book's companion DVD (or downloaded lesson files if you are using the e-book).

Before you continue, make sure you've copied all the lesson folders and contents to your hard drive. Then launch Premiere Pro. The Home screen appears.

The first few times you launch Premiere Pro, the Home screen shows links to online training videos that will help you get started.

The Home screen shows links to online training videos when you first start using Premiere Pro.

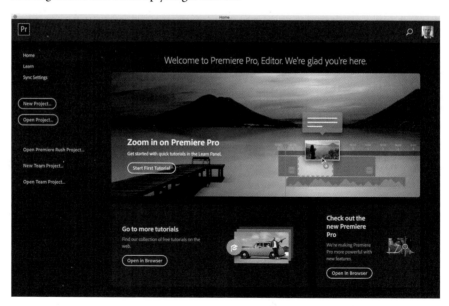

If you have opened projects previously, a list will appear in the middle of the Home screen. You can hover the pointer over a recent item to see the project file location in a pop-up window. As your list of recent projects gets longer, the links to online training videos are removed to make room for the list.

A Premiere Pro project file contains all your creative decisions for a project, links (referred to as *clips*) to your selected media files, sequences made by combining those clips, special effects settings, and more. Premiere Pro project files have the extension .prproj.

Whenever you work in Premiere Pro, you will be making adjustments to a project file. You need to create a new project file or open an existing one to use Premiere Pro.

There are a few important buttons on the Home screen, some of which look like text but can actually be clicked (look out for text that works as a button in the Premiere Pro interface):

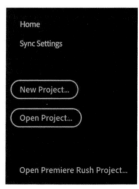

- **New Project** to create a new empty project file. You can name a Premiere Pro project file anything you like, and it's a good idea to choose a name that will be easy to identify later (in other words, don't use New Project).

- **Open Project** to open an existing project by browsing your storage drive for the project file. You can also double-click an existing project file in the macOS Finder or Windows Explorer to open it in Premiere Pro.

- **Home** takes you back to this screen if you have clicked Sync Settings.

- **Sync Settings** allows you to synchronize your user settings across multiple computers.

- **Open Premiere Rush Project** opens an existing Premiere Rush project in Premiere Pro. If you have used Premiere Rush to create a project, it will be available to open.

Lesson 01.prproj

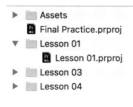

Assets
Final Practice.prproj
Lesson 01
    Lesson 01.prproj
Lesson 03
Lesson 04

Note: It's best to copy all the lesson assets to your computer storage drive and leave them there until you complete this book; some lessons refer to assets from previous lessons.

Try opening an existing project:

1 Click Open Project.

2 In the file navigation dialog box that appears, navigate to the Lesson 01 folder in the Lessons folder; then double-click the Lesson 01.prproj project file to open the first lesson.

After opening an existing project file, you may be prompted with a dialog box asking where a particular media file is. This will occasionally happen when the original media files are saved on a storage drive (or drive letter) different from the one you're using. You'll need to tell Premiere Pro where the file is.

In the dialog box that prompts you to link the media file, you'll see a list of missing items, with the first already highlighted. Select Locate, at the bottom right.

At the top of the Locate File dialog box you'll see the Last Path (that's the last known location for the file) and the Path (that's the current location you have browsed to).

Using the folders on the left, navigate to the Lessons/Assets folder, and click Search at the bottom right. Premiere Pro will locate the missing file and highlight it on the right side of the window. Select the file, and click OK. Premiere Pro will remember this location for other missing files, and relink them automatically without your needing to link each one individually.

Working with workspaces

The Premiere Pro interface is divided into panels. Each panel has a particular purpose. For example, the Effects panel lists all the effects available for you to apply to clips, while the Effect Controls panel gives you access to the settings for those effects.

A workspace is a preset arrangement of panels, organized to make particular tasks easier. There's one for editing, another for working on audio, and another for making color adjustments, for example.

Every panel is accessible from the Window menu, but workspaces are a quicker way to access several panels, and have them laid out exactly as you need them, in a single step.

Before you begin, make sure you're using the default Editing workspace by choosing the Editing workspace option in the Workspaces panel at the top of the screen.

Then, to reset the Editing workspace, click the small panel menu icon ≡ next to the Editing option on the Workspaces panel, and choose Reset To Saved Layout.

If the Workspaces panel is not visible, choose Window > Workspaces > Editing. Then reset the Editing workspace by choosing Window > Workspaces > Reset To Saved Layout.

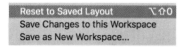

Notice the various workspace names displayed in the Workspaces panel.

Think of these words as buttons you can click; it's an elegant design feature you'll discover in a number of areas in Premiere Pro.

If you're new to nonlinear editing, the default Editing workspace might look like a lot of buttons and menus. Don't worry. Things become simpler when you know what the buttons are for. The interface is designed to make video editing easy, so commonly used controls are immediately accessible.

Workspaces consist of panels, and you can save space by gathering several panels into a *panel group*. The names of all the panels in the group are displayed across the top. Click a panel name to bring that panel to the "front" of the group.

When many panels are combined, you may not be able to see all their names. If this is the case, a list of all the panels in the group becomes available. Click the chevron in the upper-right corner of the panel group to access a panel.

Chevron

List of the panels
in the group

You can display any panel by choosing it from the Window menu, so if you can't locate a panel, just look there.

The principal elements are shown here.

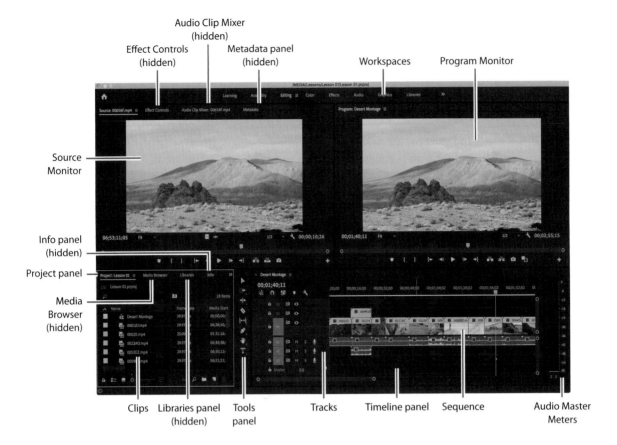

Some important interface elements are as follows:

- **Project panel:** This is where you organize the links to your media files (referred to as *clips*), sequences, and graphics in bins. Bins are similar to folders—you can place one bin inside another for more advanced organization of your media assets.

- **Timeline panel:** This is where you'll do most of your editing. You view and work on *sequences* (the term for video segments edited together) in the Timeline panel. One feature of sequences is that you can *nest* them (place one sequence inside another sequence). In this way, you can break up a production into manageable chunks or create unique special effects.

- **Tracks:** You can layer—or *composite*—video clips, images, graphics, and titles on an unlimited number of tracks. Video and graphic clips on upper video tracks cover whatever is directly below them on the timeline. Therefore, you need to give clips on higher tracks some form of transparency or reduce their size if you want clips on lower tracks to show.

- **Monitor panels:** Use the Source Monitor (on the left) to view and select parts of clips (your original footage). To view a clip in the Source Monitor, double-click it in the Project panel. The Program Monitor (on the right) is for viewing your current sequence, displayed in the Timeline panel.

- **Media Browser:** This important panel allows you to browse your storage to find media. It's especially useful for file-based camera media and RAW files.

- **Libraries:** This panel gives access to custom Lumetri color Looks, motion graphics templates, graphics, and to shared libraries for collaboration. It also acts as a browser and store for the Adobe Stock service. For more information, go to https://helpx.adobe.com/premiere-pro/using/creative-cloud-libraries.html.

- **Effects panel:** This panel contains the effects you will use in your sequences, including video filters, audio effects, and transitions. Effects are grouped by type to make them easier to find, and there's a search box at the top of the panel to quickly locate an effect. Once applied, the controls for these effects are displayed in the Effect Controls panel.

- **Audio Clip Mixer:** This panel is based on audio production studio hardware, with volume sliders and pan controls. There is one set of controls for each audio track on the timeline. The adjustments you make are applied to audio clips. There's also an Audio Track Mixer for applying audio adjustments to tracks rather than clips.

Effects panel

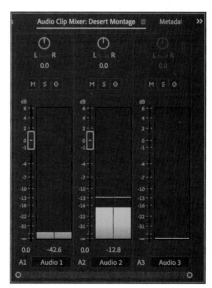

Audio Clip Mixer

- **Effect Controls panel:** This panel displays the controls for any effects applied to a clip you select in a sequence or open in the Source Monitor. If you select a visual clip in the Timeline panel, Motion, Opacity, and Time Remapping controls are always available. Most effect parameters are adjustable over time.

- **Tools panel:** Each icon in this panel gives access to a tool that performs a specific function in the Timeline panel. The Selection tool is context-sensitive, which means it changes function depending on where you click. If your pointer doesn't work as you expect, it might be because you have the wrong tool selected.

Tools panel

Effect Controls panel

Several tools have a small triangle icon, indicating a menu of additional tools. Press and hold on one of these tools to see the menu of options.

- **Info panel:** The Info panel displays information about any item you select in the Project panel or any clip or transition you select in a sequence.

- **History panel:** This panel tracks the steps you take and lets you back up easily. It's a kind of visual Undo list. When you select a previous step, all steps that came after it are also undone.

The name of each panel is displayed at the top. When a panel is displayed, the name is underlined, and a panel menu appears next to the name with options particular to that panel.

Using the Learning workspace

While other workspaces are intended to facilitate a particular creative activity, the Learning workspace is an exception. This workspace includes the Learn panel, which offers a series of tutorials to help you build familiarity with the Premiere Pro interface and several important skills.

You will find the tutorials complement the exercises in this book well, and you may find it helpful to practice first with this book and then explore the relevant tutorials to reinforce the lessons you have learned.

Customizing a workspace

In addition to choosing between the default workspaces, you can adjust the position and location of panels to create a workspace that works best for you. You can create multiple workspaces for different tasks.

- As you change the size of a panel or panel group, other panels change size to compensate.
- Every panel within a panel group is accessible by clicking its name.
- All panels are movable—you can drag a panel from one group to another.
- You can drag a panel out of a group to become a separate floating panel.

In this exercise, you'll try all these functions and save a customized workspace.

1 In the Project panel, double-click the icon for the clip 0022AO.mp4 to open it in the Source Monitor. It's the fourth item on the list. Be careful to double-click the icon and not the name, as clicking the name selects the text, making it ready for renaming.

● **Note:** Though "panel" is not part of their names, both the Source Monitor and Program Monitor behave exactly like panels.

2 Position your pointer on the vertical divider between the Source Monitor and the Program Monitor. The pointer will change to a double-headed arrow 🔀 when it's in the right position. Drag left and right to change the sizes of those panels. You can choose to have different sizes for your video displays, which is useful at different stages of post-production.

3 Now place the pointer on the horizontal divider between the Program Monitor and the Timeline panel. The pointer will change when it's in the right position. Drag up and down to change the sizes of these panels.

4 Click the name of the Media Browser panel, at the top, and drag it to the middle of the Source Monitor to dock the Media Browser panel in that panel group.

The drop zone is displayed as a center highlight.

5 Drag the Effects panel (which is grouped with the Project panel by default) by its name to a point just inside the right edge of it's own panel group to place it in its own panel group. Remember, if you can't see the Effects panel, you can choose it from the Window menu.

Before you let go of the panel, make sure you're over the drop zone. It's a blue trapezoid that covers the right portion of the Project panel. Release the panel, and your workspace should have a new panel group that contains just the Effects panel.

When you drag a panel by its name, Premiere Pro displays a drop zone. If the highlighted drop zone is a rectangle, the panel will go into the selected panel group as an additional tab when it's dropped. If the drop zone is a trapezoid, it will create a new panel group.

You can also pull panels into their own floating windows.

6 Command-drag (macOS)/Ctrl-drag (Windows) the Source Monitor out of its panel group.

7 Drop the Source Monitor anywhere, creating a floating panel. You can resize the panel by dragging a corner or a side.

Note: You may need to resize a panel to see all of its controls.

As you gain experience, you might want to create and save the layout of your panels as a customized workspace. To do so at any time, choose Window > Workspaces > Save As New Workspace. Type a name, and click OK.

If you want to return a workspace to its default layout, choose Window > Workspaces > Reset To Saved Layout, or double-click the workspace name.

8 Now, to return to a recognizable starting point, choose the preset Editing workspace, and reset it.

Note: You can change the font size in the Project panel by choosing Font Size from the panel menu and then choosing Small, Medium (Default), Large, or Extra Large from the submenu.

Introducing preferences

The more you edit video, the more you'll want to customize Premiere Pro to match your specific needs. Premiere Pro has several types of settings. For example, panel menus, which are accessible by clicking the menu button next to a panel name, have options that relate to each panel, and individual clips in a sequence have settings you can access by right-clicking them.

It's worth noting that the panel name, displayed at the top of each panel, is often referred to as the *panel tab*. This is the area of a panel you use to move the panel, almost like a handle you can grab the panel by.

Note: When panels and panel groups were first introduced in Premiere Pro, the names of panes were incorporated into a tabbed design. Over time, the interface has been restyled and cleaned up, which led to the removal of the tabs themselves—but the name remained.

There are also application-wide preferences, all grouped into one dialog box for easy access. Preferences will be covered in depth as they relate to the individual lessons in this book. Let's look at a simple example.

1   Choose Premiere Pro CC > Preferences > Appearance (macOS) or Edit > Preferences > Appearance (Windows).

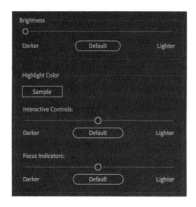

2   Drag the Brightness slider to the right to suit your preference.

The default brightness is a dark gray to help you see colors correctly (human perception of color is influenced by surrounding colors). There are additional options for controlling the brightness of interface highlights.

3   Experiment with the Interactive Controls and Focus Indicators brightness sliders. The difference in the on-screen sample is subtle, but adjusting these sliders can make quite a big difference to your editing experience.

4   Set all three settings to Default by clicking the Default buttons when you have finished.

5   Switch to the Auto Save preferences by clicking the preference name on the left.

Imagine if you had worked for hours and then there was a power outage. If you hadn't saved recently, you'd have lost a lot of work. With these options, you can decide how often you would like Premiere Pro to save an automated backup of your project file and how many versions you would like to keep in total. Auto save backups have the date and time they were created added to the filename.

● **Note:** When opening the Preferences dialog box it's not too important which pane you choose first, as you can always quickly switch to another pane.

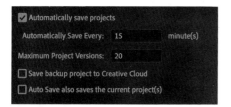

Project files are small relative to media files, so it's usually fine to increase the number of project versions without any impact on system performance.

You'll notice there's an option to save a backup project to Creative Cloud.

This option creates an additional backup of your project file in your Creative Cloud Files folder. If you suffer a total system failure while working, you can log in to any Premiere Pro editing system with your Adobe ID to access the backup project file and quickly carry on working.

There's also the option Auto Save Also Saves The Current Project(s). When this option is selected, saving or auto saving will also create an "emergency project backup"—a project file that is a copy of the current version, with the same name. If you have a sudden system failure (like a power outage), this is the file you will most likely want to open to continue working.

● **Note:** Premiere Pro allows you to open multiple projects at the same time. For this reason, you'll see options for "project(s)" rather than just "project."

6   Click Cancel to close the Preferences dialog box without applying any changes.

Using and setting keyboard shortcuts

Premiere Pro makes extensive use of keyboard shortcuts. These are usually faster and easier than clicking. Many keyboard shortcuts are shared universally by non-linear editing systems. The spacebar, for example, starts and stops playback—this even works on some websites.

Some standard keyboard shortcuts come from celluloid film-editing traditions. The I and O keys, for example, are used to set In and Out marks on footage and sequences. These special marks indicate the start and end of a desired section and were originally drawn on celluloid directly.

Other keyboard shortcuts are available but not configured by default. This allows flexibility when setting up your editing system.

Choose Premiere Pro CC > Keyboard Shortcuts (macOS) or Edit > Keyboard Shortcuts (Windows).

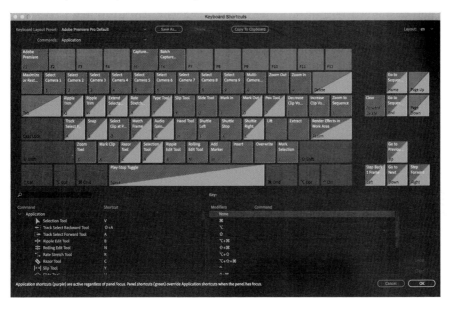

It can be a little daunting to see the number of keyboard shortcuts available, but by the end of this book you will recognize most of the options displayed here.

Some keyboard shortcuts are specific to individual panels. You can view them by opening the Commands menu and examining the list of items.

Specialized keyboards are available with shortcuts printed on them and color-coded keys. These make it easier to remember commonly used shortcuts.

Click outside of the search box (to deselect it), and try pressing Command (macOS) or Ctrl (Windows).

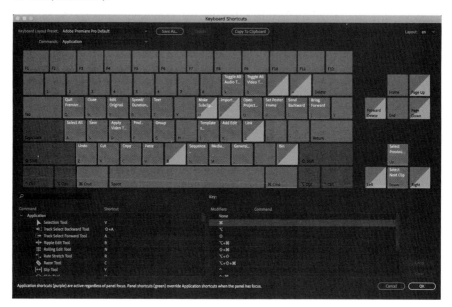

The keyboard shortcut display updates to show the results of combining the modifier key with the character keys. Notice there are many keys without shortcuts assigned when you use a modifier key. These are available for you to assign your own shortcuts.

Try combinations of modifier keys including Shift+Option (macOS) or Shift+Alt (Windows). You can set keyboard shortcuts with any combination of modifier keys.

If you press a character key, or character and modifier key combination, that particular shortcut information is displayed.

The list at the bottom left of this dialog box includes every option you can assign to a key—it's a long list, but there's a search box at the top to help you find the option you want.

Having found an option you would like to assign to a key, drag it from the list onto the key you would like to use in the upper part of the dialog box. If you hold modifier keys while performing this operation, they'll be included in the shortcut.

To remove a shortcut, click the key, and choose Clear at the bottom right.

For now, click Cancel.

Moving, backing up, and syncing user settings

User preferences include a number of important options. The defaults work well in most cases, but it's likely you'll want to make a few adjustments over time. For example, you might prefer the interface to be brighter than the default.

Premiere Pro includes the option to share your user preferences between multiple computers: When installing Premiere Pro, you will enter your Adobe ID to confirm your software license. You can use the same ID to store your user preferences in Creative Cloud, allowing you to synchronize and update them from any installation of Premiere Pro.

You can sync your preferences while on the Home screen by choosing Sync Settings. You can also sync your preferences while working with Premiere Pro by choosing Premiere Pro CC > Sync Settings > Sync Settings Now (macOS) or File > Sync Settings > Sync Settings Now (Windows).

Now close Premiere Pro by choosing Premiere Pro CC > Quit Premiere Pro (macOS) or File > Exit (Windows).

If a dialog box appears asking if you would like to save changes you have made, click No.

Review questions

1 Why is Premiere Pro considered a nonlinear editor?

2 Describe the basic video-editing workflow.

3 What is the Media Browser used for?

4 Can you save a customized workspace?

5 What is the purpose of the Source Monitor and the Program Monitor?

6 How can you drag a panel to its own floating panel?

Review answers

1 Premiere Pro lets you place video clips, audio clips, and graphics anywhere in a sequence; rearrange items already in a sequence; add transitions; apply effects; and do any number of other video-editing steps in any order that suits you. You're not tied to a particular line of action.

2 Shoot your video; transfer it to your computer; create a sequence by combining video, audio, and still-image clips in the Timeline panel; add effects and transitions; add text and graphics; mix your audio; and export the finished product.

3 The Media Browser allows you to browse and import media files without having to open an external file browser. It's particularly useful when you're working with file-based camera footage because you can easily preview footage.

4 Yes. You can save any customized workspace by choosing Window > Workspaces > Save As New Workspace.

5 You can view and trim your original footage in the Source Monitor and use the Program Monitor to view the contents of the current timeline sequence as you build it.

6 Drag the name of the panel while holding down Command (macOS) or Ctrl (Windows).

2 SETTING UP A PROJECT

Lesson overview

In this lesson, you'll learn about the following:

- Choosing project settings
- Choosing video rendering and playback settings
- Choosing video and audio display settings
- Creating scratch disks
- Using sequence presets
- Customizing sequence settings

This lesson will take about 60 minutes to complete. You will not need any of the downloadable lesson files.

Before you begin editing, you need to create a new project and choose some settings for your first sequence. If you're not familiar with video and audio technology, you might find all the options a little overwhelming. Luckily, Adobe Premiere Pro CC gives you easy shortcuts. Plus, the principles of video and sound reproduction are the same no matter what you're creating.

It's just a question of knowing what you want to do. To help you plan and manage your projects, this lesson contains information about formats and video technology. You may decide to revisit this lesson later, as your familiarity with Premiere Pro and nonlinear video editing develops.

In practice, you're unlikely to make changes to the default settings when creating a new project, but it's helpful to know what the options mean.

In this lesson, you'll learn how to create a new project and choose sequence settings that tell Premiere Pro how to play your video and audio clips.

Starting the lesson

A Premiere Pro project file stores links to all the video, graphic, and sound files you have imported. Each item is displayed in the Project panel as a clip. The name *clip* originally described sections of celluloid film (lengths of film were literally clipped to separate them from a roll), but these days the term refers to any item in the project, regardless of the type of media. You could have an audio clip or an image sequence clip, for example.

Clips displayed in the Project panel appear to be media files, but they are actually only links to those files. It's helpful to understand that a clip in the Project panel and the media file it links to are two separate things. You can delete one without affecting the other (more on this later).

When working on a project, you will create at least one *sequence*—that is, a series of clips that play, one after another, sometimes overlapping, with special effects, titles, and sound, to form your completed creative work. While editing, you will choose which parts of your clips to use and in which order they'll play.

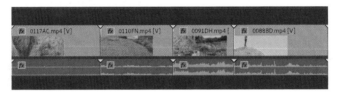

The beauty of nonlinear editing with Premiere Pro is that you can change your mind about almost anything, at any time.

Premiere Pro project files have the file extension .prproj.

Starting a new project is simple. You create a new project file, import media, choose a sequence preset, and start editing.

When you create a sequence, you'll choose playback settings (things such as frame rate and frame size) and place multiple clips in it. It's important to understand how the sequence settings change the way Premiere Pro plays your video and audio clips (clips are automatically adjusted to match the sequence settings). To speed things up, you can use a sequence preset to choose the settings and then make adjustments if necessary.

You need to know the kind of video and audio your camera records because your sequence settings will usually be based on your original source footage to minimize conversion during playback. In fact, most Premiere Pro sequence presets are named after cameras to make it easier to choose the correct option. If you know which camera was used to capture the footage and which video format was recorded, you'll know which sequence preset to choose.

In this lesson, you'll learn how to create a new Premiere Pro project and choose sequence settings that tell Premiere Pro how to play your clips. You'll also learn about different kinds of audio tracks and what preview files are.

Creating a project

Let's begin by creating a new project.

1   Launch Premiere Pro. The Home screen (sometimes also called the "Start screen") appears.

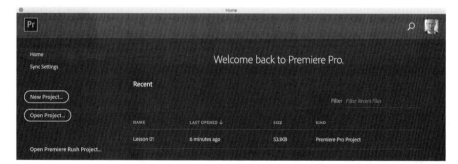

If you have opened Premiere Pro a few times, you won't see links to tutorials (as mentioned in Lesson 1). Instead, in the middle of the screen you'll find a list of previously opened projects. You should see Lesson 01. You could click that project to open it, but you're going to make a new one.

Notice that you can thin out the list of recent project files by typing some text into the Filter text box—only project files whose file names contain the text will be displayed.

There are a couple of other items in this window:

* **Magnifying glass icon:** Click the magnifying glass icon at the top right of the Home screen to open a multipurpose Search screen. If you enter text into the text box at the top of the screen, Premiere Pro will display both previously opened project files and tutorials from Adobe Premiere Pro Learn & Support that contain the text. You'll need to be connected to the Internet to access the tutorials.

* **User icon:** Next to the magnifying glass is a thumbnail of your Adobe ID profile picture. If you have just signed up, this may be a generic thumbnail. Click the icon to manage your account online.

2 Click New Project to open the New Project dialog box.

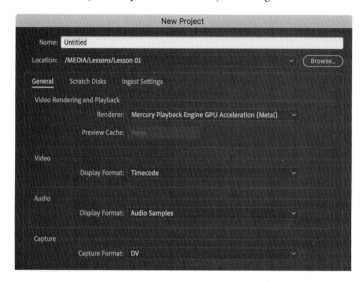

Below the new project name and location fields, this dialog box has three tabs: General, Scratch Disks, and Ingest Settings. All the settings in this dialog box can be changed later, and in most cases, you'll want to leave them as they are. For now, we'll finish creating our new project using the default settings. Afterward, we'll take a look at what all of those settings mean.

3 Click in the Name box, and name your new project First Project.

Note: When choosing a location for your project file, you may want to choose a recently used location from the Location menu.

4 Click Browse, and browse to the Lessons/Lesson 02 folder. Click Choose to establish this new folder as the location for the new project.

5 If your project is set up correctly, the General section in the New Project window should look similar to the screen shown here.

Exploring video rendering and playback settings

While you're working creatively with video clips in your sequences, it's likely you will apply some visual effects to adjust the appearance of your footage. Some special effects can be played immediately, combining your original video with the effect and displaying the results as soon as you click Play. When this happens, it's called *real-time playback.*

Real-time playback is desirable because it means you can watch the results of your creative choices right away.

If you use lots of effects on a clip or if you use effects that are not designed for real-time playback, your computer may not be able to display the results at the full frame rate. That is, Premiere Pro will attempt to display your video clips, combined with the special effects, but it will not show every single frame each second. When this happens, it's described as *dropping* frames.

Premiere Pro displays colored lines along the top of the Timeline panel, where you build sequences, to tell you when extra work is required to play back your video. No line or a yellow line means Premiere Pro expects to be able to play without dropping frames. A red line means Premiere Pro may drop frames when playing that section of the sequence.

● **Note:** A red line at the top of the Timeline panel doesn't necessarily mean frames will be dropped. It just means visual adjustments aren't accelerated, so on a less powerful machine dropped frames are more likely.

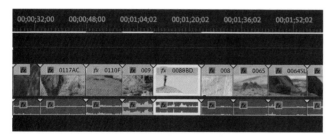

If you can't see every frame when you play your sequence, it's okay! It won't affect the final results. When you're done editing and you output your finished sequence, it'll be full quality, with all the frames intact (more on this in Lesson 16, "Exporting Frames, Clips, and Sequences").

Real-time playback can make a difference to your editing experience and your ability to preview the effects you apply with confidence. If frames are being dropped, there is a simple solution: preview rendering.

What do *rendering* and *real time* mean?

Think of *rendering* as an artist's rendering, where something is visualized, taking up paper and taking time to draw. Imagine you have a piece of video that is too dark. You add a visual effect to make it brighter, but your video-editing system is unable to both play the original video and make it brighter at the same time. In this situation, you'd have your system render the effect, creating a new temporary video file that looks like the original video combined with the visual effect that makes it brighter.

When your edited sequence plays, sections that are rendered display the newly rendered video file instead of the original clip (or clips). The process is invisible and seamless. In this example, the rendered file looks like the original video file but brighter.

When the part of your sequence with the brightened clip is finished, your system invisibly and seamlessly switches back from playing the preview file to playing your other original video files.

The downside of rendering is that it takes up extra space for media storage, and it takes time. Also, because you're viewing a new video file that is a copy of your original media, there might be some minor loss of quality. The upside with rendering is that you can be confident your system will be able to play the results of your effect at full quality, with all the frames per second. This might be important if you output to tape, but it won't change output to a file.

Real-time playback, by contrast, is instant! When using a real-time special effect, your system plays the original video clip combined with the special effect right away, without waiting for the effect to render. The only downside with real-time performance is that the amount you can do without rendering depends on how powerful your system is. More effects are more work to play back, for example. In the case of Premiere Pro, you can dramatically improve real-time performance by using the right kind of graphics card (see the sidebar "The Mercury Playback Engine"). Plus, you'll need to use effects that are designed for GPU acceleration, and not all effects are.

Many menu items display a keyboard shortcut on the right. In this case, the shortcut for Render Effects In To Out is Return (macOS) or Enter (Windows).

When you render, Premiere Pro creates new media files that look like the results of your effects work and then plays back those files in place of the original footage. The rendered preview is a regular video file, so playback is at high quality and full frame rate, without your computer having to do any extra work.

You render effects in a sequence by choosing a render command from the Sequence menu.

Back in the New Project dialog box, under Video Rendering And Playback, if the Renderer menu is available, it means you have graphics hardware in your computer that meets the minimum requirements for GPU acceleration and it is installed correctly.

The menu has two types of options:

- **Mercury Playback Engine GPU Acceleration:** If you choose this option, Premiere Pro will send many playback tasks to the graphics hardware on your computer, giving you lots of real-time effects and smooth playback of mixed formats in your sequences. You may see an option to use CUDA, OpenCL, or Metal for GPU acceleration, depending on your graphics hardware. Performance can vary and some graphics hardware configurations allow multiple types of acceleration, so you may need to experiment to find the best option for your system. Some advanced GPU configurations also allow you to choose a persistent Preview Cache to improve playback. You'll want to experiment with this option for optimum playback performance.

- **Mercury Playback Engine Software Only:** This mode will still give excellent performance that uses all of the available power in your computer. If your system does not have graphics hardware that can be used for GPU acceleration, only this option will be available, and you won't be able to open this menu.

You will almost certainly want to choose GPU acceleration and benefit from the additional performance if you can. However, if you experience performance or stability issues using GPU acceleration, choose the Software Only option in this menu.

Choose a GPU option now, if it's available.

The Mercury Playback Engine

The Mercury Playback Engine, which decodes and displays video files in Premiere Pro, has three main features.

- **Playback performance:** Premiere Pro plays back video files with great efficiency, even when working with the types of video that are difficult to play back, such as H.264, H.265, or AVCHD. If you're filming with a DSLR camera or phone camera, for example, chances are your media is recorded using the H.264 codec. Thanks to the Mercury Playback Engine, you'll find that these files play back with ease.

- **64-bit and multithreading:** Premiere Pro is a 64-bit application, which means it can use all the random access memory (RAM) on your computer. This is particularly useful when you're working with high-definition or ultra-high-definition video (HD, or 4K and above). The Mercury Playback Engine is multi-threaded, which means it uses all the CPU cores in your computer. The more powerful your computer is, the higher the performance you'll see in Premiere Pro.

- **CUDA, OpenCL, Apple Metal, and Intel graphics support:** If you have powerful enough graphics hardware, Premiere Pro can send some of the work for playing back video to the graphics card, rather than putting the entire processing burden on the CPU in your computer. The results are even better performance and responsiveness when working with sequences, and many special effects will play in real time, without dropping frames.

For more information about supported graphics cards, see http://helpx.adobe.com/premiere-pro/system-requirements.html.

Setting the video and audio display formats

The next two areas of the General tab in the New Project dialog box allow you to choose how Premiere Pro should measure time for your video and audio clips.

In most cases, you'll choose the default options: Timecode from the Video Display Format menu and Audio Samples from the Audio Display Format menu. These settings don't change the way Premiere Pro plays video or audio clips, only the way time is measured—and you can change the settings at any time.

The Video Display Format menu

There are four options for Video Display Format. The correct choice for a given project largely depends on whether you are working with video or celluloid film as your source material. It's rare to produce content using film, so if you are not sure, choose Timecode.

The choices are as follows:

- **Timecode:** This is the default option. Timecode is a universal system for counting hours, minutes, seconds, and individual frames of video. The same system is used by cameras, professional video recorders, and nonlinear editing systems all around the world.

- **Feet + Frames 16 mm or Feet + Frames 35 mm:** If your source files are captured from film and you intend to give your editing decisions to a lab so they can cut the original negative to produce a finished film, you may want to use this standard method of measuring time. Rather than measuring time as seconds and frames, this system counts the number of feet plus the number of frames since the last foot. It's a bit like feet and inches but with frames rather than inches. Because 16mm film and 35mm film have different frame sizes (and so different numbers of frames per foot), there's an option for each.

- **Frames:** This option simply counts the number of frames of video. This is sometimes used for animation projects and is another way that labs like to receive information about edits for film-based projects.

For this exercise, leave Video Display Format set to Timecode.

The Audio Display Format menu

For audio files, time can be displayed as samples or milliseconds.

- **Audio Samples:** When digital audio is recorded, sound level samples are taken (technically, air pressure level), as captured by the microphone, thousands of times a second. In the case of most professional video cameras, this happens 48,000 times per second. When playing clips and sequences, Premiere Pro gives you the choice of displaying time as hours, minutes, seconds, and frames, or as hours, minutes, seconds, and samples.

- **Milliseconds:** With this mode chosen, Premiere Pro can display time in your sequences as hours, minutes, seconds, and thousandths of a second.

By default, Premiere Pro lets you zoom the Timeline enough to view individual sequence clip segment frames. However, you can easily switch to showing the audio display format instead. This powerful feature lets you make the tiniest adjustments to your audio.

For this project, leave the Audio Display Format option set to Audio Samples.

About seconds and frames

When a camera records video, it captures a series of still images of the action. If there are enough images captured each second, it looks like moving video when played back. Each picture is called a *frame*, and the number of frames each second is usually called *frames per second* (fps) or the recording or playback *frame rate*.

The fps will vary depending on your camera/video format and settings. It could be any number, including 23.976, 24, 25, 29.97, 30, 50, or 59.94. Most cameras allow you to choose between more than one frame rate and more than one frame size. It's important to know the recording settings so you can be sure you have selected the correct playback options.

Setting the capture format

It's most common to record video as a file you can work with immediately. However, there may be times you need to capture from videotape.

The Capture Format menu (under Capture in the New Project dialog box) tells Premiere Pro what videotape format you are using when capturing video to your storage drive.

Capturing from DV and HDV cameras

Premiere Pro can capture from DV and HDV cameras using the FireWire connection on your computer, if it has one. FireWire is also known as IEEE 1394 and i.LINK.

Capturing from third-party hardware

Note: The Mercury Playback Engine can share performance with video input and output hardware for playback, thanks to a feature called Adobe Mercury Transmit.

Not all video decks use a FireWire connection, so you may need additional third-party hardware installed to be able to connect your video deck for capture.

If you have additional hardware, you should follow the directions provided by the manufacturer to install it. Most likely you'll install software supplied with your hardware. The software installer will usually discover Premiere Pro on your computer, automatically adding extra options to this menu and to others.

Follow the directions provided with your third-party equipment to configure new Premiere Pro projects.

For more information about the video capture hardware and video formats supported by Premiere Pro, visit http://helpx.adobe.com/premiere-pro/compatibility.html.

Ignore this setting for now because you will not be capturing from a tape deck in this exercise, and you can always change the setting as needed later.

Displaying the project item names and label colors

There's a check box at the bottom of the New Project dialog box described as "display the project item name and label color for all instances."

☐ Display the project item name and label color for all instances

With this option selected, when you change name of a clip, or the color of the label assigned to a clip, all copies of the clip used anywhere in the project will update accordingly. If this option is not selected, only the copy you select will be changed. Both options can be useful, depending on your chosen workflow for a particular project.

Leave this deselected for now, and click the Scratch Disks area to view the options.

Setting up the scratch disks

Existing media files are imported from wherever they are currently stored. However, whenever Premiere Pro *captures* (records) video from tape, renders special effects, saves backup copies of the project file, downloads content from Adobe Stock, or imports animated motion graphics templates, new files are created on your hard drive.

The various *scratch disks* are the locations these files are stored. Though they are described, here, as disks, they are actually folders. Some of the files that are stored will be temporary, while some will be new media created in Premiere Pro or imported.

Scratch disks can be stored on physically separate disks, as the name suggests, or any subfolder on your storage. Scratch disks can be located all in the same place or in separate locations, depending on your hardware and workflow requirements. If you're working with really large media files, you may get a performance boost by putting each scratch disk on a physically separate hard drive.

There are generally two approaches to storage for video editing:

- **Project-based setup:** All associated media files are stored with one project file in the same folder (this is the default option for scratch disks and the simplest to manage).

- **System-based setup:** Media files associated with multiple projects are saved to one central location (perhaps high-speed network-based storage), and the project file is saved to another location. This might include storing different kinds of media files in different locations.

To change the location of the scratch disk for a particular type of data, choose a location from the menu next to the data type. The choices are as follows:

- Documents (to store the scratch disk in the Documents folder in your system user account).

- Same As Project (to store the scratch disk with the project file); this is the default option.

- [Custom] Choose any location—this option is automatically chosen if you click Browse and choose a specific location for the scratch disk.

Below each Scratch Disk location menu, a file path shows the current setting and the disk space available at that location.

Your scratch disks might be stored on local hard drives or on a network-based storage system; any storage location your computer has access to will work. However, the speed of your scratch disks can have a big impact on both playback and rendering performance, so choose fast storage if possible.

Using a project-based setup

By default, Premiere Pro keeps newly created media together with the associated project file (this is the Same As Project option). Keeping everything together this way makes finding relevant files simple.

It also makes it easier to stay organized if you move media files into the same folder before you import them into the project. When you're finished with your project, you can remove everything from your system by deleting the single folder your project file is stored in.

There's a downside, though: Storing your media files on the same drive as your project file means the drive has to work harder while you edit, and this can impact playback performance.

Using a system-based setup

Some editors prefer to have all their media stored in a single location, for all projects. Others choose to store their capture folders and preview folders in a different location from their project. This is a common choice in editing facilities where multiple editors share several editing systems, all connected to the same network-based storage. It's also common among editors who have fast hard drives for video media and slower hard drives for everything else.

There's a downside with this setup too: Once you finish editing, it's likely you'll want to gather everything together for archiving. This is slower and more complex when your media files are distributed across multiple storage locations.

Typical drive setup and network-based storage

Although all file types can coexist on a single hard drive, a typical editing system will have two hard drives: Drive 1, dedicated to the operating system and programs, and Drive 2 (often a faster drive), dedicated to media, including captured video and audio, video and audio preview files, still images, and exported media.

Some storage systems use local computer networks to share storage between multiple systems. If this is the case for you, check with your system administrators to make sure you have the right settings and check performance.

Setting up a Project Auto Save location

In addition to choosing where new media files are created, you can set the location to store automatically saved project files. These are additional backup copies of your project file that are created automatically while you work. Choose a location from the Project Auto Save menu on the Scratch Disks tab.

Storage drives occasionally fail, and you may lose files stored on them without warning. In fact, any computer engineer will tell you that if you have only one copy of a file, you can't count on having the file at all. For this reason, it's a great idea to set the Project Auto Save location to a physically separate storage location.

If you use a synchronized file sharing service like Dropbox, OneDrive, or Google Drive, storing your auto-save files using that service will mean you always have access to all your automatically saved project files.

In addition to storing automatically saved project files in the location you choose, Premiere Pro can store a backup of your most recent project file in your Creative Cloud Files folder. This folder is created automatically when you install Adobe Creative Cloud. It allows you to access files in any location where Creative Cloud is installed and you are logged in.

This useful extra safety net is available by choosing Premiere Pro CC > Preferences > Auto Save (macOS) or Edit > Preferences > Auto Save (Windows).

CC Libraries Downloads

You can also use the Creative Cloud Files folder to store media files that you can access from any system. Collaborators on a project can use the Creative Cloud Files folder to store and share standard assets like logos or graphic elements.

Use the Libraries panel in Premiere Pro to access these files. When you add items to the current project in this way, Premiere Pro will create a copy of them in the scratch disk location you choose here.

Motion Graphics Template Media

Premiere Pro can import and display prebuilt animated template graphics and titles created with After Effects or Premiere Pro. When you import a motion graphics template into the current project, a copy will be stored in the location you choose.

For this project, leave all your scratch disks set to the default option: Same As Project.

Choosing ingest settings

Professional editors describe adding media to a project as *importing* or *ingesting*. The two words are often used interchangeably but actually have different meanings.

When you import a media file into a Premiere Pro project, a clip is created that is linked to the original file. The media file stays in its current location, and you're ready to include it in a sequence.

When you enable the Ingest options, the original media file may also be copied to a different location (which is useful for keeping your media files organized) and/or converted to a new format and codec before it's imported into your Premiere Pro project.

In the Ingest Settings area, you can enable the Ingest option, and choose what to do with media files before they are imported.

⬤ **Note:** There are several ways to import clips into a project. Once ingest options are enabled, they are applied regardless of the import method you use.

- **Copy** them to a new storage location—useful if you want to be sure all your media is in one folder.

- **Transcode** them to a new codec and/or format—useful if you choose to standardize your media as part of a larger-scale workflow.

- **Create Proxies**, which converts them to lower-resolution media files that are easier for a lower-powered computer to play back and that take up less storage space. The original media is always available too, and you can switch between the full-quality and proxy-quality files whenever you like.

  You'll be exploring these settings in Lesson 3, "Importing Media." They can be changed at any time; for now leave Ingest deselected.

  Now that you have checked that the settings are correct for this project, click OK to finish creating it.

Setting up a sequence

In your Premiere Pro project you will create a sequence (or several sequences) into which you'll place video clips, audio clips, and graphics. Sequences have settings, just like media files, that specify things like the frame rate and image size. Frame rates and frame sizes for clips that don't match the sequence settings are converted during playback to match the settings you chose for your sequence. This is called *conforming*.

Each sequence in your project can have different settings. You'll want to choose settings that match your original media as precisely as possible to minimize conforming during playback. Matching the settings reduces the work your system must do to play back your clips, improves real-time performance, and maximizes quality.

If you're editing a project with mixed-format media, you may have to choose which media to match with your sequence settings. You can mix formats easily, but because playback performance improves when the sequence settings match, you'll often choose settings that match the most media files.

If the first clip you add to a sequence does not match the settings of your sequence, Premiere Pro checks if you would like to change the sequence settings automatically to fit.

Creating a sequence that automatically matches your source

If you're not sure what sequence settings you should choose, don't worry. Premiere Pro can create a sequence based on your clip.

At the bottom of the Project panel, there's a New Item menu ▣. Use this menu to create new items for your project, including sequences, captions, and color mattes (full-screen color graphics useful for backgrounds).

To automatically create a sequence that matches your media, drag any clip (or multiple clips) in the Project panel onto the New Item menu. A new sequence will be created with the same name as the clip and a matching frame size and frame rate.

Using this method, you can be confident your sequence settings will work with your media. If the Timeline panel is empty, you can also drag a clip (or multiple clips) into it to create a sequence with matching settings.

Choosing the correct preset

If you do know the settings you need, you can configure the sequence settings exactly. If you're not so sure, you can use a preset.

Click the New Item button 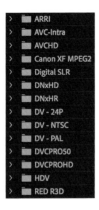 at the lower-right corner of the Project panel now, and choose Sequence.

The New Sequence dialog box has four tabs: Sequence Presets, Settings, Tracks, and VR Video.

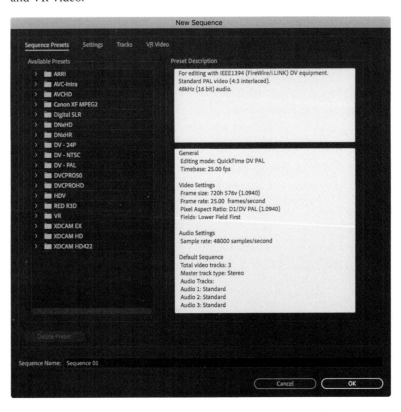

The Sequence Presets tab makes setting up a new sequence easier. When you choose a preset, Premiere Pro applies settings for the new sequence that closely match a particular video and audio format. After choosing a preset, you can adjust these settings on the Settings tab if necessary.

You'll find a wide range of preset configuration options for the most commonly used and supported media types. These settings are organized based on camera formats (with specific settings inside a folder named after the recording format).

You can click the disclosure triangle to see specific formats in a group. These are typically designed around frame rates and frame sizes. Let's look at an example.

1 Click the disclosure triangle next to the group Digital SLR.

You can now see three subfolders, based on frame sizes. Remember that video cameras can often shoot video using different frame sizes, as well as different frame rates and codecs.

2 Click the disclosure triangle next to the 1080p subgroup.

3 Choose the DSLR 1080p30 preset by clicking its name.

For this sequence, use the default settings. Take a moment to familiarize yourself with the description.

4 Click in the Sequence Name box, and name your sequence First Sequence.

5 Click OK to create the sequence.

6 Choose File > Save.

Congratulations! You have made a new project and sequence with Premiere Pro.

Formats and codecs

Video and audio files have a particular *format*, that is, a frame rate, frame size, audio sample rate, and so on.

Video file types such as Apple QuickTime, Microsoft AVI, and MXF are containers that can carry many different video and audio codecs.

Codec is a shortening of the words *coder* and *decoder*. It's the way video and audio information is stored and replayed.

The media file is referred to as the *wrapper*, and the video and audio inside the file are sometimes referred to as the *essence*.

If you output your finished sequence to a file, you'll choose a format, a file type, and a codec.

When you're starting out in video editing, you may find the number of formats available a little overwhelming. Premiere Pro can work natively with a wide range of video and audio formats and codecs and will often play back mismatched formats smoothly.

However, when Premiere Pro has to adjust video for playback because of mismatched sequence settings, your editing system must work harder to play the video, and this will impact real-time performance. It's worth taking the time before you start editing to make sure you have sequence settings that closely match your original media files.

The essential factors are always the same: the number of frames per second, the frame size (the number of pixels in the picture horizontally and vertically), and the audio format. If you were to turn your sequence into a media file without applying a conversion, then the frame rate, audio format, frame size, and so on, would all match the settings you chose when creating the sequence.

When you output your sequence to a file, you can choose any format you like (for more on exporting, see Lesson 16, "Exporting Frames, Clips, and Sequences").

Note: The Preset Description area of the Sequence Presets tab often describes the kind of camera used to capture media in this format.

Customizing a sequence preset

Once you've selected the sequence preset that most closely matches your source video, you may want to adjust the settings to meet a particular delivery requirement or in-house workflow.

Let's take a look at those settings. So you can view them while reading about them, choose File > New > Sequence. Choose the DSLR 1080p30 preset again by clicking its name.

▶ **Tip:** For now, leave the settings as they are, but review the way the preset is going to configure the new sequence. Look at each setting from top to bottom to build familiarity with the choices required to configure a sequence.

The detailed settings are accessible by clicking the Settings tab in the New Sequence dialog box. Remember, Premiere Pro will automatically conform footage you add to your timeline so that it matches your sequence settings, giving you a standard frame rate and frame size, regardless of the original clip format.

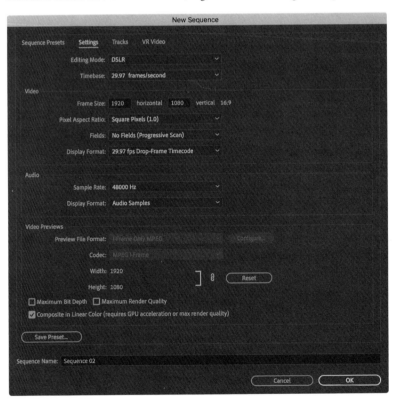

You'll notice that though you chose a 30 fps format, the Timebase menu defaults to 29.97 fps, which is a drop-frame timecode system used when broadcasting NTSC video on traditional TV networks. If you are not intending to broadcast your video this way but instead intend to distribute your creative work online, you may as well change this to 30 fps to accurately measure playback duration.

Creating a sequence preset

While the standard presets usually work, you may sometimes need to create a custom setting. To do so, first choose a sequence preset that matches your media closely and then make custom selections in the Settings and Tracks areas of the New Sequence dialog box. Having adjusted the settings, you can save your custom preset for future use by clicking the Save Preset button near the bottom of the Settings section.

If you save a preset, you can give your customized project settings preset a name in the Save Settings dialog box, add notes if you want, and click OK. The preset will appear in a Custom folder under Sequence Presets.

If your media matches one of the presets, it's not necessary to change the settings.

You'll notice that some settings cannot be changed when you use a preset. This is because they're optimized for the media type you selected on the Sequence Presets tab. For complete flexibility, change the Editing Mode menu to Custom.

Maximum Bit Depth and Maximum Render Quality settings

When editing with GPU acceleration (that's when dedicated graphics hardware graphics performs some of the visual effects rendering and playback), advanced algorithms are used, and effects are rendered in 32-bit color.

When working without GPU acceleration, you can enable Maximum Bit Depth, and Premiere Pro will render special effects at the maximum quality possible. For many effects, this means 32-bit floating-point color, which allows for trillions of color combinations. This is the best possible quality for your effects but is more work for your computer, so expect less real-time playback performance.

If you enable the Maximum Render Quality option or if you have GPU acceleration enabled in the project's settings, Premiere Pro uses a more advanced system for scaling images. Without this option, you might see minor artifacts or noise in the picture when making images smaller. Without GPU acceleration, this option will impact playback performance and file export times.

Both of these options can be turned off or on at any time, so you can edit without them to maximize performance and then turn them on when you output your finished work. Even with both options on you can use real-time effects and expect good performance from Premiere Pro.

Understanding audio track types

When you add a video or audio clip to a sequence, you'll always put it on a *track*. Tracks are horizontal areas in the Timeline panel that hold clips in a particular position in time. If you have more than one video track, any video clips placed on an upper track will appear in front of clips on a lower track. For example, if you have text or a graphic on your second video track and a video clip on your first video track (below it), you'll see the graphic in front of the video.

The Tracks tab in the New Sequence dialog box allows you to preselect the track types for the new sequence. This is perhaps most useful when creating a sequence preset with names already assigned to audio tracks.

All audio tracks are played at the same time, creating a complete audio mix. To create a mix, simply position your audio clips on different tracks, lined up in time. Narration, sound bites, sound effects, and music can be organized by putting them on different tracks. You can also rename tracks, making it easier to find your way around more complex sequences.

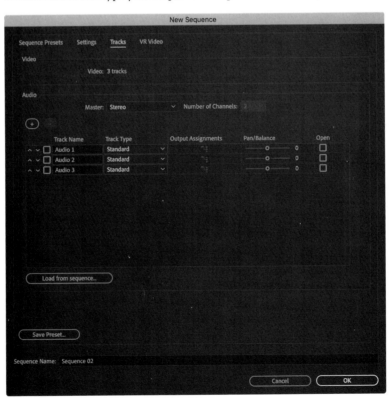

● **Note:** The Audio > Master setting configures the sequence to output audio as stereo, 5.1, multichannel, or mono.

Premiere Pro lets you specify how many video and audio tracks will be included when the sequence is created. You can easily add and remove tracks later, but you can't change the option you choose from the Master menu under Audio, which is the final audio mix type your sequence will produce. For now, choose Stereo.

An audio track can be one of several types. Each track type is designed for specific types of audio. When you choose a particular track type, Premiere Pro gives you the right controls to make adjustments to the sound, based on the number of audio channels in the track. For example, stereo clips need different controls than 5.1 surround-sound clips.

The types of audio tracks are as follows:

- **Standard:** These tracks are for both mono and stereo audio clips.

- **5.1:** These tracks are for audio clips with 5.1 audio (the kind used for surround sound).

- **Adaptive:** Adaptive tracks are for mono, stereo, or multichannel audio and give you precise control over the output routing for each audio channel. For example, you could decide the track audio channel 3 should be output to your mix in channel 5. This workflow is used for multilingual broadcast TV, where precise control of audio channels is used at transmission.

- **Mono:** This track type will accept only mono audio clips.

When you add a clip to a sequence that has both video and audio, Premiere Pro makes sure the audio channels go to the right kind of track. You can't accidentally put an audio clip on the wrong kind of track; Premiere Pro will automatically create the right kind of track if one doesn't exist already.

You'll explore audio more in Lesson 10, "Editing and Mixing Audio."

When you've finished exploring the New Project dialog box, click OK to close it, then choose File > Save to save your project.

VR video

Premiere Pro offers exceptional support for 360 video and 180 video. Both are often described as *VR video*, or immersive video, where multiple cameras, or a very wide lens, are used to capture a video image that can be viewed with a VR headset to create an immersive experience.

On the VR Video tab in the New Sequence dialog box, you can specify the angle of view captured so Premiere Pro can accurately display the image.

VR video is beyond the scope of this book, but it is well worth exploring when you have mastered the basics of video editing.

Review questions

1 What is the purpose of the Settings tab in the New Sequence dialog box?

2 How should you choose a sequence preset?

3 What is timecode?

4 How do you create a custom sequence preset?

Review answers

1 The Settings tab is used to customize an existing preset or to create a new custom preset.

2 It's generally best to choose a preset that matches your original footage to minimize conversion during playback. Premiere Pro makes this easy by describing the presets in terms of camera systems.

3 Timecode is the universal system for measuring time in hours, minutes, seconds, and frames. The number of frames per second varies depending on the recording format.

4 When you've chosen the settings you want for your custom preset on the Settings tab in the New Sequence dialog box, click the Save Preset button, give it a name and a description, and click OK.

3 IMPORTING MEDIA

Lesson overview

In this lesson, you'll learn about the following:

- Using the Media Browser to load video files

- Using the Import command to load graphic files

- Working with proxy media

- Using Adobe Stock

- Choosing where to place cache files

- Recording a voice-over

 This lesson will take about 75 minutes to complete. Please log in to your account on peachpit.com to download the lesson files for this lesson, or go to the "Getting Started" section at the beginning of this book and follow the instructions under "Accessing the lesson files and Web Edition." Store the files on your computer in a convenient location. Your Account page is also where you'll find any updates to the lesson files. Look on the Lesson & Update Files tab to access the most current content.

To create a sequence, you need to import media files into your project. This might include video footage, animation files, narration, music, atmospheric sound, graphics, or photos. Everything you include in a sequence must be imported before it can be used.

Any item included in a sequence will always also be included in the Project panel. Importing a clip directly to a sequence automatically adds the clip to the Project panel, and deleting a clip in the Project panel removes it from sequences it appears in (you'll be given the option to cancel if you do this).

Whichever way you approach editing sequences, importing clips to the Project panel and organizing them is the first step. In this lesson, you'll learn multiple methods for browsing and importing media.

Starting the lesson

In this lesson, you'll learn to import media assets into Adobe Premiere Pro CC. For most files, you'll use the Media Browser panel, a robust asset browser that works with many media types you'll import into Premiere Pro. You'll also learn about special cases such as importing graphics or capturing from videotape.

For this lesson, you can continue to use the project file you created in Lesson 2, "Setting Up a Project." If you do not have the previous lesson file, you can open the file Lesson 03.prproj from the Lesson 03 folder.

1 Continue to work with your project file from the previous lesson, or open it from your hard drive.

2 Choose File > Save As.

3 Browse to Lessons/Lesson 03, and save the project with the name My Lesson 03.prproj.

Importing assets

When you import items into a Premiere Pro project, you are creating a link to the original media file with a pointer that lives inside your project.

The pointer is called a *clip*, and you can think of a clip as a special kind of alias (macOS) or shortcut (Windows).

When you work with a clip in Premiere Pro, you are not making a copy of the original file or modifying it; instead, you're selectively playing a part of, or all of, the original media from its current location, in a nondestructive manner.

For example, if you choose to edit only part of a clip into your sequence, you're not throwing away the unused media. A copy of the clip is added to the sequence with instructions to play only the part you selected. This changes the apparent duration in the sequence, even though the full original duration in the media file is unchanged.

Also, if you add an effect to a clip to brighten the image, the effect is applied to the clip, not the media file it links to. In a sense, the original media file is played "through" the clip, with interpretation settings and effects applied.

Media can be imported in two principal ways.

Tip: Another way to open the Import dialog box is to double-click an empty area of the Project panel.

- By choosing File > Import. You can also drag media files directly from Finder (macOS) or Explorer (Windows) into the Project panel or Timeline panel.

- Using the Media Browser.

Let's explore the benefits of each.

When to use the Import command

Using the Import command is straightforward (and may match your experience in other applications). To import any file, just choose File > Import.

You can also use the keyboard shortcut Command+I (macOS) or Ctrl+I (Windows) to open the Import dialog box.

This method works best for self-contained assets such as graphics and audio or video files like .mov (QuickTime) or .mp4 (H.264), especially if you know exactly where those assets are on your drive and can quickly navigate to them.

This importing method is not ideal for file-based camera footage, which often uses complex folder structures with separate files for audio, video, and important additional data describing the footage (metadata), or for RAW media files. For most camera-originated media, you'll want to use the Media Browser panel.

When to use the Media Browser panel

In short, if in doubt, use the Media Browser panel. It's a robust tool for reviewing your media assets and then importing them into Premiere Pro. The Media Browser shows the fragmented files you might capture with a digital video camera as whole clips; you'll see each recording as a single item, with the video and audio combined, regardless of the original recording format.

This means you can avoid dealing with complex camera folder structures and instead work with easy-to-browse icons and metadata. Being able to see this metadata (which contains important information, such as clip duration, recording date, and file type) makes it easier to select the correct clip in a long list.

Tip: If you want to import assets used in another Premiere Pro project, you can browse inside that project in the Media Browser panel. Use the Media Browser to locate the project file and double-click it to view its contents. You can select and import clips and sequences to your current Project panel.

Note: You can open multiple project files at the same time. This makes it easy to copy clips from one project to another. If you do, remember you are copying the clip and not the media it links to.

By default, in the Editing workspace, you'll find the Media Browser in the lower-left corner of your Premiere Pro workspace. It's docked in the same panel group as the Project panel. You can also quickly access the Media Browser by pressing Shift+8 (be sure to use the 8 key at the top of the keyboard).

Like any other panel, you can position the Media Browser in another panel group by dragging its panel name (sometimes referred to as the *panel tab*).

You can also undock it to make it a floating panel by clicking the menu ▤ next to the panel name and choosing Undock Panel.

Browsing for files in the Media Browser is similar to browsing with Finder (macOS) or Explorer (Windows). The contents of your storage are displayed as navigation folders on the left, with buttons to navigate forward and backward at the top.

You can use arrow keys to select items.

There are several benefits to using the Media Browser:

- While browsing a folder, you can narrow the display to a specific file type, such as JPEG, Photoshop, XML, or ARRIRAW files (by choosing items from the File Types Displayed menu ▼).

- Autosensing camera data—AVCHD, Canon XF, P2, RED, Cinema DNG, Sony HDV, or XDCAM (EX and HD)—to correctly display the clips.

- Viewing and customizing the kinds of metadata to display.

- Correctly displaying media that has spanned clips across multiple camera media cards. Premiere Pro will automatically import the files as a single clip even if a longer video file filled a storage card and continued onto a second.

Working with ingest options and proxy media

Premiere Pro offers excellent performance when playing back, and applying special effects to, a broad range of media formats and codecs. However, there may be occasions that your system hardware will struggle to play media, especially if it's high-resolution RAW footage.

You may decide it will be more efficient to work with low-resolution copies of your media while you edit and to switch to the full, original resolution media just before you check your effects and output your finished work. This is a *proxy workflow*— creating low-resolution "proxy" files to use instead of your original content. You can switch between the two whenever you like.

Premiere Pro can automate creating proxy files during import. If you're happy with the performance on your system when working with original footage, you'll probably skip this feature. Still, it opens up significant advantages, both for system performance and for collaboration, particularly if you're working with high resolution media on a less powerful computer.

Let's check out the options.

1 Choose File > Project Settings > Ingest Settings.

Tip: You can also open the Project Settings dialog box to the Ingest Settings tab from the Media Browser panel by selecting Ingest or by clicking the Open Ingest Settings button.

This dialog box contains the original project setup options you saw when creating the project. You can change any setting at any time.

By default, all the Ingest options are deselected. Whichever ingest option you choose, the actions will be performed regardless of the way you import media files from now on. Files you have already imported are not affected.

2 Enable Ingest by selecting it, and open the first menu to see these options:

- **Copy:** When you import media files, Premiere Pro will copy the original files to a location you choose from the Primary Destination menu below. This is a valuable option if you are importing media files directly from your camera storage, since media files must be available to Premiere Pro when your cards are not connected to the computer.

- **Transcode:** When you import media files, Premiere Pro will convert the files to a new format and codec based on the preset you choose and will place the new files in a destination location you choose. This is useful if you are working in a post-production facility that has adopted a standard format and codec for all projects.

- **Create Proxies:** When you import media files, Premiere Pro creates additional copies that are lower resolution, based on the preset you choose, and stores them in the location you choose from the Proxy Destination menu. This is useful if you are working on a lower-powered computer or you want to temporarily save on storage space while traveling with a copy of your media. You would not want to use these files for your final delivery, but they open up the option of using a number of collaborative workflows as well as speeding up effect configuration.

- **Copy and Create Proxies:** When you import media files, Premiere Pro will copy the original files to a location you choose in the Primary Destination menu *and* create proxies that are stored in the Proxy Destination menu.

If proxy media exists for clips in your project, it's easy to switch between displaying your original, full-quality media and your low-resolution proxy versions. Choose Premiere Pro CC > Preferences > Media (macOS) or Edit > Preferences > Media (Windows) and toggle Enable Proxies.

3   Choose Create Proxies, open the Preset menu, and try choosing a few options. Look at the Summary in the lower part of the dialog box that explains each option.

```
✓ 1024x540 Apple ProRes 422 (Proxy)
  1024x540 GoPro CineForm
  1024x540 H.264
  1280x720 Apple ProRes 422 (Proxy)
  1280x720 GoPro CineForm
  1280x720 H.264
  1536x790 Apple ProRes 422 (Proxy)
  1536x790 GoPro CineForm
  1536x790 H.264
  VR 2048x1024 Monoscopic DNxHR Stereo Audio
  VR 2048x2048 Stereoscopic DNxHR Stereo Audio
```

It's most important that the preset you choose matches the aspect ratio of your original footage (the ratio of the width to the height of the image). This way, you'll be able to position titles and graphics correctly while viewing the proxy files.

4   When you have finished looking at the settings, click Cancel to exit without applying any of the options.

This was just an introduction to the proxy media workflow. For more information about managing proxy files, linking proxy media, and creating new proxy file pre-sets, see the Adobe Premiere Pro Help.

Working with the Media Browser panel

The Media Browser allows you to easily browse for files on your computer. It can stay open, it's fast and convenient, and it's optimized for locating and importing footage.

Following a file-based camera workflow

Premiere Pro can use footage from file-based cameras without conversion, including compressed native media from camera systems such as P2, XDCAM, and AVCHD; RAW media from Canon, Sony, RED, and ARRI; and post-production-friendly codecs such as Avid DNxHD, Apple ProRes, and GoPro Cineform.

For best results, follow these guidelines (no need to follow along for now):

- Create a new media folder for each project.

- Copy camera media to your editing storage with the existing folder structure intact. Be sure to transfer the complete data folder directly from the root directory of the card. For best results, consider using the transfer application that is often included by the camera manufacturer to move your video files, or explore Adobe Prelude CC, which can automate much of this process. Check that all media files have been copied and that the original card and the copied folder sizes match. See the sidebar "Importing from Adobe Prelude" for an introduction to sending a Prelude project to Premiere Pro.

- Clearly name the copied folder of the media with the camera information, including card number and the date of the shoot.

- Create a second copy of the media on a physically separate, second drive in case of hardware failure.

- Really do actually create that second copy of your media on a physically separate drive! Storage can fail without warning…

- Ideally, create a long-term archive copy of your media using another backup method, such as LTO tape (a popular long-term storage system) or an external storage drive.

Importing from Adobe Prelude

Adobe Prelude is designed to allow producers or assistants to quickly and efficiently ingest, log, and transcode media (convert format and codec) for tapeless workflows.

Here's how to send a Prelude project to Premiere Pro:

1 Launch Adobe Prelude.

2 Open the project you want to transfer, and select one or more items in the Project panel. Adobe Prelude has a similar appearance to Premiere Pro but with simplified controls.

3 Choose File > Export > Project.

4 Select the Project check box.

5 Enter a name in the Name field.

6 In the Type menu, choose Premiere Pro.

7 Click OK. The Choose Folder dialog box opens.

8 Navigate to a destination for the new project, and click Choose. A new Premiere Pro project is created.

You can open the Premiere Pro project file directly, or you can import it into an existing project.

If both Premiere Pro and Prelude are running at the same time on the same computer, you can also send clips from Prelude to Premiere Pro by selecting them, right-clicking the selection, and choosing Send To Premiere Pro.

All Supported Files

AAF

ARRIRAW Files

Adobe After Effects Projects

Adobe After Effects Text Templates

Adobe Audition Tracks

Adobe Illustrator File

Adobe Premiere Pro Projects

Adobe Rough Cut File

Adobe Sound Document

Adobe Title Designer

Audio Interchange File Format

Audio Interchange File Format AIFF-C

Biovision Hierarchy

Bitmap

CMX3600 EDLs

Canon Cinema RAW Light

Canon RAW

Character Animator Project

Cinema DNG Files

Cineon/DPX File

Comma Delimited Value

Distribution Format Exchange Profile File

EBU N19 Subtitle File

Final Cut Pro XML

GIF File

HEIF files

JPEG File

JSON

MBWF / RF64

MP3 Audio

MPEG Movie

MXF

MacCaption VANC File

Motion Graphics JSON

Motion Graphics Template

OpenEXR

PNG File

Phantom Files

Photoshop

QuickTime Movie

RED R3D Raw File

Scenarist Closed Caption File

SonyRAW Format

SubRip Subtitle Format

TIFF image file

Tab Delimited Value

Text Template

Truevision Targa File

W3C/SMPTE/EBU Timed Text File

Waveform Audio

XDCAM-EX Movie

All Files

Understanding supported video file types

It's not unusual to work on a project with video clips from multiple cameras using different file types, media formats, and codecs. This is no problem for Premiere Pro because you can mix different types of media in the same sequence. Also, the Media Browser can display almost any media file type. It's particularly well suited to file-based camera formats.

If your system hardware struggles to play back high-resolution media, you may find it helpful to use proxy files while editing.

The following are the major types of file-based media supported by Premiere Pro:

- Any DSLR camera that shoots H.264 media as QuickTime MOV or MP4 files, or H.265 (HEVC) media. H.265 requires a more powerful computer for playback.

- Panasonic P2, DV, DVCPRO, DVCPRO 50, DVCPRO HD, AVCI, AVC Ultra, AVC Ultra Long GOP.

- RED ONE, RED EPIC, RED Mysterium X, the 6K RED Dragon, the 8K REDCODE RAW Weapon.

- ARRIRAW, including ARRI AMIRA.

- Sony XDCAM SD, XDCAM 50, XAVC, SStP, RAW, HDV (when shot on file-based media).

- AVCHD cameras.

- Canon XF, Canon RAW.

- Apple ProRes.

- Image sequences, including DPX.

- Avid DNxHD and DNxHR MXF files.

- Blackmagic CinemaDNG.

- Phantom Cine camera.

Finding assets with the Media Browser panel

In many ways, the Media Browser is like Finder (macOS) or Explorer (Windows). It has Forward and Back buttons to go through your recent navigation. It also has a list of shortcuts on the side. Finding materials is easy.

● **Note:** When importing media, be sure to copy the files to your local storage, or use the project ingest options to create copies before removing your memory cards or external drives.

Continue working with your My Lesson 03.prproj project.

1   Begin by resetting the workspace to the default; in the Workspaces panel, click Editing. Then open the panel menu adjacent to the Editing option, and choose Reset To Saved Layout, or double-click the Editing workspace name.

> **Note:** If you can't see the Workspaces panel, select it by choosing Window > Workspaces (at the bottom of the menu).

Note: When you open a project created on another computer, you may see a message warning you about a missing renderer. It's fine to click OK in this message.

2   Click the Media Browser panel name to bring it to the front of the panel group (it should be docked with the Project panel by default).

3   To make the Media Browser easier to see, position your mouse pointer over the panel and then press the ` (accent grave) key (it is often in the upper-left corner of a keyboard), or double-click the panel name.

> **Tip:** Some keyboard layouts make it difficult to find the right key. If you can't locate the ` (accent grave) key, you can double-click the name of a panel to enlarge it to fill the screen.

The Media Browser panel should now fill the screen. You may need to adjust the width of columns to make it easier to see items.

4   Using the Media Browser, navigate to the folder Lessons/Assets/Video and Audio Files/Theft Unexpected.

Note: The Media Browser filters out non-media and unsupported files, making it easier to browse for video or audio assets.

5 Click the Thumbnail View button  at the bottom left of the Media Browser panel, and drag the resize slider next to it to enlarge the thumbnails of the clips. You can use any size you like.

You can hover your pointer over any unselected clip thumbnail, without clicking, to see a preview of the clip contents. Hovering over the left edge shows the start of the clip; hovering over the right edge shows the end of the clip.

6 Click any clip once to select it.

You can now preview the clip using keyboard shortcuts. When a clip is selected while in thumbnail view, a small preview timeline appears under the clip.

7 Press the L key to play a clip.

8 To stop playback, press the K key.

9 To play backward, press the J key.

10 Experiment with playing back other clips. You should be able to hear the clip audio during playback.

You can press the J or L key multiple times to increase the playback rate for fast previews. Use the K key or the spacebar to pause playback.

11 Now you'll import all these clips into your project. Press Command+A (macOS) or Ctrl+A (Windows) to select all the clips.

12 Right-click one of the selected clips and choose Import.

▶ **Tip:** You can also drag selected clips onto the Project panel's tab and then down into the empty area to import the clips.

Having completed the process of importing, the Project panel opens automatically and displays the clips you just imported.

13 Press the ` (accent grave) key or use the Project panel menu to restore the panel group to its original size.

Like the Media Browser panel, clips in the Project panel can be viewed as icons or as a list, with information about each clip displayed. Switch between these two viewing modes by clicking the List View button 📋 or Icon View button ■, at the bottom left of the Project panel.

Making the most of the Media Browser

The Media Browser has a number of features that make it easy to navigate your storage.

*   The Forward and Back buttons ← → work like those in a web browser, allowing you to navigate to locations you have viewed previously.

*   If you expect to import files from a location often, you can add the folder to a list of favorites at the top of the navigation panel. To create a favorite, right-click the folder and choose Add to Favorites.

*   You can limit the types of files displayed to make it easier to browse large folders by opening the File Types Displayed menu ▼.

*   To ignore regular media file types and just display file-based media from a particular camera system, open the Directory Viewers menu ◎.

*   You can open multiple Media Browser panels and access the contents of several different folders at once. To open a new Media Browser panel, open the panel menu and choose New Media Browser Panel.

*   By default, limited information about clips is displayed in the list view. To display more information, you can add multiple columns of metadata by clicking the panel menu and choosing Edit Columns. In the Edit Columns dialog box, select each type of metadata you would like to display.

Importing still image files

Graphics are an integral part of post-production. People expect graphics to both convey information and add to the visual style of a final edit. Premiere Pro can import just about any image and graphic file type. Support is especially excellent when you use the native file formats created by Adobe's leading graphic tools, Adobe Photoshop CC and Adobe Illustrator CC.

Anyone who works with print graphics or performs photo retouching has probably used Adobe Photoshop. Adobe Photoshop is a powerful tool with great depth and versatility, and it's an increasingly important part of the video production world. Let's explore how to properly import files from Adobe Photoshop.

First, you'll import a basic graphic.

Importing single-layer image files

Most graphics and photos you will work with will have a single layer—one flat grid of pixels that you can work with as a simple media file. Let's import one.

1 Select the Project panel.

2 Choose File > Import, or press Command+I (macOS) or Ctrl+I (Windows).

3 Navigate to Lessons/Assets/Graphics.

4 Select the file Theft_Unexpected.png, and click Import.

   This PNG graphic is a simple logo file, and it appears in the Premiere Pro Project panel.

When the Project panel is in icon view, it displays the contents of graphics as thumbnails.

Introducing Dynamic Link

One way to work with Premiere Pro is with a suite of tools. You may be using a version of Adobe Creative Cloud that includes other components for related video-editing tasks. To make things easier, you'll find several options for speeding up your post-production workflow.

A good example is Dynamic Link. This allows you to import After Effects compositions (which are a little like Premiere Pro sequences) into a Premiere Pro project in a way that creates a live connection between the two applications. Once added in this way, the After Effects compositions will look and behave like any other clip in your Premiere Pro project.

When you make changes in After Effects, the compositions automatically update in Premiere Pro, which is a great time-saver.

You can use Dynamic Link to create links between Premiere Pro and After Effects and between Premiere Pro and Audition.

Importing layered Adobe Photoshop files

Adobe Photoshop can create graphics with multiple layers. Layers are similar to tracks in a Premiere Pro sequence and allow for separation between visual elements. You can import Photoshop document layers into Premiere Pro individually to allow for isolation (when making adjustments) or animation. Let's look at the import options.

1 Double-click an empty area of the Project panel to open the Import dialog box.

2 Navigate to Lessons/Assets/Graphics.

3 Select the file Theft_Unexpected_Layered.psd, and click Import.

4 The Import Layered File dialog box appears and contains the Import As menu offering four ways of selectively importing layers:

> **Note:** There are some deselected layers in this PSD. These are layers with layer visibility turned off in Photoshop but not deleted. Premiere Pro honors the layer selection automatically on import.

- **Merge All Layers:** This merges all layers into one, importing the file into Premiere Pro as a single, flattened clip.

- **Merged Layers:** This merges only the specific layers you select in this dialog box into a single, flattened clip.

- **Individual Layers:** This imports only the specific layers you select in this dialog box, with each layer becoming a separate clip in a bin in the Project panel.

- **Sequence:** This imports only the layers you select in this dialog box, each as a single clip. Premiere Pro then automatically creates a new sequence (with its frame size based on the imported PSD dimensions) containing each clip on a separate track (matching the original stacking order).

If you choose Sequence or Individual Layers, you can choose one of the following from the Footage Dimensions menu:

- **Document Size:** This brings all the selected layers into Premiere Pro at the size of the original Photoshop document.

- **Layer Size:** This matches the frame size of the new Premiere Pro clips to the frame size of their individual layers in the original Photoshop file. Layers that do not fill the entire canvas will be cropped tightly, as transparent areas outside of the rectangle containing the layer's pixels are removed. Layers are also then centered in the frame, losing their original relative positioning.

5 For this exercise, choose Sequence, and choose Document Size. Click OK.

> **Tip:** There are good reasons to import individual PSD layers with separate layer sizes. For example, some graphic designers create multiple images for editors to incorporate into video edits, with each image occupying a different layer in the PSD. The PSD itself is a kind of one-stop image store when used this way.

6 Look in the Project panel for the newly created bin ▦ called Theft_Unexpected_Layered. Double-click it to open it.

● **Note:** Remember, bins in the Project panel look and behave a lot like folders in your computer file system. Bins exist only inside the project file and are a great way to stay organized.

7 Inside the bin, double-click the sequence Theft_Unexpected_Layered to open it in the Timeline panel.

Sequences have a unique icon in List view ▦ and displayed over their thumbnail in Icon view ▦.

If you're unsure which item is which, hover the pointer over an item name to find out whether it is a clip or a sequence by reading the tooltip.

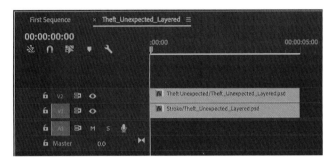

Image tips for Adobe Photoshop files

Here are a few tips for importing images from Adobe Photoshop:

- Remember that when you import a layered Photoshop document as a sequence, the frame size in Premiere Pro will be the same as the pixel dimensions of the Photoshop document.

- Even if you don't plan to zoom in or pan, try to create files with a frame size at least as large as the frame size of the project. Otherwise, you'll have to scale up the image, and it will lose some of its sharpness.

- If you do plan to zoom or pan, create images so that the resulting zoomed or panned area of the image has a frame size at least as large as the frame size of the sequence. For example, if you were working in full HD, which is 1920 × 1080 pixels, and you wanted to do a 2X zoom, you'd need 3840 × 2160 pixels to keep the image perfectly sharp without expanding the appearance of the pixels.

- Importing large image files uses more system memory and can slow down your system. If you are working with original photos and they're massive, consider processing them to make them smaller before using them.

- If possible, use 16-bit RGB color. The CMYK color mode is for print workflows only (and is not supported by Premiere Pro), while video editing uses RGB or YUV color modes.

- As with any other media you import, changes made to the PSD file will update automatically in Premiere Pro when the file is saved. This means a designer can continue to work on an image you have already incorporated into a sequence.

8　Look at the sequence in the timeline. The contents of the sequence are displayed in the Program Monitor. Try clicking the Toggle Track Output button ⊙ at the left of the timeline for each track to reveal and hide the content on each layer.

9　When you double-clicked the Theft_Unexpected_Layered bin, it opened in a new panel in the same group as the Project panel. Bins have the same options as the Project panel, and opening multiple bins to browse their contents is a common way to navigate the available media in a project.

Close the Theft_Unexpected_Layered bin by choosing Close Panel from its panel menu ☰.

Importing Adobe Illustrator files

Another graphics component in Adobe Creative Cloud is Adobe Illustrator. Unlike Adobe Photoshop, which is primarily designed to work with pixel-based (or raster) graphics, Adobe Illustrator is a vector-based application. Vector graphics are mathematical descriptions of shapes rather than drawn pixels. This means you can scale them to any size and they always look sharp.

Vector graphics are typically used for technical illustrations, line art, or complex graphics.

Let's import a vector graphic.

1　Double-click an empty area of the Project panel to open the Import dialog box.

2　Navigate to Lessons/Assets/Graphics.

3　Select the file Brightlove_film_logo.ai, and click Import.

4　A clip linked to the Illustrator file you imported will appear in the Project panel. Double-click the icon for the clip to view the logo in the Source Monitor.

Notice the black text in the logo disappears into the black background of the Source Monitor. That's because the logo has a transparent background; you'll learn more about working with layers and transparency in Lesson 14, "Exploring Compositing Techniques."

Here's the way Premiere Pro deals with Adobe Illustrator files:

- Like the Photoshop file you imported earlier, this is a layered graphic file. However, Premiere Pro doesn't give you the option to import Adobe Illustrator files in separate layers. It always merges them into a single layer clip.

- Premiere Pro uses a process called *rasterization* to convert the vector-based Adobe Illustrator art into the pixel-based image format used by Premiere Pro. This conversion happens during import automatically, so be sure your graphics are configured to be large enough in Illustrator before importing them into Premiere Pro.

Note: If you right-click Brightlove_film_logo.ai in the Project panel, you'll note that one option is Edit Original. If you have Illustrator installed on your computer, choosing Edit Original will open this graphic in Illustrator, ready to be edited. So even though the layers are merged in Premiere Pro, you can return to Adobe Illustrator, edit the original layered file, and save it; the changes will immediately appear in Premiere Pro.

- Premiere Pro automatically anti-aliases (smooths the edges of) Adobe Illustrator art.

- Premiere Pro sets all empty areas of Illustrator files as transparent so that clips on lower tracks in your sequence will show through.

Importing subfolders

When you bring media into Premiere Pro by choosing File > Import, you don't have to select individual files. You can select a whole folder. If you have already organized your files into folders and subfolders on your storage drive, when you import them, the folders are re-created as bins in Premiere Pro.

Try this now.

1   Choose File > Import, or press Command+I (macOS) or Ctrl+I (Windows).

2   Navigate to Lessons/Assets, and select the Stills folder. Don't browse inside the folder; just select it.

3   Click the Import (macOS) or Import Folder (Windows) button. Premiere Pro imports the folder and its contents, including two subfolders containing photos. In the Project panel, you'll find bins have been created to match the folders. You can click the disclosure triangle next to any bin to toggle the display of its contents.

> **Note:** If you import an entire folder, it's possible some of the files will not be media supported by Premiere Pro. If so, an information message will inform you that some files could not be imported.

Importing VR video

What is often referred to as *VR video* is really 360 video that is best viewed using a VR headset as it captures an image in all 360 degrees. When wearing a VR headset to view this kind of video, you can turn your head to look in different directions. Premiere Pro has built-in support for 360° video and a new 180° video standard, with a dedicated viewing mode, native support for VR headsets, and special effects designed for the particular needs of video footage that surrounds the viewer.

There is no special import process for 360 video—you can use the regular Import option, or you can use the Media Browser panel and import as you would any other video.

Premiere Pro expects prestitched equirectangular media, so you will have to use another application to prepare your 360 media in this way prior to import. This is the standard delivery option for 360° and 180° video.

The excellent 360 video workflows in Premiere Pro are beyond the scope of this book—check the online help for more information.

Using Adobe Stock

The Libraries panel allows you to easily share design assets between projects and users. You can also search Adobe Stock directly in the Libraries panel, choose video clips and graphics, and use a low-resolution preview in your project immediately.

Adobe Stock offers millions of images and videos you can easily incorporate into your sequences via the Libraries panel.

If you're happy with a stock item and you'd like to purchase the full-resolution version, you can click the License And Save To shopping cart icon that appears on the item in the Libraries panel. The full-resolution item will be downloaded and automatically replaces the low-resolution version in your project and sequences.

For more information about Adobe Stock, check out https://stock.adobe.com.

Customizing the media cache

When you import files in certain video and audio formats, Premiere Pro may need to process and cache (temporarily store) a version of the file. This is particularly true for highly compressed formats, and the process is called *conforming*.

If necessary, imported audio files are automatically conformed to a new CFA file (conformed audio file). Most MPEG files are *indexed*, leading to an extra .mpgindex file that makes it easier to read the file (it's a little like creating a map of the file to make playback easier).

You'll know that the cache is being built if you see a small progress indicator in the lower-right corner of the screen when importing media.

The media cache improves preview playback performance by making it easier for your editing system to decode and play media. You can customize the cache to further improve performance. A media cache database helps Premiere Pro manage these cache files, which are shared between multiple Creative Cloud applications.

Note: You may have noticed the word *conform* is used to describe both the way clip playback is adjusted to match sequence settings *and* the way certain formats are processed when imported to Premiere Pro. That's because the principle is the same—the original material is adapted to improve performance.

To access options for the cache, choose Premiere Pro CC > Preferences > Media Cache (macOS) or Edit > Preferences > Media Cache (Windows).

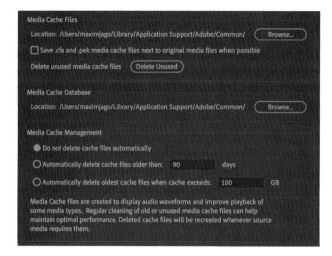

Here are the options:

- To move the media cache files or the media cache database to a new location, click the appropriate Browse button, select the desired location, and click Choose (macOS) or Choose Folder (Windows). In most cases, you should not move the media cache database during an editing project.

- Select Save .cfa And .pek Media Cache Files Next To Original Media Files When Possible to keep media cache files stored on the same drive as the media. If you want to keep everything in one central folder, leave this option unselected. Remember, the faster the drive for the media cache, the better the playback performance you're likely to experience in Premiere Pro.

- You should clean the media cache database on a regular basis to remove old conformed and indexed files that are no longer required. To do so, click the Delete Unused button. Any connected drives will have their cache files removed. It's a good idea to do this after you wrap up projects because it removes unnecessary preview render files too, saving space.

- The Media Cache Management options allow you to configure a degree of automation in the management of caches files. Premiere Pro will automatically re-create these files if they are needed, so it's safe to enable these options to save space.

Click Cancel to close the Preferences dialog box without saving your changes.

Tape vs. tapeless workflow

Tape is still sometimes used to acquire media, and it's often available as an archive storage format. To bring footage from tape into a Premiere Pro project, you can capture it.

Capture digital video from tape to your system storage before using it in a project. Premiere Pro captures video through a digital port, such as a FireWire or Serial Digital Interface (SDI) port (if you have third-party hardware). Premiere Pro saves captured footage to disk as files and imports the files into projects as clips, just as you would with file-based camera media. There are three basic approaches:

- You can capture your entire videotape as one long clip.
- You can log the beginning and end of each clip (each clip's In and Out marks) to batch capture them later.
- With some tape formats, you can use the scene detection feature in Premiere Pro to automatically create separate clips based on every time you pressed Record on your camera.

By default, you can use DV and HDV sources with Premiere Pro if your computer has a FireWire port. If you'd like to capture other, higher-end professional formats, you'll need to add a third-party capture device. These come in several form factors, including internal cards and breakout boxes that connect via FireWire, USB 3.0, SDI, and Thunderbolt.

Third-party hardware manufacturers can take advantage of Mercury Playback Engine features for previewing effects and video on a connected professional monitor. You can find a detailed list of supported hardware by visiting http://helpx.adobe.com/premiere-pro/compatibility.html.

Recording a voice-over

You may be working on a video project that includes a narration track. It's likely you will have the narration recorded by professionals (or at least recorded in a location quieter than your desk), but you can record audio right into Premiere Pro too.

This can be helpful because it will give you a sense of timing for your edits.

Try recording a scratch audio track.

1   If you're not using a built-in microphone, make sure your external microphone or audio mixer is properly connected to your computer. You may need to consult the documentation for your computer or sound card.

2   Every audio track has a set of buttons and options on the far left. This area is called the *track header*. There's a Voice-Over Record button 🎙 for each audio track. Right-click a microphone icon in the header area of the timeline

► **Tip:** If you have multiple audio input devices connected to your system, you can choose which will be used for voice over recording by right-clicking the Voice-over Record button and choosing Voice-Over Record Settings. The dialog box that appears also allows you to pre-name the new audio file.

panel, and choose Voice Over Record Settings to choose your microphone. Then click the "Close" button.

3 Turn down your computer speakers, or use headphones to prevent feedback or echo.

4 Open the Theft_Unexpected_Layered sequence, in the Theft_Unexpected_Layered bin.

5 Increase the height of the A1 track.

To increase the height of an audio track, drag down on the horizontal dividing line between two audio track headers, or hover the pointer over the track header, while holding Option (macOS) or Alt (Windows), and scroll the mouse wheel.

In the Timeline panel, time moves from left to right, just as it does with any online video. At the top of the Timeline panel, where the time ruler is displayed, a playhead 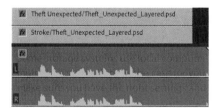 indicates the current frame displayed in the Program Monitor. You can click at any point in the time ruler and the playhead will move to show that frame. You can also drag on the time ruler itself to view the contents of the current sequence. This is called *scrubbing* (like scrubbing a floor).

6 Position the Timeline playhead at the beginning of the sequence, as far left as it will go, and click the voice-over Record button for track A1 to begin recording.

7 After a brief countdown, recording will begin. Say a few words, and press the spacebar to stop recording.

A new audio clip is created and added to the Project panel and the current sequence.

8 Choose File > Save to save the project. You may close it or leave it open for the next lesson.

Review questions

1 Does Premiere Pro CC need to convert P2, XDCAM, R3D, ARRIRAW, or AVCHD footage when it is imported?

2 What is one advantage of using the Media Browser rather than the File > Import method to import file-based media?

3 When you're importing a layered Photoshop file, what are the four different ways to import the file?

4 Where can media cache files be stored?

5 How can you enable proxy media file creation when video is imported?

Review answers

1 No. Premiere Pro CC can edit P2, XDCAM, R3D, ARRIRAW, and AVCHD, as well as many other formats, natively.

2 The Media Browser understands the complex folder structures for P2, XDCAM, and many other formats, and it shows you the clips in a visually friendly way.

3 You can merge all the visible layers in the Photoshop file into a single clip by choosing Merge All Layers from the Import As menu in the Import Layered File dialog box; or select the specific layers you want by choosing Merged Layers. If you want layers as separate clips, choose Individual Layers and select the layers to import, or choose Sequence to import the selected layers and create a new sequence from them.

4 You can store media cache files in any specified location or automatically on the same drive as the original files (when possible). The faster the storage for your cache, the better the playback performance.

5 You can enable proxy media file creation in the Ingest settings. You'll find these in the Project Settings dialog box. You can also enable proxy creation by selecting the box at the top of the Media Browser. There's an Ingest Settings button there too.

4 ORGANIZING MEDIA

Lesson overview

In this lesson, you'll learn about the following:

- Using the Project panel

- Staying organized with bins

- Adding clip metadata

- Using essential playback controls

- Interpreting footage

- Making changes to your clips

 This lesson will take about 90 minutes to complete. Please log in to your account on peachpit.com to download the lesson files for this lesson, or go to the Getting Started section at the beginning of this book and follow the instructions under "Accessing the lesson files and Web Edition." Store the files on your computer in a convenient location.

Your Account page is also where you'll find any updates to the lesson files. Look on the Lesson & Update Files tab to access the most current content.

Once you have some video and sound assets in your project, you'll begin looking through your footage and adding clips to a sequence. Before you do, it's well worth spending a little time organizing the assets you have. Doing so can save you from spending hours hunting for things later.

Starting the lesson

When you have lots of clips in your project, imported from several different media types, it can be a challenge to stay on top of everything and always find that magic shot when you need it.

In this lesson, you'll learn how to organize your clips using the Project panel. You'll create special folders, called *bins*, to divide your clips into categories. You'll also learn about adding important metadata and labels to your clips.

You'll begin by getting to know the Project panel and organizing your clips.

1 For this lesson, you'll use the project file you used in Lesson 3, "Importing Media." Continue to work with the project file from the previous lesson. Alternatively, open the project file **Lesson 04.prproj** from the Lessons/Lesson 04 folder.

2 To begin, reset the workspace to the default. In the Workspaces panel, click Editing. Then click the panel menu adjacent to the Editing option, and choose Reset To Saved Layout.

3 Choose File > Save As.

4 Rename the file to Lesson 04 Working.prproj.

5 Browse to the Lessons folder and click Save to save the project in the Lessons > Lesson 04 folder.

Using the Project panel

Everything you import into your Adobe Premiere Pro project will appear in the Project panel. As well as giving you tools for browsing your clips and working with their metadata, the Project panel has folder-like *bins* that you can use to stay organized.

Anything that appears in a sequence must also be in the Project panel. If you delete a clip in the Project panel that is already used in a sequence, the clip will automatically be removed from the sequence. Premiere Pro will warn you if deleting a clip will affect an existing sequence.

In addition to acting as the repository for all your clips, the Project panel gives you important options for interpreting media. All your footage will have a frame rate (frames per second, or fps) and a pixel aspect ratio (pixel shape), for example. You may want to change these settings for creative or technical reasons.

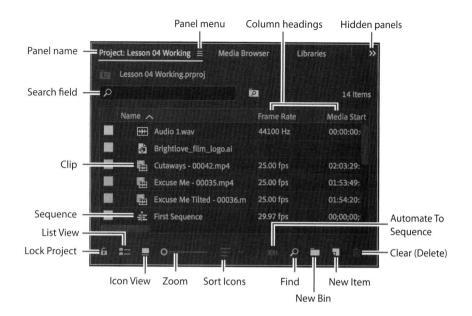

The Project panel in List view. To switch to this view, click the List View button at the bottom left of the panel.

Labels for the figure:
- Panel menu
- Column headings
- Hidden panels
- Panel name — Project: Lesson 04 Working
- Search field
- Clip
- Sequence
- List View
- Lock Project
- Icon View
- Zoom
- Sort Icons
- Find
- New Bin
- New Item
- Automate To Sequence
- Clear (Delete)

You could, for example, interpret video recorded at 60fps video as 30fps to achieve a 50-percent slow-motion effect. You might receive a video file that has the wrong pixel aspect ratio setting and want to correct it.

Name	Frame Rate	Media Start	Media End	Media Duration
Brightlove_film_logo.ai				
Cutaways - 00042.mp4	25.00 fps	02:03:29:12	02:04:34:11	00:01:05:00
Excuse Me - 00035.mp4	25.00 fps	01:53:49:17	01:54:20:21	00:00:31:05
Excuse Me Tilted - 00036.m	25.00 fps	01:54:20:22	01:56:02:19	00:01:41:23
First Sequence	29.97 fps	00;00;00;00	23;00;00;01	00;00;00;00
HS John - 00032.mp4	25.00 fps	01:46:22:12	01:50:13:08	00:03:50:22

Premiere Pro uses metadata associated with footage to know how to play it back. If you want to change the clip metadata, you can do so in the Project panel.

Customizing the Project panel

It's likely that you'll want to resize the Project panel from time to time. You'll alternate between looking at your clips as a list or as thumbnail icons. Sometimes it's quicker to resize the panel than to scroll to see more information.

The default Editing workspace is designed to keep the interface as clean as possible so you can focus on your creative work. Part of the Project panel that's hidden from view by default, called the Preview Area, gives additional information about your clips.

Let's take a look.

1 Open the Project panel menu.

Tip: You can access lots of clip information by scrolling the List view or by hovering your pointer over a clip name.

2 Choose Preview Area.

The Preview Area shows useful information about clips when you select them.

Tip: There's a quick way to toggle between seeing the Project panel in a frame and seeing it full-screen: Hover your pointer over the panel, and press the ` (accent grave) key. You can do this with any panel. If your keyboard does not have a ` (accent grave) key, you can double-click the panel name.

The Preview Area shows you several kinds of useful information about a selected clip in the Project panel, including the frame size, pixel aspect ratio, and duration.

Click the Poster Frame button to set the clip thumbnail displayed in the Project panel.

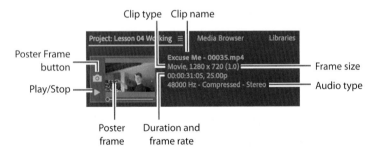

Clip type   Clip name

Poster Frame button

Play/Stop

Frame size

Audio type

Poster frame   Duration and frame rate

If it's not already selected, click the List View button ![List View icon] at the bottom left of the Project panel. In this view, you'll find a lot of information about each clip in the Project panel organized in columns, but you need to scroll horizontally to see it.

3 Choose Preview Area from the Project panel menu again to hide it.

Finding assets in the Project panel

Working with clips is a little like working with pieces of paper at your desk. If you have just one or two clips, it's easy. But when you have 100 to 200, you need an organizational system.

One way you can help make things smoother during the edit is to invest a little time in organizing your clips at the beginning. If you rename your clips after importing them, it will make it easier for you to locate content later (see "Changing names" in this lesson).

1 Click the Name column heading at the top of the Project panel. The items in the Project panel are displayed in alphabetical order or reverse alphabetical order each time you click the Name heading. A direction indicator next to the heading shows the current sort order.

Tip: You can scroll the Project panel view up and down using the scroll wheel on your mouse, or using a gesture if you have a touchpad.

If you're searching for several clips with particular features—such as a duration or a frame size—it can be helpful to change the order in which the headings are displayed.

2 Scroll to the right until you can see the Media Duration heading in the Project panel. This shows the total duration of each clip's media file.

Note: When you scroll to the right in the Project panel, Premiere Pro always maintains the clip names on the left so you know which clips you're seeing information about.

3 Click the Media Duration heading. Premiere Pro now displays the clips in order of media duration. Notice the direction arrow on the Media Duration heading. Each time you click the heading, the direction arrow toggles between showing clips in order of increasing duration and or decreasing duration.

Note: You may need to drag a heading divider to expand the width of a column before you can see its sort order indicator or all of the information available in the column.

Media Duration ∨	Media Duration ∧

4 Drag the Media Duration heading to the left until you see a blue divider between the Frame Rate heading and the Name heading. When you release the mouse button, the Media Duration heading will be repositioned right next to the Name heading.

Tip: The Project panel configuration is saved with workspaces, so if you want to always have access to a particular setup, save it as part of a custom workspace.

Name		Frame Rate	Media Start	Media End	Media Duration ∨	Video In Point
	HS John - 00032.mp4	25.00 fps	01:46:22:12	01:50:13:08	00:03:50:22	01:46:22:12
	Mid Suit - 00008.mp4	25.00 fps	01:15:20:09	01:18:28:14	00:03:08:06	01:15:20:09

Filtering bin content

Premiere Pro has built-in search tools to help you find your media. Even if you're using nondescriptive original clip names assigned in-camera, you can search for clips based on a number of factors, such as frame size or file type.

Note: Graphic and photo files such as Photoshop PSD, JPEG, and Illustrator AI files import with a default frame duration you set after choosing Preferences > Timeline > Still Image Default Duration.

At the top of the Project panel, you can type in the Search (or Filter Bin Content) field to display only clips with names or metadata matching the text you enter. This is a quick way to locate a clip if you remember its name (or even part of its name). Clips that don't match the text you enter are hidden, and clips that do match are revealed, even if they are inside a closed bin.

Try this now.

Note: The name *bin* comes from film editing. The Project panel is also effectively a bin; it can contain clips and functions like any other bin.

1   Click in the Filter Bin Content box, and type **jo**.

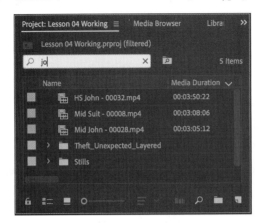

Premiere Pro displays only the clips with the letters *jo* in the name or in the metadata. Notice that the name of the project is displayed above the text-entry box, along with "(filtered)."

2   Click the X on the right of the Search field to clear your search.

3   Type **psd** in the box.

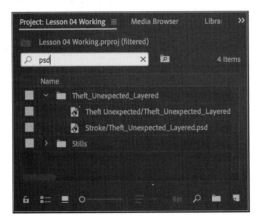

Premiere Pro displays only clips that have the letters *psd* in their name or metadata. In this case, it's the Theft_Unexpected title you imported in the previous lesson as a layered image—this is a Photoshop PSD file. Using the Filter Bin Content box in this way, you can search for particular types of files.

Be sure to click the X on the right of the Search field to clear your filter when you have found the clips you want. Do this now.

Using advanced Find

Premiere Pro also has an advanced Find option. To learn about it, start by importing some more clips.

Using any of the methods described in Lesson 3, import these items:

• Seattle_Skyline.mov from the Assets/Video and Audio Files/General Views folder

• Under Basket.MOV from the Assets/Video and Audio Files/Basketball folder

At the bottom of the Project panel, click the Find button . Premiere Pro displays the Find dialog box, which has more advanced options for locating your clip.

You can perform two searches at once with the advanced Find dialog box. You can choose to display clips that match *all* search criteria or *any* search criteria. For example, depending on the setting you choose in the Match menu, you could do either of the following:

• Search for a clip with the words *dog* and *boat* in its name.

• Search for a clip with the word *dog* or *boat* in its name.

To do this, make choices from the following menus:

• **Column:** Choose one of the columns in the Project panel. When you click Find, Premiere Pro will search only within the column you choose.

• **Operator:** Choose from a set of common search parameters to determine whether the search will return a clip for which the column chosen in the first menu contains, matches exactly, begins with, or ends with whatever you search for.

• **Match:** Choose All to find a clip with both your first and your second search text. Choose Any to find a clip with either your first or your second search text.

• **Case Sensitive:** Select this option to return only results that exactly match the uppercase and lowercase letters you enter.

• **Find What:** Type your search text here. You can add up to two sets of search text.

▷ **Tip:** You can find clips in sequences too. With a sequence open, choose Edit > Find.

When you click Find, Premiere Pro highlights a clip that matches your search criteria. Click Find again, and Premiere Pro highlights the next clip that matches your search criteria. Click Done to exit the Find dialog box.

Working with bins

Bins allow you to organize clips by dividing them into groups.

Just as with folders on your hard drive, you can have multiple bins inside other bins, creating a folder structure as complex as your project requires.

There's an important difference between bins and the folders on your storage drive: Bins exist only in your Premiere Pro project file to help organize clips. You won't find individual folders representing project bins on your storage drive.

Creating bins

Let's create a bin.

1   Click the New Bin button  at the bottom of the Project panel.

 Premiere Pro creates a new bin and automatically highlights the name, ready for you to rename it. It's a good habit to name bins as soon as you create them.

2   You have already imported some clips from a short film, so let's give them a bin. Name the new bin **Theft Unexpected** and press Return/Enter.

3   You can also create a bin using the File menu. Let's do this now: Make sure the Project panel is active, and deselect the bin you just created (if a bin is selected when you create a new bin, the new bin is placed inside the selected bin). Choose File > New > Bin.

4   Name the new bin **Graphics** and press Return/Enter.

Note: It can be difficult to find a blank part of the Project panel to click when it is full of clips. Try clicking just to the left of the icons, inside the panel, or choose Edit > Deselect All.

5   You can also make a new bin by right-clicking a blank area in the Project panel and choosing New Bin. Try this now.

6   Name the new bin **Illustrator Files** and press Return/Enter.

 One of the quickest and easiest ways to create a new bin for clips you already have in your project is to drag and drop the clips onto the New Bin button at the bottom of the Project panel.

7   Drag and drop the clip Seattle_Skyline.mov onto the New Bin button.

8   Name the newly created bin **City Views** and press Return/Enter.

9   Make sure the Project panel is active, but no existing bins are selected. Press the keyboard shortcut Command+B (macOS) or Ctrl+B (Windows) to make another bin.

 ▶ **Tip:** If you accidentally create a new bin inside an existing bin, drag the new bin out of the selected bin or choose Edit > Undo to remove the new bin and create it again after deselecting.

10 Name the bin **Sequences** and press Return/Enter.

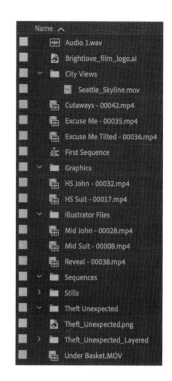

If your Project panel is set to List view, with the Name heading selected for sorting at the top of the panel, bins are displayed in alphabetical order among the clips.

● **Note:** To rename a bin, right-click it and choose Rename. Type the new name, and click away from the text to apply it.

Managing media in bins

Now that you have some bins, let's put them to use. As you move clips into bins, use the disclosure triangles to hide their contents and tidy up the view.

● **Note:** When you import a Photoshop file with multiple layers and choose to import it as a sequence, Premiere Pro automatically creates a bin for the layers and their sequence.

1 Drag the clip Brightlove_film_logo.ai into the Illustrator Files bin.

2 Drag Theft_Unexpected.png into the Graphics bin.

3 Drag the Theft_Unexpected_Layered bin (created automatically when you imported the layered PSD file as individual layers) into the Graphics bin.

4 Drag the clip Under Basket.MOV into the City Views bin. You may need to resize the panel or switch it to full-screen to see both the clip and the bin.

● **Note:** Notice the clip Under Basket.MOV has a file extension all in caps. This makes no difference for your operating system or for Premiere Pro.

5 Drag the sequence called First Sequence into the Sequences bin.

6 Drag all the remaining clips into the Theft Unexpected bin.

You should now have a nicely organized Project panel, with each kind of clip in its own bin.

You can also copy and paste clips to make extra copies if this helps you stay organized. In the Graphics bin, you have a PNG file that might be useful for the Theft Unexpected content. Let's make an extra copy.

7 Click the disclosure triangle for the Graphics bin to display the contents.

8 Right-click the Theft_Unexpected.png clip and choose Copy.

9 Click the disclosure triangle for the Theft Unexpected bin to display the contents.

10 Right-click the Theft Unexpected bin and choose Paste.

Premiere Pro places a copy of the clip in the Theft Unexpected bin.

▶ **Tip:** You can make Shift-click as well as Command-click (macOS) or Ctrl-click (Windows) selections in the Project panel, just like you can with files on your hard drive.

● **Note:** When you make copies of clips, you are not making copies of the media files they are linked to. You can make as many copies as you like of a clip in your Premiere Pro project. Those copies will all link to the same original media file.

Finding your media files

If you're not sure where a media file is on your hard drive, right-click the clip in the Project panel and choose Reveal In Finder (macOS) or Explorer (Windows).

Premiere Pro will open the folder in your storage drive that contains the media file. This can be useful if you are working with media files stored on multiple hard drives or if you have renamed your clips in Premiere Pro.

Changing bin views

Although there is a distinction between the Project panel and the bins inside it, they have the same controls and viewing options. For all intents and purposes, you can treat the Project panel as a bin; many Premiere Pro editors use the terms *bin* and *Project panel* interchangeably.

Bins have two views. You choose between them by clicking the List View button ■ or Icon View button ■ at the bottom left of the Project panel.

- **List view:** This view displays your clips and bins as a list, with a significant amount of metadata displayed. You can scroll through the metadata and use it to sort clips by clicking column headers.

- **Icon view:** This view displays your clips and bins as thumbnails you can rearrange and use to preview clip contents.

The Project panel has a zoom control, next to the List View and Icon View buttons, which changes the size of the clip icons or thumbnails.

1 Double-click the Theft Unexpected bin to open it in its own panel (the option to open bins in a new panel when double-clicking can be changed in the General preferences).

2 Click the Icon View button on the Theft Unexpected bin to display thumbnails for the clips.

3 Try adjusting the zoom control.

Premiere Pro can display large thumbnails to make browsing and selecting your clips easier.

You can also apply various kinds of sorting to clip thumbnails in Icon view by clicking the Sort Icons menu.

4 Switch to List view.

5 Try adjusting the Zoom control for the bin.

When you're in List view, it doesn't help that much to zoom, unless you turn on the display of thumbnails in this view.

6 Open the panel menu and choose Thumbnails.

Note: You can also change the font size in the Project panel or a bin by clicking the panel menu and choosing Font Size. This is particularly useful if you are working on a high-resolution screen.

Premiere Pro now displays thumbnails in List view, as well as in Icon view.

7 Try adjusting the Zoom control.

The clip thumbnails show the first frame of the media. In some clips, the first frame will not be particularly useful. Look at the clip HS Suit, for example. The thumbnail shows the clapperboard, but it would be useful to see the character.

Note: Selecting a clip by clicking its thumbnail reveals a small timeline control under it. Drag on this timeline to view the contents of the clip.

Tip: When you double-clicked the Theft Unexpected bin to open it, it opened in a new panel in the same group as the Project panel. You can keep as many bins open as you like and place them anywhere in the interface to help you stay organized.

Tip: When you've finished using the Search field, be sure to click the X on the right side to clear the filter.

8 Switch to Icon view.

In this view, you can hover the pointer over clip thumbnails to preview clips.

9 Hover your pointer over the HS Suit clip. Move the mouse until you find a frame that better represents the shot.

10 While the frame you have chosen is displayed, press the I key.

The I key is the keyboard shortcut for Mark In, a command that sets the beginning of a selection when choosing part of a clip that you intend to add to a sequence. The same selection also sets the poster frame for a clip in a bin.

11 Switch to List view.

Premiere Pro shows your newly selected frame as the thumbnail for this clip.

12 Choose Thumbnails from the panel menu to turn off thumbnails in List view.

Creating Search bins

When using the Search field to display specific clips, you have the option to create a special kind of virtual bin, called a Search bin.

After typing in the Search field, click the Create New Search Bin From Query button.

Search bins appear in the Project panel automatically. They display the results of a search performed when using the Search field. You can rename search bins and place them in other bins.

The contents of a Search bin will update dynamically, so if you add new clips to a project that meet the search criteria, they'll appear in the Search bin automatically. This can be a fantastic time-saver when working with documentary material that changes over time as you obtain new footage.

Assigning labels

Every item in the Project panel has a label color. In List view, the Label column shows the label color for every clip. When you add clips to a sequence, they are displayed in the Timeline panel with this label color.

Let's change the label color for a title.

1   In the Theft Unexpected bin, right-click Theft_Unexpected.png and choose
    Label > Forest.

You can change label colors for multiple clips in a single step by selecting them
and then right-clicking the selected clips to choose another label color.

2   Press Command+Z (macOS) or Ctrl+Z (Windows) to change the
    Theft_Unexpected.png label color back to Lavender.

    When you add a clip to a sequence, Premiere Pro creates a new *instance*, or
    copy, of that clip. You'll have one copy in the Project panel and one copy in the
    sequence.

    By default, when you change the label color for a clip in the Project panel or
    rename a clip, it won't update copies of the clip in sequences.

    You can change this by choosing File > Project Settings > General and enabling
    the option to display the project item name and label color for all instances.

▶ **Tip:** Once your clips
have the right label
colors, you can right-
click a clip at any time
and choose Label >
Select Label Group to
select and highlight all
visible items with the
same label.

Changing the available label colors

You can assign up to 16 colors as labels to items in your project. There are seven
types of items that label colors can be assigned to automatically based on the item
type (video, audio, still, etc.), which means there are nine spare label colors.

If you choose Premiere Pro CC > Preferences > Labels (macOS) or Edit >
Preferences > Labels (Windows) , you'll see the list of colors, each with a color
swatch. You can click the color swatch to change the color, and you can click the
name to rename it.

You can use the Label Defaults options to choose different default labels for each
kind of item in your project.

Changing names

Because clips in your project are separate from the media files they link to, you
can rename items in Premiere Pro and the names of your original media files on
the hard drive are left untouched. This makes it safe to rename clips—and it can be
helpful when organizing a complex project.

If you opened the Theft Unexpected bin by double-clicking it, it will have opened as a new panel in the same group as the Project panel. Let's begin by navigating between bins.

At the top left of the Theft Unexpected bin, you'll see the a button to navigate up . This button appears whenever you are viewing the contents of a bin by opening it. Just as Finder (macOS) or Explorer (Windows) have navigation buttons, you can use this button to browse "up" to the container of the current bin. In this case, it's the Project panel, but it could just as easily be another bin.

1   Click to navigate up to the Project panel.

    You now have two instances of the same Project panel in the same panel group. You're free to arrange and position multiple instances of bins or the Project panel any way you like, and they all have the same controls.

Project: Lesson 04 Working   Project: Lesson 04 Working ≡

2   Open the Graphics bin.

3   Right-click the clip Theft_Unexpected.png and choose Rename.

4   Change the name to TU Title BW (that is, *Theft Unexpected Title Black and White*).

▶ **Tip:** To rename an item in the Project panel, you can also click the item name, wait a moment, and click again, or you can select the item and press Enter.

5   Right-click the newly renamed clip, TU Title BW, and choose Reveal In Finder (macOS) or Reveal In Explorer (Windows).

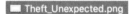

The original media file is displayed in its current location. Notice that the original filename has not changed. It's helpful to be clear about the relationship between your original media files and the clips inside the Premiere Pro project because it explains much of the way the application works.

● **Note:** When you change the name of a clip in Premiere Pro, the new name is stored in the project file. Two Premiere Pro project files can have different names representing the same clip. In fact, so could two copies of a clip in the same project—even in the same bin!

Customizing bins

When set to List view, the Project panel displays a number of columns of information about each clip heading. You can easily add or remove columns. Depending on the clips you have and the types of metadata you are working with, you might want to display or hide some columns.

1   In the Project panel, double-click the Theft Unexpected bin to open it.

2 Open the panel menu, and choose Metadata Display.

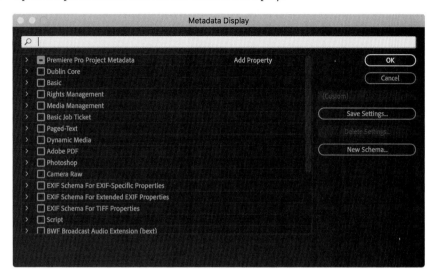

The Metadata Display panel allows you to choose any kind of metadata to display in the List view of the Project panel (and any bins). All you have to do is select the check box for the kind of information you would like to be included.

3 Click the disclosure triangle for Premiere Pro Project Metadata to show those options.

4 Select the Media Type option.

● **Note:** Notice there's a Search box at the top of the Metadata Display settings. Enter the name of an item here to locate it if you're not sure which category to browse in.

5 Click OK.

Media Type is now added as a heading for the Theft Unexpected bin only. You can apply the change to every bin in one step by using the panel menu in the Project panel to access the Metadata Display settings, rather than in an individual bin.

How Metadata display settings are stored

Metadata display settings for individual bins are saved in the project file, while Metadata display settings for the Project panel are saved with the workspace.

Any bins without modified Metadata display settings will inherit the settings from the Project panel.

Note: Several useful bin columns are displayed by default, including the Good check box. Select this box for clips you prefer, and then click the column heading to sort selected shots from unwanted content.

Some columns provide information only, while others can be edited directly in the bin. The Scene column, for example, allows you to add a scene number for each clip, while the Media Type column gives information about the original media and cannot be edited directly.

If you add information and press the Return (macOS) or Enter (Windows) key, Premiere Pro activates the same box for the next clip down. This way, you can use the keyboard to quickly enter information about several clips, jumping from one box to the next without using your mouse. You can also use the Tab key to move between boxes toward the right, and you can press Shift+Tab to move between boxes toward the left. This way, you can leave the mouse and switch to a faster keyboard workflow for metadata entry (it also leaves a hand free to hold a cup of coffee...).

Having multiple bins open at once

Every bin panel behaves in the same way, with the same options, buttons, and settings. By default, when you double-click a bin, it opens in a new panel, in the same panel group.

You can change this in Preferences by choosing Premiere Pro CC > Preferences > General (macOS) or Edit > Preferences > General (Windows).

The options in the Bins area of the General preferences allow you to choose what will happen when you double-click; Command-double-click (mac OS) or Ctrl-double-click (Windows); or Option-double-click (macOS) or Alt-double-click (Windows).

Once you are familiar and comfortable with navigating between bins, you may want to change these options to match the way Finder (macOS) or Explorer (Windows) open folders, with bins opening in place when you double-click, for example. The settings shown here are a good match.

Monitoring footage

The greater part of video editing is spent watching or listening to clips and making creative choices about them.

Premiere Pro has multiple ways to perform common tasks, such as playing video clips. You can use the keyboard, click buttons with your mouse, or use an external device like a jog/shuttle controller.

1 Continue working in the Theft Unexpected bin.

2 Click the Icon View button at the lower-left corner of the bin and use the Zoom control to set the thumbnails to a size you are happy with.

3 Hover your pointer (move the pointer without clicking) across any of the images in the bin. This is called *hover scrubbing.*

Premiere Pro displays the contents of the clip as you move your pointer. The left edge of the thumbnail represents the beginning of the clip, and the right edge represents the end. In this way, the width of the thumbnail represents the whole clip.

4 Select a clip by clicking it once (be careful not to double-click or the clip will open in the Source Monitor). Hover scrubbing is now turned off, and a mini navigator appears at the bottom of the thumbnail. Try dragging through the clip using the playhead.

When a clip is selected, you can use the J, K, and L keys on your keyboard to perform playback, just as you can in the Media Browser.

- **J:** Play backward

- **K:** Pause

- **L:** Play forward

> ▶ **Tip:** If you press the J or L key multiple times, Premiere Pro will play the video clips at multiple speeds. Pressing Shift+J or Shift+L reduces or increases playback speed in 10% increments.

5 Select a clip, and use the J, K, and L keys to play the video in the thumbnail.

When you double-click a clip, not only does Premiere Pro display the clip in the Source Monitor, but it adds it to a list of recent clips.

Touchscreen editing

If you are working on a touchscreen computer, you may see additional controls on
thumbnails in the Project panel.

These allow you to perform editing
tasks without a mouse or trackpad. To
see these controls on a nontouchscreen
computer, click the panel menu and
choose Thumbnail Controls For All Pointing Devices.

6   Double-click four or five clips from the Theft Unexpected bin to open them in
the Source Monitor.

7   Open the Source Monitor panel menu to browse your recent clips.

> ▶ **Tip:** Notice that you have the option to close a single clip or close all clips, clearing the menu
> and the monitor. Some editors like to clear the menu and then open several clips that are part of
> a scene by selecting them in the bin and dragging them into the Source Monitor together. You
> can then use the Recent Items menu to browse only the clips from that selection. You can also
> toggle between open sources by pressing the Source Monitor panel keyboard shortcut, Shift+2.

8   Open the Zoom Level menu at the bottom left of the Source Monitor.

By default, this is set to Fit, which means Premiere Pro will display the whole
frame, regardless of the original size. Change the setting to 100%.

Your clips will often be higher resolution than the monitors.

It's likely scroll bars have appeared at the bottom and on the right of your Source Monitor so you can view different parts of the image. If you are working on a very high-resolution screen, it's possible the image got smaller.

The benefit of viewing with Zoom set to 100% is that you see every pixel of the original video, which is useful for checking the quality.

9 Choose Fit from the Zoom Level menu.

Using essential playback controls

Let's look at the playback controls.

1 Double-click the shot Excuse Me (not Excuse Me Tilted) in the Theft Unexpected bin to open it in the Source Monitor.

2 At the bottom of the Source Monitor, you'll find a blue playhead marker. Drag it along the bottom of the panel to view different parts of the clip. You can also click wherever you want the playhead to go, and it will jump to that spot.

▶ **Tip:** If you're not sure which button is which, hover the pointer over each one to see the name and keyboard shortcut (in brackets).

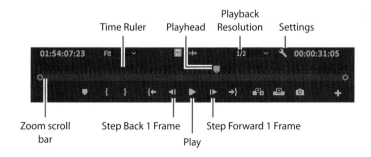

3 Below the time ruler and its playhead, there's a scroll bar that doubles as a Zoom control. Drag one end of this scroll bar to zoom in on the Time Ruler. This will make it easier to navigate longer clips.

Drag here   Drag here

4 Click the Play/Stop button to play the clip. Click it again to stop playback. You can also use the spacebar to play and stop playback.

5 Click the Step Back 1 Frame and Step Forward 1 Frame buttons to move through the clip one frame at a time. You can also use the Left Arrow and Right Arrow keys on your keyboard.

6 Try using the J, K, and L keys to play your clip.

● **Note:** Selection is important when using keyboard shortcuts (and menus). If you find the J, K, and L keys don't work, double-check that the Source Monitor is selected, with a blue outline.

Lowering the playback resolution

If you have an older or slower computer processor or are working with RAW media with large frame sizes, such as Ultra High-Definition (4K, 8K, or above), your computer may struggle to play back all the frames of your video clips. Clips will play with the correct timing (so 10 seconds of video will still take 10 seconds), but some frames may not be displayed.

To work with a wide variety of computer hardware configurations, from powerful desktop workstations to lightweight portable laptops, Premiere Pro can lower the playback resolution to make playback smoother.

The default resolution is 1/2.

You can switch the playback resolution as often as you like, using the Select Playback Resolution menu on the Source Monitor and Program Monitor panels.

Some lower resolutions are available only when working with particular media types. For other media types, the work of converting the image to lower resolution might be more than the work saved by not playing full resolution because not all codecs can be played back at a lower resolution efficiently.

▶ **Tip:** If you are working with a particularly powerful computer, you may want to turn on High Quality Playback, in the monitor Settings menu, which maximizes preview playback quality, particularly for compressed media like H.264 video, graphics, and stills, at the expense of playback performance.

Getting timecode information

At the bottom left of the Source Monitor, a timecode display shows the current position of the playhead in hours, minutes, seconds, and frames (00:00:00:00), according to the clip's timecode. For example, 00:15:10:01 is 0 hours, 15 minutes, 10 seconds, and 1 frame. Clip timecode will rarely begin at 00:00:00:00, so you should not count on this number to assess the duration of a clip.

At the bottom right of the Source Monitor, a timecode display shows the duration of your clip. By default, this shows the whole clip duration, but later you'll add special *In* and *Out* marks to make a partial selection. When you do, that duration shown will change accordingly.

In and Out marks are simple to use: Click the Mark In button 〔 to set the beginning of the part of a clip you want, and click the Mark Out button 〕 to set the end of the part of a clip you want. You'll learn more about this in Lesson 5, "Mastering the Essentials of Video Editing."

Displaying safe margins

Television monitors often crop the edges of the picture to achieve a clean edge. Open the Settings menu 🔧 at the bottom of the Source Monitor and choose Safe Margins to display useful white outlines over the image.

The outer box is the action-safe zone. Aim to keep important action inside this box so that when the picture is displayed, edge cropping does not hide what's going on.

The inner box is the title-safe zone. Keep titles and graphics inside this box so that even on a badly adjusted display, your audience will be able to read the words.

Premiere Pro also has advanced overlay options that can be configured to display useful information in the Source Monitor and Program Monitor. To enable or disable overlays, open the monitor Settings menu 🔧 and choose Overlays.

You can access the specific settings for overlays and safe margins by clicking the monitor Settings menu and choosing Overlay Settings > Settings.

You can disable Safe Margins or Overlays by choosing them from the Source Monitor or Program Monitor Settings menu again. Do so now so you can see the image clearly.

Customizing the monitors

To customize the way a monitor displays video, open each monitor's Settings menu 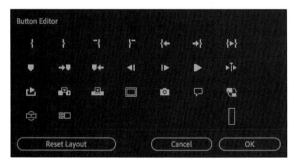.

The Source Monitor and Program Monitor have similar options. You can view an audio waveform, which shows amplitude over time (useful if you are searching for a particular sound or the start of a word), and if your video has fields, you can choose which fields are shown.

▶ **Tip:** If you are working with 360 video, you can switch to a VR video viewing mode using the Source Monitor and Program Monitor Settings menus.

Make sure Composite Video is selected in the Source Monitor and Program Monitor Settings menus for now.

You can also switch between viewing the clip audio waveform and the video by clicking Drag Video Only ▣ or Drag Audio Only ⦙⦙. These icons are mainly used when dragging the video-only or audio-only part of a clip into a sequence, but they also provide this useful shortcut to view the audio waveform.

You can add, move, or remove buttons at the bottom of the Source Monitor and Program Monitor. Note that any customizations you make to the buttons on one of the monitor panels are applied only to that panel.

1   Click the Button Editor ⊞ at the bottom right of the Source Monitor.

    The complete set of available buttons appears on a floating panel.

2   Drag the Loop Playback button 🔁 from the floating panel to a spot to the right of the Play button on the Source Monitor (the other buttons will automatically make space for it), and click OK to close the Button Editor.

3   Double-click the Excuse Me clip in the Theft Unexpected bin to open it in the
    Source Monitor if it isn't open already.

4   Click the Loop Playback button you added to enable it.

5   Click the Play button to play the clip. Play the video using the spacebar or the
    Play button on the Source Monitor. Stop the playback when you've seen the
    video start again.

    With Loop turned on, Premiere Pro continuously repeats playback of a clip or
    sequence. If there are In and Out marks set, playback loops between them. This
    is a great way to review a section of a clip.

6   Click the Step Back 1 Frame ◀ and Step Forward 1 Frame ▶ buttons to move
    through the clip one frame at a time. You can also use the Left Arrow and Right
    Arrow keys on your keyboard.

Modifying clips

Premiere Pro uses metadata associated with clips to know how to play them back.
This metadata is normally added correctly when the media is created (by the
camera, for example), but occasionally it might be wrong. Sometimes, you'll need
to tell Premiere Pro how to interpret clips.

You can change the interpretation of clips for one file or multiple files in a single
step. All clips you have selected are affected by changes you make to interpretation.

Choosing audio channels

Premiere Pro has advanced audio management features. You can create complex
sound mixes and selectively target output audio channels with original clip audio.
You can work with mono, stereo, 5.1, Ambisonics, and even 32-channel sequences
and clips with precise control over the routing of audio channels.

If you're just starting out, you'll probably want to produce sequences mastered in
stereo using mono or stereo source clips. In this case, the default settings are most
likely what you need.

When recording audio with a professional camera, it's common to have one microphone record onto one audio channel and a different microphone record onto
another audio channel. These are the same audio channels that would be used for
regular stereo audio, but they now contain completely separate sound.

Your camera adds metadata to the audio to tell Premiere Pro whether the sound is
meant to be mono (separate audio channels) or stereo (channel 1 audio and channel 2 audio combined to produce the complete stereo mix).

What is an audio channel?

When an audio recording is created, it's always captured and stored as one or more audio channels. Think of a channel as a single signal—something you could hear with one ear.

Because we have two ears, we are able to hear in stereo—sensing where a sound comes from by comparing differences in the way the sound arrives at each ear. The process happens automatically and precognitively (your conscious mind doesn't do any analysis to sense where a sound comes from).

To capture stereo (the sound two ears can detect), you need two signals, so two channels are recorded.

One signal (let's say the sound a microphone captures) becomes one channel in an audio recording. For output, one channel will play through one speaker or head-phone ear. The more channels you have for recording, the more sources you can capture independently (think of capturing an entire orchestra with many channels to be able to adjust the volume of each instrument separately in post-production).

To play audio with different volume levels on multiple speakers (for surround sound, for example), you need multiple playback channels. You'll learn more about working with audio in Lesson 10, "Editing and Mixing Audio."

You can tell Premiere Pro how to interpret audio channels when new media files are imported by choosing Premiere Pro CC > Preferences > Timeline > Default Audio Tracks (macOS) or Edit > Preferences > Timeline > Default Audio Tracks (Windows).

The Use File option means Premiere Pro will use the settings applied to the clip when it was created. You can override that option for each media type using the appropriate menu.

If the setting was wrong when you imported your clips, it's easy to set a different way to interpret the audio channels in the Project panel.

1   Right-click the Reveal clip in the Theft Unexpected bin, and choose Modify > Audio Channels.

When the Preset menu is set to Use File, as it is here, Premiere Pro will use the file's metadata to set the channel format for the audio.

In this case, Clip Channel Format is set to stereo, and Number of Audio Clips is set to 1—that's the number of audio clips that will be added to a sequence if you edit this clip into it.

Now look at the channel matrix below those options. The Left and Right audio channels of the source clip (described as Media Source Channel) are both assigned to a single clip (described as Clip 1).

When you add this clip to a sequence, it will appear as one video clip and one audio clip, with both audio channels in the same audio clip.

2 Open the Preset menu, and choose Mono.

Premiere Pro switches the Clip Channel Format menu to Mono, so the Left and Right source channels are now linked to two separate clips.

▶ **Tip:** Be sure to use the Preset menu and not the Clip Channel Format menu to correctly change this setting.

This means that when you add the clip to a sequence, each audio channel will go on a separate track, as separate clips, allowing you to work on them independently.

3 Click OK.

A few tips on audio clip channel interpretation

Here are some things to keep in mind when working with audio clip channel interpretation:

- In the Modify Clip dialog box, every available audio channel will be listed. If your source audio has channels you don't need, you can deselect them, and those empty channels won't take up space in your sequence.

- You can override the original file audio channel interpretation (mono, stereo, etc.). This will mean a different type of audio track may be needed when the clip is added to a sequence.

- The list of clips on the left (which may be as short as one clip) shows how many audio clips will be added to a sequence when edited in.

- Use the check boxes to choose which source audio channels are included in each sequence audio clip. This means you can easily combine multiple source audio channels into a single sequence clip or separate them into different clips in any way that works for your project.

Merging clips

It's common for professional video to be recorded on a camera with relatively low-quality audio, while high-quality sound is recorded on a separate device. When working this way, you'll want to combine the high-quality audio with the video by merging them in the Project panel.

The most important factor when merging video and audio files in this way is synchronization. You will either manually define a sync point—like a clapperboard mark—or allow Premiere Pro to sync your clips automatically based on their original timecode information or by matching up their audio.

If you choose to sync clips using audio, Premiere Pro will analyze both the in-camera audio and the separately captured sound and match them up. The option to sync automatically using the audio in both clips makes it worthwhile attaching a microphone to your camera, even if you know you won't use the audio in post-production.

- If you don't have matching audio in the clips you are merging, you can manually add a marker to each clip you want to merge on a clear sync point like a clapperboard. The keyboard shortcut to add a marker is M.

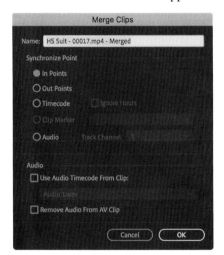

- Select the camera clip and the separate audio clip, right-click either item, and choose Merge Clips.

- Under Synchronize Point, choose your sync method, and click OK.

There's an option to use audio timecode (sometimes useful for older archived tape-based media).

There's also an option to automatically remove the unwanted audio included with the audio-video clip. You may want to keep that audio, though, just in case there's an issue with the external microphone audio.

A new clip is created that combines the video and the "good" audio in a single item.

Interpreting video footage

For Premiere Pro to play a clip correctly, it needs to know the frame rate for the video, the pixel aspect ratio (the shape of the pixels), and, if your clip is interlaced, the order in which to display the fields. Premiere Pro can find out this information from the file's metadata, but you can change the interpretation easily.

1   Use the Media Browser panel to import RED Video.R3D from the Assets/Video and Audio Files/RED folder. Double-click the clip to open it in the Source Monitor. It's full anamorphic widescreen, which is too wide for the intended sequence.

2   Right-click the clip in the Project panel and choose Modify > Interpret Footage.

The option to modify audio channels is unavailable because this clip has no audio.

3   Right now, the clip is set to use the pixel aspect ratio setting from the file: Anamorphic 2:1. This means the pixels are twice as wide as they are tall.

4   In the Pixel Aspect Ratio section, select Conform To, choose Square Pixels (1.0), and click OK. Take a look at the clip in the Source monitor.

    The clip looks almost square!

5   Try another aspect ratio. Right-click the clip in the Project panel and choose Modify > Interpret Footage. Choose DVCPRO HD (1.5) from the adjacent menu. Then click OK.

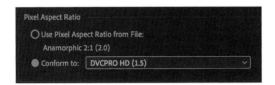

From now on, Premiere Pro will interpret the clip as having pixels that are 1.5 times wider than they are tall. This reshapes the picture to make it standard 16:9 wide-screen. You can see the result in the Source Monitor.

Working with RAW files

Premiere Pro has special settings for RAW camera media like .R3D files created by RED cameras, .ari RAW files created by ARRI cameras, and several others. These files are similar to the Camera RAW format photos created by professional digital single-lens reflex (DSLR) still cameras.

RAW files always have a layer of interpretation applied to them in order to view them. You can change the interpretation at any time without impacting playback performance. This means you can make changes, for example, to the colors in a shot without requiring any extra processing power. You could achieve a similar result using a special effect, but your computer would have to do more work to play the clip.

The Effect Controls panel gives access to controls for clips included in sequences, and in the Project panel. It also gives access to the interpretation controls for RAW media files.

1   If it isn't already open, double-click the RED Video.R3D clip to open it in the Source Monitor.

2   Using the panel name, drag the Effect Controls panel over the middle of the Program Monitor, and release the mouse button. This will place the Effect Controls panel in the same panel group as the Program Monitor so you can see both the Source Monitor and the Effect Controls panel at the same time.

    You may need to click the Source Monitor panel name to bring it back into view.

Because the RED Video.R3D clip is displayed in the Source Monitor, the Effect Controls panel now shows the RED Source Settings options for that clip, which change the way the RAW media is interpreted.

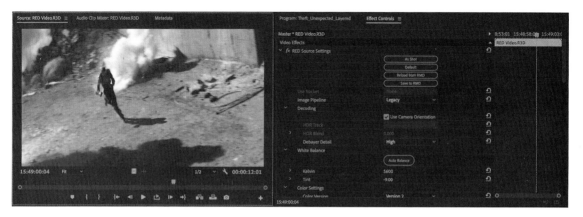

In many ways, this is a set of color adjustment controls, with automatic white balance and individual adjustments for the red, green, and blue values.

3   Scroll down to the end of the list, where you'll find Gain Settings. Increase the Red gain to about 1.5. You can click the disclosure triangle to reveal a slider control, drag the blue number directly, or click and type over the number.

4   Take another look at the clip in the Source Monitor.

The picture has updated. If you had already edited this clip into a sequence, it would update in the sequence too.

5   Scroll to the top of the list of settings in the Effect Controls panel, and click the As Shot button to reset the appearance of the video clip.

6   Choose File > Close All Projects. If you are offered the option of saving the project, click Yes.

For more information about working with RED media or other RAW media types, go to http://helpx.adobe.com/premiere-pro/compatibility.html.

Different RAW media files will give different Source Settings options in the Effect Controls panel. There are many other ways to adjust the look of your video clips, and you'll be learning about some of the options in Lesson 13, "Improving Clips with Color Correction and Grading."

Review questions

1 How do you change the List view column headings displayed in the Project panel?

2 How can you quickly filter the display of clips in the Project panel to make finding a clip easier?

3 How do you create a new bin?

4 If you change the name of a clip in the Project panel, does it change the name of the media file it links to on your hard drive?

5 What keyboard shortcuts can you use to play video and sound clips?

6 How can you change the way clip audio channels are interpreted?

Review answers

1 Open the Project panel menu and choose Metadata Display. Select the check box for any column heading you want to appear. You can also right-click a heading and choose Metadata Display to access the settings.

2 Click the Search field, and start typing the name of the clip you are looking for. Premiere Pro hides clips that don't match what you typed and reveals those that do.

3 There are several ways to create a new bin: by clicking the New Bin button at the bottom of the Project panel, by choosing File > New > Bin, by right-clicking a blank area in the Project panel and choosing New Bin, or by pressing Command+B (macOS) or Ctrl+B (Windows). You can also drag and drop clips onto the New Bin button on the Project panel.

4 No. You can duplicate, rename, or delete clips in your Project panel, and nothing will happen to your original media files.

5 The spacebar plays and stops. J, K, and L can be used like a shuttle controller to play backward and forward, and the arrow keys can be used to move one frame backward or one frame forward. If you are using a trackpad, you may be able to position your pointer over the video in a monitor or over the Timeline panel and use gestures to scrub through the content.

6 In the Project panel, right-click the clip you want to change and choose Modify > Audio Channels. Choose the correct option (usually by selecting a preset) and click OK.

5 MASTERING THE ESSENTIALS OF VIDEO EDITING

Lesson overview

In this lesson, you'll learn about the following:

- Working with clips in the Source Monitor

- Creating sequences

- Using essential editing commands

- Viewing timecode

- Understanding tracks

 This lesson will take about 75 minutes. Please log in to your account on peachpit.com to download the lesson files for this lesson, or go to the "Getting Started" section at the beginning of this book and follow the instructions under "Accessing the lesson files and Web Edition." Store the files on your computer in a convenient location.

Your Account page is also where you'll find any updates to the lesson files. Look on the Lesson & Update Files tab to access the most current content.

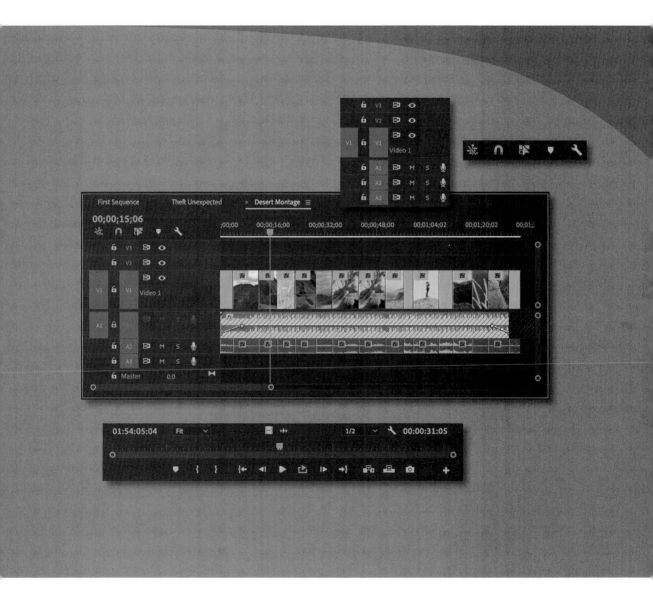

This lesson will teach you the core editing skills you will use again and again in Adobe Premiere Pro CC. Editing is much more than choosing shots. You'll choose your cuts precisely, place clips in sequences at exactly the right point in time and on the tracks you want (to create layered visual effects), add new clips to existing sequences, and get rid of unwanted content.

Starting the lesson

No matter how you approach video editing, you'll use a few simple techniques time and again. Most of the practice of video editing is carefully reviewing and making partial selections of your clips and placing them in your sequence. There are several ways of doing this in Premiere Pro.

Before you begin, make sure you're using the Editing workspace.

1　Open the Lesson 05.prproj project file from the Lesson 05 folder.

2　Choose File > Save As.

3　Rename the file **Lesson 05 Working.prproj**.

4　Choose a preferred location on your hard drive, and click Save to save the project.

5　In the Workspaces panel, click Editing; then click the panel menu next to the Editing option, and choose Reset To Saved Layout.

You'll begin by learning more about the Source Monitor and how to add In and Out points to your clips to get them ready to be added to a sequence. Then you'll learn about the Timeline panel, where you'll work on your sequences.

Using the Source Monitor

The Source Monitor is the main place you'll go when you want to check your assets before including them in a sequence.

● **Note:** Change clip interpretation by right-clicking the clip in the Project panel and choosing Modify > Interpret Footage.

When you view video clips in the Source Monitor, you watch them in their original format. They will play back with their frame rate, frame size, field order, audio sample rate, and audio bit depth exactly as they were recorded, unless you have changed the way the clip is interpreted. For more on how to do this, see Lesson 4, "Organizing Media."

However, when you add a clip to a sequence, Premiere Pro conforms it to the sequence settings. For example, if the clip and the sequence don't match, the clip frame rate and audio sample rate will be adjusted so that all the clips in the sequence play back the same way.

As well as being a viewer for multiple types of media, the Source Monitor provides important additional functions. You can use two special kinds of markers, called *In points* and *Out points*, to select part of a clip for inclusion in a sequence. You can also add comments in the form of markers that you can refer to later or use to remind yourself about important facts relating to a clip. You might include a note about part of a shot you don't have permission to use, for example.

Loading a clip

To load a clip in the Source Monitor, try the following:

1   In the Project panel, browse to the Theft Unexpected bin. With the preferences at their default settings, double-click the bin in the Project panel while holding Command (macOS) or Ctrl (Windows) to open the bin in the existing panel.

In the same way that you would double-click a folder in the Finder (macOS) or Windows Explorer (Windows), you have navigated into the bin.

When you have finished working in a bin that you have opened in the current panel, you can navigate back to the Project panel contents by clicking the Navigate Up button at the top left of the bin panel.

2   Double-click the RED Video.R3D video clip, or drag it into the Source Monitor.

Either way, the result is the same: Premiere Pro displays the clip in the Source Monitor, ready for you to watch it and add In and Out points.

3   Position your mouse pointer so that it is over the Source Monitor and press the ` (accent grave) key. The panel fills the Premiere Pro application frame, giving you a larger view of your video clip. Press the ` (accent grave) key again to restore the Source Monitor to its original size. If your keyboard does not have an ` (accent grave) key, you can double-click the panel name to toggle the full-screen view.

> **Tip:** When selecting clips, be sure to click the icon or thumbnail, rather than the name, to avoid accidentally renaming it.

> **Tip:** Notice that active panels have a blue outline. It's important to know which panel is active because menus and keyboard shortcuts sometimes give different results depending on your current selection. For example, if you press Shift+` (accent grave), the currently selected frame will toggle to full-screen, regardless of the location of your mouse.

Viewing video on a second monitor

If you have a second monitor connected to your computer, Premiere Pro can use it to display full-screen video every time you press Play.

Choose Premiere Pro CC > Preferences > Playback (macOS) or Edit > Preferences > Playback (Windows), make sure Mercury Transmit is enabled, and select the check box for the monitor you want to use for full-screen playback.

You also have the option of playing video via a DV device, if you have one connected, or via third-party hardware if it is installed. It's common to use third-party hardware to make different physical connections available for monitoring purposes. Check your third-party hardware user guide for installation and setup.

Using Source Monitor controls

As well as playback controls, there are some important additional buttons in the Source Monitor.

- **Add Marker:** This adds a marker to the clip at the location of the playhead. Markers can provide a simple visual reference or store comments.

- **Mark In:** This sets the beginning of the part of the clip you intend to use in a sequence. You can have only one In point per clip or sequence, so a new In point will automatically replace an existing one.

- **Mark Out:** This sets the end of the part of the clip you intend to use in a sequence. You can have only one Out point, so the new Out point will automatically replace an existing one.

- **Go To In:** This moves the playhead to the clip In point.

- **Go To Out:** This moves the playhead to the clip Out point.

- **Insert:** This adds the clip to the active sequence displayed in the Timeline panel using the insert edit method (see "Using essential editing commands" later in this lesson).

- **Overwrite:** This adds the clip to the active sequence displayed in the Timeline panel using the overwrite edit method (see "Using essential editing commands" later in this lesson).

- **Export Frame:** This allows you to create a still image from whatever is displayed in the monitor. See Lesson 16, "Exporting Frames, Clips, and Sequences," for more on this.

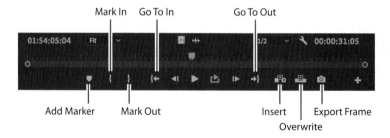

Selecting a range in a clip

You will usually want to include only a specific part of a clip in a sequence. Much of an editor's time is spent watching video clips and choosing not only which ones to use but also which parts to use. Making a selection is easy.

1 Double-click the clip Excuse Me (not Excuse Me Tilted) in the Theft Unexpected bin to open it in the Source Monitor. It's a shot of John nervously asking whether he can sit down.

2 Play the clip to get an idea of the action.

John walks on-screen about halfway through the shot but takes a moment to speak.

3 Position the playhead just before John enters the shot or just before he speaks. Around 01:54:06:00, he pauses briefly and speaks. Note that the timecode reference is based on the original recording and does not start at 00:00:00:00.

4 Click the Mark In button 〖. You can also press the I key on your keyboard.

Premiere Pro highlights the section of the clip that is selected. You have excluded the first part of the clip, but you can easily reclaim this part later if you need to do so—that's the freedom of nonlinear editing!

▶ **Tip:** If you want all of your clip timecode to be displayed as starting at 00:00:00:00, you can choose this option in the Media preferences, using the Timecode menu.

Using a numerical keypad

If your keyboard has a separate numerical keypad, you can use it to enter timecode numbers directly. For example, as long as no clips are selected, if you type **700**, Premiere Pro will position the playhead at 00:00:07:00. There's no need to enter the leading zeros or number separators. Be sure to use the numerical keypad, on the right on your keyboard, and not the numbers along the top of your keyboard (these have a different use).

5 Position the playhead just as John sits down. Around 01:54:14:00 is perfect.

6 Click the Mark Out button 〖, or press the O key on your keyboard to add an Out point.

Remember to turn off the loop playback option 🔁 if you don't want clips to loop between In and Out points when you play them.

● **Note:** In and Out points added to clips are persistent. That is, they will still be present if you close and open the clip again.

▶ **Tip:** If you hover your pointer over a button, a tooltip appears displaying the name of the button followed by the keyboard shortcut key for that button in brackets.

Note: Some editors prefer to go through all the available clips, adding In and Out points as required, before building a sequence. Some editors prefer to add In and Out points only as they use each clip. Your preference may depend on the kind of project you are working on.

Tip: To help you find your way around your footage, Premiere Pro can display timecode on the Source Monitor and Program Monitor time rulers. Toggle this option on and off by clicking the Settings menu and choosing Time Ruler Numbers.

Now you'll add In and Out points for two more clips. Double-click the icon for each clip to open it in the Source Monitor.

7 For the HS Suit clip, add an In point just after John's line, about a quarter of the way into the shot (01:27:00:16).

8 Add an Out point when John passes in front of the camera, blocking our view (01:27:02:14).

9 For the Mid John clip, add an In point just as John begins to sit down (01:39:52:00).

10 Add an Out point after he has a sip of tea (01:40:04:00).

Editing from the Project panel

Because In and Out points remain active in your project until you change them, you can add clips to a sequence directly from the Project panel, as well as from the Source Monitor. If you have already looked at all your clips and chosen the parts you want, this can be a quick way to create a rough version of a sequence. Remember, you can add In and Out points directly in the Project panel too.

Premiere Pro applies the same editing controls when you're working from the Project panel as it does when you're using the Source Monitor, so the experience is similar—and a few clicks quicker.

While it's faster to work this way, there's also value in having one last look at your clips in the Source Monitor before you add them to a sequence.

Creating subclips

If you have a long clip, you might want to use several different parts in your sequence. It can be useful to separate the sections so they can be organized in the Project panel prior to building your sequence.

This is exactly what subclips let you do. Subclips are partial copies of clips. They are commonly used when working with long clips, especially when there are several parts of the same original clip that might be used in a sequence.

Subclips have a few notable characteristics.

- They can be organized in bins, just like regular clips, though they have a different icon ![icon] in the Project panel.

- They have a limited duration based on the In and Out points used to create them, which makes it easier to view their contents when compared with viewing potentially much longer original clips.

- They share the same media files as the original clip they're based on, so if the original media file is deleted, both the original clip and any subclips will go "offline"—with no media.

- They can be edited to change their contents and even converted into a copy of the original full-length clip.

Let's make a subclip.

1　Double-click the Cutaways clip in the Theft Unexpected bin to view it in the Source Monitor.

2　While viewing the contents of the Theft Unexpected bin, click the New Bin button at the bottom of the panel to create a new bin. The new bin will appear inside the existing Theft Unexpected bin.

3　Name the bin **Subclips** and hold Command (macOS) or Ctrl (Windows) while double-clicking the new Subclips bin to have it open in the same frame, rather than in a new panel.

4　Choose a section of the clip to turn into a subclip by marking the clip with an In point and an Out point. The moment roughly halfway through when the packet is removed and replaced might work well.

As with many workflows in Premiere Pro, there are several ways to create subclips, and the outcome is always the same.

● **Note:** If you select Restrict Trims To Subclip Boundaries, you won't be able to access the parts of your clip that are outside your selection when viewing the subclip. This might be exactly what you want to help you stay organized (and you can change this setting by right-clicking the subclip in the bin and choosing Edit Subclip).

5   Try one of the following:

- Right-click in the picture display of the Source Monitor and choose Make Subclip.

- With the Source Monitor active, choose Clip > Make Subclip.

- With the Source Monitor active, press Command+U (macOS) or Ctrl+U (Windows).

- While holding Command (macOS) or Ctrl (Windows), drag the picture from the Source Monitor into the Project panel bin.

6   Name the new subclip **Packet Moved** and click OK.

The new subclip is added to the Subclips bin, with the duration you specified with your In and Out points.

Navigating the Timeline panel

The Timeline panel is your creative canvas. In this panel, you'll add clips to your sequences, make editorial changes to them, add visual and audio special effects, mix soundtracks, and add titles and graphics.

Here are a few facts about the Timeline panel:

- You view and edit clips in sequences in the Timeline panel.

- The Program Monitor shows the contents of the currently displayed sequence, at the position of the playhead.

- You can open multiple sequences at the same time, with each displayed in its own Timeline panel.

- The terms *sequence* and *Timeline* are often used interchangeably, as in "in the sequence" or "on the Timeline." Sometimes *timeline* (lowercase) is used when speaking of a sequence of clips in the abstract, without reference to a specific user interface element.

- If you add clips to a completely empty Timeline panel, you'll be invited to create a sequence.

- You can add any number of video tracks, limited only by your system's hardware resources.

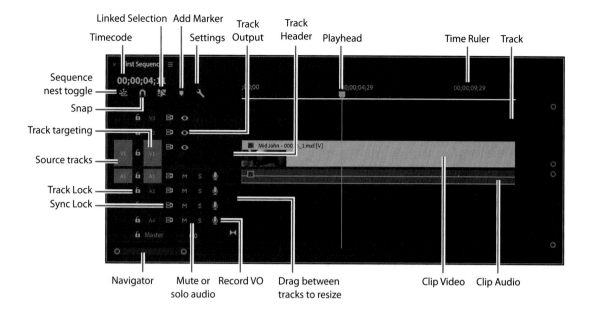

Labels around the diagram (clockwise from top):
Linked Selection | Add Marker | Track Output | Track Header | Playhead | Time Ruler | Track

Settings

Timecode

Sequence nest toggle

Snap

Track targeting

Source tracks

Track Lock

Sync Lock

Navigator | Mute or solo audio | Record VO | Drag between tracks to resize | Clip Video | Clip Audio

- Upper video tracks play "in front" of lower ones, so you would normally place foreground graphics clips on tracks above background video clips.

- You can add any number of audio tracks, and they all play at the same time to create an audio mix. Audio tracks can be mono (1 channel), stereo (2 channels), 5.1 (6 channels), or adaptive—with up to 32 channels.

- You can change the height of tracks in the Timeline panel to gain access to additional controls and thumbnails on your video clips.

- Each track has a set of controls, shown on a track header on the far left, that change the way it functions.

- Time moves from left to right in the Timeline panel, so when you play a sequence, the playhead will move in that direction.

- For most operations on the Timeline panel, you will use the standard Selection tool ▶, which you will find at the top of the Tools panel. There are several other tools that serve different purposes, and each tool has a keyboard shortcut. If in doubt, press the V key—this is the keyboard shortcut for the Selection tool.

- You can zoom in and out of the sequence using the = (equals) and – (minus) keys (at the top of your keyboard). Use the \ (backslash) key, if your keyboard has one, to toggle the zoom level between your current setting and to show your whole sequence. You can also double-click the navigator at the bottom of the Timeline panel to view the whole sequence.

  If your keyboard doesn't have dedicated = (equals) and – (minus) keys, it's easy to create new keyboard shortcuts. See Lesson 1, "Touring Adobe Premiere Pro CC," for more information about setting keyboard shortcuts.

The Tools panel includes a number of tools you'll use while working in the Timeline panel and Program Monitor.

- There are a series of buttons at the top left of the Timeline panel that give you access to alternative modes, markers, and settings.

What is a sequence?

> ▶ **Tip:** As with clips, you can edit sequences into other sequences, in a process called *nesting*. This creates a dynamically connected set of sequences for advanced editing workflows.

> ● **Note:** You may need to click the Navigate Up button to see the Theft Unexpected bin.

> ● **Note:** If you already have a sequence open, new sequences open in a new panel in the same frame.

A *sequence* is a series of clips that play one after another—sometimes with multiple blended layers and often with special effects, titles, and audio—making a complete film.

You can have as many sequences as you like in a project. Sequences are stored in the Project panel, just like clips, and have their own icon.

Let's make a new sequence for the Theft Unexpected drama.

1   In the Theft Unexpected bin, drag the clip Excuse Me (not Excuse Me Tilted) onto the New Item button 🔲 at the bottom of the panel. You may need to resize the Project panel to see the button.

 This is a shortcut to make a sequence that perfectly matches your media.

 Premiere Pro creates a new sequence, with the same name as the clip you used to create it.

2   The sequence is highlighted in the bin, and it would be a good idea to rename it right away. Right-click the sequence in the bin and choose Rename. Name the sequence **Theft Unexpected**. Note that the icon used for sequences in both List view (seen here) and Icon view is different from that used for clips.

You can zoom into the sequence, with its single clip, using the navigator at the bottom of the Timeline panel. To see a thumbnail on the clip, increase the height of the V1 track by dragging the dividing line between the V1 and V2 tracks in the track header area (where the track controls are located).

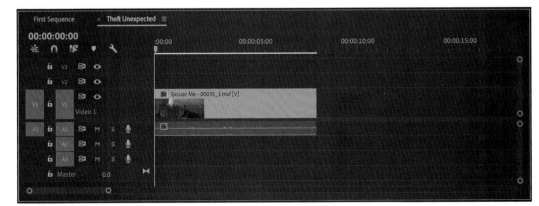

The sequence is automatically open, and it contains the clip you used to create it. This works for our purposes, but if you had used a random clip to perform this shortcut (just to make sure you had the right sequence settings), you could select it in the sequence and delete it by pressing Delete (macOS) or Backspace (Windows).

Close the sequence by clicking the X on its name tab in the Timeline panel.

▶ **Tip:** You can use the Timeline panel Settings menu  to choose Minimize All Tracks or Expand All Tracks to change the height of all tracks in a single step.

Opening a sequence in the Timeline panel

To open a sequence in the Timeline panel, do one of the following:

• Double-click the icon for the sequence in a bin.

• Right-click the sequence in a bin and choose Open In Timeline.

Open the Theft Unexpected sequence you just created.

▶ **Tip:** You can also drag a sequence into the Source Monitor to use it as if it were a clip. Be careful not to drag a sequence into the Timeline panel to open it because this will add it to your current sequence or create a new sequence from it instead.

Conforming

Sequences have a frame rate, a frame size, and an audio mastering format (mono or stereo, for example). They *conform*, or adjust, any clips you add to match these settings.

You can choose whether clips should be scaled to match your sequence frame size. For example, for a sequence with a frame size of 1920x1080 (regular high-definition) and a video clip that is 4096x2160 (Cinema 4K), you might decide to automatically scale the high-resolution clip down to match your sequence resolution or leave it as it is, viewing only part of the picture through the reduced "window" of the sequence.

When clips are scaled, the vertical and horizontal sizes are scaled equally to keep the original aspect ratio. If a clip has a different aspect ratio from your sequence, it may not completely fill the frame of your sequence when it is scaled. For example, if your clip had a 4:3 aspect ratio and you added it, scaled, to a 16:9 sequence, you'd see gaps at the sides.

Using the Motion controls in the Effect Controls panel (see Lesson 9, "Putting Clips in Motion"), you can adjust which part of the picture you see or even create a dynamic pan-and-scan effect inside the picture.

Understanding tracks

Much as railway tracks keep trains in line, sequences have video and audio tracks that constrain the positions of clips you add to them. The simplest form of sequence would have just one video track and perhaps one audio track. You add clips to tracks, one after another, from left to right, and they play in the order you place them.

Sequences can have additional video and audio tracks. They become layers of video and additional audio channels. Since higher video tracks appear in front of lower ones, you can combine clips on different tracks to produce layered compositions.

For example, you might use an upper video track to add titles to a sequence or to blend multiple layers of video using visual effects to create a complex composition.

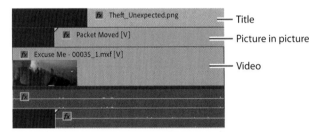

You might use multiple audio tracks to create a complete audio composition for your sequence, with original source dialogue, music, spot audio effects such as gunshots or fireworks, atmospheric sound, and voice-over.

You can scroll through clips and sequences in multiple ways, depending on the location of your pointer.

- If you hover your pointer over the Source Monitor or Program Monitor, you can navigate earlier or later using the scroll wheel; trackpad gestures work too.

- You can navigate sequences in the Timeline panel this way if you choose Horizontal Timeline Mouse Scrolling in the Timeline preferences.

- If you hold Option (macOS) or Alt (Windows) while scrolling with your pointer, the Timeline view will zoom in or out.

- If you hover your pointer over a track header and scroll while holding Option (macOS) or Alt (Windows), you'll increase or decrease the height of the track.

- If you hover your pointer over a video or audio track header and scroll while holding the Shift key, you'll increase or decrease the height of all tracks of that type (Video or Audio tracks).

▶ **Tip:** If you're scrolling to change track height while holding Option (macOS) or Alt (Windows), or while holding Shift, you can also hold Command (macOS) or Ctrl (Windows) for finer control.

Targeting tracks

The portion of each Timeline track header to the right of its Track Lock button is for selecting, or *targeting*, tracks in a sequence.

At the far left end of the track headers are the source track indicators. These represent the tracks available in the clip currently displayed in the Source Monitor or selected in the Project panel. They are numbered just like the Timeline tracks. This helps keep things clear when performing more advanced edits.

When you use a keyboard shortcut or the buttons on the Source Monitor to add a clip to a sequence, source track indicators are important. The position of a source track indicator relative to a Timeline track header sets the track the new clip will be added to.

In the example at right, the position of the source track indicators means a clip with one video track and one audio track would be added to the Video 1 and Audio 1 tracks in the Timeline panel when using buttons or a keyboard shortcut to add a clip to the current sequence.

In the following example, the source track indicators have been moved by dragging them to new positions relative to the Timeline panel track headers. In this example, the clip would be added to the Video 2 and Audio 2 tracks on the Timeline when using buttons or a keyboard shortcut to add a clip to the current sequence.

Click a source track indicator to enable it or disable it. A blue highlight indicates a track is enabled. You can make advanced edits by dragging the source track indicators up or down to different Timeline tracks and selecting which source tracks you have on or off.

When performing edits in this way, enabling or disabling timeline tracks won't affect results. Though the source track indicator and sequence track selection controls look similar, they have different functions; on the left, it's the Source track indicators, while on the right, it's the sequence track selection.

⬤ **Note:** Remember, Timeline track selection buttons matter when rendering effects or making timeline selections, but they don't affect editing clips into a sequence; only the source track indicators do.

If you drag a clip into a sequence, the position of the source track indicators is ignored, though only content on enabled source tracks is added.

Using In and Out points in the Timeline panel

The In and Out points used in the Source Monitor define the part of a clip you will add to a sequence.

Source track indicators

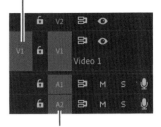

Timeline track headers

In this example, the source media contains only video, so no source audio track indicators are displayed.

The In and Out points you use in a sequence have two primary purposes.

- To tell Premiere Pro where a new clip should be positioned when it is added to a sequence.

- To select parts of a sequence you want to remove. You can make precise selections to remove whole clips, or parts of clips, from specific tracks by using In and Out points in combination with the track selection buttons.

  Selected parts of a sequence, defined by In and Out points, are highlighted in the Timeline panel. The highlighting doesn't extend to tracks that aren't selected.

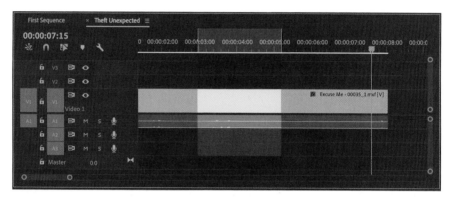

Setting In and Out points

Adding In and Out points in the Timeline panel is almost the same as adding them in the Source Monitor.

One key difference is that unlike the controls in the Source Monitor, the selection buttons on the Program Monitor also apply to the Timeline.

To add an In point to the Timeline at the current position of the playhead, make sure the Timeline panel or Program Monitor is active and then press the I key or click the Mark In button on the Program Monitor.

To add an Out point to the Timeline at the current position of the playhead, make sure the Timeline panel or Program Monitor is active and then press the O key or click the Mark Out button on the Program Monitor.

Clearing In and Out points

If you open a clip that already has In and Out points, you can change them by adding new ones; your new In and Out points will replace the existing ones.

You can also remove existing In and Out points on a clip or in a sequence. You'll use the same technique to remove In and Out points on the Timeline, in the Program Monitor, and in the Source Monitor.

1 On the Timeline, select the Excuse Me clip by clicking it once.

2 Press the X key. This adds an In point to the Timeline at the start of the clip (on the left) and an Out point at the end of the clip (on the right). Both are added to the time ruler at the top of the Timeline panel.

3 Right-click the time ruler at the top of the Timeline panel, and take a look at the menu commands.

   Choose the command you need from this menu, or use one of the following keyboard shortcuts:

   • **Option+I (macOS) or Ctrl+Shift+I (Windows):** Removes the In Point (Choose Clear In)

   • **Option+O (macOS) or Ctrl+Shift+O (Windows):** Removes the Out Point (Choose Clear Out)

   • **Option+X (macOS) or Ctrl+Shift+X (Windows):** Removes both the In Point and Out Point (Choose Clear In And Out)

4 That last option is particularly useful. It's easy to remember and quickly removes both In and Out points. Try it now to remove the In and Out points you just added.

Using time rulers

The time rulers at the bottom of the Source Monitor and Program Monitor, and at the top of the Timeline panel, all serve the same purpose: They allow you to navigate through your clips or sequences in time.

Time goes from left to right in Premiere Pro, and the location of the playhead gives you a visual reference in relation to your clips.

Drag left and right in the Timeline panel time ruler now. The playhead moves to follow your mouse. As you drag across the Excuse Me clip, you see the contents of the clip in the Program Monitor. Dragging through your content in this way is called *scrubbing*.

Notice that the Source Monitor, Program Monitor, and Timeline all have navigation bars at the bottom of the panel. You can zoom the time ruler by hovering over the navigation bar and using your mouse wheel to scroll (trackpad gestures work too). Once you have zoomed in, you can move through the time ruler by dragging the navigator. You can adjust the zoom level of the time ruler by dragging the ends of the navigator.

Double-click the navigator to fully zoom out.

Using the Timecode panel

There is a dedicated Timecode panel that, like other panels, can float in its own window or be added to a panel group. To open it, choose Window > Timecode.

The Timecode panel offers multiple lines of timecode information. Each line can be configured to show a particular type of time information.

The default configuration shows the Master time-code, the total duration, and the duration set by In and Out points for the active panel—Source Monitor, Program Monitor, or Timeline panel.

The Master timecode matches the timecode displayed at the bottom left of the Source Monitor and Program Monitor and at the top left of the Timeline panel.

You can easily add or remove lines of timecode information to make it easier to monitor your clips and sequences by right-clicking the Timecode panel and choosing Add Line or Remove Line.

To configure the type of information displayed in a line, right-click the line and choose the option you would like.

Right-click any line and choose Save Preset to store a configuration you would like to use again. The preset you create will appear in the menu when you right-click the Timecode panel.

You can also right-click and choose Manage Presets to assign a keyboard shortcut to presets or delete presets.

There's a compact mode for the Timecode panel that shows the same information in a smaller panel. Right-click the panel to choose between Compact and Full Size.

The Timecode panel doesn't have active controls—that is, you won't use it to add In or Out points or make edits—but it provides useful additional information to guide your decisions. Seeing the difference between total duration and selected duration, for example, can help you gauge your total available media for multiple edits.

Close the Timecode panel.

Customizing track headers

Just as you can customize the Source Monitor and Program Monitor controls, you can change many of the options on the Timeline track headers.

To access the options, right-click a video or audio track header and choose Customize, or click the Timeline Display Settings icon 🔧 and choose Customize Video Header or Customize Audio Header from the menu.

The Video track header button editor

The Audio track header button editor

To find out the name of an available button, hover your pointer over it to see the tooltip. Some of the buttons will be familiar to you already; others will be explained in later lessons.

To add a button to a track header, drag it from the Button Editor onto a track header. You can remove a button from a track header by dragging it away while the Button Editor is open.

All track headers update to match the one you adjust.

Experiment with this feature, and when you have finished, click the Reset Layout button on the Button Editor to return the track header to the default options.

Finally, click Cancel to leave the Button Editor.

Using essential editing commands

No matter how you add a clip to a sequence—by dragging, clicking a button on the Source Monitor, or using a keyboard shortcut—you'll choose one of two kinds of edits: an insert edit or an overwrite edit.

When a sequence has existing clips at the location where you want to add a new clip, these two choices—insert and overwrite—will produce markedly different results.

Performing one or other of these two types of edit is the absolute heart of nonlinear editing. Of all the skills you will learn in this book, this is the one you will perform most often. Fundamentally, this is nonlinear editing, so take a little extra time to be sure you are comfortable with this workflow before you continue.

Performing an overwrite edit

Continue working on the Theft Unexpected sequence. So far, you have just one clip, in which John asks if a seat is free.

First, you'll use an overwrite edit to add a reaction shot to John's request for a chair.

1   Open the shot HS Suit in the Source Monitor. You added In and Out points to this clip earlier.

2   You'll need to set up the Timeline panel carefully. This may seem like a slow process at first, but after practice, you'll find editing is fast and easy.

Position the Timeline playhead just after John makes his request. Around 00:00:04:00 is perfect.

> **Tip:** You can copy and paste timecode into the current time indicator at the bottom left of the Source Monitor or Program Monitor. Click to select the timecode, paste the new timecode, and press Return or Enter to move the playhead to that time. This is a useful feature when working with camera logs that allow you to quickly locate a particular part of a clip.

> **Tip:** The terms *shot* and *clip* are often used interchangeably by professional editors.

Unless an In or Out point has been added to the Timeline, the playhead is used to position new clips when editing with the keyboard or on-screen buttons. When you use the mouse to drag a clip into a sequence, the location of the playhead and existing In or Out points are ignored.

3   Though the new clip has an audio track, you don't need it. You'll keep the audio that is already in the Timeline. Click the source track selection indicator A1 to turn it off. The button should be gray rather than blue.

4   Check that your track headers look like the example at left. Only the Source A1 and V1 track indicators matter for this edit because the other tracks in the sequence don't have any clips on them.

5   Click the Overwrite button [icon] in the Source Monitor.

The clip is added to the sequence on the Video 1 track.

The timing might not be perfect, but you're now editing dialogue!

● **Note:** The sequence will not get any longer when you perform an overwrite edit.

By default, when you drag and drop a clip into a sequence, you'll perform an overwrite edit. You can perform an insert edit by holding down Command (macOS) or Ctrl (Windows) while you drag and drop.

6   Position the playhead at the beginning (far left end) of the Timeline panel or the Program Monitor, and click the Play button [icon] on the Program Monitor, or press the spacebar to play the result of your edit.

Performing an insert edit

Now try an insert edit.

1   In the Timeline panel, position the playhead over the Excuse Me clip, just after John says "Excuse me" (around 00:00:02:16). Make sure there is no In or Out point in the sequence.

2   From the Project panel, open the clip Mid Suit in the Source Monitor, add an In point at 01:15:46:00, and add an Out point at 01:15:48:00. This is actually from a different part of the action, but the audience won't know, and it works well as a reaction shot.

3   Check that your Timeline has the source track selection indicators lined up as in the example at right.

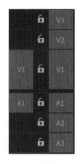

4   Click the Insert button on the Source Monitor.

> ● **Note:** When you apply an insert edit, it makes your sequence longer. The clips already on the selected track will move later (to the right) in the sequence to make room for the new clip.

Congratulations! You have completed an insert edit.

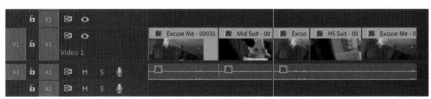

The clip Excuse Me, already in the sequence, has been split, with the part after the playhead moved later to make space for the new clip.

5   Position the playhead at the beginning of the sequence and play through your edit again. If your keyboard has a Home key, you can use it to jump to the beginning; you can drag the playhead with your pointer to move forward or back, or you can press the Up Arrow key to jump the playhead to earlier edits (the Down Arrow key jumps to later edits).

6   Now open the Mid John (not the Mid Suit) clip in the Source Monitor. You added In and Out points to this clip earlier.

7   Position the Timeline playhead at the end of the sequence—on the end of the Excuse Me clip. When dragging the playhead, you can hold the Shift key to have the playhead snap to the ends of clips.

8   Click either the Insert or Overwrite button in the Source Monitor. Because the Timeline playhead is at the end of the sequence, there are no clips in the way, and it makes no difference which kind of edit you perform.

Now you'll insert one more clip.

> ● **Note:** The words *sequence* and *edit* are often used interchangeably by editors.

> ● **Note:** If you have an In point or an Out point on the Timeline, Premiere Pro will use it in preference to the location of the playhead when performing an edit.

> ▶ **Tip:** As your sequence gets longer, you may find yourself often zooming in and out to get a better view of your clips.

Note: You can also edit clips into a sequence by dragging from the Project panel or Source Monitor into the Program Monitor. Hold the Command (macOS) or Ctrl (Windows) key to perform an insert edit.

9 Position the Timeline playhead just before John takes a sip of tea, around 00:00:14:00.

10 Open the clip Mid Suit in the Source Monitor, and use In and Out points to choose a part you think would go well between John sitting down and his first sip of tea. An In point around 01:15:55:00 and an Out point around 01:16:00:00 might work well.

Notice that the In and Out points you previously added to this clip are replaced.

11 Edit the clip into the sequence using an insert edit.

The timing of the edit may not be perfect, but that's okay; you can change your mind about the timing later—that's the beauty of nonlinear editing. The important thing, to begin with, is to get the order of the clips right.

Even from this short exercise it's clear that clip names are important. It can save hours of post-production having well organized and clearly named clips.

Performing three-point editing

To add a clip or part of a clip to a sequence, Premiere Pro needs to know its duration and when and where it should be placed in the sequence.

This means there should be four In and Out points.

- An In point for the clip

- An Out point for the clip

- An In point for the sequence setting the beginning of the clip once it has been added

- An Out point for the sequence setting the end of the clip once it has been added

In fact, you only need to specify three of these points because Premiere Pro calculates the fourth automatically, based on the selected duration.

Here's an example: If you choose four seconds of a clip in the Source Monitor, Premiere Pro automatically knows it will take four seconds of time in your sequence. Once you have set the location for the clip to be placed, you're ready to perform the edit.

Using just three points to perform edits in this way is called *three-point editing*.

When you performed your last edit, Premiere Pro aligned the In point from the clip (the start of the clip) with the In point on the Timeline (the playhead is used as the In point if no In point has been added).

Even though you didn't manually add an In point to the Timeline, you're still performing a three-point edit, with the duration calculated from the Source Monitor clip.

If you add an In point to the Timeline, Premiere Pro uses that to position the new clip, ignoring the playhead.

You can achieve a similar result by adding an Out point to the Timeline instead of an In point. In this case, Premiere Pro will align the Out point of the clip in the Source Monitor with the Out point on the Timeline when you perform the edit.

You might choose to do this if you have a piece of timed action, like a door closing at the end of a clip in the sequence, and your new clip needs to line up in time with it.

What happens if you use four points?

You can use four points to make an edit: both In and Out points in the Source Monitor *and* In and Out points on the Timeline. If the clip duration you select matches the sequence duration, the edit will take place as usual. If they're different, Premiere Pro will invite you to choose what you want to happen.

You can stretch or compress the playback speed of the new clip to fit the selected duration on the Timeline or selectively ignore one of your In or Out points.

Performing storyboard-style editing

The term *storyboard* usually describes a series of drawings that show the intended camera angles and action for a film. Storyboards are often quite similar to comic strips, though they usually include additional technical information, such as intended camera moves, lines of dialogue, and sound effects.

You can use clip thumbnails in a bin as storyboard images.

Drag the thumbnails to arrange them in the order you want the clips to appear in your sequence, from left to right and from top to bottom. Then drag them all into your sequence.

Using a storyboard to build an assembly edit

An assembly edit is a sequence in which the order of the clips is correct but the timing has yet to be worked out. It's common to build sequences as an assembly edit first, just to make sure the structure works, and then adjust the timing later.

You can use storyboard editing to quickly get your clips in the right order.

1   Save your current project.

2   Open Lesson 05 Desert Sequence.prproj in the Lessons/Lesson 05 folder.

Tip: Project file-names can become quite long. It's fine to include useful information to help you identify a project, but avoid making the name so long it's hard to manage the file.

3   Choose File menu > Save As. Save the project as **Lesson 05 Desert Sequence Working.prproj**.

This project has a Desert Montage sequence that already has music but no visuals. You'll add some shots.

The audio track A1 has been locked (click the track padlock icon to lock and unlock a track). This means you can make adjustments to the sequence without risking making changes to the music track.

Arranging your storyboard

Double-click the Desert Footage bin to open it. There are beautiful shots in this bin.

Note: Premiere Pro has the option to sort clips in Icon view based on a number of criteria. Click the Sort Icons button ☰⌄ for the options. Set the menu to User Order to be able to drag and drop the clips into a new order.

1   If necessary, click the Icon View button ▣ at the lower-left corner of the bin to see thumbnails for the clips.

2   Drag the thumbnails in the bin to position them in the order in which you want them to appear in the sequence, from left to right and from top to bottom—just like a comic strip or storyboard. You may need to resize the panel, set the panel to full screen, or scroll to see all the clips.

3   Make sure the Desert Footage bin is selected (with a blue outline). Select all the clips in the bin by pressing Command+A (macOS) or Ctrl+A (Windows).

4   Drag the clips into the sequence, positioning them on the Video 1 track right at the beginning of the Timeline, above the music clip.

The clips are added to the sequence in the order you originally selected them in the Project panel. If no clips are already selected when you select all the clips, they are selected in order from left to right, top to bottom.

If you already had a clip selected when you selected all the clips, that clip will be included first.

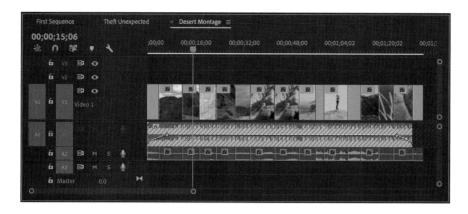

5 Though you chose an order for the clips to play in the bin, you are free to change the order, or the timing, of the clips in the sequence at any time.

Play your sequence to see the result.

You currently have two projects open at the same time. Depending on the panel you make active, it may not be clear which project you are working on. If in doubt, you can always tell by looking at the project information at the top of the Premiere Pro interface. If you see * after the project name, changes have been made to the project since it was last saved.

/MEDIA/Lessons/Lesson 05/Lesson 05 Desert Sequence Working.prproj *

6 Close each project by choosing File > Close Project twice or by choosing File > Close All Projects. If you are asked if you would like to save, do so.

Setting the duration for still images

These video clips already have In and Out points, which were used automatically when you added them to the sequence.

Graphics and photos can have any duration in a sequence. However, they have default In and Out points applied as you import them.

Choose Premiere Pro CC > Preferences > Timeline (macOS) or Edit > Preferences > Timeline (Windows) to change the duration in the Still Image Default Duration box. The change you make applies to clips when you import them, so it won't change clips that have already been imported.

Still images and still image sequences (a series of images intended to play one after another, as animation) have no *timebase*—that is, the number of frames that should play each second. You can set the default timebase for still images by choosing Premiere Pro > Preferences > Media (macOS) or Edit > Preferences > Media (Windows) and setting an option for Indeterminate Media Timebase.

Review questions

1 What do In and Out points do?

2 Is the Video 2 track in front of the Video 1 track or behind it?

3 How do subclips help you stay organized?

4 How would you select a sequence time range to work with in the Timeline panel?

5 What is the difference between an overwrite edit and an insert edit?

6 How much of your source clip will be added to a sequence if the source clip has no
   In or Out points and there are no In or Out points in the sequence?

Review answers

1   In the Source Monitor and in the Project panel, In and Out points define the part of a clip you would like to use in a sequence. On the Timeline, In and Out points are used to define parts of your sequence you want to remove, edit, render, or export as a file.

2   Upper video tracks are always in front of lower ones.

3   Though subclips make little difference to the way Premiere Pro plays back video and sound, they make it easier for you to divide your footage into different bins. For larger projects with lots of longer clips, it can make a big difference to be able to divide content this way.

4   You'll use In and Out points to define parts of your sequence you want to work with. For example, you might render when working with effects or export parts of your sequence to export as a file.

5   Clips added to a sequence using an overwrite edit replace any content already in the sequence where they are placed. Clips added to a sequence using an insert edit displace existing clips, pushing them later (to the right) and making the sequence longer.

6   If you don't add In or Out points to your source clip, the entire clip will be added the sequence. Setting an In point, an Out point, or both will limit the portion of the source clip used in the edit.

6 WORKING WITH CLIPS AND MARKERS

Lesson overview

In this lesson, you'll learn about the following:

- Understanding the differences between the Program Monitor and the Source Monitor
- Playing 360 video for virtual reality (VR) headsets
- Using markers
- Applying sync locks and track locks
- Selecting items in a sequence
- Moving clips in a sequence
- Removing clips from a sequence

This lesson will take about 90 minutes to complete. Please log in to your account on peachpit.com to download the lesson files for this lesson, or go to the "Getting Started" section at the beginning of this book and follow the instructions under "Accessing the lesson files and Web Edition." Store the files on your computer in a convenient location.

Your Account page is also where you'll find any updates to the lesson files. Look on the Lesson & Update Files tab to access the most current content.

Once you have some clips in a sequence, you're ready for the next stage of fine-tuning. You'll move clips around in your edit and remove the parts you don't want. You can also add comment markers to store information about clips and sequences, which can be useful during your edit or when you send your sequence to other Adobe Creative Cloud applications.

Adobe Premiere Pro CC makes it easy to fine-tune your
edits with markers and advanced tools for syncing and
locking tracks when you're editing clips in your video
sequence.

Starting the lesson

The art and craft of video editing is perhaps best demonstrated during the phase after the first version of your sequence is completed. Once you've chosen your shots and put them in approximately the right order, the process of carefully adjusting the timing of your edits begins.

In this lesson, you'll learn about additional controls in the Program Monitor and discover how markers help you stay organized.

You'll also learn about working with clips that are already on the Timeline—the "nonlinear" part of nonlinear editing with Adobe Premiere Pro CC.

Before you begin, make sure you are using the Editing workspace.

1 Open the file Lesson 06.prproj from the Lesson 06 folder.

2 Choose File > Save As.

3 Rename the file **Lesson 06 Working.prproj**.

4 Choose a location on your hard drive and click Save to save the project.

5 Reset the workspace to the default layout: in the Workspaces panel, click Editing, open the menu next to the Editing option, and choose Reset To Saved Layout.

Using Program Monitor controls

The Program Monitor is almost identical to the Source Monitor, but there are a small number of important differences.

What is the Program Monitor?

The Program Monitor displays the frame your sequence playhead is sitting on, or playing. The sequence in the Timeline panel shows the clip segments and tracks, while the Program Monitor shows the resulting video output. The Program Monitor time ruler is a smaller version of the one in the Timeline panel.

In the early stages of editing, you're likely to spend a lot of time working with the Source Monitor. Once your sequence is roughly edited together, you will spend most of your time using the Program Monitor and the Timeline panel.

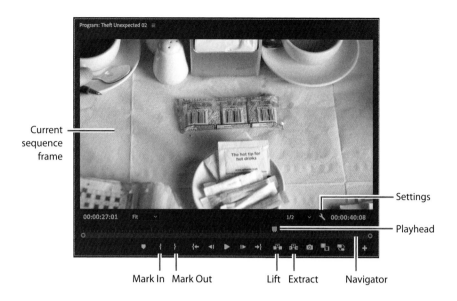

Current sequence frame

Settings

Playhead

Mark In Mark Out Lift Extract Navigator

Comparing the Program Monitor and the Source Monitor

Key differences between the Program Monitor and the Source Monitor include the following:

- The Source Monitor shows the contents of a clip; the Program Monitor shows the contents of whichever sequence is currently displayed in the Timeline panel. In particular, it shows whatever is under the playhead in the Timeline panel.

- The Source Monitor has Insert and Overwrite buttons for adding clips (or parts of clips) to sequences. The Program Monitor has equivalent Extract and Lift buttons for removing clips (or parts of clips) from sequences (more on Extract and Lift edits is coming up).

- Both monitors have a time ruler. The playhead on the Program Monitor matches the playhead in the sequence you're currently viewing in the Timeline panel (the name of the current sequence is displayed at the top left of the Program Monitor). As one playhead moves, the other moves as well, so you can use either panel to change the currently displayed frame.

- When you work with special effects in Premiere Pro, you'll see the results in the Program Monitor. There's one exception to this rule: Master clip effects are viewed in both the Source Monitor and the Program Monitor (for more information about effects, see Lesson 12, "Adding Video Effects").

- The Mark In and Mark Out buttons in the Program Monitor work in the same way as the ones in the Source Monitor. In and Out marks are added to the currently displayed sequence when you add them in the Program Monitor, and those marks are persistent in sequences in the same way they are persistent in clips.

Adding clips to the Timeline with the Program Monitor

You've already learned how to make a partial clip selection with the Source Monitor and then add the clip to a sequence by pressing a key, clicking a button, or dragging and dropping.

You can also drag and drop a clip from the Source Monitor into the Program Monitor to add it to the Timeline.

Typing timecode

You can click a timecode display, type the timecode you want the playhead to move to without punctuation, and then press Enter to send the playhead to that time.

When typing timecode, you can use a period (full stop) as a replacement for two zeros or to skip to the next number type, and there's no need to enter leading zeros.

For example, if you wanted the playhead to jump to 00:00:27:15, you could type **27.15**.

If you wanted the playhead to go to 01:29:00:15, you could type **1.29..15**.

1   In the Sequences bin, open the Theft Unexpected sequence.

> **Tip:** You can use the Left Arrow and Right Arrow keys to expand and collapse bins that are selected in the Project panel when it's in the List view.

2   Position the Timeline playhead at the end of the sequence, just after the last frame of the clip Mid John. You can hold the Shift key to snap the playhead to edits, or you can press the Up Arrow and Down Arrow keys to navigate between edits.

> **Tip:** You can press fn+Right Arrow key (macOS) or End key (Windows) to move the playhead to the end of the sequence. You can press fn+Left Arrow key (macOS) or Home key (Windows) to move the playhead to the start of the sequence.

3   Open the clip HS Suit from the Theft Unexpected bin in the Source Monitor. This is a clip that has already been used in the sequence, but you want a different part.

4   Set an In mark for the clip around 01:26:49:00. There's not much going on in the shot, so it works well as a cutaway. Add an Out point around 01:26:52:00 so you have a little time with the man in the suit.

5 Click in the middle of the picture in the Source Monitor and drag the clip into the Program Monitor, but don't release the mouse yet.

Several overlay images appear in the Program Monitor, each highlighting a drop zone that gives different options for the edit you're about to perform.

The overlays give maximum flexibility when editing by touch, with a computer screen that allows touch interaction. You can use the mouse to drag clips in, as well as drag clips by touch.

As you move the pointer over each overlay, it's highlighted to indicate the type of edit you will apply if you release the mouse button.

Here's the list of options:

- **Insert:** This performs an insert edit, using the source track indicators to choose the track (or tracks) the clip will land on.

- **Overwrite:** This performs an overwrite edit, using the source track indicators to select the track (or tracks) the clip will land on.

- **Overlay:** If you have a clip selected in the current sequence, the new clip will be added to the next available track above the selected clip. If there's already a clip on the next track, the one above that is used, and so on.

- **Replace:** The new clip will replace the clip currently under the Timeline playhead (more on replace edits in Lesson 8, "Mastering Advanced Editing Techniques").

- **Insert After:** The new clip will be inserted immediately after the clip currently under the Timeline playhead.

● **Note:** When you
drag a clip into your
sequence, Premiere Pro
still uses the Timeline
panel's source track
indicators to control
which parts of the clip
(video and audio chan-
nels) are used.

- **Insert Before:** The new clip will be inserted immediately before the clip currently under the Timeline playhead.

For this edit, no clip is selected on the Timeline, and there are no clips in the
way to overwrite. Choose Insert—just because it's the largest drop zone and
easier to aim for.

When you release the mouse button, the clip is edited into the sequence at the
playhead position, and your edit is complete.

Insert editing with the Program Monitor

Let's try an insert edit into the middle of the sequence using the same technique.

1 Position the Timeline playhead on the edit at 00:00:16:01, between the Mid Suit
and Mid John shots. The continuity of movement isn't good on this cut, so let's
add another part of that HS Suit clip.

2 Add a new In mark and Out mark to the HS Suit clip in the Source Monitor.
Choose any part you like, selecting about two seconds in total. You can see the
selected duration at the lower-right corner of the Source Monitor.

3 Once again, drag the clip from the Source Monitor into the Program Monitor, making sure to drop the clip onto the Insert overlay. When you release the
mouse button, the clip is inserted into your sequence.

If you prefer to drag clips into your sequence, rather than using keyboard shortcuts,
clicking the Insert and Overwrite buttons on the Source Monitor, or dragging into
the Program Monitor, there's still a way to bring in just the video or audio part of
a clip.

Let's try a combination of techniques. You'll set up your Timeline track headers and then drag and drop into the Program Monitor.

● **Note:** Remember, only the source track selection indicators matter when editing clips into a sequence, not the Timeline track selection controls.

1 Position the Timeline playhead at 00:00:25:20, just before John takes out his pen.

2 On the Timeline track headers, drag the Source V1 track selection button next to the Timeline Video 2 track. For the technique you're about to use, the track targeting is used to set the location of the clip you are adding.

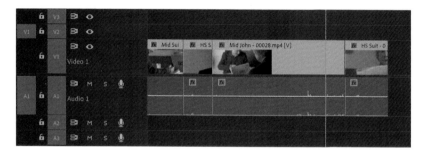

3 Open the Mid Suit clip in the Source Monitor. At about 01:15:54:00, John is wielding his pen. Add an In mark there.

4 Add an Out mark at about 01:15:56:00. You just need a quick alternative angle.

At the bottom of the Source Monitor, you'll see the Drag Video Only and Drag Audio Only icons ![icon].

These icons serve three purposes.

- They tell you whether your clip has video, audio, or both. If there is no video, for example, the filmstrip icon is dimmed. If there is no audio, the waveform is dimmed.

- You can click one or other icon to switch between viewing the audio waveform or video.

- You can drag them with the mouse to selectively edit video or audio into your sequence.

5 Drag the filmstrip icon from the bottom of the Source Monitor into the Program Monitor, and release it on the Overwrite option. When you release the mouse button, just the video part of the clip is added to the Video 2 track on the Timeline.

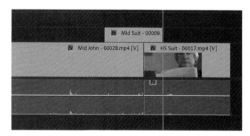

This works even if both the Source Video and Source Audio selection buttons in the Timeline panel are enabled, so it's a quick, intuitive way to select the part of a clip you want. You could achieve the same effect by selectively disabling Source track selection buttons, but it would require more clicks.

6 Play your sequence from the beginning.

The timing may not be perfect, but the edit is off to a good start. The clip you just added plays in front of the end of the Mid John clip and the start of the HS Suit clip, changing the timing. Because Premiere Pro is a nonlinear editing system, you can adjust the timing later. You'll learn how to do this in Lesson 8, "Mastering Advanced Editing Techniques."

Why are there so many ways to edit clips into a sequence?

As you continue to develop your editing skills and build experience, you'll find that some ways to add clips to sequences work better in a particular situation. Perhaps you need to be absolutely sure you've got the timing right, so you'll carefully select options in the Source Monitor and Timeline panel. Perhaps you are in a hurry to throw something together, so you'll drag clips from the Project panel into the Timeline panel and worry about timing later.

In addition, you'll find you naturally tend toward one editing style or another. To ensure editors can work flexibly according to their own style, Premiere Pro includes multiple workflows for the same outcome.

Setting the playback resolution

The Mercury Playback Engine enables Premiere Pro to play multiple media types, special effects, and more in real time. Mercury uses the power of your computer hardware to boost performance. This means the speed (and number of cores and breadth of instruction sets) of your CPU, the amount of RAM you have, the power of your GPU, and the speed of your storage drives are all factors that impact playback performance.

If your system has difficulty playing back every frame of video in your sequence (in the Program Monitor) or in your clip (in the Source Monitor), you can lower the playback resolution to make playback smoother. If you see your video playback stuttering, stopping, and starting, it usually indicates that your system is unable to play the file because of a hardware limitation.

It's worth remembering that playing high-resolution video files is *hard*! A single frame of uncompressed full HD video is roughly equivalent to more than 8 million letters of text. UHD video (often described as 4K video) is four times that! And, of course, there are usually at least 24 frames per second.

Reducing the playback resolution means you won't see every pixel in your pictures, but it can dramatically improve performance, making creative work much easier. It's common for video to have a much higher resolution than can be displayed, simply because your Source Monitor and Program Monitor are often smaller than the original media size. This means you may not actually see a difference in the display when you lower the playback resolution.

Changing playback resolution

Let's try adjusting playback resolution.

1 Open the clip Snow_3 from the Boston Snow bin in the Source Monitor. At the bottom right of the Source Monitor and Program Monitor, you'll see the Select Playback Resolution menu.

    By default, playback should be set to half-resolution. If it isn't, choose that option now.

2 Play the clip to get a sense of the quality when it's set to half-resolution.

3 Change the resolution to Full and play it again to compare. It probably looks similar.

4 Try reducing the resolution to 1/8. Now you might begin to see a difference during playback. Notice that the picture is sharp when you pause playback. This is because the pause resolution is independent of the playback resolution (see the next section).

Note: The choices on the Playback Resolution menu are the same on the Source Monitor and the Program Monitor, but the option you choose on one of the menus is independent of the other.

You'll notice the biggest differences in images with lots of detail, like text. Compare the detail in the tree branches, for example.

5 Try dropping the playback resolution to 1/16. Premiere Pro makes an assessment of each kind of media you work with, and if the benefits of reducing resolution are less than the effort it takes to drop the resolution, the option is unavailable. In this case, the media is full 4K (4096 x 2160 pixels), and the 1/16 option is available.

6 Return the setting to 1/2, ready for the other clips in this project.

If you're working on a powerful computer, you may want to maximize the playback quality when previewing at full resolution. There's an extra option to do this. You can choose High Quality Playback from the Settings menu 🔧 for the Source Monitor or Program Monitor.

With High Quality Playback selected, playback is performed at the same quality as file export. Without this option enabled, a small amount of quality loss is allowed in exchange for better playback performance.

Changing resolution when playback is paused

The playback resolution control is also available in the Settings menu 🔧 on the Source and Program Monitors.

If you look in that Settings menu on either monitor, you'll find a second set of options related to display resolution: Paused Resolution.

This menu works in the same way as the menu for playback resolution, but as you might have guessed, it changes the resolution only when the video is paused.

Most editors choose to leave Paused Resolution set to Full. That way, during playback you may see lower-resolution video, but when you pause, Premiere Pro reverts to showing you full resolution. This means when working with effects, you'll see the video at full resolution.

If you work with third-party special effects, it's possible you'll find they do not make use of your system hardware as efficiently as Premiere Pro does. As a consequence, it might take a long time to update the picture when you make changes to the effect settings. You can speed things up by lowering the paused resolution.

The playback resolution and paused resolution settings have no impact on output quality when exporting to a file.

Playing back VR video

Virtual reality headsets for the home are now more commonplace. Premiere Pro has built-in support for 360 video for VR headset display, with clip interpretation options, immersive video visual effects, desktop playback controls, integrated VR headset playback, and Ambisonics Audio support.

What's the difference between 360 video and virtual reality?

360 video is captured a little like a panoramic photo. Video is recorded in multiple directions, and the different camera angles are merged (a process called *stitching*) into a complete sphere. The sphere is flattened into 2D video footage that's described as *equirectangular*. This is the term used to describe a globe of the Earth that has been flattened into an atlas you can view in a book.

Equirectangular video looks distorted, which makes it hard to view and follow the action. However, although the appearance is strange for human eyes, it's a regular video file like any other, and Premiere Pro can work with it.

To view 360 video properly, it's usually necessary to wear a virtual reality headset. In the headset, 360 video is presented as all around you, and you can turn your head to see different parts of the image. Because a VR headset is required to see 360 video properly, it's often referred to as *VR video*.

True VR isn't actually video. It's a complete 3D environment you can move around in, viewing things from different directions, like 360 video, but also viewing things from different locations in the virtual reality space.

The key difference is this: In 360 video, you can view in different angles, but in true VR you can view from different locations within the scenario.

Let's try playing a 360 video clip.

1 Browse into the Further Media bin, and open the clip 360 Intro.mp4 in the Source Monitor. Play the clip.

This is an introduction to a 360 video film. The clip is in 4K resolution, which might be difficult for your system to play back—lower the playback resolution if you need to do so.

The center of the image is quite easy to make out, but if you look toward the edges, it gets harder to follow what you're looking at.

That's because the clip is equi-rectangular video, where a spherical video intended for VR headsets has been flattened into a 3D image. To see this clearly, you're going to need to switch to the VR Video mode.

● **Note:** The Source Monitor and Program Monitor have identical VR video playback controls.

2 Click the Source Monitor's Settings menu, and choose VR Video > Enable.

Now the clip looks more like regular video, and additional controls appear in the Source Monitor.

3 Play the clip again. This time, while it plays, click into the image, and drag to change the angle of view.

The numbers under the image and to the right of the image allow you to precisely control the angle of view. They're helpful, but they take up a lot of space.

4 Open the Source Monitor Settings menu, and choose VR Video > Show Controls to deselect the option.

You can still click the image to change the angle of view, but now the image is much larger in the Source Monitor.

Also, by choosing VR Video > Settings from the Settings menu, you'll open the VR Video Settings dialog box, where you can specify the height and width of the view in degrees to emulate different VR headsets.

By default, the height and width are quite small. Try changing the Monitor View Horizontal option to 150 degrees, and click OK.

Different VR headsets have different ranges of field of view. The ideal setting will match the intended VR headset field of view. In this sense, each VR headset you create content for is a little like a different screen you might prepare regular video for.

You'll want to preview your content for each proposed display medium to be sure your audience will have the experience you expect.

5 Now open the Source Monitor's Settings menu, and choose VR Video > Enable to deselect it.

Using markers

Sometimes it can be difficult to remember where you saw that useful part of a shot or what you intended to do with it. Wouldn't it be useful if you could mark clips with comments and flag areas of interest for later?

What you need are markers.

What are markers?

Markers allow you to identify specific times in clips and sequences and add comments to them. These temporal (time-based) markers are a fantastic aid to help you stay organized and communicate with co-editors.

You can use markers for personal reference or for collaboration. They can be connected to individual clips or a sequence.

By default, when you add a marker to a clip, it's included in the metadata for the original media file. This means you can open the clip in another Premiere Pro project and see the same markers. You can disable this option by choosing Premiere Pro CC > Preferences > Media (macOS) or Edit > Preferences > Media (Windows), and deselecting Write Clip Markers To XMP.

Exploring the types of markers

More than one type of marker is available, and like clips, each marker has a color. You can change a marker type by double-clicking it.

- **Comment Marker:** This is a general marker you can assign a name, duration, and comments.

- **Chapter Marker:** This is a marker that DVD and Blu-ray Disc design applications can convert into a regular chapter marker.

- **Segmentation Marker:** This marker makes it possible for certain video servers to divide content into parts.

- **Web Link:** Certain video formats can use this marker to automatically open a web page while the video plays. When you export your sequence to create a supported format, web link markers are included in the file.

- **Flash Cue Point:** This is a marker used by Adobe Animate CC. By adding these cue points to the Timeline in Premiere Pro, you can begin to prepare your Animate project while still editing your sequence.

Sequence markers

Let's add some markers to a sequence.

1 Open the City Views sequence from the Sequences bin.

   This is a simple assembly with a few shots from a travelogue program.

2 Set the Timeline playhead to around 00:01:12:00, and make sure no clips are selected (you can click the background of the Timeline to deselect clips).

3 Add a marker in one of the following ways:

   - Click the Add Marker button 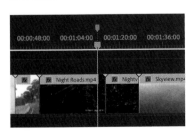 at the top left of the Timeline panel.

   - Right-click the Timeline time ruler and choose Add Marker.

   - Press M.

   Premiere Pro adds a green marker to the Timeline, just above the playhead.

Note: If a single clip is selected in a sequence on the timeline when you add a marker, the marker will be added to the selected clip rather than the sequence. See "Selecting clips" later in this lesson for more information about selecting clips in sequences.

The same marker appears at the bottom of the Program Monitor.

You can use this as a visual reminder of an important moment in time, or go into the settings and change it into a different kind of marker. You'll do that in a moment, but first let's look at this marker in the Markers panel.

4   Open the Markers panel. By default, the Markers panel is grouped with the Project panel. If you don't see it there, choose Window > Markers.

The Markers panel shows you a list of markers, displayed in time order. The same panel shows you markers for a sequence or for a clip, depending on whether the Timeline, a sequence clip, or the Source Monitor is active.

5   Double-click the thumbnail for the marker in the Markers panel. This displays the Marker dialog box.

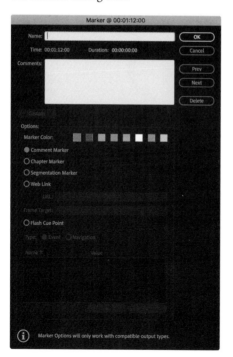

▶ **Tip:** The Markers panel has a Search box at the top that works the same way as the Search box in the Project panel. Next to the Search box are marker color filters. Click one (or several) of these to see only markers with matching colors in the Markers panel.

▶ **Tip:** You can open the Marker dialog box by double-clicking a marker in the Markers panel or by double-clicking the marker icon.

▶ **Tip:** You can quickly add a marker and immediately display the Marker dialog by pressing M twice, in quick succession.

6   Click the Duration field, and type **400**. Avoid the temptation to press Enter or Return, as this will close the panel. Premiere Pro automatically adds punctuation, turning this into 00:00:04:00 (four seconds) as soon as you click away or press the Tab key to move to the next field.

7   Click in the Name box, and type a comment, such as **Replace this shot**.

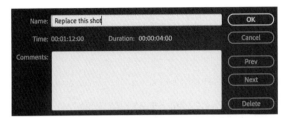

8   Click OK.

The marker now has a duration on the Timeline. Zoom in to the Timeline a little, and you'll see the text you typed into the Name field.

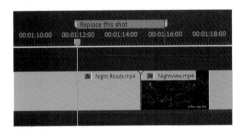

▶ Tip: Notice that the entries in the Markers menu have keyboard shortcuts. Working with markers using the keyboard is generally much faster than using the mouse.

The name of the marker is also displayed in the Markers panel.

9   Take a moment to open the Markers menu, on the main menu bar, to see the available commands.

At the bottom of the Markers menu is the Ripple Sequence Markers command. With this enabled, sequence markers will move in sync with clips when you insert and extract clips, which are editing operations that change the sequence duration and timing. With this option disabled, markers stay where they are when your clips move.

The menu includes a command with the "snappy" name Copy Paste Includes Sequence Markers. With this option enabled, when you copy a section of a sequence that you've selected using In and Out marks and then paste that content somewhere else, any sequence markers in the selection are included.

Clip markers

Let's add markers to a clip.

1 Open the clip Seattle_Skyline.mov from the Further Media bin in the Source Monitor.

2 Play the clip, and while it plays, press the M key several times to add markers.

● **Note:** Markers can be added using a button or a keyboard shortcut. If you use the keyboard shortcut, M, it's easy to add markers that match the beat of your music because you can add them during playback.

3 Look in the Markers panel. If the Source Monitor is active, every marker you added will be listed.

When clips with markers are added to a sequence, they retain their markers.

▶ **Tip:** You can use markers to quickly navigate your clips and sequences. If you single-click a marker in the Markers panel, the playhead will move to the location of the marker—a fast way to find your way around. If you double-click a marker in the Markers panel, the options for that marker will be displayed too.

4 Make sure the Source Monitor is active by clicking it. Choose Markers > Clear All Markers.

All the markers are removed from the clip.

▶ **Tip:** You can get to the same option to remove all markers—or a current marker—by right-clicking in the Source Monitor, in the Program Monitor, or on the Timeline time ruler and choosing Clear All Markers.

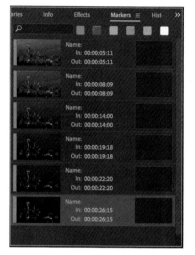

You can add a marker to a clip in a sequence by selecting it before you add the marker. Markers added to clips already edited into a sequence still appear in the Source Monitor when you view the clip.

Exporting markers

You can export markers associated with a clip or sequence as an HTML page with thumbnails, or a .csv (comma-separated value) file readable by spreadsheet-editing applications. This is great for collaboration and as a reference.

Export markers by choosing File > Export > Markers.

Adding markers with Adobe Prelude

Adobe Prelude is a logging and ingest application included with Adobe Creative Cloud. Prelude provides excellent tools for managing large quantities of footage and can add markers to footage that are fully compatible with Premiere Pro.

Markers are added to clips in the form of metadata, and like the markers you add in Premiere Pro, they will travel with your media into other applications.

If you add markers to your footage using Adobe Prelude, those markers will automatically appear in Premiere Pro when you view the clips. In fact, you can even copy and paste a clip from Prelude into your Premiere Pro project, and the markers will be included.

Finding clips in the Timeline panel

As well as searching for clips in the Project panel, you can search for them in a sequence. Depending on whether you have the Project panel active or the Timeline panel active, choosing Edit > Find or pressing Command+F (macOS) or Ctrl+F (Windows) will display search options for that panel.

When clips in a sequence are found that match your search criteria, Premiere Pro highlights them. If you choose Find All, Premiere Pro will highlight all clips that meet the search criteria.

Sync Lock

Track Lock

Using Sync Lock and Track Lock

There are two distinct ways to lock tracks on the Timeline.

- You can lock clips in sync so when you use an insert edit to add a clip, other clips stay together in time.
- You can lock a track so that no changes can be made to it.

Using sync locks

If an actor's lips move out of time with the audio of their voice, it's considered bad lip-sync. It's obvious when this kind of synchronization (sync) is wrong but other examples may be harder to detect.

It's helpful to think of syncing as coordinating any two things that are meant to happen at the same time. You might have a musical event that happens at the same time as some climactic action or something as simple as a lower-third title that identifies a speaker. If it happens at the same time, it's synchronized.

Open the Theft Unexpected sequence from the Sequences bin.

When John arrives, at the beginning of the sequence, the audience won't know what he's looking at.

1   Open the Mid Suit clip, from the Theft Unexpected bin, in the Source Monitor. Add an In mark around 01:15:35:18, and add an Out mark around 01:15:39:00.

2   Position the Timeline playhead at the beginning of the sequence, and make sure there are no In or Out marks on the Timeline.

3   Deselect Sync Lock for the Video 2 track.

4   Check that your Timeline panel is configured as in the following example, with the Source V1 track patched to the Timeline V1 track. The Timeline track header buttons are not important now, but having the right source track selection buttons enabled is.

Before you do anything else, take a look at the position of the Mid Suit cutaway clip on the Video 2 track, toward the end of the sequence.

Note: You may need to zoom out to see the other clips in the sequence.

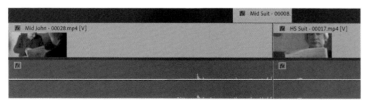

It's just over the cut between the clips Mid John and HS Suit on Video 1.

5 Insert-edit the source clip into the beginning of the sequence.

Take another look at the location of the Mid Suit cutaway clip.

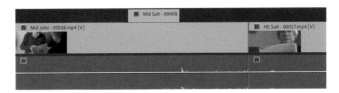

The Mid Suit cutaway clip on the Video 2 track has not moved, while the other clips, on the Video 1 track, have moved to the right to accommodate the new clip. This is a problem because the cutaway is now out of position with the clips to which it relates—it no longer covers the cut.

6 Undo by pressing Command+Z (macOS) or Ctrl+Z (Windows) and try it again with the Video 2 track Sync Lock turned on.

● **Note:** Overwrite edits do not change the duration of your sequence, so of course they are not affected by sync locks.

7 Turn on Sync Lock ⊟ for the Video 2 track, and perform the insert edit again.

This time, the cutaway clip moves with the other clips on the Timeline, even though nothing is being edited onto the Video 2 track. This is the power of sync locks—they keep things in sync!

Using track locks

Track locks prevent you from making any changes at all to a track. They are an excellent way to avoid making accidental changes to your sequence and to fix clips on specific tracks in place while you work.

For example, you could lock your music track while you insert different video clips. By locking the music track, you can simply forget about it while editing because no changes can be made to it.

Lock and unlock a track by clicking the Toggle Track Lock button 🔒. Clips on a locked track are highlighted with diagonal lines.

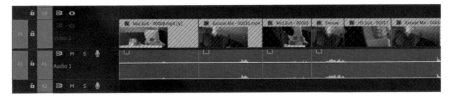

Finding gaps in the sequence

Until now, you've been exclusively adding clips to a sequence (not removing them). Part of the power of nonlinear editing is in having the freedom to move clips around in a sequence and remove the parts you don't want.

When removing clips or parts of clips, you'll either leave a gap by performing a lift edit or not leave a gap by performing an extract edit.

An extract edit is a little like an insert edit but in reverse. Rather than other clips in a sequence moving out of the way to make space for a new clip, the other clips move in to fill the gap left behind by a clip you are removing.

When you zoom out of a complex sequence, it can be difficult to see smaller gaps left behind after performing an edit. To automatically locate the next gap, choose Sequence > Go To Gap > Next In Sequence.

Once you've found a gap, you can remove it by selecting it and pressing Delete.

You can remove multiple gaps by choosing Sequence > Close Gap.

If you have set In and Out marks in the sequence, only gaps between the marks will be removed.

Let's learn a little more about working with clips in a sequence. Continue working with the Theft Unexpected sequence.

Selecting clips

Selection is an important part of working with Premiere Pro. For example, depending on the panel you have selected, different menu options will be available. You'll want to select clips in your sequences carefully before applying adjustments.

When working with clips that have video and audio, you'll have two or more segments for each clip: one video segment and one or more audio segments.

When the video and audio clip segments come from the same original media file, they are automatically treated as linked. If you select one, the other is automatically selected.

You can switch linked selections on and off in the Timeline panel globally by clicking the Linked Selection button  at the top left of the Timeline panel. When Linked Selection is on, video and audio clips in a sequence are automatically selected together when you click them. When Linked Selection is off, clicking the video or audio part of a clip selects only that part. If there's more than one audio clip, you'll select just the one you click.

Selecting a clip or range of clips

When selecting clips in a sequence, there are two approaches.

- Make time selections by using In and Out marks.
- Make clip segment selections.

The simplest way to select a clip in a sequence is to click it. Be careful not to double-click, which will open the sequence clip in the Source Monitor, ready for you to adjust the In or Out marks (these will update, live, in the Timeline panel).

When making selections, you'll want to use the Selection tool ▶ which is selected in the Tools panel by default. This tool has the keyboard shortcut V.

If you hold the Shift key while you click sequence clips with the Selection tool, you can select or deselect additional clips.

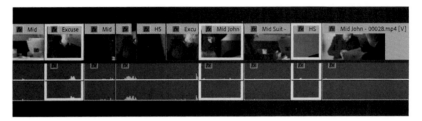

You can also drag the Selection tool over multiple clips to select them. Begin by pressing the mouse button in an empty part of the Timeline panel and then dragging to create a selection box. Any clip you drag over (even partially) with the selection box will be selected.

Premiere Pro also gives you the option to automatically select whichever clip the Timeline playhead passes over. This is particularly useful for a keyboard-based editing workflow. You can enable the option by choosing Sequence > Selection Follows Playhead. You can also press the keyboard shortcut D to select the current clip under the Timeline playhead. The clip on the highest enabled track will be selected.

Selecting all the clips on a track

If you want to select every clip on a track, there are two handy tools to do just that: the Track Select Forward Tool ▦, which has the keyboard shortcut A, and the Track Select Backward Tool ◀, which has the keyboard shortcut Shift+A. Try this now. Select the Track Select Forward tool, and click any clip on the Video 1 track.

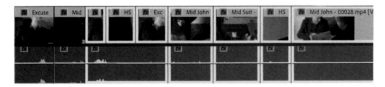

Every clip on every track, from the one you select until the end of the sequence, is selected. This is useful if you want to add a gap to your sequence to make space for more clips; you can drag all the selected clips to the right.

Look at the Track Select Forward tool icon in the Tools panel. Notice the tiny triangle next to the icon—this indicates the button is also a menu. If you press and hold on this tool, a menu appears with the Track Select Backward tool. When you click a clip with this tool, every clip up to the one you clicked is selected.

If you hold the Shift key while using either of the tools, you'll select clips on only one track.

When you have finished, switch to the Selection tool by clicking it in the Tools panel or by pressing the V key.

Selecting audio or video only

It's common to add a clip to a sequence and later realize you don't need the audio or video part of the clip. You may want to remove one or the other to keep your Timeline panel tidy, and there's an easy way to make the correct selection: If Linked Selection is on, you can temporarily override it.

Switch to the Selection tool and try clicking some clip segments in the Timeline panel while holding the Option (macOS) or Alt (Windows) key. Premiere Pro ignores the link between video and audio parts of your clips. You can even drag a selection across multiple clips in this way!

Splitting a clip

It's also common to add a clip to a sequence and then realize you need it in two parts. Perhaps you want to take just a section of a clip and use it as a cutaway, or maybe you want to separate the beginning and the end to make space for new clips.

You can split clips in several ways.

- Use the Razor tool ![Razor tool icon]. If you hold the Shift key while clicking with the Razor tool, you'll split the clips on every track.

- Make sure the Timeline panel is selected and choose Sequence > Add Edit. Premiere Pro adds an edit at the location of your playhead to clips on any tracks that are targeted (with the track selection button on). If you have selected clips in the sequence, Premiere Pro adds the edit only to the selected clips, ignoring track selections.

- If you choose Sequence > Add Edit To All Tracks, Premiere Pro adds an edit to clips on all tracks, regardless of whether they are targeted.

- Use the Add Edit keyboard shortcuts. Press Command+K (macOS) or Ctrl+K (Windows) to add an edit to targeted tracks or selected clips, or press Shift+Command+K (macOS) or Shift+Ctrl+K (Windows) to add an edit to all tracks.

> **Tip:** The keyboard shortcut for the Razor tool is C.

Clips that were originally continuous will still play back seamlessly unless you move them or make separate adjustments to different parts.

If you click the Timeline Display Settings icon , you can choose Show Through Edits to see a special icon on edits of this kind.

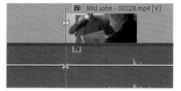

You can rejoin clips that have the Through Edit icon by right-clicking the edit and choosing Join Through Edits.

Using the Selection tool, you can also click a Through Edit icon and press Delete (macOS) or Backspace (Windows) to rejoin the two parts of a clip.

Try it with this sequence. Be sure to use Undo to remove the new cuts you add.

Linking and unlinking clips

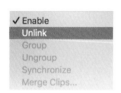

You can switch off and on the link between connected video and audio segments easily. Just select the clip or clips you want to change, right-click the selected clips, and choose Unlink.

You can also use the Clip menu. You can link a clip with its original audio again by selecting both clip segments, right-clicking one of them, and choosing Link. There's no harm in linking or unlinking clips—it won't change the way Premiere Pro plays your sequence. It just gives you the flexibility to work with clips in the way you want.

Even if video and audio clip segments are linked, you'll need to make sure the Timeline Linked Selection option is enabled to select linked clips together.

Moving clips

Insert edits and overwrite edits add new clips to sequences in dramatically different ways. Insert edits push existing clips out of the way, whereas overwrite edits simply replace them. This theme of having two ways of working with clips extends to the techniques you'll employ to move clips around the sequence and to remove clips from the sequence.

When moving clips using the Insert mode, you may want to ensure the sync locks are on for all tracks to avoid any possible loss of sync.

Let's try a few examples.

Dragging clips

At the top left of the Timeline panel, you'll see the Snap button 🔒. When snapping is enabled, clip segments snap automatically to each other's edges. This simple but useful feature will help you position clip segments frame-accurately.

1   Select the last clip on the Timeline, HS Suit, and drag it a little to the right.

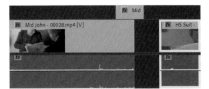

Because there are no clips after this one, you simply introduce a gap before the clip. No other clips are affected.

2   Make sure the Snap option is enabled, and drag the clip back to its original position. If you move the mouse slowly, you'll notice that the clip segment jumps into position at the last moment. When this happens, you can be confident it's perfectly positioned. Notice that the clip also snaps to the end of the cutaway shot on the Video 2 track.

3   Drag the clip left until the end of the clip snaps to the end of the previous clip so they are overlapping. When you release the mouse button, the clip replaces the end of that clip.

When you drag and drop clips, the default editing mode is Overwrite.

4   Undo repeatedly until the clip is in its original position.

Nudging clips

Many editors prefer to use the keyboard as much as possible, minimizing the use of the mouse because working with the keyboard is usually faster.

It's common to move clip segments in a sequence using the arrow keys in combination with a modifier key, nudging the selected items left and right (earlier or later in time) or up and down between tracks.

Because of the separator between the video and audio tracks in the Timeline panel, when you nudge linked video and audio clips up or down, one or other clip may be left in its original position. This introduces a vertical gap between the linked clips. This won't impact playback but can make it a little harder to see which clips are linked.

Default clip-nudging shortcuts

Premiere Pro includes many keyboard shortcut options, some of which are available but not yet assigned keys. You can set these up, prioritizing the use of available keys to suit your workflow.

Here are the default shortcuts for nudging clips:

- Nudge Clip Selection Left 1 Frame (add Shift for five frames): Command+Left Arrow (macOS) or Alt+Left Arrow (Windows)
- Nudge Clip Selection Right 1 Frame (add Shift for five frames): Command+Right Arrow (macOS) or Alt+Right Arrow (Windows)
- Nudge Clip Selection Up: Option+Up Arrow (macOS) or Alt+Up Arrow (Windows)
- Nudge Clip Selection Down: Option+Down Arrow (macOS) or Alt+Down Arrow (Windows)

Rearranging clips in a sequence

If you hold the Command (macOS) or Ctrl (Windows) key while you drag clips on the Timeline, Insert mode (rather than Overwrite mode) is used to place the clip when you release the mouse button.

▶ **Tip:** You may need to zoom in to the Timeline to see the clips clearly and move them easily.

The HS Suit shot around 00:00:20:00 might work better if it appeared before the previous shot—and it might help to hide the poor continuity between the two shots of John.

1 Drag and drop the HS Suit clip to the left of the clip before it. The left edge of the HS Suit clip should easily line up with the left edge of the Mid Suit clip if snapping is enabled.

   After you have begun dragging, hold the Command (macOS) or Ctrl (Windows) key. Release the modifier key after you've dropped the clip.

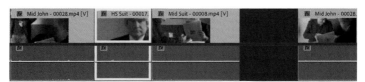

2 Play the result. This creates the edit you want, but it introduces a gap where the clip HS Suit was originally placed.

   Let's try that again with an additional modifier key.

3 Undo to restore the clips to their original positions.

4 Holding Command+Option (macOS) or Ctrl+Alt (Windows), drag and drop the HS Suit clip to the beginning of the previous clip again.

This time, no gap is left in the sequence. Play through the edit to see the result.

▶ **Tip:** Be careful when dropping the clip into position. The ends of clips snap to edges just as the beginnings do.

Using the clipboard

You can copy and paste clip segments on the Timeline just as you might copy and paste text in a word processor.

1 In a sequence, select any clip segment (or segments) you want to copy and then press Command+C (macOS) or Ctrl+C (Windows) to add them to the clipboard.

2 Position your playhead where you would like to paste the clips you copied and press Command+V (macOS) or Ctrl+V (Windows).

Premiere Pro adds copies of the clips to your sequence based on the tracks you enable. The lowest enabled track receives the clip (or clips). If no tracks are targeted, the clips will be added to their original tracks, which can be useful when rearranging clips.

Extracting and deleting segments

Now that you know how to add clips to a sequence and how to move them around, all that remains is to learn how to remove them. Once again, you'll be operating in a kind of Insert or Overwrite mode.

There are two ways to select parts of a sequence you want to remove. You can use In and Out marks combined with track selections, or you can select clip segments.

Performing a lift edit

A lift edit will remove the selected part of a sequence, leaving blank space. It's similar to an overwrite edit but in reverse.

Open the sequence Theft Unexpected 02 in the Sequences bin. This sequence has some unwanted extra clips. They have different label colors to make them easy to identify.

Set In and Out marks on the Timeline to select the part that will be removed. You can do this by positioning the playhead and pressing I or O. You can also use a handy shortcut.

1 Position the playhead so that it's somewhere over the first unwanted clip, Excuse Me Tilted.

2 Make sure the Video 1 track header is turned on and that the clip is not selected; then press X.

   Premiere Pro automatically adds an In mark and an Out mark that match the beginning and end of the clip. You'll see a highlight that shows the selected part of the sequence.

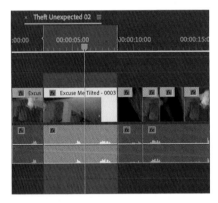

   Make sure Video 1 and Audio 1 tracks are targeted to prepare for the lift edit.

Different shortcuts to add In and Out marks

You can set In and Out points at the beginning and end of a select clip (or multiple clips) by pressing / (forward slash). You can also use X. Position the playhead over the clip (without selecting it) and having the correct tracks selected. The difference is subtle, but X is perhaps even faster than using the selection-based / key if your track selections are already set up.

3 Click the Lift button at the bottom of the Program Monitor. If your key-board has a ; (semicolon) key, you can press it instead.

Premiere Pro removes the part of the sequence you selected, leaving a gap. This might be fine on another occasion, but in this instance you don't want the gap. You could remove the gap now, but for this exercise you'll use an extract edit so no gap is left.

Performing an extract edit

An extract edit removes the selected part of your sequence and does not leave a gap. It's similar to an insert edit but in reverse.

1 Undo the last edit.
2 Click the Extract button ⊞ at the bottom of the Program Monitor. If your keyboard has an ' (apostrophe) key, you can press it.

This time, Premiere Pro removes the selected part of the sequence, and the other clips in the sequence move to close the gap.

Performing a delete and ripple delete edit

Just as there are two ways to remove part of a sequence based on In and Out marks, there are also two similar ways to remove clips by selecting clip segments: Delete and Ripple Delete.

Click once to select the second unwanted clip, called Cutaways, and try these two options:

• Pressing the Delete/Backspace key removes the selected clip (or clips), leaving a gap behind. This is the same as a lift edit.

• Pressing Shift+Forward Delete (macOS) or Shift+Delete (Windows) removes the selected clip (or clips) without leaving a gap behind. This is the same as an extract edit. If you're using a Mac keyboard without a dedicated Forward Delete key, you can convert the Delete key into a Forward Delete key by pressing the Function (fn) and Delete keys together.

The result seems similar to that achieved by using In and Out marks because you used In and Out marks earlier to select a whole clip. However, you can use In and Out marks to choose parts of clips, while selecting clip segments and pressing Delete will always remove whole clips.

Disabling a clip

Just as you can turn a track output off or on, you can also turn individual clips off or on. Clips that you disable are still in your sequence, but they cannot be seen or heard during playback or while scrubbing.

This is a useful feature for selectively hiding parts of a complex, multilayered sequence when you want to see background layers or compare different versions, or different performance takes that you have placed on different tracks.

Try this on the cutaway shot on the Video 2 track, toward the end of the sequence.

1 Right-click the Mid Suit clip on the Video 2 track, and choose Enable to deselect it.

    ● **Note:** When right-clicking clips in a sequence, be careful not to right-click the FX badge as this will give you options relating to effects instead of the general clip options.

    Play through that part of the sequence, and you'll notice that the clip is present, but you can no longer see it.

2 Right-click the clip again and choose Enable. This reenables the clip.

Review questions

1 When dragging clips directly into the Timeline panel, what modifier key (Command/Ctrl, Shift, or Option/Alt) should you use to make an insert edit rather than an overwrite edit?

2 How do you drag just the video or audio part of a clip from the Source Monitor into a sequence?

3 How do you reduce the playback resolution in the Source Monitor or Program Monitor?

4 How do you add a marker to a clip or sequence?

5 What is the difference between an extract edit and a lift edit?

6 What is the difference between Delete and Ripple Delete?

Review answers

1 Hold the Command (macOS) or Ctrl (Windows) key when dragging a clip into the Timeline panel to make an insert edit rather than an overwrite edit.

2 Rather than grabbing the picture in the Source Monitor, drag and drop the filmstrip icon or the audio waveform icon at the bottom of the monitor to select only the video or audio part of the clip. You can also use the Source selection indicators in the Timeline panel to deselect the parts you want to exclude.

3 Use the Select Playback Resolution menu at the bottom of the monitor to change the playback resolution.

4 To add a marker, click the Add Marker button at the bottom of the monitor or on the Timeline panel, press the M key, or use the Marker menu.

5 When you extract a section of your sequence using In and Out marks, no gap is left behind. When you lift, a gap remains.

6 When you delete one or more clip segments in a sequence, a gap is left behind. When you ripple delete, no gap is left.

7 ADDING TRANSITIONS

Lesson overview

In this lesson, you'll learn about the following:

- Understanding transitions

- Understanding edit points and handles

- Adding video transitions

- Modifying transitions

- Fine-tuning transitions

- Applying transitions to multiple clips at once

- Using audio transitions

This lesson will take about 75 minutes to complete. Please log in to your account on peachpit.com to download the lesson files for this lesson, or go to the "Getting Started" section at the beginning of this book and follow the instructions under "Accessing the lesson files and Web Edition." Store the files on your computer in a convenient location.

Your Account page is also where you'll find any updates to the lesson files. Look on the Lesson & Update Files tab to access the most current content.

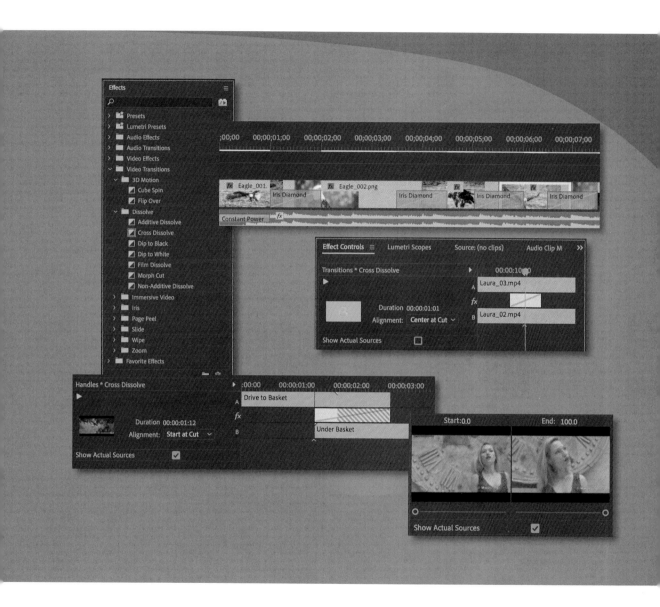

Transitions can help create a seamless flow between two video or audio clips. Video transitions are often used to signify a change in time or location. Audio transitions provide a useful way to avoid abrupt edits that jar the listener. While the most common transition is a cut—where one clip abruptly ends and another begins—there are great opportunities for creativity using transition effects you can animate.

Starting the lesson

In this lesson, you'll learn to use transitions between video and audio clips. Video editors often use transitions to help an edit flow more smoothly. You'll learn best practices for choosing transitions selectively.

For this lesson, you'll use a new project file.

1 Start Adobe Premiere Pro CC, and open the project Lesson 07.prproj in the Lessons/Lesson 07 folder.

2 Save the project as **Lesson 07 Working.prproj** in the same folder.

● **Note:** If you have been using Premiere Pro for a while, there's a small chance your settings will prevent the Workspaces panel from being displayed. You can always restore it by choosing the correct workspace from the Window menu and then going back to the Window menu and choosing Workspaces > Reset To Saved Layout.

3 Choose Effects in the Workspaces panel, or choose Window > Workspaces > Effects. Reset the workspace to the saved layout.

This changes the workspace to the preset that was created to make it easier to work with transitions and effects.

This workspace uses stacked panels to maximize the number of panels that can be on-screen at a time.

You can enable stacked panels for any panel group by opening the panel menu ▤ and choosing Panel Group Settings > Stacked Panel Group. The same option will toggle off stacked panels.

You can click the name of any panel in a stack to view its contents. Start with the Effects panel.

As you click effect category disclosure triangles to display their contents, the panel will automatically change height to accommodate the list.

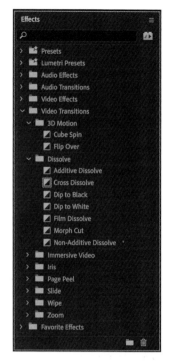

What are transitions?

Adobe Premiere Pro offers several special effects and preset animations to help you bridge neighboring clips in the sequence. These transitions—such as dissolves, page wipes, dips to color, and so on—provide a way to ease viewers from one scene to the next. A transition can also be used to grab viewers' attention to signify a major jump in the story.

Adding transitions to your project is an art. Applying them is simple enough; drag the transition you want onto the cut between two clips. The skill comes in their placement, length, and settings, such as direction, motion, and start/end positions.

You can adjust some transition settings in the Timeline panel, but it's usually easier to make precise adjustments in the Effect Controls panel. To view the settings for a transition in the Effect Controls panel, select a transition effect in a sequence.

In addition to the unique options for each transition, the Effect Controls panel features an *A/B timeline display*. This makes it easy to change the timing of transitions relative to the edit point, change the transition duration, and apply transitions to clips that don't have enough head or tail frames—that is, additional content to provide an overlap at the beginning/head or end/tail of a clip.

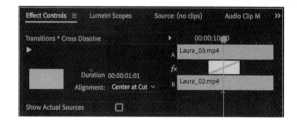

You can also apply a transition effect to all the edit points in a group of selected clips.

VR video transitions

Though it is beyond the scope of this book, Premiere Pro includes excellent support for 360 video and includes effects and transitions intended for this format.

Unlike 2D or stereoscopic video, 360 video requires visual effects and transitions designed to deal with wraparound video with no edges.

The techniques described here also apply to 360 video transitions—just be sure to use one of the options available in the Video Transitions > Immersive Video category in the Effects panel.

Knowing when to use transitions

The rules for transitions are similar to the rules of screenwriting. They're effective when they help the viewer understand the story or a character. For example, you may switch from indoors to outdoors in a video, or you may jump forward in time by several hours in the same location. An animated transition, a fade to black, or a dissolve helps the viewer understand that time has passed or that the location has changed.

Transitions are a standard storytelling tool in video editing. A fade to black at the end of a scene is a clear indication that the scene has finished. The trick with transitions is to be intentional—and this often means using restraint—unless, of course, a total lack of restraint is the result you want to achieve.

Only you can know what is right for your creative work. As long as it looks like you meant to include a particular effect, your audience will tend to trust your decision (whether or not they agree with your creative choices). It takes practice and experience to develop sensitivity for the right time, and the wrong time, to use effects such as transitions. If in doubt, less is usually better.

Following best practices with transitions

New editors sometimes overuse transitions, perhaps because it's an easy way to add visual interest. You may be tempted to use a transition on every cut. Don't! Or at least, get them out of your system with your first project.

Most TV shows and feature films use cuts-only edits. You'll rarely see any transition special effects. Why? An effect should be used only if it gives a particular additional benefit; transition effects can sometimes be a distraction from the story, reminding viewers they are watching a story and not experiencing it.

If a news editor uses a transition effect, it's for a purpose. The most frequent use in newsroom editing is to take what would have been a jarring or abrupt edit and make it more acceptable.

A *jump cut* is a good example of a scenario where a transition effect can help. A jump cut is a cut between two similar shots. Rather than looking like a continuation of the story, they look a little like a piece of the video was missing unintentionally. By adding a transition effect between the two shots, you can make a jump cut look intentional and less distracting.

Dramatic transition effects do have their place in storytelling. Consider the *Star Wars* movies with their highly stylized transition effects, such as obvious, slow wipes. Each of those transitions has a purpose. In this case, it's to create a look reminiscent of old serialized movies and TV shows. The transition effects send a clear message: "Pay attention now. We're transitioning across space and time."

Using edit points and handles

To understand transition effects, you'll need to understand edit points and handles. An edit point is the point in your sequence where one clip ends and the next begins. This is often called a *cut*. These are easy to see because Premiere Pro displays vertical lines to show where one clip ends and another begins (much like two bricks next to each other).

When you edit part of a clip into a sequence, the unused sections at the beginning and end are still available but hidden. Those unused sections are referred to as *clip handles*, or simply *handles*.

When you first edited a clip into a sequence, you set In and Out marks (also known as In and Out points) to select the part you wanted. There's a handle between the clip's original beginning and the In mark you chose. There's also a handle between the clip's original end and the Out mark you chose.

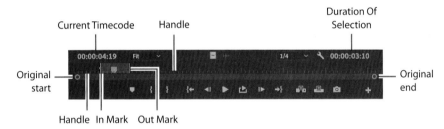

Of course, you may not have used In or Out marks, or you may have set just one or other mark at the beginning or end of the clip. In this case, you would have either no unused media or unused media at only one end of the clip.

In the sequence, if you see a little triangle in the upper-right or upper-left corner of a clip, it means you've reached the end of the original clip and there are no additional frames available.

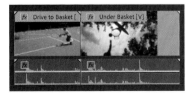

In this example, the first clip has no handles (triangles at both ends). The second clip has a handle available at the start (on the left) but no handle at the end (on the right).

For transitions to work, you need handles because they provide the overlap needed when creating a transition effect.

These unused sections of clips are not visible unless you apply a transition effect. The transition effect automatically creates an overlap between the outgoing clip and the incoming clip. For example, if you wanted to add a two-second Cross Dissolve transition centered between two video clips, you'd need at least a one-second handle on both clips (one additional second each that would not normally be visible in the sequence).

The transition effect icon gives a visual indication of the duration of the effect and the clip overlap.

Adding video transitions

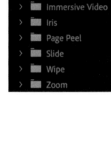

Premiere Pro gives you multiple video transition effects to choose from. Most options are available in the Video Transitions group in the Effects panel.

The transitions are organized into eight effect subcategories. You'll find some additional transitions in the Video Effects > Transition group in the Effects panel. These effects are meant to be applied to an entire clip and can be used to reveal the visual contents of the clip between its start and end frames (not using clip handles). This second category works well for superimposing text or graphics.

● **Note:** If you'd like more transitions, check the Adobe website. Visit https://helpx.adobe.com/premiere-pro/compatibility.html and click the Plug-ins link. There, you'll find several third-party effects to explore.

Applying a single-sided transition

The easiest transition to understand is one that applies to just one end of a single clip. This could be a fade from black on the first clip in a sequence or a dissolve into an animated graphic that leaves the screen on its own.

● **Note:** You can use the Search field, at the top of the Effects panel, to locate an effect by name or keyword, or you can browse the folders of effects.

Let's give it a try.

1   If necessary, open the sequence Transitions.

    This sequence has four video clips and background music. The clips have handles long enough for transition effects to be applied between them.

2   In the Effects panel, open the Video Transitions > Dissolve group. Find the Cross Dissolve effect.

3 Drag the effect onto the start of the first video clip. A highlight shows you where the transition effect will be added. When the transition is in the right position, release the mouse button.

4 Drag the Cross Dissolve effect onto the end of the last video clip.

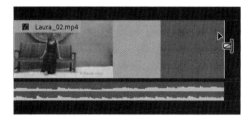

The Cross Dissolve icon shows the timing for the effect. For example, the effect you just applied to the last clip in the sequence will start before the end of the clip and complete by the time it reaches the clip's end.

Because you're applying the Cross Dissolve transition effect at the ends of clips, where there is no connected clip, the picture dissolves into the background of the Timeline (which happens to be black).

Transitions of this kind don't extend the clip (using the handle) because the transition doesn't reach past the end of the clip.

5 Play the sequence to see the result.

You should see a fade from black at the start of the sequence and a fade to black at the end.

When you apply a Cross Dissolve effect in this way, the result looks similar to the Dip to Black effect, which transitions to black. However, in reality you are causing the clip to become gradually transparent in front of a black background. The difference is clearer when you work with multiple layers of clips, with different-colored background layers.

Applying a transition between two clips

Let's apply transitions between several clips. For the purposes of exploration, you'll break some artistic rules and try a few different options. As you go through these steps, play the sequence regularly to view the results.

1   Continue working with the previous sequence, called Transitions.

Tip: It's easy to remember that pressing the = key (if your keyboard has one) zooms in because it normally has a + symbol on the same key.

2   Move the playhead to the edit point between clip 1 and clip 2 on the Timeline and then press the equal sign (=) key two or three times to zoom in fairly close. If your keyboard does not have the = key, use the navigator at the bottom of the Timeline panel to zoom. You can also create a custom keyboard shortcut for this purpose—see Lesson 1, "Touring Adobe Premiere Pro CC."

3   Drag the Dip to White transition from the Dissolve group in the Effects panel onto the edit point between clip 1 and clip 2. The effect will snap to one of three positions. Be sure to line up the effect with the middle of the edit, not the end of the first clip or beginning of the second clip.

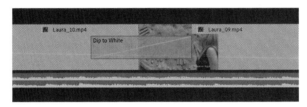

The Dip to White transition effect gradually builds to a completely white screen, which obscures the cut between the first clip and the next.

4   In the Effects panel, click the disclosure triangle for the Slide category to display its contents. Drag the Push transition onto the edit point between clip 2 and clip 3 in the sequence.

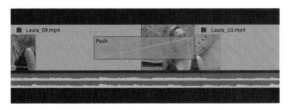

5   Play through the transition to see the result. Then position the playhead on the edit between clip 2 and clip 3 by pressing the Up arrow on your keyboard. The Up and Down arrow keys are shortcuts to move the Timeline playhead to the previous or next edit.

6   Click the Push transition effect icon in the Timeline panel to select it, and open the Effect Controls panel (remember, if you can't see a panel, it will always be listed in the Window menu).

7 Change the direction of the clip from West to East to East to West by clicking the small direction control on the thumbnail, at the top left of the Effect Controls panel.

Each small white triangle changes the direction for the Push transition effect. Hover the pointer over a triangle to see a tooltip describing the option.

Play through the transition to see the result.

8 Drag the Flip Over transition from the 3D Motion group onto the edit point between clip 3 and clip 4.

9 Review the sequence by playing it from beginning to end.

Having watched this sequence, you can probably see why it's a good idea to use transitions with restraint!

Let's try replacing an existing effect.

10 Drag the Split transition from the Slide category onto the existing Push transition effect icon, between clip 2 and clip 3. The new transition effect replaces the old one, taking the duration of the old effect.

11 Select the Split transition effect icon on the Timeline so its settings will be displayed in the Effect Controls panel. Using that panel, set Border Width to 7 and Anti-aliasing Quality to Medium to create a thin black border at the edge of the wipe.

● **Note:** When you drag a new video or audio transition effect from the Effects panel on top of an existing transition, it replaces the existing effect. It also preserves the alignment and duration of the previous transition. This is an easy way to swap transition effects and experiment.

The anti-aliasing method reduces potential flicker when the line animates during the effect.

● **Note:** You may need to scroll down in the Effect Controls panel to access further controls.

12 Play through the transition to view the result. The best way to do this is probably to click a little farther back in the sequence to watch the video leading up to the transition.

If the video does not play smoothly during the transition, press the Return/ Enter key to prerender the effect (more on this later), and try again.

Video transitions have a default duration, which can be set in seconds or frames (it's frames by default). The duration of the effect will change depending on the sequence frame rate, unless the default duration is set in seconds. The default transition duration can be changed in the Timeline section of the Preferences panel.

13 Choose Premiere Pro CC > Preferences > Timeline (macOS) or Edit > Preferences > Timeline (Windows).

Depending on your region, you may see a default Video Transition Duration setting of 30 Frames or 25 Frames.

14 This is a 24-frames-per-second sequence, but this doesn't matter if you change the Video Transition Default Duration option to 1 second. Do so now, and click OK.

Existing transition effects keep their existing settings when you change the preference, but any future transitions you add will have the new duration.

The duration of an effect can dramatically change its impact, and later in this lesson, you'll learn about adjusting the timing of transitions.

Applying transitions to multiple clips at once

So far, you've been applying transitions to video clips. However, you can also apply transitions to still images, graphics, color mattes, and even audio, as you'll see in the next section of this lesson.

It's common for editors to create a photo montage, which might look good with transitions between photos. Applying transitions one at a time to 100 images would take a long time. Premiere Pro makes it easy to automate this process by allowing the default transition effect (that you set) to be added to any group of clips.

1 In the Project panel, find and open the sequence Slideshow.

This sequence consists of several images placed in a particular order. Notice that a Constant Power audio crossfade has already been applied to the beginning and end of the music clip to create a fade in and out.

2 Play the sequence by making sure the Timeline panel is active and pressing the spacebar.

There's a cut between each clip.

3 Press the backslash (\) key to zoom out the Timeline so the whole sequence is visible.

4 Increase the height of the V1 track to see thumbnails on the clips (you can drag the dividing line between V1 and V2 in the track header).

5 With the Selection tool, draw a marquee around all the clips to select them. You'll need to begin outside of the clips to make this selection, or you'll move the first clip you click on instead.

6 Choose Sequence > Apply Default Transitions To Selection.

This applies the default transition between all the currently selected clips. Notice that the Constant Power audio crossfade at the beginning and end of the music clip is now shorter.

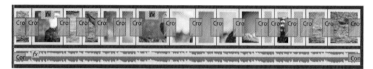

The default video transition effect is a one-second Cross Dissolve, and the default audio transition effect is a one-second Constant Power Crossfade. The shortcut you just used replaced the existing audio crossfades with new, shorter ones.

You can change the default transition by right-clicking a transition effect in the Effects panel and choosing Set Selected As Default Transition.

7 Play the sequence to see the difference the Cross Dissolve transitions make to the montage.

⬤ **Note:** If you're working with clips that have linked video and audio, you can select just the video or audio portions if you Option-drag (macOS) or Alt-drag (Windows) with the Selection tool. Then choose Sequence > Apply Default Transitions To Selection.

▶ **Tip:** You'll find the option to apply audio-only or video-only transition effects in the Sequence menu too.

You can also copy an existing transition effect to multiple edits using the keyboard. Let's try it.

1 Press Command+Z (macOS) or Ctrl+Z (Windows) to undo the last step, and press Esc to deselect the clips.

2 Choose any transition effect in the Effects panel, and drag it onto the cut between the first two video clips in the Slideshow sequence.

3 Select the transition you just applied by clicking its effect icon once on the Timeline.

4   Press Command+C (macOS) or Ctrl+C (Windows) to copy the effect. Then hold Command (macOS) or Ctrl (Windows) while you drag out a marquee with the Selection tool around multiple other edits to select them, rather than clips.

5   With the edits selected, press Command+V (macOS) or Ctrl+V (Windows) to paste the transition effect onto all the selected edits.

This is a great way to add transition effects with matching settings to multiple edits, especially if you have taken the time to customize an effect.

Sequence display changes

When you add a transition to a sequence, a red or yellow horizontal line may appear above it in the Timeline panel. A yellow line indicates that Premiere Pro expects to be able to play the effect smoothly. A red line means that this section of the sequence may need to be rendered before you can record it to tape or view a preview without dropped frames.

Rendering happens automatically when you export your sequence as a file, but you can choose to render at any time to make these sections preview more smoothly on a slower computer.

The easiest way to render is to use the keyboard shortcut Return (macOS) or Enter (Windows). You can also add In and Out marks to select a part of your sequence and then render. Only the selected section of the sequence will render. This is useful if you have many effects that need to render, but you're concerned with only one part for now.

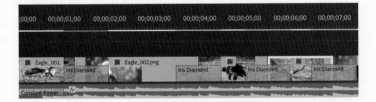

Red or yellow lines will turn to green. Premiere Pro creates a video file for each section where the line turns green. The new video files are stored in the Preview Files folder (as set in the Scratch Disk settings). As long as the line is green, playback should be smooth.

Using A/B mode to fine-tune a transition

When you review transition effect settings in the Effect Controls panel, you have access to an *A/B editing mode* that splits a single video track into two. What would normally be displayed as two consecutive and contiguous clips on a single track are now displayed as individual clips on separate tracks, with a transition between them. Separating the elements of the transition in this way allows you to manipulate the head and tail frames (or handles) and to change other transition options.

Changing parameters in the Effect Controls panel

All transitions in Premiere Pro can be customized. Some effects have just a few customizable properties (such as duration or starting point). Other effects offer more options, such as direction, color, border size, and so on. A major benefit of the Effect Controls panel is that you can see the outgoing and incoming clip handles (unused media in the original clip). This makes it easy to adjust the position of an effect.

Let's modify a transition.

1 In the Timeline, switch back to the Transitions sequence.

2 Position the Timeline playhead over the Split transition you added between clips 2 and 3, and click the transition effect icon to select it.

3 In the Effect Controls panel, select Show Actual Sources to view frames from the actual clips.

This makes it easier to assess the changes you'll make.

4 In the Effect Controls panel, open the Alignment menu, and choose Start At Cut.

The transition icon in the Effect Controls panel and the Timeline panel switches to show the new position.

5 Click the small Play The Transition button at the upper-left corner of the Effect Controls panel to preview the transition.

6 Now change the transition duration. In the Effect Controls panel, click the blue numbers for the effect Duration, type **300**, and click away or press the Tab key to apply the new number for an effect that is three seconds in duration (remember, Premiere Pro will add the correct punctuation automatically).

The Alignment menu changes to Custom Start because the effect now reaches beyond the beginning of the next transition effect. To make the new transition duration fit, Premiere Pro sets the start a little earlier.

Examine the right side of the Effect Controls panel, which displays the transition in the context of a timeline.

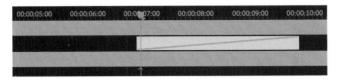

In this example, the Effect Controls panel playhead is centered on the cut, and you can see the way the effect timing has been adjusted automatically. These adjustments can be subtle, so always double-check the results of new settings.

Play the transition to see the change.

It's important to play through transitions to be sure you're happy with the newly revealed media in the handles—this media was hidden from view until you added the transition effect. While it's useful that Premiere Pro automatically modifies the timing of effects when necessary, it makes it even more important to check the transition before you move on.

Let's customize the transition.

Note: The Effect Controls Timeline may not currently be visible. Clicking the Show/Hide Timeline View button in the Effect Controls panel toggles it on and off. You might need to resize the Effect Controls panel to make the tiny Show/Hide Timeline View button visible.

Tip: The bottom of the Effect Controls panel timeline includes a zoom navigator that works the same way as the one in the Monitors and Timeline panel.

Tip: You may need to move the playhead out of the way—earlier or later—to see the edit point between two clips.

7 In the Effect Controls panel timeline, hover the pointer over the thin vertical black line that crosses all three layers (both clips and the transition effect between them). The line is the edit point between the two clips.

This edit line is close to the left edge of the effect, so you will probably want to zoom in to the Effect Controls panel timeline to conveniently make adjustments.

The pointer changes to a red Rolling Edit tool.

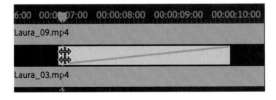

Note: When trimming, it's possible to shorten a transition to a duration of one frame. This can make it hard to grab and position the transition effect icon, so try using the Duration and Alignment controls. If you want to remove a transition, select it in the sequence in the Timeline panel and press Delete (macOS) or Backspace (Windows).

In the Effect Controls panel, the Rolling Edit tool lets you reposition the edit point by dragging the edit line.

8 In the Effect Controls panel, drag the Rolling Edit tool left and right. As you do, you're changing the timing of the cut. The Out mark of the clip on the left of the edit and the In mark of the clip on the right of the edit update in the Timeline panel when you release the mouse button. This is also called *trimming*.

You'll explore trimming in more detail in Lesson 8, "Mastering Advanced Editing Techniques."

9   Move the pointer to the left or right of the edit line in the Effect Controls panel, and the cursor changes to the Slide tool. The blue line is the Timeline playhead.

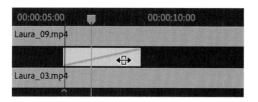

The edit line is the small black vertical line on the effect icon in the Effect Controls panel.

Using the Slide tool changes the start and end points of the transition without changing its overall duration. Unlike using the Rolling Edit tool, moving the transition rectangle by using the Slide tool does not change the edit point between the two sequence clips. Instead, it changes the timing of the transition effect.

10 Use the Slide tool to drag the transition rectangle left and right and compare the results.

Tip: You can position the start time of a dissolve asymmetrically by dragging it. This means you don't have to settle for the Centered, Start At Cut, and End At Cut options. You can drag the position of a transition effect directly on the Timeline too; there's no need to use the Effect Controls panel.

Using a Morph Cut effect

Morph Cut is a special transition effect that aims to be invisible. It's designed specifically to help with "talking head" video interviews, where a single speaker looks in the direction of the camera. If your subject pauses a lot or there is inappropriate content in the footage, you may want to remove a section of the interview.

This would normally produce a jump cut (when the image seems to jump suddenly from one piece of content to another), but with the right media and a little experimentation, the Morph Cut effect might yield an invisible transition that seamlessly hides what you have removed. Let's try it.

1   Open the sequence Morph Cut. Play the beginning of the sequence.

    This sequence has one clip, with a jump cut near the start. It's a small jump cut but enough to jar the audience.

2   In the Effects panel, look in the Video Transitions > Dissolve group for the Morph Cut effect. Drag this effect to the join between the two clips.

    The Morph Cut transition effect begins by analyzing the two clips in the background. You can continue to work on your sequence while this analysis takes place.

    Depending on your media, you may achieve improved results with the Morph Cut transition effect by experimenting with different durations.

3 Double-click the Morph Cut transition effect to display the Set Transition Duration dialog. Change the duration to **18** frames (you can double-click in this way on any transition effect to access the duration setting).

4 When the analysis is complete, press Return (macOS) or Enter (Windows) to render the effect (if your system requires it) and play a preview.

The result is not perfect, but it's close, and it's unlikely an audience will notice the join. It's worthwhile experimenting with the duration of this effect to achieve the best results.

Dealing with inadequate (or nonexistent) head or tail handles

If you try to extend a transition for a clip that doesn't have enough frames as a handle, the transition still appears but has diagonal warning bars through it. This means Premiere Pro is using a freeze frame to extend the duration of the clip.

You can adjust the duration and position of the transition to resolve the issue.

1 Open the sequence Handles.

2 Locate the edit between the two clips.

These two sequence clips have no heads or tails. You can tell this immediately because of the little triangles in the corners of the clips; a triangle indicates the last frame of an original clip.

3 Select the Ripple Edit tool ![icon] in the Tools panel, and use it to drag the right edge of the first clip to the left (begin dragging just to the left of the cut between the two clips). Drag to shorten the duration of the first clip to about 1:10 and then release. A tooltip appears while you trim to show the new clip duration.

The clip to the right of the edit point ripples to close the gap. Notice that the little triangle at the end (the right edge) of the clip you have trimmed is no longer present.

4 Drag the Cross Dissolve transition effect from the Effects panel onto the edit point between the two clips.

You can drag the transition onto the right side of the edit but not the left. That's because there's no handle available at the beginning of the second clip to create a dissolve overlapping the end of the first clip without using freeze frames.

5 Press V to select the Selection tool , or click to select the tool in the Tools panel. Click the Cross Dissolve transition effect icon once to select it. You may need to zoom in to make it easier to select the transition.

6 In the Effect Controls panel, set the duration of the effect to **1:12**.

There aren't enough frames of video to create this effect; the diagonal lines on the transition, both in the Effect Controls panel and on the Timeline, indicate still frames that have been automatically added to fill the duration you set. The result is a freeze frame wherever you see the diagonal lines.

7 Play the transition to see the result.

8 In the Effect Controls panel, change the alignment of the transition to Center At Cut.

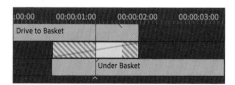

9 Drag the Timeline playhead slowly through the transition and watch the result.

- For the first half of the transition (up to the edit point), the B clip is a freeze frame, while the A clip continues to play.

- At the edit point, the A clip and the B clip start to play.

- After the edit, a short freeze frame is used.

There are several ways to fix this kind of issue.

Note: The Rolling Edit tool lets you move the transition left or right but does not change the overall length of the sequence.

- You can change the duration or alignment of the transition effect.

- You can use the Rolling Edit tool , accessible by pressing and holding the Ripple Edit tool in the Tools panel, to change the timing of the transition in the Timeline panel. This won't necessarily remove all the freeze frames, but it may improve the overall result. Be sure to click the edit between the clips and not the transition effect icon.

- You can use the Ripple Edit tool to shorten a clip. Again, be sure to click the edit between the clips and not the effect icon.

You'll learn more about the Rolling Edit and Ripple Edit tools in Lesson 8.

Adding audio transitions

Audio transitions can dramatically improve a sequence's soundtrack by removing unwanted audio pops or abrupt edits. Audiences are usually much more aware of inconsistency in the soundtrack than they are of the overall quality of the soundtrack, and crossfade transitions can have a big impact in smoothing variation between clips.

Creating a crossfade

There are three styles of crossfade.

- **Constant Gain:** The Constant Gain crossfade (as its name implies) transitions audio by using a constant audio gain (volume) adjustment between the clips. Though this transition leads to a slight perceived dip in the audio level, some find it useful. It can result in a slight drop in overall level as the sound of the outgoing clip fades out and the incoming clip then fades in at an equal gain. It's most useful in situations where you do not want much blending between two clips but rather more of a dip out and in between the clips.

- **Constant Power:** The default audio transition in Premiere Pro creates a smooth, gradual transition between two audio clips. The Constant Power crossfade works in a similar way to a video dissolve. The outgoing clip fades out slowly at first and then faster toward the end of the clip. For the incoming clip, the opposite occurs—the audio level increases quickly at the start of the incoming clip and more slowly toward the end of the transition. This crossfade is useful in situations where you want to blend the audio between two clips, without a noticeable drop in level in the middle.

- **Exponential Fade:** The Exponential Fade transition creates a fairly smooth fade between clips. It uses a logarithmic curve to fade out and fade up audio. Some editors prefer the Exponential Fade transition when performing a single-sided transition (such as fading in a clip from silence at the start or end of a program).

Applying audio transitions

There are several ways to apply an audio crossfade to a sequence. You can, of course, drag and drop an audio transition effect just as you would a video transition effect, but there are also useful shortcuts to speed up the process.

Audio transitions have a default duration, measured in seconds or frames. You can change the default duration by choosing Premiere Pro CC > Preferences > Timeline (macOS) or Edit > Preferences > Timeline (Windows).

Let's take a look at the three methods for applying audio transitions.

1   Open the sequence Audio.

   The sequence has several clips with audio.

2   Open the Audio Transitions > Crossfade group in the Effects panel.

3   Drag the Exponential Fade transition to the start of the first audio clip.

4   Navigate to the end of the sequence.

5   Right-click the final edit point in the Timeline and choose Apply Default Transitions.

   New video and audio transitions are added.

   ● **Note:** To add only an audio transition, hold Option (macOS) or Alt (Windows) when right-clicking to select only the audio clip.

   The Constant Power transition is added to the end audio clip as a transition to create a smooth blend as the audio ends.

6 You can change the length of any transition by dragging its edge in the Timeline. Drag to extend the audio transition you just created and then listen to the result.

7 To polish the project, add a Cross Dissolve transition at the beginning of the sequence. Move the playhead near the beginning, select the first clip, and press Command+D (macOS) or Ctrl+D (Windows) to add the default video transition.

You now have a fade from black at the beginning and a fade to black at the end. Now let's add a series of short audio dissolves to smooth out the sound mix.

8 With the Selection tool, press Option (macOS) or Alt (Windows) and marquee all the audio clips on track Audio 1, being careful not to select any video clips—drag from below the audio clips to avoid accidentally selecting items on the video track.

● **Note:** The selection of clips does not have to be contiguous. You can Shift-click clips to select individual clips in a sequence.

Pressing Option (macOS) or Alt (Windows) lets you temporarily unlink the audio clips from the video clips to isolate the transitions.

▶ **Tip:** You could choose Apply Audio Transition in the Sequence menu to add transitions exclusively to audio clips, but if you have already chosen audio-only clips, there's no need, as the default transition option will have the same effect.

9 Choose Sequence > Apply Default Transitions To Selection.

10 Play the sequence to see and hear the changes you made.

11 Choose File > Close to close the current project. Click Yes to save the file if you are prompted.

▶ **Tip:** To add the default audio transition to an edit point near the playhead, between selected clips, or at selected cut points, press Shift+Command+D (macOS) or Shift+Ctrl+D (Windows). Track selection (or clip selection) is used to work out where exactly the effects should be applied.

It's common for audio editors to add one- or two-frame audio transitions to every cut in a sequence to avoid jarring pops when an audio clip begins or ends. If you set your default duration for audio transitions to two frames, you can use the Apply Default Transitions To Selection option in the Sequence menu to quickly smooth your audio mix.

Review questions

1 How can you apply the default transition to multiple clips in a sequence?

2 In the Effects panel, how can you locate a transition effect by name?

3 How do you replace a transition with another one?

4 Explain three ways to change the duration of a transition.

5 What is an easy way to gradually increase the audio level at the beginning of a clip?

Review answers

1 Select the clips, and choose Sequence > Apply Default Transitions To Selection. You can also use the keyboard shortcut Shift+D.

2 Start typing the transition name in the Contains text box in the Effects panel. As you type, Premiere Pro displays all effects and transitions (audio and video) that have that letter combination anywhere in their names. Type more letters to narrow your search.

3 Drag the replacement transition on top of the transition you're rejecting. The new one automatically replaces the old one while adopting its timing.

4 Drag the edge of the transition icon in the Timeline, do the same thing in the Effect Controls panel's A/B timeline display, or change the Duration value in the Effect Controls panel. You can also double-click the transition icon in the Timeline panel and change the Duration value in the dialog box that appears.

5 Apply an audio-crossfade transition to the beginning of the clip.

8 MASTERING ADVANCED EDITING TECHNIQUES

Lesson overview

In this lesson, you'll learn about the following:

- Performing a four-point edit

- Changing the speed or duration of clips in your sequence

- Replacing a clip in a sequence

- Replacing footage in a project

- Creating a nested sequence

- Performing basic trimming on media to refine edits

- Applying slip and slide edits to refine your edit

- Dynamically trimming clips

 This lesson will take about 120 minutes to complete. Please log in to your account on peachpit.com to download the lesson files for this lesson, or go to the "Getting Started" section at the beginning of this book and follow the instructions under "Accessing the lesson files and Web Edition." Store the files on your computer in a convenient location.

Your Account page is also where you'll find any updates to the lesson files. Look on the Lesson & Update Files tab to access the most current content.

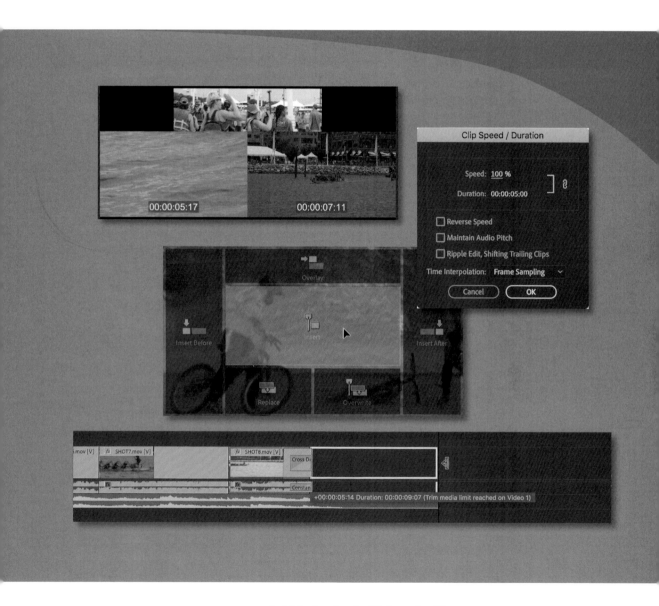

In Adobe Premiere Pro CC, the main editing commands are easy to master. More advanced techniques take a little time to learn, but they're worth it! They'll accelerate your editing and provide the understanding you'll need to produce the highest-level professional results.

Starting the lesson

In this lesson, you'll use several short sequences to explore advanced editing concepts in Adobe Premiere Pro CC. The goal is to get hands-on with the techniques you'll need for advanced editing.

1   Open the project Lesson 08.prproj in the Lesson 08 folder.

2   Save the project as **Lesson 08 Working.prproj** in the Lesson 08 folder.

3   Choose Editing in the Workspaces panel, or choose Window > Workspaces > Editing.

4   Reset the workspace to the saved version by clicking the Editing menu in the Workspaces panel or by choosing Window > Workspaces > Reset To Saved Layout, or by double-clicking the Editing workspace name.

Performing four-point editing

In previous lessons, you used the standard technique of three-point editing. You used three In and Out points (split between the Source Monitor as well as the Program Monitor or Timeline panel) to set the source, duration, and location of an edit.

But what happens if you have four points defined?

The short answer is that you have to make a choice. It's likely that the duration you've marked in the Source Monitor differs from the duration you've marked in the Program Monitor or in the Timeline panel.

In this case, when you attempt to perform the edit using a keyboard shortcut or on-screen button, a dialog box warns you the durations don't match and asks you to make a decision about what to change. Most often, you'll discard one of the points.

Setting editing options for four-point edits

If you perform a four-point edit, Premiere Pro opens the Fit Clip dialog to alert you to the problem. You'll need to choose from five options to resolve the conflict. You can ignore one of the four points or change the speed of the clip.

• **Change Clip Speed (Fit To Fill):** The first choice assumes that you set four points with different durations deliberately. Premiere Pro preserves the source clip's In and Out points but adjusts its playback speed to match the duration you set in the Timeline panel or in the Program Monitor. This is an excellent choice if you want to precisely adjust clip playback speed to fill a gap.

- **Ignore Source In Point:** If you choose this option, Premiere Pro ignores the source clip's In point, converting your edit back to a three-point edit. When you have an Out point and no In point in the Source Monitor, the In point is worked out automatically based on the duration set in the Timeline panel or Program Monitor (or the end of the clip). This option is available only if the source clip is longer than the duration set in the sequence.

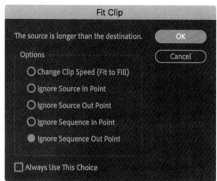

- **Ignore Source Out Point:** When you select this option, the source clip's Out point is ignored, converting your edit back to a three-point edit. When you have an In point and no Out point in the Source Monitor, the Out point is worked out based on the duration set in the Timeline panel or Program Monitor (or the end of the clip). This option is available only if the source clip is longer than the targeted duration.

- **Ignore Sequence In Point:** When you select this option, the In point you've set in the sequence is ignored, making this a three-point edit using only the sequence Out point. The duration is taken from the Source Monitor.

- **Ignore Sequence Out Point:** This option is similar to the previous one. It tells Premiere Pro to ignore the Out point in the sequence you set and perform a three-point edit. Again, the duration is taken from the Source Monitor.

▶ **Tip:** You can choose to set a default behavior when a four-point edit occurs by selecting an option and selecting Always Use This Choice. If you change your mind, open the Preferences dialog box, click Timeline, and select Fit Clip Dialog Opens For Edit Range Mismatches. The Fit Clip dialog box will then open when an edit range mismatch occurs.

Making a four-point edit

Let's perform a four-point edit. You'll change the playback speed of a clip to fit a duration set in the sequence.

1 Open the sequence 01 Four Point. Play through the sequence to review the content.

2 Scroll through the sequence and locate the section with In and Out points already set. You should see a highlighted range in the Timeline panel.

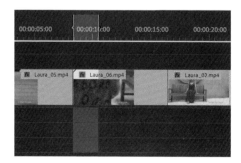

3 Browse inside the bin called Clips To Load, and open the clip called Laura_04 in the Source Monitor.

Clip In and Out points should already be set on this clip.

4 In the Timeline panel, check that the source track indicators are patched correctly, with Source V1 positioned next to Timeline Video 1. There's no audio in this source clip, so you just need to check the Source V1.

5 In the Source Monitor, click the Overwrite button to make the edit.

6 In the Fit Clip dialog box, select the Change Clip Speed (Fit To Fill) option, and click OK.

7 The edit is applied. Zoom in to the Timeline panel using the Navigator controls at the bottom of the panel until you can see the name and speed information on the Laura_04 clip you just edited into the sequence.

The percentage shows the new playback speed. The speed has been adjusted perfectly to fit the new duration.

8 Play the sequence now to see the effects of your edit and the speed change.

Changing playback speed

Slow motion is one of the most commonly used effects in video post-production. You might change the speed of a clip for technical reasons or for artistic impact. It can be an effective way to add drama or to give the audience more time to experience a moment.

● **Note:** When changing the speed of a clip, you will usually achieve smoother playback if the new speed is an even multiple or fraction of the original clip playback speed. For example, changing a 24fps clip to play back at 25% speed will result in 6fps, and this will usually look smoother than if the clip is set to a nonequally divided playback speed, like 27.45%. Sometimes you'll get the best results by changing clip playback speed and then trimming to get a precise duration.

The fit to fill edit you just learned about is one way to change clip playback speed, and its results can vary. If the media originally had clear smooth motion, you'll probably get better results. Also, because fit to fill edits often result in precise partial frame rates, they may produce inconsistent motion.

Usually the best way to achieve high-quality slow motion is to record at a higher frame rate than your sequence playback frame rate. If you play the video at a slower frame rate than it was recorded at, you'll see slow motion—provided the new frame rate is still at least as high as your sequence frame rate.

For example, imagine a 10-second video clip was recorded at 48 frames per second but your sequence is set to 24 frames per second. You can set your footage to play at 24 frames per second, matching the sequence. Playback will be smooth, with no frame rate conversion when the clip is added to the sequence. However, the clip will be playing at half its original frame rate, resulting in 50% slow motion. It will take twice as long to play back, so the clip will now have a 20-second duration.

Overcranking

This technique is often called *overcranking* because early film cameras were driven by turning a crank handle.

The faster the handle was turned, the more frames per second were captured. Slower turning would capture fewer frames per second. This way, when the film was played back at a regular speed, filmmakers would achieve fast motion or slow motion.

Modern cameras often allow recording at faster frame rates to provide excellent-quality slow motion in post-production. The camera assigns a frame rate to the clip metadata that might differ from the recorded rate (the system frame rate is used).

This means clips may play in slow motion automatically when you import them into Premiere Pro. Use the Interpret Footage dialog box to tell Premiere Pro how to play clips.

Let's try this.

1   Open the sequence 02 Laura In The Snow. Play the clip in the sequence.

The clip plays in slow motion for the following reasons:

- The clip was recorded at 96 frames per second.

- The clip is set to play back at 24 frames per second (this was actually set by the camera).

- The sequence is configured for 24 frames per second playback.

2   In the Timeline panel, right-click the clip and choose Reveal In Project.

    This highlights the clip in the Project panel.

3   Right-click the clip in the Project panel and choose Modify > Interpret Footage.
    We'll use the Interpret Footage dialog box to tell Premiere Pro how to play back
    this clip.

4   Select the Assume This Frame Rate option, and enter **96** in the box. This tells
    Premiere Pro to play the clip at 96 frames per second. Click OK.

    Look back at the Timeline panel. The clip has changed appearance.

    You have given the clip a faster frame rate, so the original clip duration is no
    longer used. Because the clip plays faster, its duration is shorter, and diagonal
    lines indicate the portion of the clip that has no media.

    Premiere Pro does not change the duration of the Timeline clip segment
    because doing so might change the timing of your sequence. Instead, the part of
    the sequence clip that has no media is empty.

5   Play the sequence again.

    The clip plays at regular speed because it was originally recorded at 96 frames
    per second. It's much less smooth—not because there's anything wrong with the
    clip but because the original camera recording was bumpy.

6   Drag the Laura_01.mp4 clip onto the sequence close to the first instance, so you
    can see both versions side by side.

    The new clip instance is shorter and matches the total playback time at the new
    frame rate. If you slow down the playback speed of the clip now, to 25%, it will
    restore the original frames, producing slow motion.

Note: If you're using
a system with slow
storage, you may need
to lower the playback
resolution in the Pro-
gram Monitor to play
the clip at a fast frame
rate without dropping
frames.

Changing clip speed or duration

Although it's more common to slow clips down, speeding up clips is a useful effect as well. The Speed/Duration command in the Timeline panel can change the playback speed for a clip in two different ways. You can set the duration of a clip to match a certain time, or you can set the playback speed as a percentage.

For example, if you set a clip to play at 50% speed, it will play back at half-speed; 25% would be one-quarter speed. Premiere Pro allows you to set playback speeds up to two decimal places, so you could have 27.13% if you wanted.

Let's explore this technique.

1   Open the sequence 03 Speed and Duration. Play the sequence to get a sense of the normal playback speed.

2   Right-click the Eagle_Walk clip in the sequence and choose Speed/ Duration. You can also select the clip in the sequence and choose Clip > Speed/Duration.

The Clip Speed/Duration dialog box gives you several options for controlling the clip playback speed.

If you click the small chain icon ⛓, you can toggle on and off keeping the clip duration and speed ganged together. If this is on, changing one updates the other.

- Clicking the chain icon now so that it shows a broken link ⛓; indicates that the duration and speed are unganged. Now, if you enter a new speed, the duration won't update.

- Once the settings are unganged, you can also change the duration without changing the speed. If there's another clip immediately after this one in the sequence, shortening a clip will leave a gap. By default, if you make the clip longer than the space available, the speed change will have no effect. That's because the clip can't move the next clip to make room for the new duration when you change these settings. If you select the Ripple Edit, Shifting Trailing Clips option, the clip will make space for itself, pushing other clips later in the sequence.

- To play a clip backward, select the Reverse Speed option. You'll see a negative symbol next to the new speed displayed in the sequence.

- If you're changing the speed of a clip that has audio, consider selecting the Maintain Audio Pitch check box. This will keep the clip's original pitch at the new speed. With this option disabled, the pitch will naturally go up or down as the speed changes. This option is more effective for small speed changes; dramatic resampling can produce unnatural results—consider adjusting the audio in Adobe Audition if you need to make a more significant speed change. See the *Adobe Audition Classroom in a Book* for audio speed change workflows and more.

Note: There's one exception to the way the chain icon works in the Clip Speed/Duration dialog box: If a new, higher speed reduces the duration so much that all the original clip media is used and the result has a shorter duration than the Timeline clip segment, then the Timeline clip will still shorten to fit. This way, you won't have blank video frames in your sequence.

3 Make sure Speed and Duration are linked with the chain icon on, change the speed to 50%, and click OK.

Play the clip in the Timeline panel. You may need to render the clip by pressing Return (macOS) or Enter (Windows) to see smooth playback. Notice that the clip is now 10 seconds long. That's because you slowed it to 50%: Half the playback speed means twice the original length.

4 Choose Edit > Undo or press Command+Z (macOS) or Ctrl+Z (Windows).

5 Select the clip on the Timeline and press Command+R (macOS) or Ctrl+R (Windows) to open the Clip Speed/Duration dialog box.

6 Click the chain icon to make sure the Speed and Duration settings are unlinked 🔗. Then change Speed to 50%.

▶ **Tip:** You can change the speed of multiple clips at the same time. To do so, select multiple clips and choose Clip > Speed/Duration. When you change the speed of multiple clips, be sure to pay attention to the Ripple Edit, Shifting Trailing Clips option. This will automatically close or expand gaps for all the selected clips after the speed change.

7 Click OK; then play the clip. The clip plays back slower, with unlinked duration, so it's the same length on the Timeline.

The clip is now playing at 50% speed, so it should play for twice as long. But because you've turned off the link between playback speed and duration, the second half has been trimmed to maintain the five-second duration in the sequence.

Now try reversing playback.

8 Select the clip and open the Clip Speed/Duration dialog box again.

9 Leave Speed at 50%, but this time select Reverse Speed; then click OK.

10 Play the clip. Now it plays in reverse at 50% slow motion.

Changing clip speed/duration with the Rate Stretch tool

Sometimes you'll have a clip that has perfect content to fill a gap in your sequence, but it is just a little too short or a little too long. This is where the Rate Stretch tool helps.

1 Open the sequence 04 Rate Stretch.

   This sequence is synchronized to music, and the clips contain the desired content, but the first video clip is too short. You can make a guess and try to make an exact Speed/Duration adjustment, but it's much easier and faster to use the Rate Stretch tool to drag the end of the clip to fill the gap.

2 In the Tools panel, press and hold the Ripple Edit tool ◄►▶ to select the Rate Stretch tool 🔳.

3 With this tool, drag the right edge of the first video clip to the left edge of the second video clip.

   The speed of the clip changes to fill the gap. The contents haven't changed; the clip is playing more slowly.

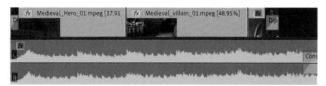

4 Using the same tool, drag the right edge of the second video clip to the left edge of the third clip.

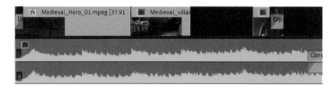

▶ **Tip:** If you change your mind about a change made with the Rate Stretch tool, you can always use it to stretch a clip back. Alternatively, you can use the Speed/Duration command and enter a Speed value of 100% to restore the clip to its default speed.

5 Drag the right edge of the third clip until it matches the end of the audio. Notice that you must drag somewhere other than the transition effect icon to be able to change the duration this way.

   The duration of the video now matches that of the music. You may need to zoom in to the Timeline panel to see the new playback speed of a clip.

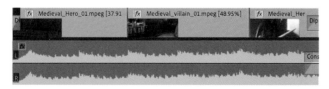

6 Play the sequence to view the result.

7 Press the shortcut key V or click the Selection tool in the Tools panel to select it.

8 Right-click the third clip and choose Time Interpolation > Optical Flow. This smooths playback when changing clip speed. This is a more advanced system for rendering motion changes and takes longer to render and preview.

9 Render and play the sequence to see the result.

Recognizing the downstream effects of changing time

If you change the speed of a clip at the beginning of a sequence with multiple clips placed after it, it's important to understand the way this will affect the those other clips "downstream." You might cause the following:

- Unwanted gaps caused by clips growing shorter because they are playing faster than they did originally

- Unwanted duration changes to the overall sequence because of the Ripple Edit option

- Potential audio problems created by changes in speed—including changing pitch

When you're making speed or duration changes, be careful to view the overall impact on the sequence. You may want to change the zoom level of the Timeline panel to view the entire sequence or segment at once.

Replacing clips and footage

During the editing process, it's common to swap one clip in a sequence for another as you try different versions of an edit.

This might mean making a global replacement, such as replacing one version of an animated logo with a newer file. You might also want to swap out one clip in a sequence for another that you have in a bin. Depending on the task at hand, you'll use different methods.

Dragging in a replacement clip

You can drag a new shot onto the existing sequence clip you'd like to replace. This is called a replace edit.

Let's try it.

1 Open the 05 Replace Clip sequence.

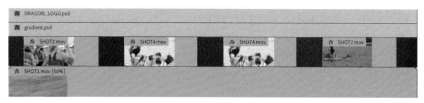

2 Play the sequence.

On the Video 2 track, clips 2 and 3 are actually the same SHOT4 clip repeated. The clip has motion keyframes applied to make it spin onto the screen and spin off again. You'll learn how to create these kinds of animation effects in Lesson 9, "Putting Clips in Motion."

Let's replace the first instance of the clip (SHOT4) with a new clip called Boat Replacement. You don't want to have to re-create the effects and animation, as these are already set perfectly. This is an ideal scenario for replacing a sequence clip.

3 From the Clips To Load bin, drag the Boat Replacement clip straight from the Project panel over the first instance of the SHOT4 clip in the sequence, but don't release the mouse button yet.

For this technique, it's not necessary to position the pointer precisely; just make sure it's over the clip you want to replace.

The clip is longer than the existing clip that you intend to replace.

4 Hold the Option (macOS) or Alt (Windows) key. While you're holding this modifier key, the replacement clip snaps to fit the exact length of the clip it's replacing. Just enough of the new clip will be used to replace the existing clip in the sequence.

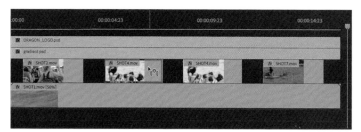

Release the mouse button while still holding the modifier key to replace the clip.

5 Play the sequence. All the picture-in-picture clips have the same effect applied to different footage. The new clip inherits the settings and effects from the clip it replaced. This is a quick and easy way to try different shots in a sequence.

Performing a synchronized replace edit

When you drag and drop to replace a sequence clip, Premiere Pro synchronizes the first frame (or In point) of the replacement clip with the first visible frame of the existing clip in the sequence. This is often fine, but what if you need to synchronize a particular moment in the action, such as hands clapping or a door closing?

If you'd like to have more control, you can use additional options of the Replace Edit command. This allows you to synchronize a particular frame of the replacement clip with a particular frame of the clip it's replacing.

1 Open the sequence 06 Replace Edit.

This is the same sequence you previously fixed, but this time you'll position the replacement clip precisely.

2 Position the playhead in the sequence at approximately 00:00:06:00. The playhead will be the sync point for the edit you are about to perform.

3 Click the first instance of the SHOT4 clip in the sequence to select it.

4 From the Clips To Load bin, open the clip Boat Replacement in the Source Monitor.

5 In the Source Monitor, position the playhead to choose a good piece of action for the replacement. There's a marker on the clip for guidance. You can click the marker to line up the playhead with it.

6 Make sure the Timeline panel is active, with the first instance of SHOT4.mov selected, and choose Clip > Replace With Clip > From Source Monitor, Match Frame.

The clip is replaced.

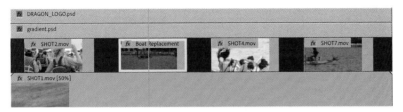

7 Play the newly edited sequence to check the edit.

The playhead position in the Source Monitor and Program Monitor was synchronized. The sequence clip duration, effects, and settings are all applied to the replacement clip. This technique can be a huge time-saver when the precise timing of action needs to be matched.

Using the Replace Footage feature

While a replace edit replaces a clip in a sequence, the Replace Footage feature replaces footage in the Project panel so that the clip links to a different media file. This can be of great benefit when you need to replace a clip that occurs several times in a sequence or in multiple sequences. You might use this to update an animated logo or a piece of music, for example.

When you replace footage in the Project panel, all instances of the clip you replace are changed anywhere the clip is used.

1 Load the sequence 07 Replace Footage.

2 Play the sequence.

Let's replace the graphic on the fourth video track with something more interesting.

3 In the Clips To Load bin, click to select the clip DRAGON_LOGO.psd in the Project panel.

4 Choose Clip > Replace Footage, or right-click the clip and choose Replace Footage.

5 Navigate to the Lessons/Assets/Graphics folder, and choose the DRAGON_LOGO_FIX.psd file. Double-click to select it.

  ● **Note:** The Replace Footage command cannot be undone. To switch back to the original clip, choose Clip > Replace Footage again to navigate to and relink the original file, or choose File > Revert to restore the current project to the last saved version (you'll lose changes made since you last saved).

6 Play the sequence. The graphic has been updated throughout the sequence and project.

Even the clip name in the Project panel has updated to match the new file.

Nesting sequences

A *nested* sequence is a sequence contained within another sequence. You can break up a long project into more manageable parts by creating separate sequences for each section. Then, you can drag each sequence—with all its clips, graphics, layers, multiple audio/video tracks, and effects—into another, "master" sequence. Nested sequences look and behave like single audio/video clips, but you can edit their contents and see the changes update inside the master sequence.

Nesting sequences is quite an advanced workflow, but if you can get to grips with treating sequences as clips, it can be a powerful addition to your post-production workflow. Nest sequences do the following:

- Simplify editing by allowing you to create complex sequences in separate parts. This can help you avoid running into conflicts or accidentally moving clips and ruining your edit.

- Allow you to apply an effect to a group of clips in a single step.

- Let you use sequences as a source in multiple other sequences. You can create one intro sequence for a multipart series and add it to each episode. If you need to change the intro sequence, you can do so once and see the results update everywhere it's nested.

- Allow you to organize your work in the same way you might create subfolders in the Project panel.

- Allow you to apply transitions to a group of clips as a single item.

When editing one sequence into the Timeline for another sequence, an important button in the upper-left corner of the Timeline panel lets you choose between adding the contents of the sequence ⬚ or nesting it ⬚.

Adding a nested sequence

One reason to use a nest is to reuse an existing edited sequence. Let's add an edited opening title into a sequence now.

1 Open the sequence 08 Bike Race, and make sure the option is set to nest sequences .

2 Set an In point at the start of the sequence.

3 When a clip or sequence is selected in the Project panel, or open in the Source Monitor, its source track indicators appear in the Timeline panel, so you can configure track patching.

   In the Project panel, single-click on the sequence 09 Race Open to select it. In the Timeline panel, make sure that source track V1 is patched to the Video 1 track.

4 You can use any method to edit a sequence into another sequence—sequences really do behave just like clips when you nest. On this occasion, drag the sequence 09 Race Open into the Program Monitor (rather than the Timeline panel), dropping the clip onto the Insert option.

▶ Tip: A quick way to create a nested sequence is to drag a sequence from the Project panel into the appropriate track or tracks of the currently active sequence. You can also drag a sequence into the Source Monitor, apply In and Out points, and perform insert and overwrite edits to add a selected section to another sequence.

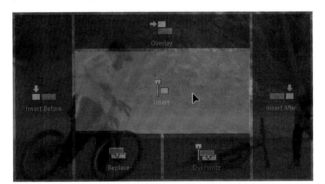

This performs an insert edit. Because you set an In point in the sequence, it's not important where the Timeline playhead is—the In point will be used for timing.

5 Play the 08 Bike Race sequence to see the result.

   The 09 Race Open sequence is added as a single clip, even though it contains multiple video tracks and audio clips.

6 Undo that last edit by pressing Command+Z (macOS) or Ctrl+Z (Windows).

Tip: If you need to make a change to a nested sequence, double-click it, and it will open in a new Timeline panel.

7 Turn off sequence nesting 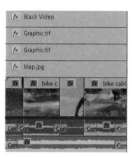.

8 Drag the sequence 09 Race Open into the Program Monitor, choosing the Insert option again.

The individual clips in the Race Open sequence are added to the current sequence.

Performing regular trimming

You can adjust the part of a clip used in a sequence in several ways. This process is generally called *trimming*. When you trim, you can make the selected part of the original clip shorter or longer in the sequence. Some trimming types affect a single clip, and others adjust the relationship between two adjacent clips, or even multiple clips.

Trimming in the Source Monitor

A clip edited into a sequence is a separate instance from the original clip in the Project panel. You can view a sequence clip in the Source Monitor by double-clicking it in the Timeline panel. The clip will open in the Source Monitor, where you can adjust its In and Out points. The clip will update in the sequence.

By default, when you open a sequence clip segment in the Source Monitor, the Source Monitor navigator will be set to zoom in to the existing selection.

You may need to adjust the navigator zoom to easily explore all of the available content in the clip.

There are two basic ways to change existing In and Out points in the Source Monitor.

- **Add new In and Out points:** In the Source Monitor, set new In or Out points, replacing the current selection. If the clip has another clip adjacent to it in the sequence, before or after the current clip, you cannot extend the In or Out point in that direction.

- **Drag In and Out points:** Position your pointer over an In or Out point in the mini timeline at the bottom of the Source Monitor. The cursor changes into a red-and-black icon, indicating that a trim can be performed. Now you can drag left or right to change the In or Out point.

  Once again, if the clip has another clip adjacent to it in the sequence, you cannot extend the current clip in that direction.

Trimming in a sequence

Another, faster way to trim clips is directly in the Timeline panel. Making a single clip shorter or longer is called a *regular* trim, and it's fairly easy.

1 Open the sequence 10 Regular Trim.

2 Play the sequence.

   The last shot is cut off, and it needs to be extended to match the end of the music.

3 Make sure you have the Selection tool ▶ selected.

4 Position the pointer inside the right edge, at the end of the last clip in the sequence.

   The pointer changes into the red Trim Out pointer with directional arrows.

Tip: The keyboard shortcut for the Selection tool is V.

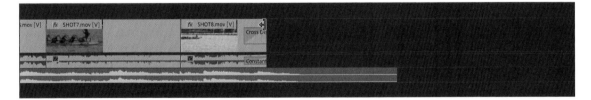

Precisely hovering the mouse cursor over the end of a clip changes it between trimming the Out point (open to the left) and trimming the In point of the next clip (open to the right). In this case, there's no next clip, of course.

Note: If you make a clip shorter, it will leave a gap between it and any adjacent clips. Later in this lesson you'll learn to use the Ripple Edit tool to automatically remove any gaps or push clips later in a sequence when you trim a clip longer.

This clip has a transition effect applied to the end. You may need to zoom in to make it easier to trim the clip and not retime the transition effect.

5   Drag the edge to the right until it meets the end of the audio file.

A tooltip shows you how much you've trimmed.

6   Release the mouse button to apply the trim.

Performing advanced trimming

The trimming methods you've learned so far have their limitations. They can leave unwanted gaps in the sequence caused by shortening a clip. They can also prevent you from lengthening a shot if there's an adjacent clip.

Fortunately, Premiere Pro offers several more ways of trimming.

Making ripple edits

⬤ **Note:** When per-
forming a ripple edit,
you might shift items on
other tracks out of sync.
By default, sync locks
keep items on all tracks
in sync.

You can avoid introducing gaps when trimming by using the Ripple Edit tool rather than the Selection tool.

You use the Ripple Edit tool to trim a clip in the same way you use the Selection tool. When you use the Ripple Edit tool to change the duration of a clip, the adjust-ment ripples through the sequence. That is, clips after the clip you adjust slide to the left to fill the gap, or they slide to the right to make room for the longer clip.

▶ **Tip:** The keyboard
shortcut for the Ripple
Edit tool is B.

Let's try it.

1   Open the sequence 11 Ripple Edit.

2   In the Tools panel, press and hold the Rate Stretch tool to reveal the tools hidden underneath and select the Ripple Edit tool in the Tools panel.

3   Hover the Ripple Edit tool cursor over the inside-right edge of the seventh clip (SHOT7) until it turns into a yellow, left-facing bracket and arrow.

The shot is too short, so let's add some more footage from the clip handle.

4 Drag to the right until the timecode in the tooltip reads +00:00:01:10.

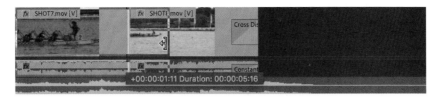

Notice that while you're using the Ripple Edit tool, the Program Monitor displays the last frame of the clip on the left side of the edit, and the first frame of the clip on the right side. The image updates dynamically while you trim.

5 Release the mouse button to complete the edit.

The clip you have trimmed expands, and the clip to its right slides along with it. Play that portion of the sequence to see whether the edit works smoothly.

Making ripple edits with keyboard shortcuts

Though the Ripple Edit tool gives fine control when trimming, there are two useful keyboard shortcuts that apply the same type of trim adjustment, based on the location of the Timeline panel playhead.

For these shortcuts to work, the correct Timeline Track Indicators must be enabled. Whichever tracks are enabled will be trimmed.

Position the Timeline playhead over a clip (or multiple layers of clips), and press one of the following shortcuts:

Q: Ripple trims clips from their current start to the playhead position.

W: Ripple trims clips from their current end to the playhead position.

This can be a fast way to trim clips, particularly in the early stages of editing, when you may simply want to "top and tail" (remove unwanted content at the start or end) your clips.

6 Trim again—this time add another +2:00 seconds to the SHOT7 clip and play through the newly trip edit between SHOT7 and SHOT8.

> ▶ **Tip:** You can temporarily use the Selection tool as a Ripple Edit tool by holding Command (macOS) or Ctrl (Windows). Be sure to click to one side of the edit to avoid performing a rolling edit (described next).

This time, the trim has exposed a slight on-camera shake that you'll work on next.

Making rolling edits

When you use the Ripple Edit tool, it makes changes to the overall length of the sequence. This is because one clip gets longer or shorter while the rest of the sequence moves to close the gap (or moves out of the way).

There's another way to change the timing of an edit: a rolling edit.

With a rolling edit, the overall length of the sequence does not change. Instead, a rolling edit shortens one clip and lengthens another at the same time, adjusting the clips by the same number of frames.

For example, if you use the Rolling Edit tool to extend a clip by two seconds, you will also shorten the adjacent clip by two seconds.

1 Continue working with the sequence 11 Ripple Edit.

Several clips are already in the sequence, with enough leftover handle frames to allow the edits you're about to perform.

2 Press and hold the Ripple Edit tool ◀▶ to select the Rolling Edit tool ✛ in the Tools panel.

3 Drag the edit point between SHOT7 and SHOT8 (the last two clips on the Timeline). Use the Program Monitor split screen to find a better-matching edit between the two shots, dragging the edit left to remove the camera shake.

> ● **Note:** You can use the Selection tool with the Command (macOS) or Ctrl (Windows) key as a shortcut for the Ripple Edit tool or Rolling Edit tool.

Try rolling the edit to the left 1 second and 20 frames (−01:20). You can use the Program Monitor timecode or the pop-up timecode in the Timeline panel to find the edit, and if you pre-position the playhead, the edit will snap to it as you drag.

Marginal notes:

● **Note:** A rolling edit trim is sometimes referred to as a *double-roller* or *dual-roller* trim.

▶ **Tip:** Zoom in to the Timeline panel to make more accurate adjustments.

● **Note:** When trimming, it's possible to trim a clip to a 0 (zero) duration (removing it from the Timeline altogether).

▶ **Tip:** The keyboard shortcut for the Rolling Edit tool is N.

Making slip edits

A slip trim changes both the In point and Out point of a sequence clip segment at the same time, by the same amount, rolling the visible contents in position.

Because a slip trim changes the beginning and end by equal amounts, it doesn't change the duration of your sequence. In this way, it's the same as a rolling trim.

Slip trims change only the clip you select; adjacent clips before or after the clip you adjust are not affected. Using the Slip tool to adjust a clip is a little like moving a conveyor belt: The visible part of the original clip changes inside the Timeline clip segment without changing the length of the clip or the sequence.

1 Continue working with the sequence 11 Ripple Edit.

2 Select the Slip tool . The keyboard shortcut for the Slip tool is Y.

3 Drag SHOT5 left and right.

4 Take a look at the Program Monitor while you perform the slip edit.

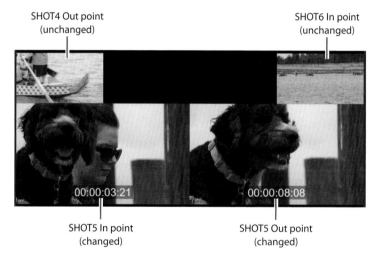

SHOT4 Out point (unchanged)

SHOT6 In point (unchanged)

SHOT5 In point (changed)

SHOT5 Out point (changed)

The two top images are the Out point of SHOT4 and the In point of SHOT6, before and after the clip you are adjusting; they don't change. The two larger images are the In point and Out point of SHOT5, the clip you are adjusting; these edit points do change.

The Slip Trim tool is well worth taking time to get to grips with. It can be the fastest tool for adjusting timing when cutting action.

Making slide edits

The Slide tool works by leaving the duration of the clip you're sliding unchanged. Instead, the Out point of the clip to the left and the In point of the clip to the right are changed by equal amounts, in opposite directions. It's another form of dual-roller trim.

Because you're changing the other clip durations by an equal number of frames, the length of the sequence doesn't change.

1 Continue working with the sequence 11 Ripple Edit.

2 Press and hold the Slip tool in the Tools panel to select the Slide tool . The keyboard shortcut for the Slide tool is U.

3 Position the Slide tool over the middle of the second clip in the sequence, SHOT2.

4 Drag the clip left or right.

5 Take a look at the Program Monitor as you perform the slide edit.

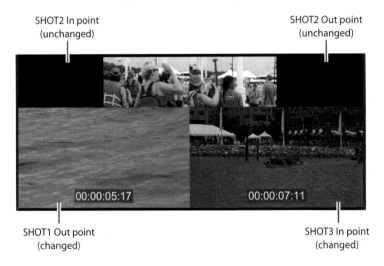

SHOT2 In point
(unchanged)

SHOT2 Out point
(unchanged)

00:00:05:17   00:00:07:11

SHOT1 Out point
(changed)

SHOT3 In point
(changed)

The two top images are the In point and Out point of SHOT2—the clip you are dragging. They do not change because you are not changing the selected part of SHOT2.

The two larger images are the Out point and In point of the previous and next clips. These edit points change as you slide the selected clip over those adjacent clips.

Trimming in the Program Monitor

If you'd like to trim with more control, you can use the Program Monitor Trim mode. This allows you to see both the outgoing and incoming frames of the trim you're working on and has dedicated buttons for making precise adjustments.

When the Program Monitor is set to Trim mode, pressing the spacebar to play the sequence loops playback around the edit you have selected. This means you can continually adjust the timing of an edit and view the result immediately.

You can perform three types of trim using the Program Monitor Trim mode controls. You learned about each of these earlier in this lesson.

- **Regular trim:** This basic type of trim moves the edge of the selected clip. This method trims only one side of the edit point. It moves the selected edit point either forward or backward in the sequence, but it doesn't shift any of the other clips.

- **Roll trim:** The roll trim moves the tail of one clip and the head of the adjacent clip. It lets you adjust an edit point (provided there are handles). No gap is created, and the sequence duration doesn't change.

- **Ripple trim:** This moves the selected edge of the edit either earlier or later. Clips after the edit shift to close a gap or make room for a longer clip.

Using Trim mode in the Program Monitor

When you're in Trim mode, some of the Program Monitor controls change to make it easier to focus on trimming. To use Trim mode, you need to activate it by selecting an edit point between two clips. There are three ways to do this.

- Double-click an edit point (the left or right end of a clip) on the Timeline with a selection tool or trimming tool.

- With the correct Timeline track indicator enabled, press Shift+T. The playhead will move to the nearest edit point, and Trim mode will open in the Program Monitor.

- Drag around one or more edits using the Ripple Edit tool or Rolling Edit tool to select them and open the Program Monitor to Trim mode.

▶ **Tip:** You also can select edits by dragging around them using the Selection tool if you hold Command (macOS) or Ctrl (Windows).

When invoked, Trim mode shows two video clips. The box on the left shows the outgoing clip (also called *A side*). The box on the right shows the incoming clip (also called *B side*). Below the frames are five buttons and two indicators.

Callouts are on the following page.

A Out Shift counter

B Trim Backward Many

C Trim Backward

D Apply Default Transitions to Selections

E Trim Forward

F Trim Forward Many

G In Shift counter

A **Out Shift counter:** This shows how many frames the Out point for the A side has changed.

B **Trim Backward Many:** This performs the selected trim, adjusting by multiple frames earlier. The size of the adjustment depends on the Large Trim Offset option in the Trim Preferences tab of Preferences.

C **Trim Backward:** This performs the selected trim, adjusting by one frame at a time earlier.

D **Apply Default Transitions to Selection:** This applies the default transition (usually a dissolve) to video and audio tracks that have their edit points selected.

E **Trim Forward:** This is like Trim Backward except it adjusts the edit one frame later.

F **Trim Forward Many:** This is like Trim Backward Many except it adjusts the edit multiple frames later.

G **In Shift counter:** This shows how many frames the In point for the B side has changed.

Choosing a trimming method in the Program Monitor

You've already learned about the three types of trims you can perform (regular, roll, and ripple). Using Trim mode in the Program Monitor makes the process easier because it provides rich visual feedback. It also provides subtle control when dragging, regardless of the Timeline panel view scale: Even if the Timeline panel is zoomed a long way out, you'll be able to make frame-accurate trim adjustments in the Program Monitor Trim view.

1 Open the sequence 12 Trim View.

2 With the Selection tool (keyboard shortcut V), hold down Option (macOS) or Alt (Windows) and double-click the video edit between the first video clip and the second video clip in the sequence. Holding this modifier key selects just the video edits and leaves the audio tracks untouched.

3 In the Program Monitor, hover the pointer over the A and B clip images (but don't click yet).

   As you move the pointer from left to right, you'll see the tool change from Trim Out (left side) to Roll (center) to Trim In (right).

4 Drag in between both clips in the Program Monitor to perform a rolling edit trim.

Adjust the timing until the time display on the lower-right side of the Program Monitor, as an overlay on the B clip image, reads 01:26:59:01.

5 Press the Down Arrow key three times to jump between edits until you have selected the edit between the third and fourth clips (the cut in the audio track counts as one jump).

The outgoing shot is too long and shows the actor sitting down twice.

6 When dragging in the Program Monitor to trim, the color of the tool indicates the type of trim you'll perform. Red indicates a regular trim and yellow indicates a ripple trim.

You can quickly change the trim type by holding Command (macOS) or Ctrl (Windows) and clicking one of the images in the Program Monitor. After clicking, you'll need to move the pointer in order for the color of the tool to update.

Now, Command-click (macOS) or Ctrl-click (Windows) one of the images in the Program Monitor until the trim tool pointer turns yellow. This indicates that you've selected the Ripple Trim tool.

● **Note:** Clicking the A or B side will switch which side is being trimmed. Clicking in the center will switch to a rolling edit.

7 Drag to the left on the outgoing clip (on the left side of the Program Monitor) to make the clip shorter.

Make sure the time display on the left reads 01:54:12:18.

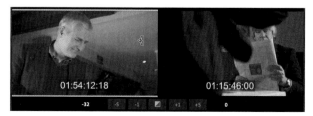

8 Play the edit by pressing the spacebar. Notice that playback loops over the edit to allow you to review it.

Modifier keys

You can use multiple modifier keys to refine a trim selection.

- Hold down Option (macOS) or Alt (Windows) when selecting clips to temporarily ignore links between audio and video clip segments in a sequence.
- Hold down the Shift key to select multiple edit points. You can trim multiple tracks or even multiple clips at the same time. Wherever you see a trim "handle," adjustments will be made when you apply a trim.
- Combine these two modifier keys to make advanced selections for trimming.

Performing dynamic trimming

Much of the trimming work you will perform will be to tune the rhythm of an edit. In many ways, achieving perfect timing for a cut is the point at which the craft of editing becomes the art.

Because playback using the spacebar will loop in Trim mode, it's easier to get a feel for the timing of an edit. You can also trim using keyboard shortcuts or buttons while the sequence plays back in real time.

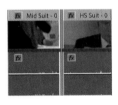

Note: To control the pre-roll and post-roll durations, go to Premiere Pro Preferences and select the Playback category. You can set the duration in seconds. Most editors find a duration of two to five seconds most useful.

1 Continue working with the sequence 12 Trim View.

2 Press the Down Arrow key to move to the next video edit point, between the fourth and fifth video clips. Set the trim type to a rolling trim.

You can stay in Trim mode while switching between edit points.

3 Press the spacebar to loop playback.

You'll see a playback loop lasting a few seconds, with the shot before and after the cut playing back. This helps you get a feel for the content of the edit.

4 Try adjusting the trim using the methods you've learned while the playback loops.

The Trim Forward and Trim Backward buttons at the bottom of Trim mode view work well and can adjust the edit while the clip plays back.

Now let's try using the keyboard for more dynamic control. The same J, K, and L keys you use to control playback can also be used to control trimming.

5 Click Stop or press the spacebar to stop the playback loop.

6 Press the L key to shuttle the trim to the right.

Pressing once trims in real time. You can tap the L key multiple times to trim faster.

If you are in regular trim mode and trimming a clip extends to the next clip, the trim will be blocked. If you are in ripple trim mode, clips will move to accommodate the new clip duration.

These clips are quite short, so you'll reach the end quickly. Let's refine and trim with a little more precision.

7 Press the K key to stop trimming.

8 Hold down the K key and press the J key to shuttle left in slow motion.

9 Release both keys to stop the trim.

10 Exit Trim mode by clicking away from the edit on the Timeline to deselect the edit.

Note: Timeline clip segment durations update when you press K to stop trimming.

Trimming with the keyboard

Here are some of the most useful keyboard shortcuts to use when trimming.

macOS	WINDOWS
Trim Backward: Option+Left Arrow	**Trim Backward:** Ctrl+Left Arrow
Trim Backward Many: Option+Shift+Left Arrow	**Trim Backward Many:** Ctrl+Shift+Left Arrow
Trim Forward: Option+Right Arrow	**Trim Forward:** Ctrl+Right Arrow
Trim Forward Many: Option+Shift+Right Arrow	**Trim Forward Many:** Ctrl+Shift+Right Arrow
Slide Clip Selection Left Five Frames: Option+Shift+, (comma)	**Slide Clip Selection Left Five Frames:** Alt+Shift+, (comma)
Slide Clip Selection Left One Frame: Option+, (comma)	**Slide Clip Selection Left One Frame:** Alt+, (comma)
Slide Clip Selection Right Five Frames: Option+Shift+. (period)	**Slide Clip Selection Right Five Frames:** Alt+Shift+. (period)
Slide Clip Selection Right One Frame: Option+. (period)	**Slide Clip Selection Right One Frame:** Alt+. (period)
Slip Clip Selection Left Five Frames: Command+Option+Shift+Left Arrow	**Slip Clip Selection Left Five Frames:** Ctrl+Alt+Shift+Left Arrow
Slip Clip Selection Left One Frame: Command+Option+Left Arrow	**Slip Clip Selection Left One Frame:** Ctrl+Alt+Left Arrow
Slip Clip Selection Right Five Frames: Command+Option+Shift+Right Arrow	**Slip Clip Selection Right Five Frames:** Ctrl+Alt+Shift+Right Arrow
Slip Clip Selection Right One Frame: Command+Option+Right Arrow	**Slip Clip Selection Right One Frame:** Ctrl+Alt+Right Arrow

Review questions

1 If you change the playback speed of a clip to 50%, what effect will this have on the clip duration?

2 Which tool allows you to stretch a sequence clip to change its playback speed?

3 What's the difference between a slide edit and a slip edit?

4 What is the difference between replacing a clip and replacing footage?

Review answers

1 The clip will be twice as long. Reducing a clip's speed causes the clip to become longer, unless the Speed and Duration parameters are unlinked in the Clip Speed/Duration dialog box or the clip is blocked by another clip.

2 The Rate Stretch tool allows you to adjust playback speed as if you were trimming. This is useful when you need to fill a small extra amount of time in a sequence, or shorten a clip just a little.

3 You slide a clip over adjacent clips, retaining the selected clip's original In and Out points. You slip a clip under adjacent clips (or roll the contents like a conveyor belt), changing the selected clip's In and Out points.

4 Replacing a clip replaces a single sequence clip on the Timeline with a new clip from the Project panel. Replacing footage replaces a clip in the Project panel with a new source clip. Any instance of the clip in any sequence in the project is replaced. In both cases, effects applied to the replaced clip are maintained.

9 PUTTING CLIPS IN MOTION

Lesson overview

In this lesson, you'll learn about the following:

- Adjusting the Motion effect for clips

- Changing clip size and adding rotation

- Adjusting the anchor point to refine rotation

- Working with keyframe interpolation

- Enhancing motion with shadows and beveled edges

 This lesson will take about 75 minutes to complete. Please log in to your account on peachpit.com to download the lesson files for this lesson, or go to the "Getting Started" section at the beginning of this book and follow the instructions under "Accessing the lesson files and Web Edition." Store the files on your computer in a convenient location.

Your Account page is also where you'll find any updates to the lesson files. Look on the Lesson & Update Files tab to access the most current content.

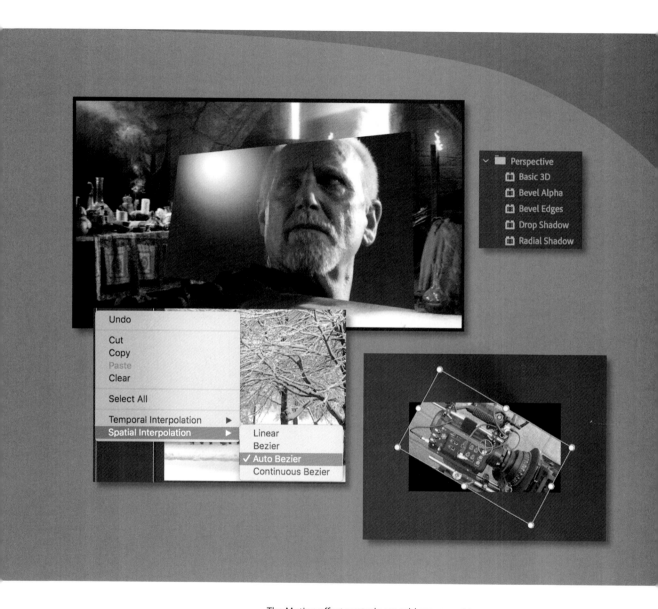

The Motion effect controls can add movement to a clip. You can animate a graphic or resize and reposition a video clip within the frame. You can animate an object's position using keyframes and enhance that animation by controlling the way those keyframes are interpreted.

Starting the lesson

Video projects are often motion graphics-oriented, and it's common to see multiple shots combined as complex compositions. These are often put into motion. Perhaps you'll see multiple video clips streaming past in floating boxes, or you'll see a video clip shrunk down and placed next to an on-camera host. You can create those effects (and many more) in Premiere Pro using the Motion settings in the Effect Controls panel, or a number of clip-based effects that offer Motion settings.

The Motion effect controls allow you to position, rotate, or change the size of a clip within the frame. Some adjustments can be made directly in the Program Monitor. It's important to be clear that the adjustments you make in the Effect Controls panel relate exclusively to the clip you have selected and not to the sequence it is in. Think of the sequence settings, in the Sequence menu, as the output settings.

A *keyframe* is a special kind of marker that stores settings at a particular point in time. If you use two (or more) keyframes, Premiere Pro can automatically animate the settings for an adjustment between them. You can use advanced controls to control the timing of that animation using different types of keyframes.

Adjusting the Motion effect

Every visual clip in a Premiere Pro sequence automatically has a number of effects applied. These are referred to as *fixed effects* (also sometimes called *intrinsic effects*). Motion is the name of one of these effects.

To adjust a clip's Motion effect, select the clip in a sequence and look in the Effect Controls panel. Expand the Motion effect to adjust the settings.

> **Tip:** Unlike other effect controls, if you expand or collapse the settings for the Motion effect, the settings will remain expanded or collapsed for all clips.

The Motion effect allows you to adjust the position, scale, or rotation of a clip. Let's look at the way this effect has been used to reposition a clip in a sequence.

1 Open Lesson 09.prproj in the Lesson 09 folder.

2 Save the project as **Lesson 09 Working.prproj**.

> **Tip:** As you have been saving projects with new names while working on them, you can go back to earlier lessons and experiment again with a fresh copy of the original project file.

3 Choose Effects in the Workspaces panel, or choose Window > Workspaces > Effects. Reset the workspace.

4 If necessary, open the sequence 01 Floating. This simple sequence has just one clip in it (Gull.mp4).

5 Make sure Fit is chosen from the Select Zoom Level menu in the Program Monitor. It's important to see the whole composition when setting up visual effects. This menu does not change the contents of the sequence, only the way

the contents are viewed. It can be helpful to zoom in or out to see fine details in an image or set up effects, but generally you will want to keep this menu set to Fit.

6 Play the sequence.

This clip's Position, Scale, and Rotation properties have been changed. Key-frames have been added, with different settings at different points in time, so the clip animates.

Understanding Motion settings

Though these controls are called Motion, there's no movement until you add it. By default, clips are positioned in the center of the Program Monitor, at their original scale. Select the clip in the sequence and then click the disclosure triangle next to Motion in the Video Effects section of the Effect Controls panel to display the available settings.

Here are the options:

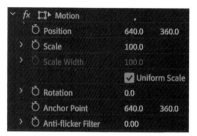

- **Position:** This places the clip along the x-axis (horizontal) and y-axis (vertical). The position is calculated based on the position of an anchor point (covered later in this list) measured from the upper-left corner of the image. So the default position for a 1280x720 clip would be 640, 360 (which is the exact center of the image).

- **Scale (Scale Height, when Uniform Scale is deselected):** Clips are set to their full size by default (100%). To shrink a clip, reduce this number. You can scale up to 10,000%—though be warned, scaling up will make images pixelated and soft.

- **Scale Width:** Deselect Uniform Scale to make Scale Width available. This lets you change the clip width and height independently.

- **Rotation:** You can rotate an image along the z-axis—a flat spin (as if viewing a spinning turntable or carousel from above). You can enter degrees or a number of rotations. For example, 450 is the same as 1x90 (one full 360° turn plus an additional 90°). Positive numbers give clockwise rotation, and negative numbers give counterclockwise rotation.

- **Anchor Point:** Rotation and position adjustments are all based on the anchor point, which is a point at the center of a clip by default. This can be changed to any point, including one of the clip's corners or even a point outside the clip.

  For example, if you set the anchor point to the corner of the clip, when you adjust the Rotation setting, the clip will rotate around that corner rather than around the center of the image. If you change the anchor point in relation to the image, you may have to reposition the clip in the frame to compensate for the adjustment.

▶ **Tip:** The Anchor point position can be animated, just like every other Motion control, for more complex motion.

Note: If the panel group containing the Effect Controls panel is too narrow, some of the controls will overlap, making it difficult to interact with them. If this is the case, make the group wider before working with the Effect Controls panel.

- **Anti-flicker Filter:** This feature is useful for interlaced video clips and for images that contain high detail, such as fine lines, hard edges, or parallel lines (which can cause moiré effects). These high-detail images can flicker during motion. To add some blurring and reduce flicker, use 1.00.

Let's look closer at the animated clip, continuing to work with the sequence 01 Floating.

1 Click the clip in the Timeline panel once to make sure it is selected.

2 Make sure the Effect Controls panel is visible. It should have appeared when you reset the Effects workspace, but if you can't find it, look for it in the Window menu.

3 In the Effect Controls panel, if necessary, expand the Motion effect controls by clicking the disclosure triangle ▸ next to the word *Motion*.

4 At the upper right of the Effect Controls panel settings, to the right of the master clip name and sequence clip name (these can be different if you choose), a small triangle toggles the display of an integrated timeline ▶. Make sure the Effect Controls timeline is visible.

   If it isn't, click the triangle to show it. The timeline in the Effect Controls panel displays keyframes.

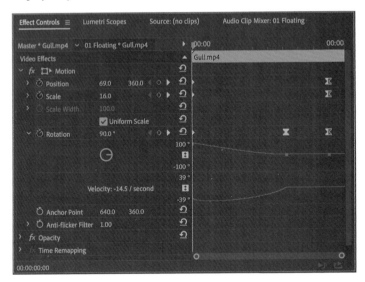

5 Each setting control has its own keyframes. Click the Go To Previous Keyframe or Go To Next Keyframe arrows to jump between existing keyframes for a particular control.

   Note: It can be difficult to line up the playhead with an existing keyframe. Using the Previous/Next Keyframe buttons helps you avoid adding unwanted keyframes. You can assign a keyboard shortcut to position the playhead at the next or previous keyframe.

6 Drag the playhead back and forth in the Effect Controls panel, Timeline panel, or Program Monitor to see the way the position of the keyframe markers relates to the animation.

Now that you know how to view the settings for an existing animation, let's begin by resetting the clip.

7 The Toggle Animation stopwatch button ⏱ for each setting turns animation on or off. When the stopwatch is blue, animation is enabled for a setting. Click the stopwatch for the Position property to turn off its keyframes.

8 Because the setting already has some keyframes, a warning message lets you know they will be deleted if you continue. Click OK to continue.

9 Turn off keyframes for the Scale and Rotation properties in the same way.

10 Click the curved-arrow Reset Effect button ↺ to the right of the Motion effect heading in the Effect Controls panel.

Now the Motion settings are all set to their default values.

● **Note:** When the Toggle Animation button is on, clicking the Reset button will not change any existing keyframes. Instead, a new keyframe is added with default settings. It's important to turn off animation before resetting the effect to avoid this.

● **Note:** Each control has its own Reset button. If you reset the whole effect, every control is returned to its default state.

Examining Motion properties

The Position, Scale, and Rotation properties are spatial. That means the changes you make are easy to see because the object will change in size and position. You can adjust these properties by entering numerical values, by using the scrubbable numbers (drag on the blue numbers), or by dragging the Transform controls.

1 Open the sequence 02 Motion.

2 In the Program Monitor, make sure the zoom level is set to 25% or 50% (or a zoom amount that allows you to see space around the active frame).

Setting the zoom small like this makes it easy to position items outside the frame.

3 Drag the Timeline panel playhead anywhere in the sequence so you can see the video clip contents displayed in the Program Monitor.

4   Click the clip in the sequence once so it's selected, with its settings displayed in the Effect Controls panel.

5   Click the Motion effect heading in the Effect Controls panel to select it.

When you select the motion effect, a bounding box with a crosshair and handles appears around the clip in the Program Monitor.

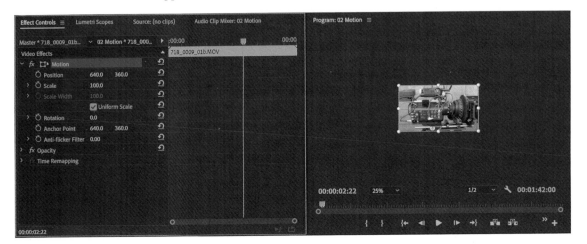

6   Click inside the clip bounding box in the Program Monitor, avoiding the crosshair in the center, and drag the clip around.

Position values in the Effect Controls panel update as you move the clip.

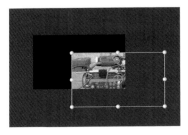

● **Note:** Several
effects, like the Motion
effect, have a Transform
icon ▣ next to the
effect name to indicate
that you can use direct
manipulation in the
Program Monitor when
you select the effect
heading. Try this with
Corner Pin, Crop, Mirror,
Transform, and Twirl.

7   Position the clip so that it's centered in the upper-left corner of the screen. Make sure the anchor point ⊕ is aligned with the upper-left corner of the frame.

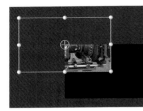

The crosshair is the anchor point, which is used for position and rotation controls. Be careful not to click the anchor point control, or you'll move it in relation to the image.

The Position settings in the Effect Controls panel should be 0, 0 (or close to that, depending on where you placed the center of the clip).

This is a 720p sequence, so the lower-right corner of the screen is 1280, 720.

8   Click the Reset button for the motion settings to restore the clip to its default position.

9   Drag the blue number for the Rotation setting in the Effect Controls panel. As you drag left or right, the clip rotates.

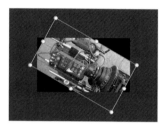

10   Click the Reset button for the Motion heading in the Effect Controls panel to restore the clip to its default position.

● **Note:** Premiere Pro uses a coordinate system that has the upper-left corner of the screen as 0, 0. All x and y values, respectively, to the left of and above that point are negative. All x and y values to the right of and below that point are positive.

▶ **Tip:** Hold Shift while dragging numbers and they'll change ten times faster, for a more dramatic adjustment. Hold Command (macOS) or Ctrl (Windows) and they'll change ten times slower, for a more precise adjustment.

Changing clip position, size, and rotation

Sliding a clip around the screen only begins to exploit the possibilities of the Motion effect controls. One feature that makes the Motion effect so useful is the ability to change the scale of the clip as well as rotate it. In the next example, you'll build a simple intro segment for a behind-the-scenes featurette.

Changing position

Let's begin by using keyframes to animate the position of a layer. For this exercise, the first thing you'll do is change the clip position. The picture will begin off-screen and then move across the screen from right to left.

1   Open the sequence 03 Montage.

The sequence has several tracks, some of which are currently disabled. You'll use them later.

2   Position the playhead to the start of the sequence.

3   Set the Program Monitor zoom level to Fit.

4 Click once to select the first video clip on track V3.

You might want to make the track taller to see it better.

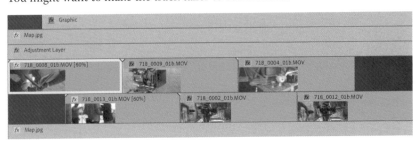

The clip's controls appear in the Effect Controls panel.

5 In the Effect Controls panel, click the Toggle Animation stopwatch button ⏱ for Position. This turns on keyframing for that setting and automatically adds a keyframe ◆ at the playhead position, visible in the Effect Controls panel. The keyframe icon is partially obscured because it's applied to the first frame of the clip.

Now that animation is enabled for Position, when you change the setting, Premiere Pro will add (or update) a keyframe automatically.

6 The Position control has two numbers. The first is the x-axis value, and the second is the y-axis value. Enter a Position setting of **−640** for the x-axis value (the first number) as a starting position.

The clip moves off-screen to the left, revealing the clips on the V1 and V2 tracks below.

The clip Map.jpg on track V1 is revealed when the selected clip is moved off-screen.

7 Drag the playhead to the last frame of the selected clip (00:00:4:23). You can do this in the Timeline panel or in the Effect Controls panel.

8 Enter **1920** for the position x-axis. The clip moves off the right edge of the screen.

Where there are two numbers for a control, they often represent the x-axis and y-axis.

9 Play the sequence from the beginning. The clip moves from off-screen left to off-screen right.

The second clip on V3 appears suddenly. You'll animate this clip and others next.

Reusing Motion settings

Now that you've applied keyframes and effects to a clip, you can save time by reusing them on other clips. It's as easy as copying and pasting to apply effects from a clip to one or more other clips. In this example, you'll apply the same left-to-right floating animation to other clips in the project.

There are several methods for reusing effects. Let's try one now.

1 In the Timeline panel, select the clip you just animated. It's the first clip on V3.

2 Choose Edit > Copy.

The clip and its effects and settings are now temporarily stored on your computer's clipboard.

3 With the Selection tool (V), drag from right to left across the five other clips on the V2 and V3 tracks to select them (you may need to zoom out a little to see all the clips). You could also hold the Shift key and select the first and last of the five clips.

4 Choose Edit > Paste Attributes.

The Paste Attributes dialog opens, letting you selectively apply effects and keyframes copied from another clip.

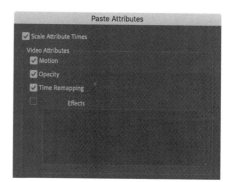

> **Note:** As an alternative to copying a whole clip in the Timeline panel, you can always select one or more specific effect headings in the Effect Controls panel. Command-click (macOS) or Ctrl-click (Windows) to select multiple noncontiguous effects, and choose Edit > Copy. You can then select another clip (or clips) and choose Edit > Paste to paste the effects onto other clips.

5 Leave the check boxes with their default values, and click OK.

6 Play the sequence to see the result.

Adding rotation and changing the anchor point

Moving clips around the screen can be effective, but you can really bring things to life using two more properties. Let's start with Rotation.

The Rotation property revolves a clip around its anchor point on the z-axis. By default, the anchor point is in the center of the image. However, you can change the relationship between the anchor point and the image for more interesting animation.

Let's add some rotation to a clip.

1 In the Timeline panel, click the Toggle Track Output button ![icon] for V6 to enable it ![icon] . The clip on the track is a title graphic that reads *Behind The Scenes*.

This clip is a title graphic created in Premiere Pro, using vector-based design tools. This means it can be scaled to any size and will always look sharp, with smooth curves and no pixelation. Vector graphics work the same way as non-vector graphics; you can use the same controls, effects, and adjustments.

2 Move the playhead to the start of the graphic clip (00:00:01:13). Try holding the Shift key while you drag the playhead to do this.

3 Select the graphic clip in the sequence. The clip's controls appear in the Effect Controls panel.

Because this is a vector graphic, there are two types of Motion effect available.

- **Motion:** Treats the contents of the graphic as pixels. When you scale up, the pixels will increase in size, producing jagged edges and softening the image.

- **Vector Motion:** Treats the contents of the graphic as vectors, allowing you to scale up the image and retain clean lines without pixelation.

4 Select the Vector Motion effect heading to see the anchor point and bounding-box controls in the Program Monitor. Notice the position of the anchor point, a small circle with a cross in the center of the title.

Let's adjust the Rotation property in the Effect Controls panel and see the effect it has.

5 Click the disclosure triangle to reveal the Vector Motion effect controls, and enter a value of **90.0** into the Rotation field.

The title rotates in the center of the screen.

6 Choose Edit > Undo.

7 Make sure the Vector Motion settings heading is still selected in the Effect Controls panel.

8 In the Program Monitor, drag the anchor point until the crosshair sits in the upper-left corner of the letter *B* in the first word.

The Position settings in the Effect Controls panel control the location of the anchor point in relation to the sequence frame. The Anchor Point settings control the position of the anchor point in relation to the clip image.

Now that you have moved the anchor point in the image, both the Anchor Point and Position settings have updated in the Effect Controls panel.

9 Your playhead should still be on the first frame of the clip. Still in the Vector Motion effect settings, click the Animation stopwatch button for Rotation to toggle on animation. This adds a keyframe automatically.

10 Set the rotation to **90.0**. This updates the keyframe you just added.

11 Move the playhead forward to 00:00:06:00, and set the clip rotation to 0.0. This adds another keyframe automatically.

12 Play the sequence to see your animation.

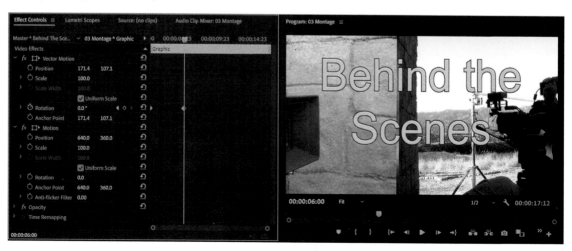

Changing clip size

There are a few approaches to changing the size of items in a sequence. By default, items added to a sequence come in at 100% of their original size. However, you can choose to manually adjust the size or let Premiere Pro do it for you automatically.

You can choose from these methods:

- Use the Scale property of the Motion effect or Vector Motion effect in the Effect Controls panel.

- If the clip has a different frame size compared to your sequence, right-click the clip in the sequence and choose Set To Frame Size. This automatically adjusts the Scale property of the Motion effect to match the frame size of the clip with the size of the sequence.

- If the clip has a different frame size compared to your sequence, right-click the clip in the sequence and choose Scale To Frame Size. This has a similar result to the Set To Frame Size option, but Premiere Pro resamples the image at the new (often lower) resolution. If you scale back up now using the Motion > Scale setting, the image might look soft, even if the original clip was very high resolution.

- You can also select Scale To Frame Size or Set To Frame Size automatically by choosing Premiere Pro CC > Preferences > Media > Default Media Scaling (macOS) or Edit > Preferences > Media > Default Media Scaling (Windows). The setting is applied to assets as you import them (but won't change assets you have already imported).

For maximum flexibility, use the first or second method so you can scale as needed without sacrificing quality. Let's try this.

1 Open the sequence 04 Scale.

2 Scrub through the sequence to view the clips.

   The second and third clips on the V1 track are much larger than the first clip. In fact, your system may struggle to play such high-resolution clips without dropping frames. They are dramatically cropped by the edge of the frame.

   Move the Timeline playhead over the last clip in the sequence, on the V1 track.

3 Right-click the clip, and choose Scale To Frame Size.

This conveniently scales the image to fit the sequence resolution, though it resamples the image, losing the original picture quality. However, there's an issue: The clip is full 4K, with a resolution of 4096x2160, and that is not a perfect 16:9 image. It doesn't fit the aspect ratio of the sequence, and black bars are introduced at the top and bottom of the image. These bars are often called *letterboxing*.

This is a common outcome when working with content that has a different aspect ratio than your sequence, and there is no easy way around it. You'll need to make a manual adjustment.

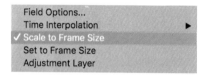

4 Right-click the clip again and select Scale To Frame Size again to deselect it. This is an option you can turn off and on at any time.

5 With the clip selected, open the Effect Controls panel.

6 Use the Scale setting to adjust the frame size until the clip image fits the sequence frame without showing letterboxing; a setting of roughly 34% should work. You can choose any framing and adjust the Position settings to reframe the shot if necessary.

When you scale an image to avoid letterboxing, you'll have to crop the sides. When aspect ratios don't match, you have to choose between letterboxing, cropping, and changing the aspect ratio of the image by deselecting the Uniform Scale option in the Effect Controls panel.

Animating clip size changes

In the previous example, the clip image has a different aspect ratio compared to the sequence.

Let's try another example and animate the adjustment.

1 Position the Timeline playhead over the first frame of the second clip in the 04 Scale sequence, at 00:00:05:00.

Note: The settings in the Effect Controls panel don't indicate if they are pixels, percentages, or degrees. This can take a little getting used to, but you'll find with experience the controls do make sense for each setting.

This clip is 3840x2160-pixel ultra-high definition (UHD), which is the same image aspect ratio as the sequence, which is 1280x720 (16:9). It's also the same aspect ratio as full HD, at 1920x1080. This makes shooting UHD content convenient if you intend to include it in an HD production.

2 Select the clip and look in the Effect Controls panel. The scale setting is 100%.

3 Right-click the clip in the Timeline panel and choose Set To Frame Size.

When you select Set To Frame Size, Premiere Pro resizes the clip using the Scale setting so that it fits inside the frame of the sequence. The amount of adjustment varies depending on the image size of the clip and the resolution of the sequence.

This clip scales down to 33.3% to fit the image. You now know you can scale this clip between 33.3% and 100% and maintain quality, while still filling the frame.

4 Turn on keyframing for Scale by clicking the Toggle Animation stopwatch button 🕓 for Scale in the Effect Controls panel.

5 Position the playhead over the last frame of the clip.

6 Click the Reset button 🔄 for the Scale setting in the Effect Controls panel.

7 Scrub through the clip to see the result.

This creates an animated zoom effect for the clip. Because the clip never scales to more than 100%, it maintains full quality.

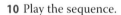

8 Turn on the Track Output option for the V2 track.

This track has an adjustment layer clip on it. Adjustment layers apply effects to all footage on lower video tracks.

9 Select the Adjustment Layer clip to display its values in the Effect Controls panel.

You'll see that two visual effects have been added: a Black and White effect, which removes color saturation, and a Brightness & Contrast effect, which increases contrast. You'll learn more about adjustment layers in Lesson 12, "Adding Video Effects."

10 Play the sequence.

You may need to render the sequence to see smooth playback because some of the clips are high resolution and will take a lot of computer processing power to play. To render the sequence, make sure the Timeline panel is active and choose Sequence > Render In To Out.

Working with keyframe interpolation

Throughout this lesson you've been using keyframes to define your animation. The term *keyframe* originates from traditional animation, where the lead artist would draw the key frames (or major poses) and then assistant animators would animate the frames in between. When animating in Premiere Pro, you're the master animator, and the computer does the rest of the work as it interpolates values in between the keyframes you set.

Using different keyframe interpolation methods

While you've already used keyframes to animate, that's only some of their power. One of the most useful yet least utilized features of keyframes is their interpolation method. This is a fancy way of saying how to get from point A to point B. Think of it as describing the sharp ramp-up as a runner takes off from the starting line and the gradual slowdown after they cross the finish line.

Premiere Pro has five interpolation methods. Changing the method can create a very different animation. You can access the available interpolation methods by right-clicking a keyframe icon to see the options (some effects have both spatial and temporal options).

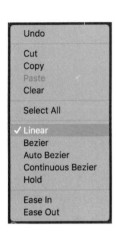

- **Linear:** This is the default method of keyframe interpolation. This method gives a uniform rate of change between keyframes. Changes begin instantly at the first keyframe and continue to the next keyframe at a constant speed. At the second keyframe, the rate of change switches instantly to the rate between it and the third keyframe, and so on. This can be effective, but it can also look a little mechanical.

- **Bezier:** This gives the most control over keyframe interpolation. Bezier keyframes (named after the French engineer Pierre Bézier) provide manual handles you can adjust to change the shape of the value graph or motion path on either side of the keyframe. By dragging the Bezier handles that appear when the keyframe is selected, you can create smooth curved adjustments or sharp angles. For example, you could have an object move smoothly to a position on-screen and then sharply take off in another direction.

- **Auto Bezier:** Auto Bezier keyframes create a smooth rate of change through the keyframe. They automatically update as you change settings. This is a good quick-fix version of Bezier keyframes.

- **Continuous Bezier:** This option is similar to the Auto Bezier option, but it provides some manual control. The motion or value path will always have smooth transitions, but you can adjust the shape of the Bezier curve on both sides of the keyframe with a control handle.

- **Hold:** This is available only for temporal (time-based) properties. Hold-style keyframes hold their value across time, without a gradual transition. This is useful if you want to create staccato-type movements or make an object suddenly disappear. When the Hold style is used, the value of the first keyframe will hold until the next hold keyframe is encountered, and then the value will change instantly.

▷ **Tip:** If you are familiar with Adobe Illustrator or Adobe Photoshop, you will recognize Bezier handles; they work the same way in Premiere Pro CC.

Temporal vs. spatial interpolation

Some properties and effects offer a choice of temporal and spatial interpolation methods for transitioning between keyframes. You'll find that all properties have temporal controls (which relate to time). Some properties also offer spatial interpolation (which refers to space or movement).

Here's what you need to know about each method:

- **Temporal interpolation:** Temporal interpolation deals with changes in time. It's an effective way to determine the speed at which an object moves. For example, you can add acceleration and deceleration with special kinds of keyframes called Ease or Bezier.

- **Spatial interpolation:** The spatial method deals with changes in an object's position. It's an effective way to control the shape of the path an object takes across the screen. That path is called a *motion path*. For example, does an object create hard angular ricochets as it moves from one keyframe to the next, or does it have a more sloping movement with round corners?

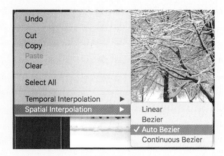

Adding Ease to Motion

A quick way to add a feeling of inertia to clip motion is to use a keyframe preset. For example, you can create a ramp-up effect for speed by right-clicking a keyframe and choosing Ease In or Ease Out. Ease In is used for approaching a keyframe, and Ease Out is used when leaving a keyframe.

Continue working with the 04 Scale sequence.

1 Select the second video clip in the sequence.

2 In the Effect Controls panel, locate the Rotation and Scale properties.

3 Click the disclosure icon next to the Scale property, and select the Scale property heading to reveal the control handles and velocity graphs.

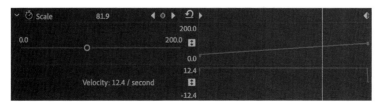

You might want to increase the height of the Effect Controls panel to make room for the extra controls.

Don't be overwhelmed by the next numbers and graphs. Once you understand one of these, you'll understand them all because they all use a common design.

The graph makes it easier to view the effects of keyframe interpolation. A straight line means essentially no change in speed or acceleration.

4 Right-click the first Scale keyframe, displayed in the Effect Controls panel mini-timeline, and choose Ease Out. The keyframe is partially obscured by the left edge of the mini-timeline.

5 Right-click the second Scale keyframe and choose Ease In.

The graph now shows a curved line, which translates as a gradual acceleration and deceleration of the animation.

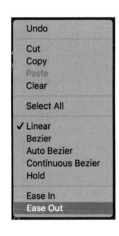

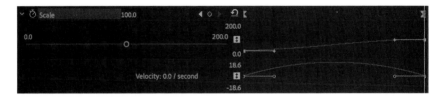

6 Play the sequence to see your animation.

7 Experiment by dragging the blue Bezier handles in the Effect Controls panel to see their effects on speed and ramping.

The steeper the curve you create, the more sharply the animation's movement or speed increases. After experimenting, you can choose Edit > Undo repeatedly if you don't like the changes.

Adding a drop shadow and bevel

Premiere Pro offers a number of other effects to control motion. While the Motion effect is the most intuitive, you may find yourself wanting more.

The Transform and Basic 3D effects are also useful and give more control over an object (including 3D rotation).

Adding a drop shadow

A drop shadow creates perspective by adding a small shadow behind an object. This is often used to help create a sense of separation between foreground and background elements.

Try adding a drop shadow.

1   Open the sequence 05 Enhance.

2   Make sure the Program Monitor zoom level is set to Fit.

3   In the Effects panel, browse into Video Effects > Perspective.

4   Drag the Drop Shadow effect onto the Journey to New York Title clip on the V3 track.

5   Experiment with the Drop Shadow settings in the Effect Controls panel. You may need to scroll down to see them. When you have finished experimenting, choose the following settings:

*   Set Distance to **15** so the shadow is further offset from the clip.

*   Drag the Direction value to about 320° to see the shadow's angle change.

*   Darken the shadow by changing Opacity to **85%**.

*   Set Softness to **25** to soften the edges of the shadow. Generally, the greater the Distance setting, the more softness you should apply.

6   Play the sequence to view the result.

You'll learn how to add drop shadows to graphics in a later lesson. However, adding a Drop Shadow effect in this way maintains the position of the shadow if you adjust or animate settings like rotation, giving a more natural-looking result.

Note: To make shadows fall away from a light source, add or subtract 180° from a perceived light source direction to get the correct direction for the shadow to fall.

Adding a bevel

Another way to enhance the edges of a clip is to add a bevel. This type of effect is useful on a picture-in-picture effect or on text. There are two bevels to choose from. The Bevel Edges effect is useful when the object is simply a standard video clip. The Bevel Alpha effect works better for text or logos because it detects the complex transparent areas in the image before applying the beveled edge.

Note: The Bevel Edges effect produces slightly harder edges than the Bevel Alpha effect. Both effects work well on rectangular clips, but the Bevel Alpha effect is better suited to text or logos.

Let's enhance the title a little.

1   Continue working with the 05 Enhance sequence.

2   Select the Journey to New York Title clip on V3 to see its controls in the Effect Controls panel.

▶ **Tip:** You can apply effects by dragging them onto clips, by dragging them into the Effect Controls panel when a clip is selected, or by double-clicking them in the Effects panel after selecting one or more clips.

3   In the Effects panel, choose Video Effects > Perspective and drag the Bevel Alpha effect into the Effect Controls panel, under the Drop Shadow effect.

The edges of the text should now appear slightly beveled, but the effect is perhaps too subtle.

4   In the Effect Controls panel, increase Bevel Alpha Edge Thickness to **10** to make the edge more pronounced. You might need to scroll down in the Effect Controls panel to see all the settings.

5   Increase Light Intensity to **0.80** to see a brighter edge effect.

The effect looks subtle because it's currently applied to both the text and the drop shadow. This is because the effect is below the drop shadow in the Effect Controls panel (the stacking order matters).

● **Note:** If you're not getting the look you want when applying multiple effects to a clip, drag the order around and see whether that produces a better result.

6   In the Effect Controls panel, drag the Bevel Alpha effect heading up, until it's just above the Drop Shadow effect. You'll see a black line where the effect will be placed. This changes the rendering order.

7 Reduce the Edge Thickness amount to **8**.

8 Examine the subtle differences in the bevel.

9 Play the sequence to see view the result.

● **Note:** You may need to render the sequence to see smooth playback because of the high-resolution clips and nonaccelerated effect.

Adding motion with the Transform effect

An alternative to the Motion effect settings is the Transform effect. These two effects offer similar controls, but there are two key differences.

- The Transform effect processes changes to a clip's Anchor Point, Position, Scale, and Opacity settings in the stack with other effects, unlike the Motion settings. This means effects such as drop shadows and bevels can behave differently.

- The Transform effect includes Skew, Skew Axis, and Shuttle Angle settings to allow a visual angular transformation to clips.

Let's compare the two effects using a prebuilt sequence.

1 Open the sequence 06 Motion and Transform.

2 Play the sequence to familiarize yourself with it.

There are two sections in the sequence. Each has a picture-in-picture (PIP), rotating twice over a background clip, while moving from left to right. Look carefully at the position of the shadow on each pair of clips.

- In the first example, the shadow follows the bottom edge of the PIP and appears on all four sides of the clip as it rotates, which obviously isn't realistic because the light source producing the shadow wouldn't be moving.

- In the second example, the shadow stays on the lower right of the PIP, which is more realistic.

3 Click the first clip on the V2 track, and view the effects applied in the Effect Controls panel: the Motion effect and the Drop Shadow effect.

4   Now click the second clip on the V2 track. The Transform effect is producing the motion this time, with the Drop Shadow effect again producing the shadow.

The Transform effect has many of the same options as the Motion effect, with the addition of Skew, Skew Axis, and Shutter Angle. As you can see, the Transform effect also works more realistically with the Drop Shadow effect than the Motion effect because of the order in which the effects are applied; the Motion effect is always applied after other effects.

> **Note:** When applying the Transform effect, deselect Use Composition's Shutter Angle to allow the Shutter Angle setting to introduce natural-looking motion blur.

Manipulating clips in 3D space with Basic 3D

Another option for creating movement is the Basic 3D effect, which can manipulate a clip in 3D space. It allows you to rotate the image around horizontal and vertical axes as well as move it toward or away from you. You'll also find an option to enable a specular highlight, which creates the appearance of light reflecting off the rotating surface.

Let's explore the effect using a prebuilt sequence.

1   Open the sequence 07 Basic 3D.

2   Drag the playhead over the sequence in the Timeline panel (scrub) to view the contents.

The light that follows the motion comes from above, from behind, and from the left of the viewer. Since the light comes from above, you won't see the effect until the image is tilted backward to catch the reflection. Specular highlights of this kind can be used to enhance the realism of a 3D effect.

The following are four major properties of the Basic 3D effect:

- **Swivel:** This controls the rotation around the vertical y-axis. If you rotate past 90°, you'll see the back of the image, which is a mirror of the front.

- **Tilt:** This controls the rotation around a horizontal x-axis. If you rotate beyond 90°, the back will also be visible.

- **Distance to Image:** This moves the image along the z-axis to simulate depth. As the distance value gets larger, the image moves farther away.

- **Specular Highlight:** This adds a glint of light that reflects off the surface of the rotated image, as though an overhead light were shining on the surface. This option is either on or off.

3 Experiment with the Basic 3D options. Note that the Draw Preview Wireframe option applies only when working in Software Only mode (without GPU acceleration enabled in the Project settings).

With this option enabled, only an outline of the clip frame will be shown. This is a quick way to set up the effect without your computer rendering the image. If you're working with GPU acceleration enabled, the full image will always be shown.

Review questions

1 Which fixed effect will move a clip in the frame?

2 You want a clip to appear full-screen for a few seconds and then spin away. How do you make the Motion effect's Rotation feature start within a clip rather than at the beginning?

3 How can you start an object rotating gradually and have it stop rotating slowly?

4 If you want to add a drop shadow to a clip, why might you choose to use a different motion-related effect from the Motion fixed effect?

Review answers

1 The Motion effect lets you set a new position for a clip. If keyframes are used, the effect can be animated.

2 Position the playhead where you want the rotation to begin, and click the Add/Remove Keyframe button or the stopwatch icon. Then move to where you want the spinning to end and change the Rotation parameter; another keyframe will appear.

3 Use the Ease Out and Ease In options to change the keyframe interpolation to be gradual rather than sudden.

4 The Motion effect is the last effect applied to a clip. Motion takes whatever effects you apply before it (including Drop Shadow) and spins the entire assemblage as a single unit. To create a realistic drop shadow on a spinning object, use Transform or Basic 3D and then place a Drop Shadow effect below that in the Effect Controls panel.

10 EDITING AND MIXING AUDIO

Lesson overview

In this lesson, you'll learn about the following:

- Working in the Audio workspace
- Understanding audio characteristics
- Adjusting clip audio volume
- Adjusting audio levels in a sequence
- Automatically lowering music level
- Using the Audio Clip Mixer

This lesson will take about 90 minutes to complete. Please log in to your account on peachpit.com to download the lesson files for this lesson, or go to the "Getting Started" section at the beginning of this book and follow the instructions under "Accessing the lesson files and Web Edition." Store the files on your computer in a convenient location.

Your Account page is also where you'll find any updates to the lesson files. Look on the Lesson & Update Files tab to access the most current content.

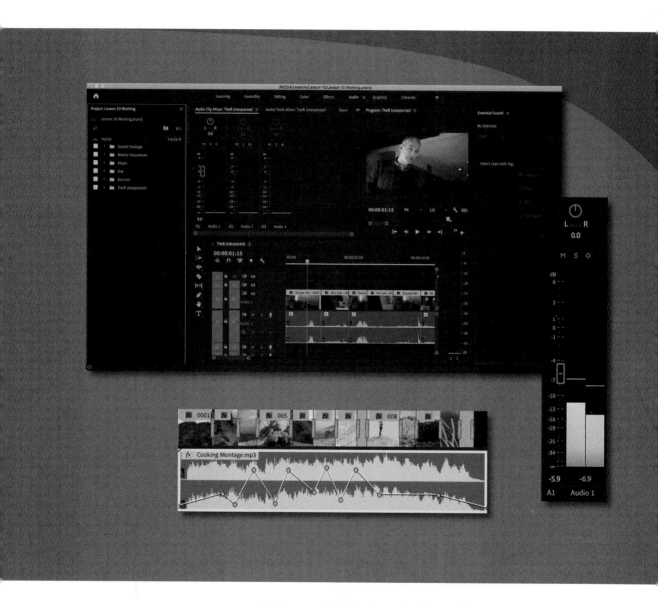

Until now, our focus has been primarily on working with visuals. No doubt about it, the pictures count, but professional editors generally agree that sound is at least as important as the images on the screen—sometimes more important! In this lesson, you'll learn some audio-mixing fundamentals using the powerful tools provided by Adobe Premiere Pro CC.

Starting the lesson

It's rare to have audio recorded on-camera that is perfect for your final output. There are several things you might want to do with sound in Premiere Pro.

- Set Premiere Pro to interpret recorded audio channels differently from the way they were recorded in-camera. For example, audio recorded as stereo can be interpreted as separate mono tracks.

- Clean up background sound. Whether it's system hum or the sound of an air-conditioning unit, Premiere Pro has tools for adjusting and tuning your audio.

- Adjust the volume of different frequencies in your clips (different tones) using EQ effects.

- Adjust the volume level on clips in the bin and on clip segments in your sequence. The adjustments you make to clips in a sequence can vary over time, creating a complete sound mix.

- Add music and mix levels between music clips and dialogue clips.

- Add audio spot effects, such as explosions, door slams, or atmospheric environmental sound.

Consider the difference it makes if you turn the sound off when watching a horror movie. Without an ominous soundtrack, scenes that were scary a moment ago can seem like comedy.

Music works around many of our critical faculties and directly influences our emotions. In fact, your body reacts to sound whether you want it to or not. For example, it's normal for your heart rate to be influenced by the beat of the music you're listening to. Fast music tends to raise your heart rate, and slow music tends to lower your heart rate. Powerful stuff!

In this lesson, you'll begin by learning how to use the audio tools in Premiere Pro and then make adjustments to clips and a sequence. You'll also use the Audio Clip Mixer to make changes to your volume "on the fly" while your sequence plays.

Setting up the interface to work with audio

Let's begin by switching to the Audio workspace.

1 Open Lesson 10.prproj.

2 Save the project as **Lesson 10 Working.prproj**.

3 In the Workspaces panel, click Audio. Then double-click the Audio workspace name and click Yes in the Confirm Workspace Reset dialog box. This is a convenient shortcut to reset the workspace to the saved layout.

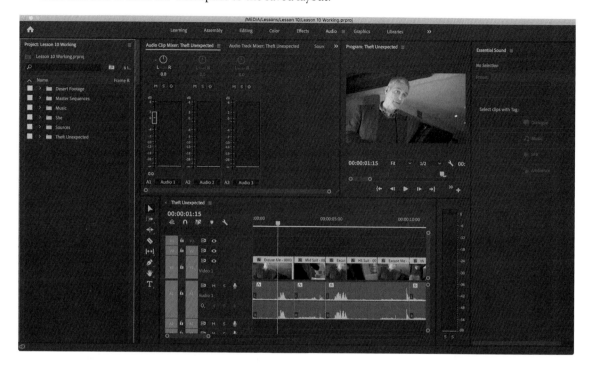

Working in the Audio workspace

You'll recognize most of the components of the Audio workspace from the video-editing workspaces you've used. One obvious difference is that the Audio Clip Mixer is displayed in place of the Source Monitor. The Source Monitor is still there; it's just hidden right now, grouped with the Audio Clip Mixer.

You can modify the appearance of timeline track headers to include an audio meter for each track, along with track-based level and pan controls. This is useful when mixing audio as it helps you locate the sources of audio levels you might want to adjust.

Try it now:

1 In the Project panel (on the left side of the Premiere Pro interface), open the Theft Unexpected sequence in the Master Sequences bin.

2 Open the Timeline Display Settings menu and choose Customize Audio Header.

The Audio Header Button Editor appears.

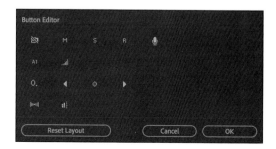

3 Drag the Track Meter button 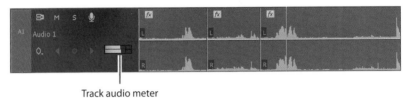 onto a Timeline audio header and click OK.

When you click OK, the audio track headers return to their previous size. You may need to resize an audio header vertically and horizontally to see the new meter.

Now every audio track will have a small built-in audio meter.

Track audio meter

There are two audio mixer panels in Premiere Pro. Let's look at the differences between the two.

- **Audio Clip Mixer:** This provides controls to adjust the audio level and pan of sequence clips. As you play your sequence, you can make adjustments, and Premiere Pro will add keyframes to clips as the playhead moves over them.

- **Audio Track Mixer:** This adjusts audio level and pan on tracks rather than clips. The controls are similar, but the Audio Track Mixer offers more advanced mixing options.

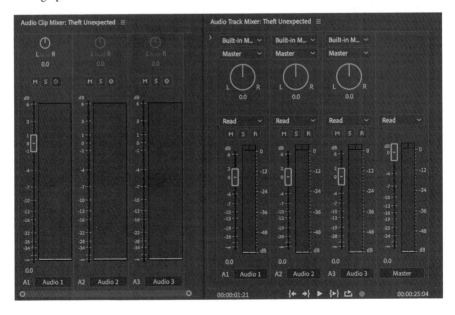

Clip adjustments and track adjustments are combined for final output. So if you reduce a clip's audio level by –3 dB *and* reduce the track audio level by –3 dB, you'll have a total drop of –6 dB.

You can apply clip-based audio effects and modify their settings in the Effect Controls panel, but track-based audio adjustments can be modified only in the Audio Track Mixer or directly on the timeline.

Clip-based audio adjustments and effects are applied before track-based adjustments and effects. The order in which adjustments are applied can have a big impact on results, especially when working with effects.

Defining master track output

Sequences have settings that closely match the way a media file would be defined. These settings include a frame rate, frame size, and pixel aspect ratio, for example.

The audio mastering setting defines the number of audio channels the sequence outputs. This is a little like configuring the audio channels for a media file. In fact, if you export the sequence using the option to match sequence settings, the sequence audio mastering configuration will be the audio format for the new file.

When you create a new sequence, the audio mastering setting is in the Tracks tab of the New Sequence dialog box, under Audio.

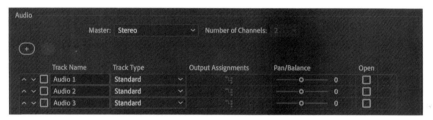

- Stereo has two audio channels: Left and Right. This is the most common option for delivered content.

- 5.1 has six audio channels: Middle, Front-Left, Front-Right, Rear-Left, Rear-Right, and Low Frequency Effects (LFE)—that's the sound that gets played through the subwoofer.

- Multichannel has between 1 and 32 audio channels you can choose (this option is commonly used for more advanced multichannel broadcast television workflows).

- Mono has one audio channel, which is useful for web video if you want to minimize file size.

You can change most sequence settings later, but not the audio master setting. This means that, with the exception of multichannel sequences, you cannot change the number of channels that your sequence will output.

You can add or remove audio tracks at any time, but the audio master setting is fixed. If you need to change your audio master setting, you can easily copy and paste clips from a sequence with one setting to a new sequence with a different setting.

What is an audio channel?

It's common to think that Left and Right audio channels are in some way identifiably different. In fact, they are both simply mono audio channels designated as Left or Right. When recording sound, it's the standard configuration to have Audio Channel 1 as Left and Audio Channel 2 as Right.

What makes Audio Channel 1 Left is simply the following:

- It's recorded from a microphone pointing left.
- It's interpreted as Left in Premiere Pro.
- It outputs to a speaker positioned on the left.

It is still a single mono channel.

If you perform the same recording from a microphone pointing right (but with Audio Channel 2), then you have stereo audio. They are, in fact, two mono audio channels.

Using the audio meters

The primary function of the audio meters is to give you the overall mix output volume for your sequence. As your sequence plays, you'll see the level meter dynamically change to reflect the volume.

To view the audio meters, you can do either of the following:

- If the audio meters are not already displayed, choose Window > Audio Meters.

  In the default Audio workspace, the audio meters are displayed, but they are relatively narrow. You may want to make the panel wider when working with them.

- There is a Solo button at the bottom of each audio meter, which allows you to exclusively hear the selected channel (or multiple channels). If the Solo buttons are displayed as small circles, drag the edge of the panel a little to make the meters wider. Larger Solo buttons will be displayed.

> **Note:** The Solo buttons are not displayed when using the more advanced multichannel audio mastering option.

If you right-click the audio meters, you can choose a different display scale. The default is a range from 0 dB to –60 dB, which clearly shows the main information about the audio level you'll want to see.

You can also choose between static and dynamic peaks. When you get a loud "spike" in audio levels that makes you glance at the meters, the sound is usually gone by the time you look. With static peaks, the highest peak is marked and maintained in the meters so you can see what the loudest level was during playback.

You can click the audio meters to reset the peak. With dynamic peaks, the peak level will continually update; keep watching to check the levels.

About audio level

The scale displayed on the audio meters is decibels, denoted by dB. The decibel scale is a little unusual in that the highest volume is designated as 0 dB. Lower volumes become larger and larger negative numbers until they reach negative infinity.

If a recorded sound is too quiet, it might get lost in the background noise. Background noise might be environmental, such as an air-conditioning system making a hum. It also might be system noise, such as the quiet hiss you hear from your speakers when no sound is playing.

When you increase the overall volume of your audio, background noise gets louder too. When you decrease the overall volume, background noise gets quieter. This means it's often better to record audio at a higher level than you need (while avoiding over-driving) and then reduce the volume later to remove (or at least reduce) the background noise.

Depending on your audio hardware, you may have a bigger or smaller signal-to-noise ratio; that's the difference between the sound you want to hear (the signal) and the sound you don't want to hear (the background noise). Signal-to-noise ratio is often shown as SNR, also measured in dB.

Viewing samples

Let's look at an individual audio sample.

1   In the Project panel, open the Music bin, and double-click the clip Cooking Montage.mp3 to open it in the Source Monitor. This is music created by composer Patrick Cannell.

    Because this clip has no video, Premiere Pro displays the waveforms for the two audio channels.

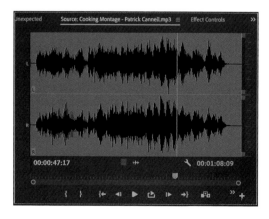

At the bottom of the Source Monitor and Program Monitor, the time ruler represents the total duration of the clip.

2 Open the Source Monitor Settings menu and choose Time Ruler Numbers. The time ruler now shows timecode indicators on the time ruler.

Try zooming in to the time ruler using the navigator just below the time ruler (drag the handles all the way together). The maximum zoom shows you an individual frame.

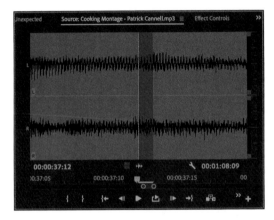

3 Open the Source Monitor Settings menu again and choose Show Audio Time Units.

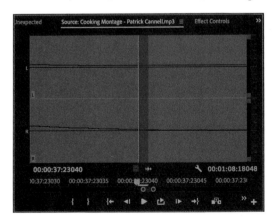

This time, you'll see individual audio samples counted on the time ruler. Try zooming in a little more. Now you can zoom in to an individual audio sample—in this case, one 48,000th of a second, the sample rate of this audio!

● **Note:** The audio sample rate is the number of times per second the recorded sound source is sampled. It's common for professional camera audio to take a sample 48,000 times per second.

The Timeline panel has the same option to view audio samples in the panel menu (rather than the Timeline Settings menu).

4 For now, use the Source Monitor Settings menu to disable Time Ruler Numbers and Show Audio Time Units.

Showing audio waveforms

When you use the waveform display option in the Source Monitor or Program Monitor, you'll see an extra navigator zoom control for each channel, to the right of the waveform. These controls work in a way that's similar to the navigator zoom control at the bottom of the panel. You can resize the vertical navigator to view the waveforms larger or smaller, which is particularly useful when navigating quiet audio.

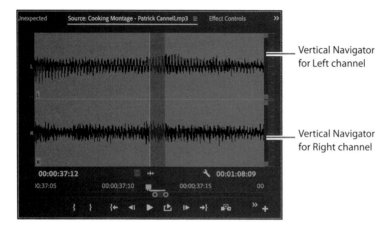

Vertical Navigator
for Left channel

Vertical Navigator
for Right channel

● **Note:** Viewing an audio waveform is great if you are trying to locate specific dialogue and you are not so concerned about the visuals.

You can choose to display audio waveforms for any clip that has audio by choosing Audio Waveform in the Source Monitor Settings menu.

If a clip has video as well as audio, the video will be displayed in the Source Monitor by default. You can switch to viewing the audio waveform by clicking the Drag Audio Only button ⬌.

Let's look at some waveforms.

1 Open the clip HS John from the Theft Unexpected bin.

2 Open the Source Monitor Settings menu and choose Audio Waveform.

You can easily see where the dialogue begins and ends. Notice the clip's In and Out marks are shown as a highlighted region on the waveform.

Notice also, you can click the waveform to move the Source Monitor playhead.

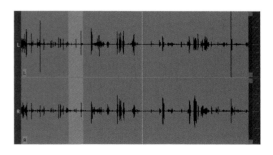

3   Switch back to viewing the composite video using the Source Monitor Settings menu.

You can also turn off and on the display of waveforms for clip segments on the Timeline.

4   The sequence Theft Unexpected should already be open in the Timeline panel. If not, open it from the Master Sequences bin.

5   Open the Timeline Display Settings menu, and make sure the Show Audio Waveform option is enabled.

6   Resize the Audio 1 track to make sure the waveform is fully visible. Notice that two audio channels are displayed on the audio clips in this sequence: The clips have stereo audio.

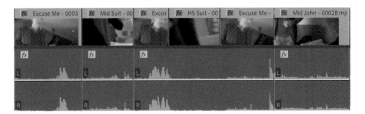

The audio waveform on these clips looks a little different from the waveform in the Source Monitor. That's because it's a Rectified audio waveform, which makes it easier to see lower-volume audio, like the dialogue in this scene. You can switch between Rectified and regular audio waveforms.

7   Open the Timeline panel menu ☰ (not the Settings menu), and choose Rectified Audio Waveforms to deselect it.

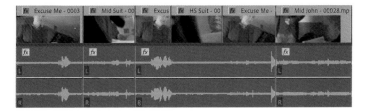

The regular waveform display works well for louder audio, but notice the quieter parts of the speech; it's much harder to follow the level changes.

8   Open the Timeline panel menu and restore the Rectified Audio Waveforms option.

Working with standard audio tracks

In a sequence, the standard audio track type can accommodate both mono audio clips and stereo audio clips. The controls in the Effect Controls panel, the Audio Clip Mixer, and the Audio Track Mixer work with both kinds of media.

If you're working with a combination of mono and stereo clips, you'll find it more convenient to use the standard track type than the traditional separate mono or stereo tracks.

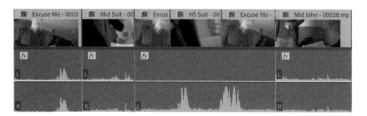

This standard audio track has a mix of stereo and mono clips.

Monitoring audio

You can choose which sequence audio channels you hear when monitoring.

Let's try this with a sequence.

1 Open the Desert Montage sequence.

2 Play the sequence, and while you do, try clicking each of the Solo buttons at the bottom of the audio meters.

Each Solo button allows you to hear only the channel you select. You can solo multiple channels to hear a specific combination—though in this example it wouldn't help much, as you have only two channels to choose between. When working with multichannel sequences, you'll solo output channels more often.

Soloing is particularly useful if you're working with audio where the sound from different microphones is recorded onto different tracks. This is common with professionally recorded location sound.

The number of channels and associated Solo buttons you'll see depends on your current sequence audio master setting.

You can also use the track header Mute button M or Solo button S for individual audio tracks in the Timeline panel. This gives you precise control over what's included or excluded in your mix.

Examining audio characteristics

When you open a clip in the Source Monitor and view the waveform, you're seeing each channel displayed. The taller the waveform is, the louder the audio for that channel will be.

Three factors affect the way audio sounds to your ears. Consider them in terms of a television speaker.

- **Frequency:** This refers to how fast the surface of the speaker moves. The number of times the surface of the speaker beats the air per second is measured as Hertz (Hz). Human hearing ranges from approximately 20 Hz to 20,000 Hz. Many factors, including age, affect the frequency range you can hear. The higher the frequency, the higher the perceived tone.

- **Amplitude:** This is how far the speaker moves. The bigger the movement, the louder the sound will be because it produces a higher air pressure wave, which carries more energy to your ears.

- **Phase:** This is the precise timing with which the surface of the speaker moves out and in. If two speakers push out air and pull in air in sync, they are considered "in phase." If they move out of sync, they become "out of phase," and this can produce problems with sound reproduction. One speaker can reduce the air pressure at exactly the moment the other speaker is attempting to increase it. The result is that you may not hear parts of the sound.

The movement of the surface of a speaker as it emits sound provides a simple example of the way sound is generated, but, of course, the same rules apply to all sound sources.

What are audio characteristics?

Imagine the surface of a speaker moving as it beats the air. As it moves, it creates a high- and low-pressure wave that moves through the air until it arrives at your ear in much the way that surface ripples move across a pond.

As the pressure wave hits your ear, it makes a tiny part of it move, and that movement is converted into energy that is passed to your brain and interpreted as sound. This happens with extraordinary precision, and since you have two ears, your brain does an impressive job of balancing the two sets of sound information to produce an overall sense of what you can hear.

Much of the way you hear is active, not passive. That is, your brain is constantly filtering out sounds it decides are irrelevant and identifying patterns so you can focus your attention on things that matter. For example, you have probably had the experience of being at a party where the general hubbub of conversation sounds like a wall of noise until someone across the room mentions your name. You perhaps didn't realize your brain was listening to the conversation the whole time because you were concentrating on listening to the person standing next to you.

There's a body of research on this subject that broadly falls under the title *psycho-acoustics*. For these exercises, we'll be focusing on the mechanics of sound more than on the psychology, though it's a fascinating subject worthy of further study.

Recording equipment makes no such subtle discrimination, which is part of the reason why it's so important to listen to location sound with headphones and to take care to get the best possible recorded sound. It's usual practice to try to record location sound with no background noise at all. The background noise is added in post-production at precisely the right level to add atmosphere to the scene but not drown out the dialogue.

Recording a voice-over track

If you have a microphone set up, you can record audio directly to the into a sequence using the Audio Track Mixer or a special Voice-over Record button on each audio track header. To record audio in this way, check that your Audio Hardware preferences are set up to allow input. You can check your audio hardware input and output settings by choosing Premiere Pro CC > Preferences > Audio Hardware (macOS) or Edit > Preferences > Audio Hardware (Windows).

Try the Voice-over Record button by following these steps:

1   Open the Voice Over sequence in the Master Sequences bin. This is a simple sequence with visuals only; you'll add the voice-over.

2   Take a look at the header for the A1 track. You should already be able to see the Voice-over Record button .

3   Mute your speakers or wear headphones while recording voice-over to avoid getting microphone feedback.

4   Position the playhead at the beginning of the sequence and click the Voice-over Record button. The Program Monitor gives a short countdown, and you can begin. Describe the shots that come up to create an accompanying voice-over.

As you record, the Program Monitor shows that you are recording, and the audio meter shows the input level.

5 When you're finished recording, press the spacebar or click the Voice-over Record button to stop.

The new audio appears in the Timeline panel, and an associated clip appears in the Project panel.

In the following example, audio was recorded onto a stereo track, and so two audio channels were recorded. If this were a mono track, only one channel would be recorded.

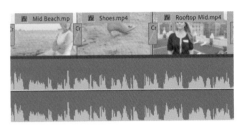

Premiere Pro will create a new audio file in the location specified in the Scratch Disks settings (in the project settings). By default, this is the same location as your project file.

You can use this technique to record professional-quality audio using a studio microphone and sound booth. Or you can use it with the built-in microphone on a laptop to record guide-track voice-over while on your way back from a shoot. That voice-over can form the basis for an outline edit, saving significant time later.

Adjusting audio volume

There are several ways to adjust the volume of clips with Premiere Pro, and they are all nondestructive. Changes you make don't affect your original media files, so you can experiment freely.

Adjusting audio in the Effect Controls panel

Earlier, you used the Effect Controls panel to make adjustments to the scale and position of clips in a sequence. You can also use the Effect Controls panel to adjust volume.

1 Open the Excuse Me sequence from the Master Sequences bin.

This is a simple sequence with two clips in it. In fact, it's the same clip added to the sequence twice. One version has been interpreted as stereo, and the other has been interpreted as mono channels. For more on clip interpretation, see Lesson 4, "Organizing Media."

2 Click the first clip to select it, and open the Effect Controls panel.

3 In the Effect Controls panel, expand the Volume, Channel Volume, and Panner controls.

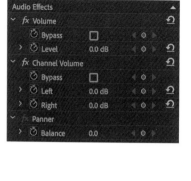

Each control gives the right options for the type of audio you have selected.

- **Volume** adjusts the combined volume of all the audio channels in the selected clip.

- **Channel Volume** allows you to adjust the audio level for individual channels in the selected clip.

- **Panner** gives you overall stereo left/right output balance control for the selected clip.

Notice that the keyframe toggle stopwatch icon is automatically enabled (in blue) for all the controls, so every change you make adds a keyframe.

If you add just one keyframe to a setting and use it to apply an adjustment, the adjustment will apply to the whole clip.

4 Position the Timeline playhead somewhere over the first clip where you would like to add a keyframe (it doesn't make too much difference where you choose if you intend to make only one adjustment).

5 Click the Timeline Display Settings menu, and make sure Show Audio Keyframes is selected.

6 Increase the height of the Audio 1 track so you can see the waveform and special thin white line for adding keyframes, often referred to as a *rubber band*.

7 In the Effect Controls panel, drag left on the blue number that sets the volume level.

Premiere Pro adds a keyframe, and the rubber band has moved down, indicating the reduced volume. The difference is subtle, but as you become more familiar with the Premiere Pro interface, it'll stand out more and more clearly.

Note: The rubber band uses the entire height of the audio clip to adjust the volume.

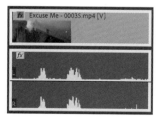

Before

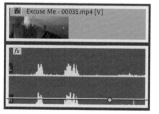

After

8 Now select the second version of the Excuse Me clip in the sequence.

You'll notice you have similar controls available in the Effect Controls panel, but now there is no Channel Volume option. This is because each channel is its own clip segment, so the Volume control for each channel is already an individual one.

The Balance control has now become a Pan control. This has a similar purpose but is suited to multiple-mono channel audio.

9 Experiment with adjusting the volume for these two independent clips.

Adjusting audio gain

Most music is created with the loudest possible signal to maximize the difference between the signal and the background noise. This is too loud to use in most video sequences. To address this issue, you can adjust the clip's audio gain.

This method works in a similar way to the adjustment you made in the last exercise but is applied to the clip in the Project panel, so any parts of the clip you use in a sequence will already include the adjustment. You can also apply audio gain adjustments to multiple clips in a single step, both in the Project panel and in the Timeline panel.

1 Open the clip Cooking Montage.mp3 from the Music bin. You may need to adjust the zoom level on the Source Monitor to see the waveform.

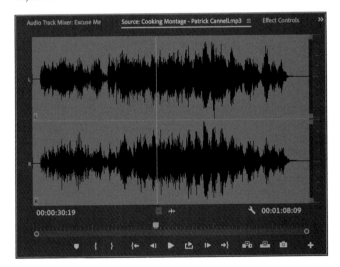

2 Right-click the clip in the bin and choose Audio Gain.

There are two options in the Audio Gain dialog box that you should learn about now.

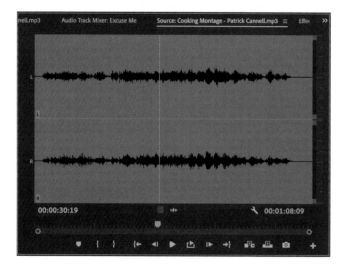

- **Set Gain To:** Use this option to specify a particular adjustment for your clip.
- **Adjust Gain By:** Use this option to specify an incremental adjustment for your clip.

For example, if you apply −3 dB, this will adjust the Set Gain To amount to −3 dB. If you go into this menu a second time and apply another −3 dB adjustment, the Set Gain To amount will change to −6 dB, and so on.

3 Select Set Gain To, set the gain to **−12 dB**, and click OK.

Right away, you'll see the waveform change in the Source Monitor.

Note: None of the changes you make to the volume of your clips will change the original media files. You can make a change to the overall gain here, in the bin, or in the Timeline panel, in addition to any changes you make using the Effect Controls panel, and your original media files will remain unmodified.

Changes like this, where you are adjusting the audio gain in the bin, will not update clips already edited into a sequence. However, you can right-click one or more clips in a sequence, choose Audio Gain, and make the same kind of adjustment there.

Normalizing audio

Normalizing audio is similar to adjusting gain. In fact, normalization results in an adjustment to the clip gain. The difference is that normalization is based on automated analysis rather than on your subjective judgment.

When you normalize a clip, Premiere Pro analyzes the audio to identify the single highest peak—in other words, the loudest part of the audio. The gain for the clip is then adjusted automatically so that the highest peak matches a level you specify.

You can have Premiere Pro adjust the volume for multiple clips so that they match any perceived volume you like.

Imagine working with multiple clips of a voice-over, recorded over several days. Perhaps because of different recording setups or working with different microphones, several clips might have different volumes. You can select all the clips and, in a single step, have Premiere Pro automatically set their volumes to match. This saves significant time you might have spent manually going through each clip, one by one, to make adjustments.

Try normalizing some clips by following these steps:

1 Open the Journey to New York sequence.

● **Note:** You may need to adjust the track size to see the audio waveforms. Do this by dragging the divider on the track header.

2 Play the sequence, and watch the level on the audio meters.

The voice level varies quite a lot, with clip one noticeably quieter than the third and fourth clips.

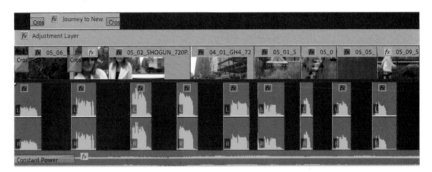

3 Select all the voice-over clips in the sequence on Track A1. To do so, you can lasso them or make an item-by-item selection.

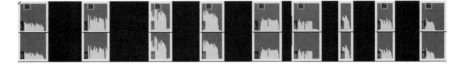

4 Right-click any of the selected clips and choose Audio Gain, or press the G key.

5 Select Normalize All Peaks To, enter **−8 dB**, and click OK.

Listen again.

Every selected clip is adjusted so that the loudest peaks are at −8 dB.

Tip: You can apply normalization in the bin too. Just select all the clips you want to automatically adjust, go to the Clip menu, and choose Audio Options > Audio Gain, or you can select the clips and press the G key.

The music adds to the overall level displayed in the Audio Meters. To see the level for the voice-over clips only, enable the Solo S option for the Audio 1 track. Be sure to disable this option before continuing.

Notice the way the waveforms for the clips level out.

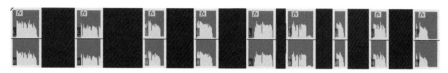

If you choose Normalize Max Peak To, rather than Normalize All Peaks To, Premiere Pro will make an adjustment based on the loudest moment of all the clips combined, as if they were one clip. That same amount of adjustment will be applied to every clip, maintaining the relative levels of all the clips.

Sending audio to Adobe Audition CC

While Premiere Pro has advanced tools to help you achieve most audio-editing tasks, it can't compete with Adobe Audition, which is a dedicated audio post-production application.

Audition is a component of Adobe Creative Cloud. It integrates neatly into your workflow when editing with Premiere Pro.

You can send an individual sequence to Adobe Audition, bringing all your clips and a video file based on your sequence, to produce an audio mix that follows along with the pictures. Audition can even open a Premiere Pro .pproj project file natively and convert sequences into multitrack sessions for advanced audio finishing.

If you have Audition installed, you can send a sequence to it by following these steps:

1 Open the sequence you want to send to Adobe Audition.

2 Choose Edit > Edit In Adobe Audition > Sequence.

3 You'll be creating new files to work with in Adobe Audition to keep your original media unchanged, so choose a name and browse for a location, then choose the remaining options as you prefer, and finally click OK.

4 In the Video menu, you can choose Send Through Dynamic Link to view the video part of your Premiere Pro sequence live in Audition.

Adobe Audition has fantastic tools for working with sound. It has a special spectral display that helps you identify and remove unwanted noises, a high-performance multitrack editor, and advanced audio effects and controls.

continues on next page

It's also easy to send an individual clip to Audition for editing, effects, and adjustment features. To send an audio clip to Audition, right-click the clip in your Premiere Pro sequence and choose Edit Clip In Adobe Audition.

Premiere Pro duplicates the audio clip, replaces the current sequence clip with the duplicate, and opens the duplicate in Audition, ready to work on it.

From now on, every time you save changes you have made to the clip in Audition, they'll automatically update in Premiere Pro.

For more information about Adobe Audition, go to www.adobe.com/products/audition.html.

Auto-duck music

One of the most common tasks when working on an audio mix is reducing music level during sections of speech. If there's a voice-over track, for example, you may want the music to get quieter just when information is being shared and then become the dominant element in the mix again. This is commonly the way radio DJs will speak over music, with the music automatically getting quieter when the DJ speaks. The technique is called *ducking*.

You can manually add audio keyframes to apply ducking (and you'll explore this technique later), but there's an automated way to do it too, with the Essential Sound panel.

You'll learn about the Essential Sound panel in more detail in Lesson 11, "Sweetening Sound." Still, this is a quick and easy workflow that saves time when creating your mix, and it's worth learning right away.

1   Continue working in the Journey to New York sequence. Make sure all the voice-over clips on the Audio 1 track are selected.

2   In the Essential Sound panel, click the Dialogue button to assign the dialogue audio type to the selected clips. Assigning the dialogue audio type gives access to tools and controls that are relevant to dialogue.

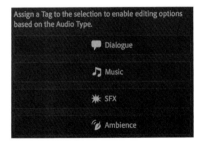

3 Resize the Audio 2 track so you can see the music clip's audio waveform clearly. Select the clip, and in the Essential Sound panel select the Music audio type.

4 In the Essential Sound panel, select the box to enable Ducking, and take a look at the options.

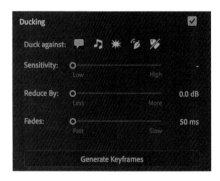

- **Duck Against:** There are multiple types of audio. You can select whether one, several, or all types of audio will trigger automatically ducking.

- **Sensitivity:** The higher the sensitivity, the lower the trigger audio will need to be to cause ducking.

- **Reduce By:** The amount the music level will be reduced in dB.

- **Fades:** The slower the fade setting, the longer it will take for the music to get quieter and then louder again.

- **Generate Keyframes:** Click this button to apply the settings and add keyframes to the music clip.

5 Applying the right settings for audio ducking is a science and an art, and the type of audio you are working with will influence the choices you make. Experimentation is the key.

For this audio, choose these settings:

- **Duck Against:** Dialogue Clips should already be selected (it's the default).

- **Sensitivity: 6.0**

- **Reduce By: -8.0 dB**

- **Fades: 500 ms**

6 Click Generate Keyframes.

Keyframes are added to the music clip, appearing in the Effect Controls panel and on the clip segment in the sequence.

7 Play the sequence to listen to the result. It's not perfect, but it's closer to a finished mix.

You can adjust the settings and click the Generate Keyframes button repeatedly to remove and replace existing keyframes, making it easy to experiment.

You can also manually adjust the keyframes that have been added. You can remove, move, and add keyframes at any time.

Creating a split edit

A split edit is a simple, classic editing technique that offsets the cut point for audio and video. The audio from one clip is played with the visuals from another, carrying the feeling of one scene into another.

Adding a J-cut

The J-cut gets its name from the shape of the edit. Picture the letter *J* over an edit. The lower part (the audio cut) is to the left of the upper part (the video cut).

1 Open the Theft Unexpected sequence.

2 Play the last cut in the sequence. The join in the audio between the last two clips is rather abrupt. You may need to turn up your speaker volume to hear the join. You'll improve things by adjusting the timing of the audio cut.

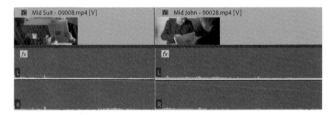

3 Select the Rolling Edit tool ⊞, accessible by pressing and holding the Ripple Edit tool icon ◄▮►.

▶ **Tip:** With the default Premiere Pro preferences, you can use the Selection tool to apply a rolling edit if you hold Command (macOS) or Ctrl (Windows).

4 Press and hold Option (macOS) or Alt (Windows)—this temporarily overrides linked selections—and drag the audio segment edit (not the video) a little to the left. Congratulations! You've created a J-cut!

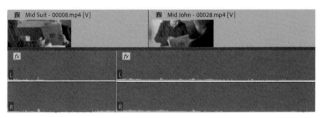

▶ **Tip:** For more information on keyboard shortcuts, see "Using and setting keyboard shortcuts" in Lesson 1, "Touring Adobe Premiere Pro CC."

5 Play through the edit.

You might want to experiment with the timing to make the cut seem more natural, but for practical purposes the J-cut works. You can smooth it over and improve it further with an audio crossfade later.

Remember to switch back to the Selection tool (V).

Adding an L-cut

An L-cut works in the same way as a J-cut but in reverse. Repeat the steps in the previous exercise, but drag the audio segment edit a little to the right while holding Option (macOS) or Alt (Windows). Play through the edit and see what you think.

Adjusting audio levels for a clip

As well as adjusting clip gain, you can use the rubber band to change the volume of clips in a sequence. You can also change the volume for tracks, and the two volume adjustments will combine to produce an overall output level.

If anything, using rubber bands to adjust volume is more convenient than adjusting gain because you can make incremental adjustments at any time, with immediate visual feedback.

The result of adjusting the rubber bands on a clip is the same as adjusting the volume using the Effect Controls panel. In fact, one control automatically updates the other.

Adjusting overall clip levels

Try this now.

1 Open the Desert Montage sequence in the Master Sequences bin.

   The music already fades up and down at the beginning and end. Let's adjust the volume between those fades.

2 Use the Selection tool to drag the bottom of the A1 track header down, or hover the pointer over the track header and scroll to make the track taller. This will make it easier to apply fine adjustments to the volume.

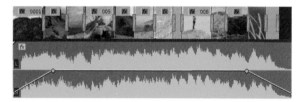

3 The music already fades up and down, and keyframes have been added to slow down those fades. The middle part of the music is a little too loud. Drag the middle part of the rubber band on the clip down a little.

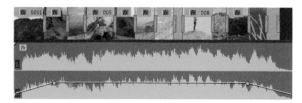

As you drag, a tooltip appears, displaying the amount of adjustment you are making.

4 Each time you make an adjustment of this kind, the only way to review the result is to play the audio. Try this now, and if you are not happy with the result, you can adjust the level and review the result again.

Because you're dragging a segment of the rubber band rather than a keyframe, you're adjusting the overall level for the clip between the two existing keyframes. If the clip did not have existing keyframes, you'd be adjusting the overall level for the entire length of the clip.

Changing clip volume with keyboard shortcuts

If the Timeline playhead is over a clip, you can also raise and lower clip volume using keyboard shortcuts. The result is the same, although you won't see a tooltip informing you about the amount of adjustment. These are particularly convenient shortcuts for quick, precise audio level adjustments:

- Use the [key to decrease clip volume by 1 dB.
- Use the] key to increase clip volume by 1 dB.
- Use Shift + [to decrease clip volume by 6 dB.
- Use Shift +] to increase clip volume by 6 dB.

If your keyboard does not have square bracket keys and you would like to use these shortcuts, choose Premiere Pro CC > Keyboard Shortcuts (macOS) or Edit > Keyboard Shortcuts (Windows) to set alternative keys.

Keyframing volume changes

You can use the Selection tool to adjust audio keyframes added to sequence clips in the same way that you might adjust visual keyframes. If you drag a keyframe up, the audio will get louder; drag a keyframe down to make the audio quieter.

▶ **Tip:** If you adjust the clip audio gain, Premiere Pro combines the effect with the keyframe adjustments dynamically. You can change either at any time.

The Pen tool ✎ adds keyframes to rubber bands. You can also use it to adjust existing keyframes or to lasso lots of keyframes to adjust them together.

You don't need to use the Pen tool, though. If you want to add a keyframe where there is none, you can hold Command (macOS) or Ctrl (Windows) when you click the rubber band.

The result of adding and adjusting the position of keyframes up or down on audio clip segments is that the rubber band is reshaped. Just as before, the higher the rubber band, the louder the sound.

Add a few keyframes now, with dramatic level adjustments to the music, and listen to the results. Go crazy with the keyframes so the adjustments are clear, and then play the sequence to hear the results.

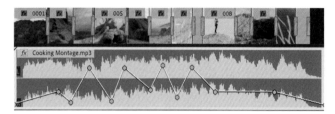

Smoothing volume between keyframes

The adjustments you made in the previous exercise are probably pretty overwhelming. You might want to smooth the adjustments over time.

To do so, right-click any of your keyframes. You'll see a range of standard options, including Ease In, Ease Out, and Delete. If you use the Pen tool, you can lasso multiple keyframes and then right-click any one of them to apply a change to them all.

The best way to learn about the different kinds of keyframes is to select each kind, make some adjustments, and see or listen to the results.

● **Note:** Adjustments you make to your clips are applied before adjustments you make to your tracks.

Using clip vs. track keyframes

Until now, you've made all your keyframe adjustments to sequence clip segments. When working with the Audio Clip Mixer, as you will in a moment, all adjustments are made directly to clips in the current sequence.

Premiere Pro has similar controls for the audio tracks those clips are placed onto. Track-based keyframes work in the same way as the clip-based ones. The difference is that they don't move with the clips.

This means you can set up keyframes for your audio level using track controls and then try different music clips. Each time you put new music into your sequence, you'll hear it via the adjustments you have made to your track.

As you develop your editing skills with Premiere Pro and create more complex audio mixes, explore the flexibility offered by combining clip and track keyframe adjustments.

Working with the Audio Clip Mixer

The Audio Clip Mixer provides intuitive controls to adjust clip volume and pan keyframes over time.

Each sequence audio track is represented by a set of controls. You can mute or solo a track, and you can enable an option to write keyframes to clips during playback by dragging a fader or adjusting a pan control.

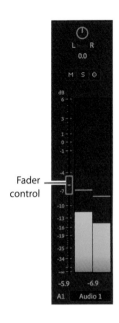

Fader control

What's a fader? Faders are industry-standard controls based on real-world audio-mixing decks. You move the fader up to increase the volume and move it down to decrease the volume. You can also use the volume faders to add keyframes to clip audio rubber bands while you play a sequence.

Try this now.

1 Continue working with the Desert Montage sequence. Make sure the Audio 1 track is set to show audio keyframes, using the Timeline Display Settings menu.

2 Open the Audio Clip Mixer (not the Audio Track Mixer), and play the sequence from the beginning.

Because you already added keyframes to this clip, the Audio Clip Mixer fader moves up and down during playback.

3 Position the Timeline playhead at the beginning of the sequence again. In the Audio Clip Mixer, enable the Write Keyframes button ⊙ in the fader for Audio 1.

4 Keyframes appear when you stop playback. Play the sequence, and while it plays, make some dramatic adjustments to the Audio 1 fader.

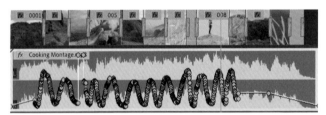

This example is a little over the top (it would be very unusual to make such wild adjustments to audio level), but it illustrates the challenge of having too many keyframes.

● **Note:** You won't see new keyframes until you stop playback.

5 If you repeat the process, you'll notice that the fader follows existing keyframes until you make a manual adjustment.

When you use the fader control to add keyframes, a *lot* of keyframes are added. By default, a keyframe is added with every adjustment. You can set a minimum time gap for keyframes.

6 Choose Premiere Pro CC > Preferences > Audio (macOS) or Edit > Preferences > Audio (Windows). Select Minimum Time Interval Thinning and set a minimum time of **500 milliseconds** (half a second is relatively slow, but it provides a balance between precise adjustment and keyframe overload). Click OK.

7 Set the playhead to the beginning of the sequence, and use the Audio Clip Mixer to add level keyframes using the fader control.

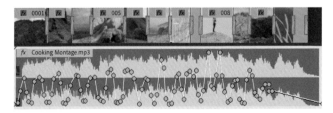

The result is a much more orderly adjustment. Even with dramatic adjustments, the smaller number of keyframes is much more manageable.

You can adjust keyframes you have created this way just as you would adjust keyframes that were created using the Selection tool or the Pen tool.

Tip: You can adjust pan in the same way as you would adjust volume using the Audio Clip Mixer. Simply enable keyframing, play your sequence, and make adjustments using the Audio Clip Mixer's Pan control.

The difference between Pan and Balance

Mono and stereo audio clips have different panner controls to set the level for each output when producing a stereo or 5.1 audio sequence.

- Mono audio clips have a Pan control. In a stereo sequence, this allows you to distribute the single audio channel between available output channels. In the case of a stereo sequence, this would mean choosing how much of the audio is in the left or right side of the mix.

- Stereo audio clips have a Balance control, which adjusts the relative levels of the left and right channels in the clip.

The controls displayed vary depending on your sequence audio mastering setting and the available audio in each clip you select.

You have now discovered several ways to add and adjust keyframes in Premiere Pro. There's no right or wrong way to work with keyframes; it's entirely a matter of personal preference or the needs of a particular project.

Review questions

1 How can you isolate an individual sequence audio channel to hear only that channel?

2 What is the difference between mono and stereo audio?

3 How can you view the waveforms for any clip that has audio in the Source Monitor?

4 What is the difference between normalization and gain?

5 What is the difference between a J-cut and an L-cut?

6 Which option in the Audio Clip Mixer must be enabled before you can use the fader controls to add keyframes to sequence clips during playback?

Review answers

1 Use the Solo buttons at the bottom of the audio meters to selectively hear an audio channel.

2 Stereo audio has two audio channels, and mono audio has one. It's the universal standard to record audio from a Left microphone as Channel 1 and audio from a Right microphone as Channel 2 when recording stereo sound.

3 Use the Settings menu on the Source Monitor to choose Audio Waveform. You can also click the Drag Audio Only button at the bottom of the Source Monitor. Clips in a sequence can display waveforms in the Timeline panel.

4 Normalization automatically adjusts the Gain setting for a clip based on the original peak amplitude. You use the Gain setting to make manual adjustments.

5 The sound for the next clip begins before the visuals when using a J-cut (sometimes described as "audio leads video"). With L-cuts, the sound from the previous clip remains until after the visuals begin (sometimes described as "video leads audio").

6 Enable the Write Keyframes option for each track you would like to add keyframes to.

11 SWEETENING SOUND

Lesson overview

In this lesson, you'll learn about the following:

- Working with the Essential Sound panel
- Improving the sound of speech
- Cleaning up noisy audio

This lesson will take about 75 minutes to complete. Please log in to your account on peachpit.com to download the lesson files for this lesson, or go to the "Getting Started" section at the beginning of this book and follow the instructions under "Accessing the lesson files and Web Edition." Store the files on your computer in a convenient location.

Your Account page is also where you'll find any updates to the lesson files. Look on the Lesson & Update Files tab to access the most current content.

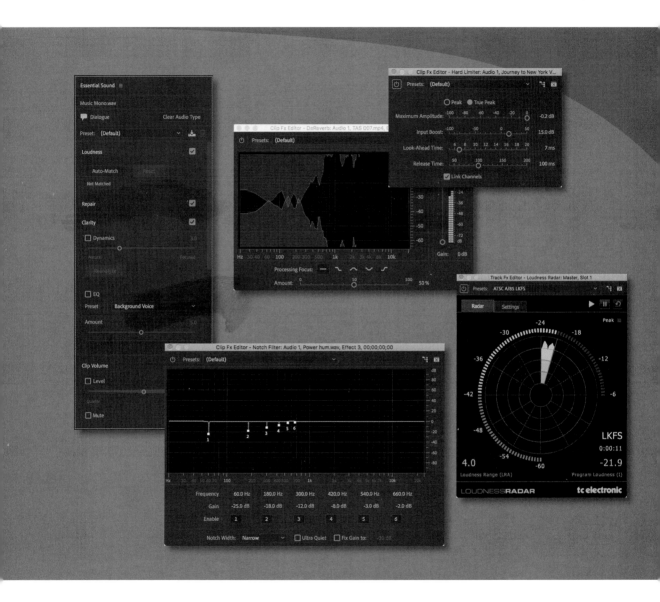

Audio effects in Adobe Premiere Pro CC can dramatically change the feel of your project—and clean up audio. To take your sound mix to the next level, leverage the integration and power of Adobe Audition CC. In this lesson, you'll learn some quick, easy ways to improve the quality of your sound mix.

Starting the lesson

You'll find many audio effects in Adobe Premiere Pro CC. These effects can be used to change pitch, create an echo, add reverb, and remove tape hiss. You can set keyframes for effects and adjust their settings over time.

1　Open the project Lesson 11.prproj.

2　Save the project as **Lesson 11 Working.prproj**.

3　In the Workspaces panel, click Audio. Then open the menu adjacent to the Audio option and choose Reset To Saved Layout, or double-click the Workspace panel name and click Yes in the Confirm Workspace Reset dialog box to reset the layout.

Sweetening sound with the Essential Sound panel

Ideally, your audio would be captured perfectly. Unfortunately, video production is rarely an ideal process. At some point, you'll need to turn to audio effects to fix problems.

Not all audio hardware plays all audio frequencies evenly. For example, listening to deep bass notes on a laptop is never the same as listening on larger speakers.

It's important to listen to your audio using high-quality headphones or studio monitor speakers to avoid accidentally compensating for a flaw in your playback hardware as you adjust the sound. Professional audio-monitoring hardware is carefully calibrated to ensure that all frequencies play evenly—a "flat" response, giving you confidence that you'll produce a consistent sound for your listeners.

It can be helpful to listen to your audio on low-quality speakers too. This allows you to confirm that enough of the audio is clear and that low frequency sound doesn't cause distortion.

Premiere Pro offers a variety of helpful effects, including the following, all of which are available in the Effects panel:

- **Parametric Equalizer:** This effect allows you to make subtle and precise adjustments to the audio level at different frequencies.

- **Studio Reverb:** This can increase the "presence" in the recording with reverb. Use it to simulate the sound of a larger room.

- **Delay:** This effect can add a slight (or pronounced) echo to your audio track.

- **Bass:** This effect can adjust the low-end frequencies of a clip. It works well on narration clips, particularly for male voices.

- **Treble:** This effect adjusts the higher-range frequencies in an audio clip.

● **Note:** Expand your knowledge of audio effects in Premiere Pro by experimenting. These effects are nondestructive, which means they do not change your original audio files. You can add any number of effects to a clip, change settings, and then delete them and start again.

Apply effects by dragging them from the Effects panel onto clips, just as you dragged transition effects onto edits earlier. Select a clip to find its effect controls in the Effect Controls panel. There are often presets to help you get a feel for the ways you can use effects.

You can remove an effect in the Effect Controls panel by selecting it and pressing Delete (macOS) or Backspace (Windows).

Use the 01 Effects sequence to experiment with audio effects. The clips in this sequence have a range of audio to make it easy to hear the results of your adjustments.

This lesson focuses on the Essential Sound panel, which offers a range of easy-to-apply professional adjustments and effects that are based on common workflows for standard media types like dialogue and music.

You are likely to find the Essential Sound panel is your go-to set of options for audio cleanup and improvement.

Adjusting dialogue

The Essential Sound panel has a comprehensive list of features to help you work with dialogue audio.

To use the Essential Sound panel, select one or more clips in a sequence, and select a tag that corresponds to the type of audio in the clip.

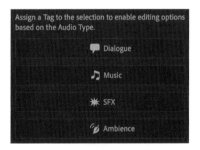

Selecting each tag displays different tools that are suitable for that type of media. There are more options for dialogue audio than any other—and for good reason! Your dialogue sound is probably the most important, and music, preprepared special effects (SFX), and ambient sound files are probably already mixed and ready to use.

Every adjustment you apply with the Essential Sound panel actually adds one or more effects to your selected clips and modifies the settings for those effects. This is an excellent shortcut to achieving great results. You can always select a clip and go into the detailed effect settings in the Effect Controls panel too.

In the following exercises, you'll try several of the adjustments available in the Essential Sound panel. All of the options you set can be stored as a preset, accessible at the top of the Essential Sound panel.

You can apply a preset without first assigning the audio type. To create a preset, select an audio type, apply some settings, and click the Save Settings As A Preset button  at the top of the Essential Sound panel.

Presets are not fixed—you can apply one and make changes to the settings—and even create a new preset based on the adjustments you have made.

If you expect to use some settings often, for a lot of the clips in your project, consider creating a preset. Anytime you know you'll do something more than five times, try making a preset—and name it carefully so you can easily locate it later. You'll find a name like Another Preset 15 becomes difficult to differentiate a few weeks later.

Setting loudness

The Essential Sound panel makes it easy to set the audio level for multiple clips to an appropriate volume for broadcast television.

Let's try this.

1 Open the sequence 02 Loudness.

This is the same sequence you worked with previously when learning about normalization.

About the Loudness scale

Until now, audio level has been described in decibels (dB). You'll find the decibel scale a useful reference all throughout production and post-production.

Peak level (the loudest moment of a clip's audio level) is often used to set limits for broadcast television soundtracks. Each broadcast television station will have its own official limit for audio level.

While peak level is a useful reference, it doesn't account for the overall energy in a soundtrack, and it's common to produce a mix that sets every part of the soundtrack louder than is natural. A whisper, for example, can sound as loud as a shout. As long as the peak level of the audio is within prescribed limits, it might be allowed for broadcast television.

This is why so many commercials sound as loud as they do—the peak level is no louder than any other content but even the quiet sections of the soundtrack are also often loud.

The Loudness scale is intended to resolve this issue. It measures the total energy over time. When a Loudness limit is used, it's okay for content to have loud sections, but overall the total amount of energy in the soundtrack can't rise above the level set. This forces content creators to produce more natural ranges of volume.

If you are producing content for broadcast television, you will almost certainly be delivering your content using the Loudness scale, and this is the scale used in the Essential Sound panel.

2 Increase the height of the Audio 1 track, and zoom in a little so you can see the voice-over clips clearly.

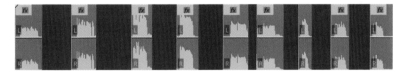

3 Play the sequence to hear the different levels for the voice-over clips.

4 Select all the voice-over clips. The easiest way is to lasso across them, being careful not to select any of the other clips in the sequence.

5 In the Essential Sound panel, click the Dialogue button. This assigns the Dialogue audio type to these clips.

6 Click the title of the Loudness category to display the Loudness options. Clicking a category in this way is a little like clicking a disclosure triangle in the Effect Controls panel—options are displayed or hidden when you click.

7 Click Auto-Match.

Each clip is automatically analyzed and Audio Gain is adjusted to match a standard level for broadcast television dialogue.

As with normalization, which also adjusts clip gain, this adjustment updates the waveforms for the clips.

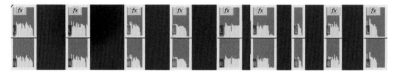

8 Play the sequence to hear the adjustment.

Repairing audio

However hard you try to capture clean audio on location, it's likely some of your footage will have unwanted background noise.

The Essential Sound panel has a number of ways to clean up dialogue clips. Click the title of the Repair category to reveal the options for repairing dialogue.

- **Reduce Noise:** Reduce the level of unwanted noises in the background, like the sound of an air-conditioning unit, rustling clothes, or system noise.

- **Reduce Rumble:** Reduce low-frequency sound, such as engine noise or some wind noise.

- **DeHum:** Reduce electrical interference hum. In North and South America, this is in the 60Hz range, while in Europe, Asia, and Africa, it's in the 50Hz range. If your microphone cable was lying next to a power cable, you may have this intrusive but easy-to-remove unwanted sound.

- **DeEss:** Reduce harsh, high-frequency "ess"-like sounds common in the sibilance part of voice recordings.

- **Reduce Reverb:** When recording in an environment with a lot of reflective surfaces, some of the sound may be reflected back to the microphone as reverb. This can be reduced to make vocals clearer.

Different clips are likely to benefit from one or more of these cleanup features, and often you will use a combination.

The default settings have high enough intensity to make it clear when a repair is enabled. In most cases, you will obtain the best results by starting with a setting of 0 and increasing the intensity until you are happy with the result, minimizing potential distortion.

Let's try cleaning up some power hum.

1 Open the sequence 03 Noise Reduction.

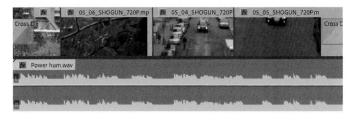

2 Play the sequence to listen to the voice-over.

   This is a simple sequence, with voice-over accompanying some visuals. There's a loud electrical interference power hum in the audio.

3 Select the voice-over clip.

   This clip has already been designated as dialogue, so the dialogue audio options are displayed in the Essential Sound panel.

4 If it's not open already, click the Repair heading in the Essential Sound panel to display the options. Enable DeHum by selecting the check box.

Tip: You can enable and disable audio and video sequence clip names by choosing an option from the Time-line Settings menu.

5 Play the sequence to hear the difference.

The impact is significant! The electrical interference hum was loud but at a specific frequency, which makes removing it relatively straightforward.

This clip has 60Hz hum, so the default option of 60Hz is suitable. If the default option doesn't work, try switching to 50Hz.

Tip: For more challenging audio cleanup, where the repair options in Premiere Pro don't give you a result that is clean enough, try Adobe Audition, which has advanced noise reduction features. Learn more in *Adobe Audition CC Classroom in a Book*.

Reducing noise and reverb

In addition to specific types of background noise like hum and rumble, Premiere Pro offers advanced noise and reverb reduction tools. These audio cleanup effects have simple controls in the Essential Sound panel and more advanced options when accessed via the Effect Controls panel.

Reducing noise

Let's try reducing noise first.

1 Open the sequence 04 Noise and Reverb. This is a simple sequence with clips suffering from background noise and reverb. Play the sequence to familiarize yourself with this challenging audio—lots of unwanted background noise and reverb recorded at noisy location.

The clips in this sequence have already been assigned the Dialogue audio type in the Essential Sound panel, and the Auto-Match option in the Loudness category has been applied.

2 Select the first clip in the sequence. In the Repair section of the Essential Sound panel, select the box to enable the Reduce Noise option. The default setting for the effect intensity is 5.

3 Play the clip in the sequence to hear the difference. The loud rumble that begins at about 00:00:10:00 is immediately much quieter.

4 As with many effects, trial and error will usually yield the best results. Try adjusting the effect intensity—if the effect is too strong, speech might begin to sound like it's underwater or distorted. If the effect is not strong enough, too much of the unwanted background sound might remain. When you have finished experimenting, leave the setting on 5.

▷ **Tip:** You can reset any setting in the Essential Sound panel by double-clicking the control.

Part of the challenge in working with this audio is that some of the low-frequency background sound is close to speech, making it harder to automatically remove. Let's use the more advanced settings.

As soon as you enable the Reduce Noise option in the Essential Sound panel, a DeNoise effect is applied to the selected clip, visible in the Effect Controls panel. If you can't see the Effect Controls panel now, you can access it via the Window menu.

5   Open the Effect Controls panel and make sure the first clip is still selected in the Timeline panel. In the Effect Controls panel, click the Edit button to access the advanced controls for the DeNoise effect. The Clip Fx Editor – DeNoise window opens.

During playback and scrubbing, the DeNoise effect graph shows the original audio (at the bottom) and cleanup adjustment applied (at the top). While the effect controls are open, you can still interact with the Timeline panel, placing the playhead and playing the sequence.

The left end of the graph shows low frequencies, and the right end shows high frequencies.

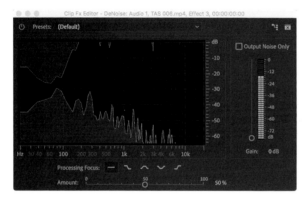

6   Play the clip again and pay particular attention to the activity in the graph when there is no speech, only rumble.

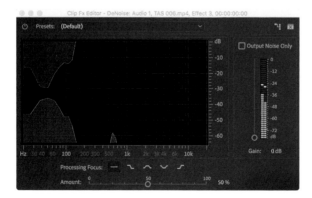

It's clear that the rumble is in the low frequencies.

Several of the controls are quite straightforward.

- **Presets:** You can choose Heavy or Light Noise Reduction—though in fact these two options just adjust the Amount setting.

- **Amount:** This is a more precise version of the slider in the Essential Sound panel. Use this to adjust the intensity of the effect.

- **Output Noise Only:** Enable this option to hear only the noise that is being removed—helpful when assessing whether you're removing too much of the desired audio.

- **Gain:** When reducing noise, you'll naturally be reducing the overall level of the audio. You can adjust the overall gain here to compensate. By looking at the level meter before and after applying the effect, you can see how much gain to apply to keep the overall audio at the original level.

The Processing Focus control is a little less self-explanatory.

By default, the DeNoise effect is applied to the full frequency range of a clip—that means it applies equally to low, medium, and high tone sounds. Using the Processing Focus control, you can selectively apply the effect to particular frequencies. If you hover your pointer over an option, a tooltip describes it, but you'll probably be able to guess which is which from the shape of the button icons.

7 Click to enable the Focus On Lower Frequencies option ![icon] and play the clip again. This sounds good, but let's push the effect a little harder.

● **Note:** When you modify effect settings, related options in the Essential Sound panel are marked ![A] to remind you the settings have been customized.

8 Drag the Amount slider up to around 80%, and play the clip again. Next, try setting the slider to 100% and play the clip.

With the focus on the lower frequencies, even setting the effect to full allows the speech to be audible, and the rumble is almost gone. Even with this more advanced control, you will need to experiment to get the ideal result.

9 For now, set the amount to 80% and close the Clip Fx Editor – DeNoise window.

Reducing reverb

The Reduce Reverb option works in a similar way to the Reduce Noise option. Let's try it.

1 Listen to the the second clip in the sequence. The audio has strong reverb caused by the hard surfaces at the recording location bouncing audio back to the microphone.

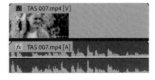

The background noise is less of a challenge in this clip, but the reverb is quite intense.

2   Select the clip and enable the Reduce Reverb option in the Essential Sound panel.

The difference is dramatic! Just as you finessed the Reduce Noise setting, you should experiment with the Reduce Reverb setting to get the optimum balance between the effect being applied with enough intensity and the speech remaining clear.

When you enabled the Reduce Reverb option, a DeReverb effect was applied to the clip, accessible in the Effect Controls panel.

3   The DeReverb effect has similar options to the DeNoise effect, with one significant difference. Click the Edit button for the effect in the Effect Controls panel now.

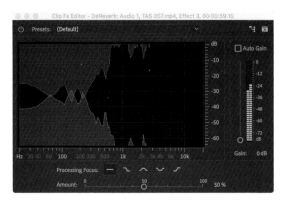

The colors are a little different, but the DeReverb settings are otherwise almost identical to the DeNoise settings. However, you'll notice there's an Auto Gain option in the upper-right corner.

When reducing reverb, reduced overall level is inevitable. The Auto Gain option automatically compensates, making this effect even easier to set up.

4   Make sure the Auto Gain option is enabled, and play the clip to compare the result. Next, close the DeReverb settings window.

5 There are two more clips in this sequence for you to experiment with. Try combining the Reduce Noise and Reduce Reverb options with lower values for a subtler result.

Improving clarity

The Clarity category in the Essential Sound panel gives you three quick and easy ways to improve the quality of spoken audio.

- **Dynamics:** Increases or decreases the dynamic range of the audio—that is, the range of volume between the quietest and loudest parts of the recording.

- **EQ:** Applies different amplitude (volume) adjustments at different frequencies. A list of presets makes selecting useful settings easy.

- **Enhance Speech:** Improves clarity at different frequencies, depending on your selection of a male or female voice.

It's worth experimenting with all three controls, as you'll find dialogue recordings will benefit from different combinations of settings.

Let's try these settings.

1 Open the sequence 05 Clarity.

This sequence has the same content as the 03 Noise Reduction sequence, but there are two versions of the voice-over. The first version is cleaner than the second, which is the same as the version in the original sequence, with the DeHum effect already applied.

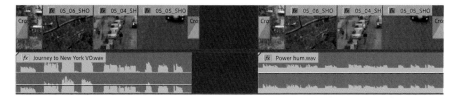

2 Listen to the first voice-over clip.

3 Select the first voice-over clip, and in the Essential Sound panel, expand the Clarity options.

4 Enable Dynamics, and experiment with different levels of adjustment. You can play the sequence while making adjustments in the Essential Sound panel, and the effect will be applied "live." Disable Dynamics when you have tried a few settings.

5 Enable the EQ option, and experiment with the Preset options.

When you apply an EQ preset, a diagram illustrating the adjustment appears. This diagram is based on a Parametric EQ effect (see the "Using the Parametric Equalizer effect" section for more on this effect). You can adjust the Amount slider to add more or less of the effect.

 Vocal Presence EQ preset

6 Play the second voice-over clip.

7 Select the second voice-over clip, and in the Clarity section of the Essential Sound panel select the Enhance Speech option and select Female.

8 Play the second voice-over clip. Try enabling and disabling the Enhance Speech option during playback.

The difference is subtle. In fact, you may need headphones or good-quality studio monitors to clearly detect the improvement. This option clarifies speech to make it more apprehensible, and in some cases this means reducing the power in the lower frequencies.

Making creative adjustments

Below the Clarity section of the Essential Sound panel is the Creative section.

This has just one adjustment, Reverb. The effect can be similar to recording in a large room with lots of reflective surfaces, or it can be subtler.

Experiment with this effect on the first voice-over clip in the 05 Clarity sequence.

Just a small amount of reverb can "thicken" a voice to give it more presence.

Adjusting volume

In addition to adjusting the gain for clips in the Project panel, setting the volume level for clips in a sequence, and applying an automated Loudness adjustment, there's an option to set the clip level at the bottom of the Essential Sound panel.

It's curious that this additional option exists—especially considering the number of ways you can already adjust the volume of your clips.

But there's something special about this volume control: No matter how much you change the volume of your clips with this control, the level will not distort. That is, they won't become so loud that they distort.

Try this now.

1   Open the sequence 06 Level.

This sequence simply contains a reasonably loud version of the voice-over clip you have heard already.

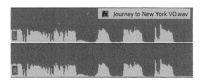

2   Select the clip, and play the sequence. While the sequence plays, use the Clip Volume Level adjustment to increase and decrease the playback level.

Note: Any control in the Essential Sound panel can be reset to its default value by double-clicking it. Knowing this, you don't need to worry about remembering the default settings.

3   Try increasing the level to the maximum, +15dB.

No matter how much you adjust the audio level, it won't distort. Even if you combine a clip gain increase with a clip volume increase (using the rubber band) and then apply this adjustment, the clip will not override.

While it's important to understand all the ways to make audio adjustments, this makes the Essential Sound panel the easiest way to adjust audio level without risking distortion.

4   Reset the Clip Volume Level adjustment by double-clicking the slider.

Using additional audio effects

As mentioned at the beginning of this lesson, there are many additional audio effects available in the Effects panel.

Most of the adjustments you have made until now with the Essential Sound panel have actually been the result of regular audio effects that were added to clips automatically as you worked.

Setting up effects in this way is quicker because all of the Essential Sound panel adjustments work like presets—as soon as you have set things the way you want them in the Essential Sound panel, the effects are set up appropriately in the Effect Controls panel.

Take a look now at the Effect Controls panel, with the clip you worked on in the 06 Level sequence selected.

When you made a Clip Volume Level adjustment in the Essential Sound panel, a Hard Limiter effect was applied to the clip, with settings to match the change you set.

Click the Edit button for the Hard Limiter effect in the Effect Controls panel, and you'll discover all of the settings for this advanced effect are available in case you'd like to change them. If you make changes in the Essential Sound panel, you can watch the controls update for effects in the Effect Controls panel.

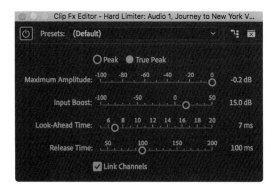

In most cases, the settings applied by the Essential Sound panel will be suitable, but the option to make further subtle changes will always be available.

Close the settings for now, and let's look at some of the other useful audio effects.

Using the Parametric Equalizer effect

Effects listed in the Effects panel can be applied to clips by dragging them onto a clip, or onto multiple selected clips in a sequence.

The Parametric Equalizer effect is a popular effect. It offers a nuanced and intuitive interface for precise audio level adjustment at different frequencies.

It includes a graphic interface you can use to drag level adjustment controls that are linked together to achieve nuanced, natural-sounding audio.

Let's try this effect.

1 Open the sequence 07 Full Parametric EQ. This sequence has one musical clip.

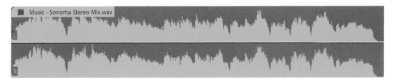

2 Locate the Parametric Equalizer effect in the Effects panel (try using the Search box at the top of the window) and drag the effect onto the clip.

3 Make sure the clip is selected, and in the Effect Controls panel, click the Edit button to access the Custom Setup controls for the Parametric Equalizer effect.

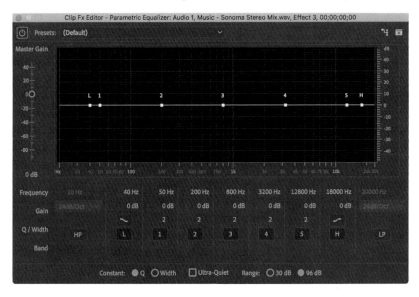

The horizontal axis of the graphic control area indicates frequency, while the vertical axis (labeled on the right) shows amplitude. The blue line across the middle of the graph represents any adjustments you have made, and you can reshape the line directly. Wherever the blue line is higher or lower in the display, adjustments are made to audio level at those frequencies.

You can drag any of the five control points directly, as well as the Low Pass and High Pass controls at the ends.

On the left is an overall Master Gain level adjustment, which offers a quick fix if the changes you make result in audio that is too loud or too quiet overall.

4 Play the clip to get familiar with its sound.

5 Drag Control Point 1 quite a long way down in the graph to reduce the audio level at low frequencies. Listen to the music again.

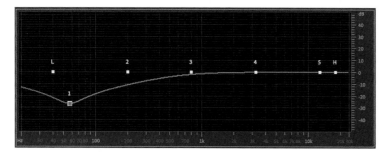

What's special about this interface is that changes you make to one area of the blue line impact surrounding frequencies, resulting in a more natural sound.

The control points you drag have a range of influence that is defined by their Q setting.

In the previous example, Control Point 1 has been set to 57Hz (which is very low frequency), with a gain adjustment of −26.8dB (which is a big gain reduction) and a Q of 2 (which is quite wide).

▶ **Tip:** Another way to use the Parametric EQ effect is to target a specific frequency and either boost it or cut it. You can use this effect to cut a particular frequency, like a high-frequency noise or a low hum.

6 Change the Q factor for Control Point 1 from 2 to 7. You can click the 2 and type in a new setting directly.

The line has a much sharper curve, so the adjustment you have made now applies to fewer frequencies.

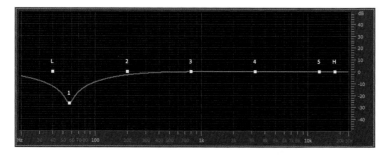

7 Play the sequence to hear the changes.

Let's refine the vocals.

8 Drag Control Point 3 down to about −20dB, and set the Q factor to 1 for a very broad adjustment.

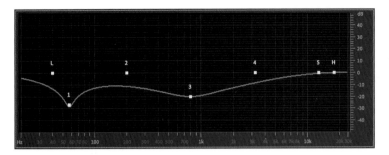

9 Play the sequence to hear the changes—the vocals are much quieter.

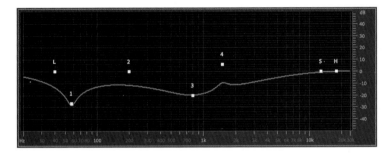

10 Drag Control Point 4 to around 1500Hz, with a gain of +6.0dB. Adjust the Q factor to 3 for more precise adjustment on the EQ adjustment.

Note: Avoid setting the volume too high (the Peak meter line will turn red, and the peak monitors will light up). This can lead to distortion.

▶ **Tip:** If your audio meters are not displayed, you can access them by choosing Window > Audio Meters.

11 Play the sequence to hear the changes.

12 Drag the High frequency filter (the H control) down, to set its gain around −8.0dB to make the highest frequencies quieter.

13 Use the Master Gain control to adjust the overall level. You may need to see your audio meters to find out whether your mix is right.

14 Close the Parametric Equalizer settings.

Note: Listing all the attributes of all the audio effects in Premiere Pro is beyond the scope of this book. To learn more about audio effects, search Premiere Pro Help.

15 Play the sequence to hear the changes.

These are dramatic changes intended to illustrate a technique. You'll usually make subtler adjustments.

Audio adjustments and effects can be modified during playback. You might want to enable looping playback in the Program Monitor rather than clicking repeatedly to play a clip or sequence.

Enable looping playback in the Program Monitor by clicking the Settings menu and choosing Loop.

There are also useful additional buttons available in the Program Monitor Button Editor ![+].

- **Loop** ![icon]: This toggles looped playback on and off.
- **Play Video In To Out** ![icon]: If you have set In and Out marks, the sequence will play just between those marks.

The combination of looped playback and selecting the Play Video In To Out option makes it easier to repeat playback of an individual clip or a group of clips in a sequence.

Audio Plug-in Manager

It's easy to install third-party plug-ins. Choose Premiere Pro CC > Preferences > Audio (macOS) or Edit > Preferences > Audio (Windows). Then click the Audio Plug-in Manager button.

1　Click the Add button to add any directories that contain AU or VST plug-ins. AU plug-ins are Mac only.

2　If needed, click the Scan For Plug-Ins button to find all available plug-ins.

3　Click the Enable All button to activate all of the plug-ins, or select individual plug-ins to activate them alone.

4　Click OK to commit your changes.

Using the Notch effect

The Notch effect removes frequencies near a specified value. The effect targets a frequency range and eliminates those sounds. The effect works well for removing power-line hum and other electrical interference.

1　Open the sequence 08 Notch Filter.

2　Play the sequence, and listen for the electrical hum. You can hear fluorescent light bulbs buzzing.

3　In the Effects panel, locate the Notch Filter effect (not the Simple Notch Filter effect) and apply it to the clip in the sequence. When you do, the clip is auto- matically selected, so the effect controls will appear in the Effect Controls panel.

4　In the Effect Controls panel, click the Edit button for the Notch filter.

The Notch Filter effect looks a lot like the Parametric Equalizer effect and func- tions in a similar way. However, you will notice there's no Q control, which sets the sharpness of the curves. By default each adjustment is extremely acute, and a Notch Width menu allows you to adjust the curves.

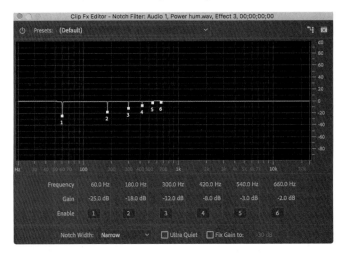

5 While playing the sequence, experiment with presets and listen to the results.

The presets usually apply multiple adjustments. This is because signal interference is often found in multiple harmonic frequencies.

6 Choose 60Hz And Octaves from the Presets menu and then listen to the sequence again to find out whether it's improved.

7 Often, when working with the Notch effect, you'll listen, adjust, and listen again until you get the settings you need.

This audio has hum at 60 Hz, 120 Hz, and 240 Hz. These and more have been targeted by the preset you chose. Turn off control points 4, 5, and 6 by clicking the enable buttons.

Now play the sequence again to review the effect.

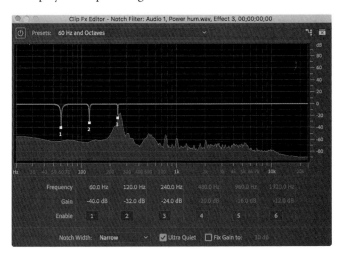

8 Close the effect settings.

Even though the interference was at precise frequencies, it made it difficult to take in the vocals. Now it's removed, and everything sounds much clearer.

When you used the Essential Sound panel to apply the DeHum option, a similar effect was applied to the clip—the DeHummer.

The Notch Filter effect has slightly more advanced controls, so if you don't get the result you need using the Essential Sound panel, try this next.

Removing background noise with Adobe Audition

Adobe Audition offers advanced mixing and effects to improve your overall sound. If you have Audition installed, you can try the following:

1   In Premiere Pro, open the sequence 09 Send to Audition from the Project panel.

2   Right-click the Noisy Audio.aif clip in the Timeline and choose Edit Clip In Adobe Audition.
    A new copy of the audio clip is created and added to your project.

    Audition opens, along with the new clip.

3   In Audition, the stereo clip should be visible in the Editor panel. Audition shows a large waveform for the clip. To use Audition's advanced noise reduction tools, you need to identify part of the clip that's just the noise so Audition knows what to remove.

4   If you don't see Spectral Frequency Display under the waveform, choose View > Show Spectral Frequency Display. Play the clip. The beginning contains a few seconds of just noise, which is perfect for making a selection.

5   Using the Time Selection tool (the I-bar tool in the toolbar), drag to highlight the section of noise you just identified.

continues on next page

6   With the selection active, choose Effects > Noise Reduction/Restoration > Capture Noise Print. You can also press Shift+P. If a dialog appears informing you that the noise print will be captured, click OK to confirm.

7   Choose Edit > Select > Select All to select the entire clip.

8   Choose Effects > Noise Reduction/Restoration > Noise Reduction (process). You can also press Shift+Command+P (macOS) or Shift+Ctrl+P (Windows). A new panel opens so you can process the noise.

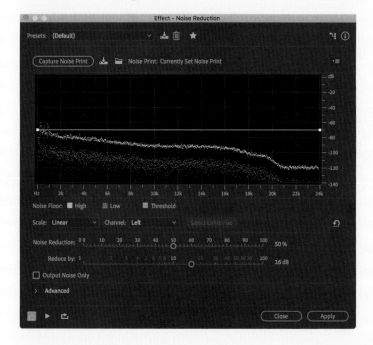

9   Select the Output Noise Only check box. This option allows you to hear only the noise you're removing, which helps you make an accurate selection so you don't accidentally remove too much of the audio you want to keep.

10 Click the Play button at the bottom of the window, and adjust the Noise Reduction and Reduce By sliders to remove noise from the clip. Try not to pull down much or any of the voice.

11 Deselect the Output Noise Only check box and listen to your cleaned-up audio.

12 Sometimes noise reduction results in distortion in vocals. In the Advanced section, there are a number of controls for refining the noise reduction. Experiment with the following:

- Reduce the Spectral Decay Rate option (this will shorten the delay between reducing noise and allowing it to be heard).
- Increase Precision Factor (this will take longer to process but improve results).
- Increase Smoothing (this will soften the adjustment from no noise reduction to full noise reduction based on an automatic selection of specific frequencies).
- Increase Transition Width, which allows some variation in level without applying full noise reduction.

13 When you're happy with the results, click the Apply button to apply the cleanup.

14 Choose File > Close, and save your changes.

15 Saving in Audition automatically updates the clip in Premiere Pro. Switch back to Premiere Pro, where you can listen to the cleaned-up audio clip. You can quit Audition.

Using the Loudness Radar effect

If you are producing content for broadcast television, it's likely you will be supplying media files according to strict delivery requirements.

One of those requirements will relate to the maximum volume for the audio—and there is more than one approach to this.

As described earlier, a popular modern way of measuring the audio level for broadcast is called the Loudness scale, and there's a way to measure your sequence audio using this scale.

You can measure the loudness for clips, for tracks, or for whole sequences. The precise settings you'll require for your audio should be given to you as part of your delivery specifications.

To measure the loudness for a whole sequence, follow these steps—you can try this with the 09 Send to Audition sequence:

1   Switch to the Audio Track Mixer panel (rather than the Audio Clip Mixer). You may need to resize the frame to see all the controls in the Audio Track Mixer.

The Audio Track Mixer allows you to add effects to tracks, rather than clips, and the Master output track is no exception. Unlike the Audio Clip Mixer, the Audio Track Mixer includes the Master track, and this is the part of the interface you want.

2 The controls in the Audio Track Mixer are arranged in columns, one column per audio track plus the Master track at the right. At the top of the Master control, click the tiny triangle to open the Effect Selection menu and choose Special > Loudness Radar.

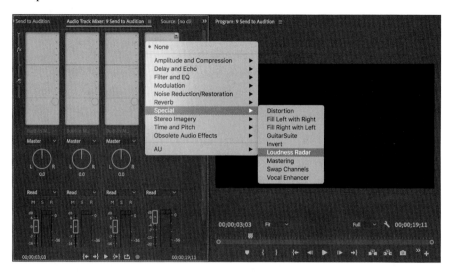

3 The effect appears at the top of the stack, with controls at the bottom.

4 Right-click the Loudness Radar effect name in the Audio Track Mixer and choose Post-Fader.

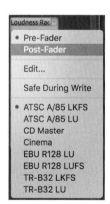

The Fader controls on the Audio Track Mixer adjust the audio level for the track. It's important that the Loudness Radar analyzes the audio level after any Fader adjustments because otherwise adjustments made with the fader are ignored.

5 Double-click the name of the Loudness Radar effect to display the full controls.

6   Press the spacebar to play, or click Play on the Program Monitor.
    During playback, the Loudness Radar monitors loudness and
    displays it as a range of values illustrated in blue, green, and
    yellow (there's also a peak indicator).

    The goal is to keep loudness generally within the green band
    on the Loudness Radar, though what that level will be depends
    on the standard you are working to, and this will be defined by
    your broadcast specifications.

7   When the analysis is complete, close the Loudness Radar
    settings.

The Loudness Radar won't change the audio level. It gives you a
precise measure of Loudness that you can use to guide changes
you'll make to the mix.

You can change the measurement levels indicated by the various
bands in the Loudness Radar by clicking Settings. You can also use a preset, based
on widely used standards, by choosing the Presets menu.

If you set level automatically using the Essential Sound panel you are likely to produce a mix that is within appropriate limits for broadcast. Still, nothing compares
to a professionally produced audio mix where levels for each clip are checked.

Review questions

1 How would you use the Essential Sound panel to set an industry-standard audio level for dialogue clips?

2 What's a quick, easy way to remove electrical interference hum from clips?

3 Where can you find the more detailed controls for the options you set using the Essential Sound panel?

4 How can you send a clip to Adobe Audition directly from the Premiere Pro timeline?

Review answers

1 Select the clips you want to adjust. In the Essential Sound panel, choose Dialogue as the audio type. Then, in the Loudness section, click Auto-Match.

2 Use the DeHum option in the Essential Sound panel to remove electrical interference hum. Try the 60Hz or 50Hz option, depending on the origin of your source footage.

3 Most adjustments you make using the Essential Sound panel are applied as effects to clips. You can find the detailed controls by selecting a clip and looking in the Effect Controls panel.

4 It's easy to send a clip to Audition. Right-click the clip and choose Edit Clip In Adobe Audition.

12 ADDING VIDEO EFFECTS

Lesson overview

In this lesson, you'll learn about the following:

- Working with fixed effects
- Browsing effects with the Effects panel
- Applying and removing effects
- Using effect presets
- Masking and tracking visual effects
- Using keyframing effects
- Exploring frequently used effects
- Using special virtual reality (VR) video effects
- Rendering effects

 This lesson will take about 120 minutes to complete. Please log in to your account on peachpit.com to download the lesson files for this lesson, or go to the "Getting Started" section at the beginning of this book and follow the instructions under "Accessing the lesson files and Web Edition." Store the files on your computer in a convenient location. Your Account page is also where you'll find any updates to the lesson files. Look on the Lesson & Update Files tab to access the most current content.

Adobe Premiere Pro CC features more than 100 video effects. In this lesson, you'll learn the main skills you need to work with all kinds of effects, as well as the some of the more advanced effects. Most effects come with an array of controls, all of which you can change over time using keyframes.

Starting the lesson

You might use video effects for many reasons. They can solve problems with image quality, such as exposure or color balance. They can create complex visual effects through compositing with techniques such as chromakey. They can also help solve a number of production problems, such as camera shake and poorly calibrated color balance.

1 Open Lesson 12.prproj.

2 Save the project as **Lesson 12 Working.prproj**.

3 Switch to the Effects workspace by clicking Effects in the Workspaces panel or by choosing Window > Workspaces > Effects.

4 Reset the workspace by double-clicking the Effects workspace name in the Workspaces panel.

Effects can also serve stylistic purposes. You can alter the color or distort footage, and you can animate the size and position of a clip within the frame. The challenge can be knowing when to use effects and when to keep it simple.

Standard effects can be constrained to elliptical or polygon masks, and these masks can automatically track your footage. For example, you might blur someone's face to hide their identity and have the blur follow them as they move through the shot. You can use the same feature to relight a scene in post-production.

Working with effects

Adobe Premiere Pro makes working with effects easy. You can drag a visual effect onto a clip, as you have already done with audio effects, or you can select the clip and double-click the effect in the Effects panel. In fact, you already know how to apply effects and change their settings. You can combine as many effects as you want on a single clip, which can produce surprising results. Moreover, you can use an adjustment layer to add the same effects to a collection of clips.

When it comes to deciding which video effects to use, the number of choices in Premiere Pro can be a little overwhelming. Many additional effects are available from third-party manufacturers for sale or free of charge.

While the range of effects and their controls can be complex, the techniques you'll use to apply, adjust, and remove effects are straightforward.

Modifying fixed effects

When you add a clip to a sequence, it will automatically have a few effects applied. These effects are called *fixed* effects, or intrinsic effects, and you can think of them as controls for the usual geometric, opacity, speed, and audio properties that every clip should have. You can modify all fixed effects using the Effect Controls panel.

1   If it's not already in the Timeline panel, open the sequence 01 Fixed Effects.

2   Single-click the first clip in the timeline to select it. In the Effect Controls panel, look at the fixed effects applied to this clip.

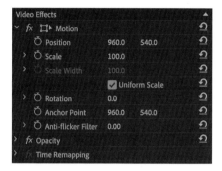

Fixed effects are automatically applied to every clip in a sequence, but they don't change anything until you modify the settings.

3   You may need to click the disclosure triangle ❯ next to a heading or an individual control to display its properties.

- **Motion:** The Motion effect allows you to animate, rotate, and scale a clip. You can also use the Anti-flicker Filter control to decrease shimmering edges for an animated object. This comes in handy when you scale down a high-resolution or interlaced source, and Premiere Pro must resample the image.

- **Opacity:** The Opacity effect lets you control how opaque or transparent a clip is. You can also access special blend modes to create visual effects from multiple layers of video. You'll explore this more in Lesson 14, "Exploring Compositing Techniques."

- **Time Remapping:** This effect lets you slow down, speed up, or reverse playback, and it even lets you freeze a frame.

- **Audio Effects:** If a clip has audio, Premiere Pro displays its Volume, Channel Volume, and Panner controls. You learned about these in Lesson 10, "Editing and Mixing Audio."

4 Click to select the second clip in the sequence and look at the Effect Controls panel.

These effects have keyframes, meaning that their settings change over time. In this case, a small Scale and Pan animation was applied to the clip to create a digital zoom that didn't exist before and to recompose the shot.

You'll explore keyframes later in this lesson.

5 Play the current sequence to compare the two clips.

Using the Effects panel

In addition to the fixed video effects, Premiere Pro has standard effects that change a clip's appearance. Because there are so many to choose from, effects are organized into 17 categories. If you install third-party effects, you may have more choices.

There's an additional category of Obsolete effects. These effects have been replaced with newer, better-designed versions, but they have been kept in Premiere Pro to ensure compatibility with older project files.

Effects are grouped into functions, including Distort, Keying, and Time, to make it easier to navigate them.

Each category has its own bin in the Effects panel.

1 Open the Effects panel.

> **Tip:** The keyboard shortcut to display the Effects panel is Shift+7.

2 In the Effects panel, expand Video Effects.

3 Click the New Custom Bin button  at the bottom of the panel.

> **Note:** With so many Video Effect subfolders, it's sometimes tricky to locate the effect you want. If you know part or all of an effect's name, start typing it in the Find box at the top of the Effects panel. Premiere Pro will display all effects and transitions that contain that letter combination, narrowing the search as you type.

The new custom bin appears in the Effects panel at the bottom of the list (you may need to scroll down to see it). Let's rename it.

4 Click once to select the bin.

5 Click once more, directly on the bin's name (Custom Bin 01), to select it.

6 Change its name to something like **Favorite Effects**.

> Favorite Effects

7 Open any Video Effects folder, and drag a few effects to copy them into your custom bin. You may need to resize the panel to make it easier to drag and drop effects. Choose any effects that sound interesting to you. You can add or remove effects from a custom bin whenever you like. Click the Delete Custom Items button 🗑 to remove a copied effect.

> **Note:** When you add an effect to a custom bin in the Effects panel, you're making a duplicate of that effect. The original effect remains in its original folder. You can use custom bins to create effect categories to suit your work style.

As you browse the video effects, you'll notice icons next to many of the effect names. Understanding these icons might influence your choices when working with effects.

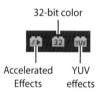

32-bit color

Accelerated Effects YUV effects

Accelerated effects

The Accelerated Effect icon 🔳 indicates that the effect can be accelerated by your graphics processing unit (GPU). The GPU (often called the *video card* or *graphics card*) can greatly enhance the performance of Premiere Pro. The range of cards supported by the Mercury Playback Engine is broad, and with the right card installed, these effects often offer accelerated or even real-time performance and need rendering only on final export, which is also hardware accelerated. You'll find a list of recommended cards on the Premiere Pro product page.

32-bit color (high-bit-depth) effects

Effects with the 32-Bit Color Support icon 🔳 can process in a 32-bits-per-channel mode, which is also called *high-bit-depth* or *float* processing.

You should use high-bit-depth effects whenever possible for maximum quality.

> **Note:** When using any 32-bit effects on a clip, try to use only combinations of 32-bit effects for maximum quality. If you mix and match effects, the non-32-bit effects switch processing back to 8-bit space for that clip.

If you are editing without GPU acceleration, in Software mode, take advantage of high-bit-depth effects by making sure your sequence settings have the Maximum Bit Depth video-rendering option selected. If your project is set to use a hardware-accelerated renderer (in the Project settings), supported accelerated effects will automatically be rendered in 32-bit.

YUV effects

Effects with the YUV icon  process color in YUV. This is particularly important if you're applying color adjustments. Effects without the YUV icon are processed in the computer's native RGB space, which might make adjusting exposure and color less accurate.

YUV effects break down the video into a Y (or luminance) channel and two channels for color information, which is how most video footage is structured natively. Because the brightness of the image is separate from the colors, it's easy to adjust contrast and exposure without shifting colors.

Applying effects

Once you have applied an effect, virtually all the video effect settings are accessible in the Effect Controls panel. You can add keyframes to nearly every setting, making it easy to apply changes over time (just look for settings with a stopwatch icon). In addition, you can use Bezier curves to adjust the velocity and acceleration of those changes.

1 Open the sequence 02 Browse.

© Copyright Maxim Jago 2017

2 Type **white** into the Effects panel Find box to narrow the results. Locate the Black & White video effect.

▶ **Tip:** If you type **black** instead of **white** into the Effects panel Find box, you'll see a fantastic list of presets for lens distortion removal because they relate to a particular camera with the word black in the name. Typing the word **white** instead displays a shorter list of effects to scroll through.

3 Drag the Black & White video effect onto the Run Past clip in the Timeline panel.

This effect immediately converts your full-color footage to black and white, or more accurately, *grayscale*.

4 Make sure the Run Past clip is selected in the Timeline panel, and open the Effect Controls panel.

5 Toggle the Black & White effect off and on by clicking the "fx" button ![fx] next to the effect name in the Effect Controls panel. Be sure the sequence playhead is over this footage clip to view the effect.

Toggling an effect on and off is a good way to see how it works with other effects.

6 Make sure the clip is selected so its settings are displayed in the Effect Controls panel. Click the Black & White effect heading to select it, and press Delete/Backspace.

This removes the effect.

7 Type **direction** into the Effects panel search box to locate the Directional Blur video effect.

8 In the Effects panel, double-click the Directional Blur effect to apply it to the selected clip.

9 In the Effect Controls panel, expand the Directional Blur effect's controls.

10 Set Direction to **75.0** degrees and Blur Length to **45**.

● **Note:** Remember, if you have a clip selected, you can apply effects by double-clicking them in the Effects panel or by dragging them into the Effect Controls panel directly.

▶ **Tip:** The slider limit may be smaller than the number you can enter by typing.

11 It's certainly an interesting result, but now it's impossible to tell what's going on in the image. Click the disclosure triangle to expand the Blur Length control and move the slider to reduce the strength of the effect.

As you change the setting, the result is displayed in the Program Monitor.

12 Click the panel menu for the Effect Controls panel and choose Remove Effects. The Remove Attributes dialog box opens.

● **Note:** You won't always use visual effects to create dramatic results. Sometimes effects are intended to look like in-camera results.

13 The Remove Attributes dialog box lets you select which effects to remove and deselect which effects you want to keep. You want to remove them all, so click OK. This is an easy way to start fresh.

▶ **Tip:** Effects are processed in a particular order, which can lead to unwanted scaling or resizing. You can't reorder fixed effects, but you can bypass them and use other, similar effects. For example, you can use the Transform effect instead of the Motion fixed effect, or you can use the Alpha Adjust effect instead of the Opacity fixed effect. These effects are not identical, but they're a close match, they behave similarly, and they can be placed in any order you choose.

Other ways to apply effects

To make working with effects more flexible, there are three ways to reuse an effect you have already configured.

- You can select an effect from the Effect Controls panel, choose Edit > Copy, select a destination clip (or several clips), and choose Edit > Paste.

- You can copy all the effects from one clip so you can paste them onto another clip, select the clip in the Timeline and choose Edit > Copy, select the destination clip (or clips), and choose Edit > Paste Attributes.

- You can create an effect preset to store a particular effect (or multiple effects) with settings for reuse later. You'll learn about this technique later in this lesson.

Using adjustment layers

Sometimes you'll want to apply an effect to multiple clips. One easy way to do this is to use an *adjustment layer*. The concept is simple: Create an adjustment layer clip that can hold effects, and position it above other clips on the Timeline, on a higher video track. Everything beneath the adjustment layer clip is viewed through it, receiving any effects it contains.

You can easily adjust the duration and opacity of an adjustment layer clip, as you would adjust any graphics clip, making it easy to control which other clips are seen through it. An adjustment layer makes it faster to work with effects because you can change the settings on the layer (a single item) to influence the appearance of several other clips.

Let's add an adjustment layer to a sequence that's already been edited.

1   Open the sequence 03 Multiple Effects.

2   At the bottom right of the Project panel, click the New Item button ⬛ , and choose Adjustment Layer. You may need to resize the Project panel to see the New Item button.

The Adjustment Layer dialog box allows you to specify settings for the new item you're creating. The settings in the dialog box will reflect the settings in the current sequence.

3 Click OK.

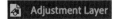

Premiere Pro adds a new adjustment layer to the Project panel.

4 Drag the adjustment layer from the Project panel to the beginning of the Video 2 track in the current sequence in the Timeline panel.

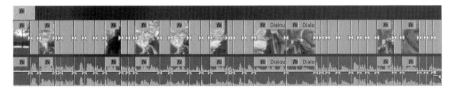

5 Drag to trim the right edge of the adjustment layer so it extends to the end of the sequence.

Let's apply an effect to the adjustment layer. Once the effect is set up, you can adjust the adjustment layer's opacity to change the intensity of the effect.

6 In the Effects panel, search for and locate the Gaussian Blur effect.

7 Drag the effect onto the adjustment layer clip in the sequence.

8 Move the timeline playhead to 27:00 to have a good close-up shot to use when designing the effect.

9 By default, the Guassian Blur effect doesn't change the image. Make sure the adjustment layer clip is selected. In the Effect Controls panel, set Blurriness to a heavy value, like **25.0** pixels. Select the Repeat Edge Pixels option to apply the effect evenly.

Let's blend the adjustment layer with the clips beneath it using a blend mode to create a film look. *Blend modes* let you mix two layers together based on their brightness and color values. You'll learn more about them in Lesson 14, "Exploring Compositing Techniques."

10 With the adjustment layer still selected in the sequence, click the disclosure triangle next to the Opacity control in the Effect Controls panel to view the settings.

11 Choose Soft Light from the Blend Mode menu to create a gentle blend with the footage.

12 Set Opacity to **75%** to reduce the effect.

You can enable and disable the visibility icon ⊙ for the Video 2 track in the Timeline panel to see the before and after states of the effect.

Sending a clip to Adobe After Effects

If you're working with a computer that also has Adobe After Effects installed, you can easily send clips back and forth between Premiere Pro and After Effects. Thanks to the close relationship between Premiere Pro and After Effects, you can seamlessly integrate the two applications more easily than with any other editing platform. This is a useful way to significantly extend the effects capabilities of your editing workflow.

You don't need to learn to use After Effects to get the most out of Premiere Pro. Still, many editors find working with both applications expands their creative toolset in exciting ways.

The process you use to share clips is called Dynamic Link. With Dynamic Link you can seamlessly exchange clips with no unnecessary rendering.

If you'd like to try this, follow these steps:

For After Effects to complete installation, it needs to be started at least once so that you can confirm the default preferences. Do this before following this workflow.

1   Open the sequence AE Dynamic Link.

2   This sequence has the same clip repeated multiple times, so you can experiment and compare multiple examples. Right-click the first instance of the clip in the sequence and choose Replace With After Effects Composition.

3   If it's not running already, After Effects launches. If the After Effects Save As dialog appears, enter a name and location for the After Effects project. Name the project **Lesson 12-01.aep** and save it to a new folder inside the Lessons folder.

    After Effects creates a new composition, which inherits the sequence settings from Premiere Pro. The new composition is named based on the Premiere Pro project name, followed by "Linked Comp."

    After Effects compositions are analogous to Premiere Pro sequences.

    Clips become layers in After Effects compositions to make it easier to work with advanced controls on the Timeline panel.

    There are lots of ways to apply effects with After Effects. To keep things simple, let's work with animation presets (these are similar to effect presets in Premiere Pro).

    For more on effects workflows, see *Adobe After Effects CC Classroom in a Book*.

4 If the composition isn't already open, look for it in the After Effects project panel, and double-click to load it. It should be called Lesson 12 Working Linked Comp 01 (the number may be higher if you have tried this workflow before). Click the Laura_02.mp4 layer in the Timeline panel to select it.

5 Locate the Effects & Presets panel (you can find this in the Window menu if it's not on-screen already). Click the disclosure triangle to expand the *Animation Presets category.

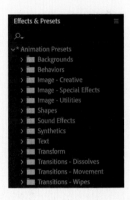

The animation presets in After Effects use standard built-in effects to achieve impressive results. They are an excellent shortcut to producing a professional finish for your work.

6 Expand the Image – Creative folder. You may need to resize the panel a little to read the full preset names.

7 Double-click the Contrast – Saturation preset to apply it to the selected layer.

8 In the Timeline panel, make sure the clip is still selected, and press the E key to view any applied effects. You can click the disclosure triangles for each effect and effect setting to see the controls, right inside the Timeline panel.

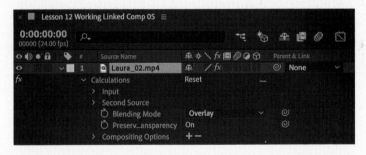

The Contrast – Saturation preset actually uses an effect with a different name, Calculations, to make changes to the appearance of the clip.

9 Now look at the Effect Controls panel. The same effect is displayed here.

10 Press the spacebar to play the clip.

After Effects displays the clip, with the effect applied, as fast as possible (depending on the power of your editing system). The green line at the top of the Timeline panel indicates a temporary preview has been created. Only playback of the highlighted section of the timeline is likely to be smooth.

The effect is subtle but gives richer color saturation and stronger contrast to a shot that would otherwise be a little flat.

11 Choose File > Save.

continues on next page

12 Switch back to Premiere Pro and play the sequence to view the results. You can repeat this process with other clips. If an After Effects project is already open when you send a clip, it will be added as a new composition to the existing project, rather than needing a new project.

13 Quit After Effects.

The original clip on the Timeline in Premiere Pro has been replaced with the dynamically linked After Effects composition. Any changes made in After Effects will updated automatically in Premiere Pro

The frames are processed in the background and handed off from After Effects to Premiere Pro. To improve preview playback performance in Premiere Pro, you can select the clip in the Timeline and choose Sequence > Render Effects In To Out.

Working with master clip effects

While all the effects work you have performed so far has been applied to clips on the Timeline, Premiere Pro also allows you to apply effects to master clips in the Project panel. You use the same visual effects and work with them in the same way. With master clips, any instance of a clip, or part of a clip, you add to a sequence will inherit the effects you have applied. You can even apply master clip effects *after* adding clips to sequences and the sequences will update—a powerful way to make adjustments to multiple clips segments in a single step.

For example, you could add a color adjustment to a clip in the Project panel so that it matches other camera angles in a scene. Each time you use that clip or part of that clip in a sequence, the adjustment will already be applied. Even if you don't make the adjustment until after the scene is edited, you can use a master clip effect to quickly match the colors.

Try working with a master clip effect now.

1 Open the sequence 04 Master Clip Effects.

This has one clip, Laura_02, edited five times into the same sequence. The copies of the clip are divided by a series of other, similar shots. Position the playhead over the first instance of the Laura_02 clip.

2 Locate the clip Laura_02 in the Project panel.

3 In the Project panel, double-click the Laura_02.mp4 clip to view it in the Source Monitor. Don't double-click the clip in the sequence because this will open the wrong instance for master clip effects.

You now have the same clip open in the Source Monitor (the master clip) and displayed in the Program Monitor (the sequence segment), so you can see how the changes affect the sequence as you apply them.

Note: If you want to open the Project panel instance of a clip you are viewing on the Timeline, position the playhead over the clip, select it, and press the F key. This is the keyboard shortcut for Match Frame, which opens the original master clip in the Source Monitor at the same frame as that displayed in the Program Monitor.

4 In the Effects panel, type **100** in the Find box to quickly locate the Lumetri Look effect preset named Cinespace 100.

5 Drag the Cinespace 100 effect into the Source Monitor.

This applies the effect to the master clip.

6 Click the Source Monitor to make sure it's the active panel, and open the Effect Controls panel to see the effect options.

Tip: You can also apply an effect to a master clip by dragging the effect onto the clip directly in the Project panel, or by selecting a clip in a sequence and clicking the master clip name at the top left of the Effect Controls panel and dragging the effect into that panel.

Note: Selection is critical in Premiere Pro. Clicking to activate the Source Monitor before going to the Effect Controls panel is necessary to see the correct options.

Because you applied the effect to the clip in the Source Monitor and then selected the Source Monitor to make it active, the Effect Controls panel shows the effect applied to the master clip, rather than the Timeline instance of the clip.

This is a Lumetri Color effect, and you will be learning a lot more about these in Lesson 13, "Improving Clips with Color Correction and Grading."

7   Because the effect has been applied to the master clip, every instance of the clip in the sequence shows the results. Play some of the sequence to see the effect is applied to every copy of the Laura_02 clip.

> **Tip:** You can quickly tell whether you're looking at Source effect settings or sequence clip effect settings by seeing whether the fixed effect controls are displayed.

The result of the effect is displayed in the Source Monitor *and* the Program Monitor because sequence clips inherit their master clip effects dynamically.

From now on, anytime you use this clip, or part of it, in a sequence, Premiere Pro will include the same effect.

However, while the master clip has the effect applied, none of the Timeline instances of the clip (the sequence clips) has the effect applied.

8   Click once on any of the sequence instances of the Laura_02 clip on the Timeline to select it, and look in the Effect Controls panel—no Lumetri Color effect, just the usual fixed effects (which are applicable only to sequence clips, not clips in the Project panel).

At the top of the Effect Controls panel there are two tabs. The tab on the left shows the name of the master clip, Master * Laura_02.mp4.

The tab on the right shows the name of the sequence followed by the name of the sequence clip, 04 Master Clip Effects * Laura_02.mp4.

Because you selected the clip in the sequence, the tab on the right is highlighted in blue, showing that you're working on that instance of the clip.

There's no Lumetri Color effect displayed because you haven't applied the effect to the Timeline instance of the clip.

9   In the Effect Controls panel, click the tab at the top that shows the master clip name.

You'll see the master clip effect options.

10 Experiment with the controls for the Lumetri Color effect and then play the sequence. You'll see the changes you apply on an instance of the clip.

Master clip effects provide a powerful way to manage effects in Premiere Pro. You may need to experiment a little to make the most of them. You use the same visual effects as you would use on the timeline, so the techniques you're learning in this book will work the same way, but the planning is a little different.

You can tell a master clip effect is applied to a clip because the "fx" badge has a red underline ▣ .

Masking and tracking visual effects

All standard visual effects can be constrained to elliptical, polygon, or custom masks, which you can manually animate using keyframes. Premiere Pro can also motion-track your shots to animate the position of the masks you create, following the action with the constrained special effect.

Masking and tracking effects are great ways to hide a detail like a face or logo behind a blur. You can also use the technique to apply subtle creative effects or modify the lighting in a shot.

Continue working with the 04 Master Clip Effects sequence.

1 Position the playhead over the second clip in the sequence, Evening Smile.

It looks good, but it would benefit from a stronger light on the subject to help separate the foreground from the background.

2 Search the Effects panel for the Brightness & Contrast effect.

3 Apply this effect to the clip.

4 In the Effect Controls panel, scroll down to the Brightness & Contrast controls. Choose the following settings:

- Brightness **35**

- Contrast **25**

You can set these levels by clicking the blue numbers and typing the new setting, by dragging the blue numbers, or by expanding the controls and using the sliders.

This effect changes the entire picture. You're going to constrain the effect to just one area of the shot.

⬤ **Note:** This example uses a vivid adjustment to illustrate a technique. You will usually make subtler adjustments.

Just under the name of the Brightness & Contrast effect in the Effect Controls panel, you'll see three buttons that allow you to add a mask to the effect.

5   Click the first button to add an elliptical mask.

Immediately, the effect is constrained to the mask you just created. You can add multiple masks to an effect. If you select a mask in the Effect Controls panel, you can click and modify the shape in the Program Monitor.

6   Position the playhead at the start of the clip, and use the mask handles in the Program Monitor to reposition the mask so it covers subject's face and hair. You may find it helpful to adjust the Zoom level for the Program Monitor to see beyond the edges of the image.

If you deselect the mask, the controls will disappear—select the name of the mask, Mask (1), to display the controls again.

7   Feathering softens the edge of the mask. Set Mask Feather to about **240**.

If you deselect the mask in the Effect Controls panel, to hide the mask handles in the Program Monitor, you'll see that you have lifted the area around the subject's face, with a natural return to regular lighting in the rest of the picture. Now you just need the mask to follow the moving video.

8 Make sure the playhead is still on the first frame of the clip. Click the Track Selected Mask Forward button ▶ in the Effect Controls panel, just under the mask name, Mask (1).

The movement is quite subtle, so it should be easy for Premiere Pro to follow the action. If the mask stops following the clip, click Stop, reposition the mask, and begin again.

9 Deselect the mask by clicking the background of the Effect Controls panel, or an empty track in the Timeline panel, and play the sequence to view the result.

Premiere Pro can also track backward so that you can select an item partway through a clip and then track in both directions to create a natural path for the mask to follow.

In this example you're making a subtle lighting adjustment, but almost any visual effect can be constrained to a mask in this way. You can even add multiple masks to the same effect.

Using keyframing effects

When you add keyframes to an effect, you're setting particular values at that moment in time. One keyframe will keep information for one setting. If, for example, you were intending to keyframe Position, Scale, and Rotation, you would need three separate keyframes.

Set keyframes at precise moments where you need a particular setting and let Premiere Pro work out how to animate the controls between them.

Note: Be sure to move the playhead over the clip you're working with when applying effects so you can view your changes as you work. Selecting the clip alone will not make it visible in the Program Monitor.

Adding keyframes

You can change almost all parameters for all video effects over time using keyframes. For example, you can have a clip gradually become out of focus, change color, or lengthen its shadow.

1 Open the sequence 05 Keyframes.

2 View the sequence to get familiar with the footage and then position the Timeline playhead over the first frame of the clip.

3 In the Effects panel, locate the Lens Flare effect and apply it to the clip in the sequence. This is not a subtle effect, but it illustrates keyframes beautifully.

4 In the Effect Controls panel, select the Lens Flare effect heading. With the effect selected, the Program Monitor displays a small control handle. Use the handle to reposition the lens flare to match the following figure so that the center of the effect is near the top of the waterfall.

5 Make sure the Effect Controls panel timeline is visible. If it isn't, click the Show/Hide Timeline View button ▶ next to the clip name at the top right of the panel to toggle the display.

6 Click the stopwatch icons to toggle animation for the Flare Center and Flare Brightness properties. Clicking the Stopwatch icon enables keyframing and adds a keyframe at the current location with the current settings.

7 Move the playhead to the last frame of the clip.

You can drag the playhead directly in the Effect Controls panel. Make sure you see the last frame of video and not black (which would be the first frame of the next clip if there were one).

8 Adjust Flare Center and Flare Brightness settings so the flare drifts across the screen with the camera pan and gets brighter. Use the following figure for guidance.

9 Deselect the Lens Flare effect and play the sequence to watch the effect animate over time. You may need to render the sequence for full frame rate playback, by choosing Sequence > Render Effects In To Out.

Adding keyframe interpolation and velocity

Keyframe interpolation changes the behavior of an effect setting as it moves between keyframes with different settings. The default behavior you've seen so far is linear; in other words, a constant change between keyframes. What generally works better is something that mirrors your real-world experience or exaggerates it, such as gradual acceleration or deceleration.

Premiere Pro offers a way to control those changes: keyframe interpolation and the Velocity graph. Keyframe interpolation is easy and simplified, whereas adjusting the Velocity graph can be complex but more precise.

The Velocity graph appears on the right side of the Effect Controls panel, along with the keyframes, when you expand a property by clicking its disclosure triangle ❯.

1 Open the sequence 06 Interpolation.

2 Position the playhead at the beginning of the clip and select the clip.

A Lens Flare effect has already been applied to this clip and is currently animated. However, the movement begins before the camera, which isn't very natural-looking.

3 Toggle the Lens Flare effect off and on by clicking the "fx" button 𝑓𝑥 next to the effect name in the Effect Controls panel so you can see the result.

▶ **Tip:** Be sure to use the Next Keyframe and Previous Keyframe buttons to move between keyframes efficiently. This will keep you from adding unwanted keyframes.

4   In the Timeline view of the Effect Controls panel, right-click the first keyframe for the Flare Center property.

5   Choose the Temporal Interpolation > Ease Out method to create a gentle transition into the move from the keyframe.

6   Right-click the second keyframe for the Flare Center property and choose Temporal Interpolation > Ease In. This creates a gentle transition from the stationary position of the last keyframe.

7   Let's modify the Flare Brightness property. Click the first keyframe for Flare Brightness and then hold down the Shift key and click the second keyframe so both are active, highlighted in blue.

You could also click the Flare Brightness property name, which selects keyframes for the property. However, there will be occasions when you'll want to select specific keyframes, so it's worth remembering the Shift key.

Keyframes

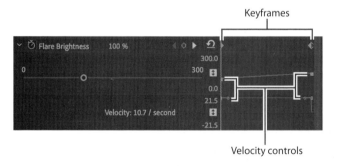

Velocity controls

8   Right-click either one of the Flare Brightness keyframes and choose Auto Bezier to create a gentle animation between the two properties. Because both keyframes were selected, both are changed.

Note: When working with position-related parameters, the context menu for a keyframe will offer two types of interpolation: spatial (related to location) and temporal (related to time). You can make spatial adjustments in the Program Monitor as well as in the Effect Controls panel if you select the effect in the Effect Controls panel. You can make temporal adjustments on the clip in the Timeline and in the Effect Controls panel. These motion-related topics are covered in Lesson 9, "Putting Clips in Motion."

Understanding interpolation methods

Here's a rundown of the keyframe interpolation methods available in Premiere Pro:

- **Linear:** This is the default behavior and creates a uniform rate of change between keyframes.
- **Bezier:** This lets you manually adjust the shape of the graph on either side of a keyframe. Beziers allow for sudden or smooth acceleration into or out of a keyframe.
- **Continuous Bezier:** This method creates a smooth rate of change through a keyframe. Unlike regular Bezier keyframes, if you adjust one handle of a Continuous Bezier keyframe, the handle on the other side moves equally to maintain a smooth transition through the keyframe.
- **Auto Bezier:** This method creates a smooth rate of change through a keyframe even if you change the keyframe value. If you choose to manually adjust the keyframe's handles, it changes to a Continuous Bezier point, retaining the smooth transition through the keyframe. The Auto Bezier option can occasionally produce unwanted motion, so try one of the other options first.
- **Hold:** This method changes a property value without a gradual transition (a sudden effect change). The graph following a keyframe with the Hold interpolation applied appears as a horizontal straight line.
- **Ease In:** This method slows down the value changes entering a keyframe and converts it to a Bezier keyframe.
- **Ease Out:** This method gradually accelerates the value changes leaving a keyframe and converts it to a Bezier keyframe.

9 Play back the animation to watch the changes you've made.

Let's refine the keyframes with the Velocity graph.

10 Hover the pointer over the Effect Controls panel and then, if your keyboard has the key, press ` (accent grave) to maximize the panel full-screen; or double-click the panel name. This will give you a clearer view of the keyframe controls.

11 If necessary, click the disclosure triangles next to the Flare Center and Flare Brightness properties to show the adjustable properties.

The Velocity graph shows the velocity between keyframes. Any sudden drops or jumps represent sudden changes in acceleration—*jerks*, in physics parlance. The farther the point or line is from the center, the greater the velocity.

12 Select a keyframe and then adjust its extended handle to change the steepness of the velocity curve.

 After adjusting the second keyframe for the Flare Center control

13 Press the ` (accent grave) key, or double-click the panel name, to restore the Effect Controls panel.

14 Play back your sequence to see the impact of your changes. Experiment some more until you have the hang of keyframes and interpolation.

Perhaps the change to the velocity of the keyframes for the Flare Center isn't enough to make the movement appear perfectly natural. Try dragging the first keyframe later to better match the camera movement, and adjust the velocity keyframes accordingly.

Using effect presets

To save time on repeated tasks, Premiere Pro supports effect presets. You'll find that there are several prebuilt presets included for specific tasks already, but the true power of effects lies in creating your own presets to solve repetitive tasks. A single preset can contain more than one effect and can even include keyframes for animation.

Using built-in presets

The effect presets provided with Premiere Pro are useful for tasks such as beveling, picture-in-picture (PIP) effects, and stylized transitions.

1 Open the sequence 07 Presets.

This sequence has a slow start—the emphasis is on the texture of the background. Let's use a preset to add visual interest to the opening of the shot.

2 In the Effects panel, click the X to clear the Search box at the top of the panel. Browse inside the Presets > Solarizes category to find the Solarize In preset.

3 Drag the Solarize In preset onto the clip in the sequence.

4   Play back the sequence to watch the Solarize effect transform the opening.

© Maxim Jago 2016

5   Select the clip and view its controls in the Effect Controls panel.

6   There are two keyframes, relatively close together. You may need to zoom in by adjusting the navigator at the bottom of the Effect Controls panel to see them both.

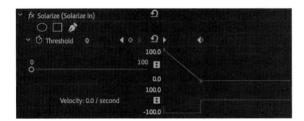

Experiment with adjusting the position of the second keyframe in the Effect Controls panel to customize the effect. If you extend the timing of the effect, it creates a more pleasing start to the shot.

Saving effect presets

Although there are several built-in effect presets to choose from, creating your own is also easy. You can also import and export presets to share them between editing systems.

1   Open the sequence 08 Creating Presets.

    This sequence has two clips, each with an adjustment layer on the V2 track and a title on the V3 track.

2   Play the sequence to watch the initial animation.

3   Select the first instance of the "Laura in the snow" title clip on V3 and take a look at the Effect Controls panel. A Fast Blur effect has been applied to the title, and there are keyframes animating several settings.

4   Click in the Effect Controls panel to make it active and choose Edit > Select All to select all the effects applied to the clip.

You can also select individual effects if you want to include only some of them in the preset.

5   Right-click any of the selected effects in the Effect Controls panel and choose Save Preset.

6   In the Save Preset dialog, name the effect **Title Animation**. Click in the Description box and type **Clip blurs into view**.

When you apply an animated preset to a clip with a different duration, Premiere Pro needs to know how to distribute the keyframes.

There are three options.

- **Scale:** Proportionally scales the source keyframes to the length of the target clip. Any existing keyframes on the original clip are deleted.

- **Anchor To In Point:** Preserves the position of the first keyframe as well as the relationship of other keyframes in a clip. Other keyframes are added to the clip relative to its In point.

- **Anchor To Out Point:** Preserves the position of the last keyframe as well as the relationship of other keyframes in a clip. Other keyframes are added to the clip relative to its Out point.

7   For this preset, choose Anchor To In Point so the timing matches at the start of each clip the preset is applied to.

8   Click OK to store the effects and keyframes as a new preset.

9   In the Effects panel, locate the Presets category and your newly created Title Animation preset. Hover the pointer over the preset to see the description you added appear as a tooltip.

10 Drag the new Title Animation preset onto the second instance of the "Laura in the snow" title clip on the V3 track in the Timeline.

11 Watch the sequence play back to see the newly applied title animation.

You can change the settings for a preset by right-clicking it and choosing Preset Properties, or by double-clicking it.

▶ **Tip:** Effect presets can be exported and imported so they can be shared. You'll find a number of free presets at https://premierepro.net/presets

Using multiple GPUs

If you'd like to speed up the rendering of effects or the export of clips, consider adding a GPU card, or external GPU. If you're using a tower or workstation, you may have an additional slot that can support a second graphics card. An additional GPU won't improve playback performance when previewing real-time effects or displaying multiple layers of video, but Premiere Pro takes full advantage of computers with multiple GPU cards to significantly accelerate render and export times. You can find additional details about supported cards on the Adobe website.

Using frequently used effects

In this lesson, you've explored several effects. Although it's beyond the scope of this book to explore all the options, here are a few additional effects that are useful in many editing situations. We'll be exploring color adjustments in the next lesson.

Applying image stabilization and rolling shutter reduction

The Warp Stabilizer effect can remove jitter caused by camera movement (which is more and more common with today's lightweight cameras). The effect is useful because it can remove unstable parallax-type movements (where images appear to shift on planes).

Let's explore the effect.

1 Open the sequence 09 Warp Stabilizer.

2 Play the first clip in the sequence to see the wobbly shot.

3 In the Effects panel, locate the Warp Stabilizer VFX effect and apply it to the shot.

As the clip is analyzed, a banner across the footage lets you know you'll need to wait before working with the effect. There's also a detailed progress indicator in the Effect Controls panel. The analysis takes place in the background, so you can carry on working while waiting for it to complete.

▶ **Tip:** If you notice that some of the details in the shot appear to wobble, you may be able to improve the overall effect. In the Advanced section, select Detailed Analysis. This makes the Analysis phase do extra work to find elements to track. You can also use the Enhanced Reduction option from the Rolling Shutter Ripple option in the Advanced category. These options are slower to calculate but produce superior results.

4 Once the analysis has completed, you can adjust settings in the Effect Controls panel to improve results by choosing options that better suit the shot.

- **Result:** You can choose Smooth Motion to retain the general camera movement (albeit stabilized), or you can choose No Motion to attempt to remove all camera movement. For this exercise, choose Smooth Motion.

- **Method:** You can use the four methods available. The two most powerful, because they warp and process the image more heavily, are Perspective and Subspace Warp. If either method creates too much distortion, you can try switching to Position, Scale, Rotation or just to Position.

- **Smoothness:** This option specifies how much of the original camera movement should be retained for Smooth Motion. Use a higher value to smooth out the shot the most. Experiment with this shot until you're happy with its stability.

5   Play back the clip. The impact is pretty dramatic.

6   Repeat the process for the second clip in the sequence. This time, set the Warp
    Stabilizer Result menu to No Motion.

This is a common example of a shot that was intended to be static but, being
handheld, has a little wobble. Warp Stabilizer is effective at locking these kinds
of shots in position.

Using the Timecode and Clip Name effects

If you need to send a review copy of a sequence to a client or colleague, the Timecode and Clip Name effects are useful. You can apply the Timecode effect to an
adjustment layer and have it generate a visible timecode for the entire sequence.
You can enable a similar timecode overlay when exporting media, but the effect has
more options.

Note: If you
work with multiple
sequences with differ-
ent format settings in a
single project, it's worth
naming adjustment lay-
ers to make it easier to
identify their resolution.

This is helpful because it allows others to make specific feedback based on a unique
point in time. You can control the display of position, size, opacity, the timecode
itself, and its format and source.

1   Open the sequence 10 Timecode Burn-In.

2   At the bottom right of the Project panel, click the New Item button ⬛, and
    choose Adjustment Layer. Click OK.

    A new adjustment layer is added to the Project panel, with settings that match
    your current sequence.

3   Drag the new adjustment layer to the beginning of track V2 in the current
    sequence.

4   Drag the right edge of the new adjustment layer to the right to trim it to the end
    of the sequence. The adjustment layer should cover all three clips.

5　In the Effects panel, locate the Horizontal Flip effect. Drag it onto the adjustment layer to apply it. This switches the video horizontally, giving the effect of changing the direction of movement.

This effect works well with this kind of content but may not work if there is visible text or a recognizable logo in the picture.

There are no additional controls for this effect.

Now let's apply an effect that will display the name of each clip in the exported movie. This will make it easier to get specific feedback from a client or collaborator.

6　In the Effects panel, search for the Clip Name effect.

7　Apply the Clip Name effect to the adjustment layer clip.

By default, the effect shows the name of the clip you applied it to, which in this case is Adjustment Layer—not very useful!

Tip: You can click the Clip Name effect heading in the Effect Controls panel and then drag the anchor point for the name displayed in the Program Monitor to reposition it.

8　In the Effect Controls panel, in the Clip Name section, choose Video 1 from the Source Track menu, and set the size to **25%**. Now the clip names from the V1 track are displayed.

9　Clear the Effects panel Search box by clicking the X.

Using immersive video effects

Premiere Pro includes comprehensive tools and effects for equirectangular 360 video (often referred to as *VR video* or *immersive video*).

The effects workflow for 360 video is similar to the workflow for any other kind of video. However, there are dedicated effects available that take into account the wraparound nature of 360 video.

The fact that 360 video seamlessly surrounds the viewer and can connect on all sides (depending on the configuration) does not impact most visual effects. The exception is any effect that generates changes to surrounding pixels, such as blurs and glows. These effects make changes to multiple pixels, and only effects specially designed to work with seamless 360 video images will result in an image without a visible join along the original edges.

Let's try this.

1 Open the sequence 11 Immersive Video.

This is equirectangular 360 video, so let's switch to the VR video viewing mode in the Program Monitor.

2 Use the Program Monitor Settings menu to choose VR Video > Enable.

3 The viewing angle is a little narrow by default. Go to the Program Monitor Settings menu again, and choose VR Video > Settings.

4 Set Monitor View Horizontal to **150** and click OK.

When producing immersive video, you'll want to choose the viewing angle of the intended VR headset.

5 In the Effects panel, find the VR Glow effect, in the Video Effects > Immersive Video category. Add the effect to the video clip in the sequence.

This is a processing-intensive effect, and you may find the preview is slower to update than when working with other effects.

6 Try dragging the image in the Program Monitor to see different views.

The original video clip has some minor "stitching" errors, where the overlap between sections of the image is visible. However, the glow effect is seamless.

7 Like other effects, you'll find settings for the VR Glow effect in the Effect Controls panel. Experiment with the VR Glow settings.

8 When you have finished, use the Program Monitor Settings menu to deselect VR video mode.

Removing lens distortion

Action and point-of-view (POV) cameras such as the GoPro and DJI Phantom are popular, especially with the advent of affordable aerial camera mounts. While the results can be amazing, the wide-angle lenses can introduce unwanted distortion.

The Lens Distortion effect can be used to introduce the appearance of lens distortion as a creative look. It can also be used to correct lens distortion. Premiere Pro has a number of built-in presets intended to correct distortion from popular cameras. You'll find the presets in the Effects panel, under Lens Distortion Removal.

Remember, you can make a preset from any effect, so if you are working with a camera that has no existing preset, you can always create your own.

Rendering all sequences

If you have several sequences with effects you want to render, you can render them all as a batch, without opening each sequence to render it individually.

Simply select the sequences you would like to render in the Project panel and choose Sequence > Render Effects In To Out.

All effects that need to render in the selected sequences will be rendered.

Rendering and replacing

If you are working on a low-powered system and your media is high resolution, you may find media tends not to preview without dropping frames. You may also see dropped frames when working with dynamically linked After Effects compositions or complex third-party visual effects that don't support GPU acceleration.

If all your media is high resolution, you may decide to use the proxy workflow, which allows you to switch between full-resolution and lower-resolution media file playback.

However, if just one or two clips are difficult to play back, you also have the option to render the clips as a new media file and replace the original item in a sequence quickly and easily.

To replace a sequence clip segment with a version that's easier to play back, right-click the clip and choose Render And Replace.

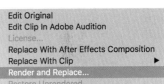

The Render And Replace dialog has similar options to the proxy work-flow. Here are the main settings:

- **Source:** Create a new media file that matches the frame rate and frame size of the sequence or of the original media, or use a preset.

- **Format:** Specify your preferred file type. Different formats give access to different encoders.

- **Preset:** While you can use a custom preset created with Adobe Media Encoder, several are included by default—choose one here.

Once you have chosen a preset and a location for the new file, click OK and the sequence clip is replaced.

A rendered and replaced clip is no longer directly linked to the original media—it's a new media file. This means, for example, changes made to a dynamically linked After Effect composition will not update in Premiere Pro. To restore the link to the original item, right-click the clip and choose Restore Unrendered.

Review questions

1 What are two ways to apply an effect to a clip?

2 List three ways to add a keyframe.

3 Dragging an effect onto a clip turns on its parameters in the Effect Controls panel, but you don't see the effect in the Program Monitor. Why not?

4 Describe how you can apply one effect to a range of clips.

5 Describe how to save multiple effects to a custom preset.

Review answers

1 Drag the effect to the clip, or select the clip and double-click the effect in the Effects panel.

2 Move the playhead in the Effect Controls panel to where you want a keyframe and activate keyframing by clicking the "Toggle animation" button; move the playhead and click the Add/Remove Keyframe button; and with keyframing activated, move the playhead to a position and change a parameter.

3 You need to move the Timeline playhead to the selected clip to see it in the Program Monitor. Selecting a clip does not move the playhead to that clip.

4 You can add an adjustment layer above the clips you want to affect. You can then apply an effect that will modify all the clips below the layer. You can also select the clips you would like to apply the effect to and then drag the effect onto the group or double-click the effect in the Effects panel.

5 You can click the Effect Controls panel and choose Edit > Select All. You can also Command-click (macOS) or Ctrl-click (Windows) multiple effects in the Effect Controls panel. Once the effects are selected, choose the Save Preset command from the Effect Controls panel menu.

13 IMPROVING CLIPS WITH COLOR CORRECTION AND GRADING

Lesson overview

In this lesson, you'll learn about the following:

- Working in the Color workspace
- Using the Lumetri Color panel
- Using vectorscopes and waveforms
- Comparing and matching clip colors
- Using color correction effects
- Fixing exposure and color balance problems
- Working with special color effects
- Creating a look

 This lesson will take about 150 minutes to complete. Please log in to your account on peachpit.com to download the lesson files for this lesson, or go to the "Getting Started" section at the beginning of this book and follow the instructions under "Accessing the lesson files and Web Edition." Store the files on your computer in a convenient location.

Your Account page is also where you'll find any updates to the lesson files. Look on the Lesson & Update Files tab to access the most current content.

Editing your clips together is just the first part of the creative process. Now it's time to work with color. In this lesson, you'll learn some key techniques for improving the look of your clips to give them a distinctive atmosphere.

Starting the lesson

So far you've organized your clips, built sequences, and applied special effects. All of these skills come together when working with color correction.

Consider the way your eyes register color and light, the way cameras record it, and the way your computer screen, a television screen, a video projector, a phone, a tablet, or a cinema screen displays it. There are a great many factors when considering the final look of your production.

Premiere Pro has multiple color correction tools and makes it easy to create your own presets. In this lesson, you'll begin by learning some fundamental color correction skills and then meet some of the most popular color correction special effects, before using them to deal with some common color correction challenges.

1   Open Lesson 13.prproj in the Lesson 13 folder.

2   Save the project as **Lesson 13 Working.prproj**.

3   Select Color in the Workspaces panel, or choose Window > Workspaces > Color, to switch to the Color workspace.

4   Choose Window > Workspaces > Reset To Saved Layout, or double-click the Color workspace name to reset the workspace to its default layout.

    This changes the workspace to the preset that was created to make it easier to work with color correction effects and, in particular, the Lumetri Color panel and Lumetri Scopes panel.

About 8-bit video

Eight-bit video works on a scale from 0 to 255. That means each pixel has red, green, and blue (RGB) values somewhere on that scale, which combine to produce a particular color. You can think of 0 as 0% and 255 as 100%. A pixel that has a red value of 127 is equivalent to having a red value of 50%.

However, we're talking about RGB images, and broadcast video uses a similar but different range, with a color system called YUV.

If you compare the YUV scale with RGB scale, when the waveform scope is set to show 8 Bit, you'll find that 8-bit YUV pixel values range from 16 to 235, while RGB values range from 0 to 255.

TVs usually use YUV color, not RGB. However, your computer screen is RGB. If you are producing video for broadcast television, this can create issues because you are looking at your video footage on a different kind of screen than the kind it will ultimately be viewed on. There is only one sure way of overcoming the uncertainty this creates: Connect a TV or broadcast monitor to your editing system and view your footage on that screen.

> The difference is a little like comparing a photograph you view on-screen with a printed version. The printer and your computer screen use different color systems, and it's an imperfect translation from one to the other.
>
> Sometimes you will view footage with visible detail on an RGB screen like your computer display that disappears when viewed on a TV screen. You'll need to make adjustments to the color to bring those details into the TV screen range.
>
> Some TVs give you the option to display color as RGB, using a range of names such as Game Mode or Photo Color Space. If your screen is set up this way, you may see the full 0 to 255 RGB range.
>
> With some computer screens, Premiere Pro can adjust the video colors to more accurately mimic other display types (see the "Understanding display color management" section).

Understanding display color management

Computer monitors generally use a different system for displaying color than do TV screens and cinema projectors (see the sidebar "About 8-bit video" for more on this).

If you're producing video for online distribution, knowing your audience will be using a computer monitor similar to yours to view your content, you can be confident the colors and brightness levels of your images will be comparable. If you're delivering video for TV or the cinema screen, you'll need a way to view video that matches the type of screen it's intended for.

Professional colorists have multiple display systems to check their work on. If they're working on a film intended for theaters, they'll have the same kind of projector a theater would use.

Some computer monitors actually offer excellent color reproduction—better than television screens. If you have enabled GPU acceleration (see Lesson 2, "Setting Up a Project") and you are using a computer monitor of this kind, Premiere Pro can adjust the way video is displayed in the Source Monitor and Program Monitors to match another type of screen.

This is a great help if you don't have access to the right kind of screen.

Premiere Pro automatically detects if you have the right kind of monitor. To enable this feature, choose Premiere Pro CC > Preferences > General (macOS) or Edit > Preferences > General (Windows), and select Enable Display Color Management (requires GPU acceleration).

✓ Enable Display Color Management (requires GPU acceleration)

For more information about this feature, as well as a helpful breakdown of the types of color displays and the ways colors will be adjusted by Premiere Pro, including examples, check out the excellent article by Jarle Leirpoll on Display Color Management at premierepro.net: https://premierepro.net/color-management-premiere-pro/.

Following a color-oriented workflow

Now that you've switched to the Color workspace, it's a good time to switch to a different kind of thinking. With your clips in place, it's time to look at them less in terms of the action and more in terms of whether they fit together and have the right look.

There are two main phases to working with color.

- Make sure clips in each scene have matching colors, brightness, and contrast so they look like they were shot at the same time, in the same place, and with the same camera.

- Give everything a "look"—in other words, a particular tonality or color tint.

You'll use the same tools to achieve both of these goals, but it's common to approach them in this order, separately. If two clips from the same scene don't have matching colors, it creates a jarring continuity problem.

Color correction and color grading

You've probably heard of both color correction and color grading. There is often confusion about the difference. In fact, both types of color work use the same tools, but there's a difference of approach.

Color correction is usually aimed at standardizing the shots to make sure they fit together and to improve the appearance in general—to give brighter highlights and stronger shadows or to correct a color bias captured in-camera. This is more craft than art.

Color grading is aimed at achieving a look that conveys the atmosphere of the story more completely. This is more art than craft.

There is, of course, a debate about where one ends and the other begins.

Working with the Color workspace

The Color workspace displays the Lumetri Color panel, which has a number of sections offering color adjustment controls, and places the Lumetri Scopes panel behind the Source Monitor. The Lumetri Scopes are a set of image analysis tools.

The remaining screen area is devoted to the Program Monitor, Timeline, and Project panels. The Timeline panel shrinks to accommodate the Lumetri Color panel.

Remember, you can open and close any panel at any time, but this workspace focuses on finishing work, rather than organizing or editing your project.

While the Lumetri Color panel is displayed, clips on the Timeline are selected automatically as the playhead moves over them. Only clips on tracks that are enabled will be selected this way.

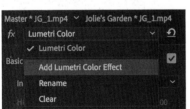

This feature is important because adjustments made with the Lumetri Color panel are always applied to the selected clip. You can apply an adjustment and move the Timeline panel playhead over the next clip to select it, and work on it.

You can enable or disable automatic clip selection by choosing Sequence > Selection Follows Playhead.

Getting an overview of the Lumetri Color panel

There is an effect available in the Effects panel called Lumetri Color, which provides all the controls and options available in the Lumetri Color panel. Like any other effect, its controls are displayed in the Effect Controls panel.

The first time you make an adjustment using the Lumetri Color panel, a Lumetri Color effect is applied to the selected clip. If there is a Lumetri Color effect already applied to the clip, the settings for that effect are adjusted.

In a sense, the Lumetri Color panel is a kind of remote control for the Lumetri Color effect settings in the Effect Controls panel. As with any other effect, you can create presets, copy and paste Lumetri Color effects from one clip to another, and change the settings in the Effect Controls panel.

You can apply more than one Lumetri Color effect to the same clip, each making different types of adjustment to produce a combined result. This can make it easier to stay organized when working on complex projects.

At the top of the Lumetri Color panel, you can choose which Lumetri Color effect you're currently working on. You can also add a new Lumetri Color effect to work on.

The same menu allows you to rename the current Lumetri Color effect to make it easier to navigate your effects. You can also rename effects in the Effect Controls panel by right-clicking the effect name and choosing Rename.

The Lumetri Color panel is divided into six sections. Each section provides a group of controls with different approaches to color adjustment. You can use any or all of the sections to achieve the result you want.

● **Note:** You can expand or collapse a section in the Lumetri Color panel by clicking its heading.

Let's take a look at each section.

Basic Correction

This section provides you with simple controls to apply quick fixes to your clips.

At the top of the section, a menu allows you to apply a preset adjustment to your media in the form of an Input LUT (Lookup Table), which makes standard adjustments to media that might otherwise look quite flat.

A LUT is actually a file, a little like an effect preset intended to adjust the appearance of clips. LUTs can be imported and exported for advanced color grading workflows.

If you're familiar with Adobe Lightroom, you'll recognize the list of simple controls in the Basic section. You can work your way down the list making adjustments to improve the look of your footage, or you can click the Auto button to let Premiere Pro work out some settings for you.

Creative

As the name suggests, the Creative section allows you to go a little further into developing a look for your media.

A number of creative looks are included, with a preview based on your current clip. Click the arrows on the preview to review different Looks, and click the image to apply a Look to the clip.

You can make subtle adjustments to the color intensity, and there are color wheels configured to adjust the color for the shadow (darker) pixels or highlight (lighter) pixels in the image.

Note: Each section has a check box to enable and disable it, making it easy to toggle the result and check the effect against the original image.

Curves

Curves allow quick but precise adjustments to visuals and make it easier to achieve more natural-looking results with just a few clicks.

▶ **Tip:** You can reset most controls in the Lumetri Color panel by double-clicking the control.

These are some of the more advanced controls, providing nuanced adjustments to the luminance, red, green, and blue pixels.

Adjustments are made in a similar way to those you applied to the Parametric Equalizer effect graph, or the audio rubber bands on clips. The position of the line indicates the adjustment.

In addition to a traditional RGB curves control, there are multiple Hue Saturation Curve controls. Each of these gives precise control over a specific adjustment.

For example, the first control, Hue vs Sat, allows you to add (by clicking) and position (by dragging) control points to increase or decrease color saturation for specific hues.

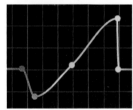

The next, Hue vs Hue, allows you to change one hue into another.

Color Wheels & Match

This section provides precise control over the shadow, midtone, and highlight pixels in the image. Simply drag the control puck from the center of a wheel toward the edge to apply an adjustment.

Each color wheel also has a luminance control slider on the left, which allows you to make simple adjustments to the brightness and, by appropriate adjustment, the contrast of your footage.

There's also a button that opens the Program Monitor Comparison View and another button that automatically color matches clips.

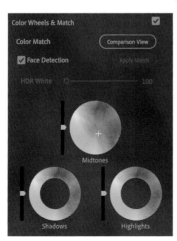

HSL Secondary

The HSL Secondary setting is a color adjustment made to specific areas of an image, selected using Hue, Saturation, and Luminance ranges.

This is the section of the Lumetri Color panel you would use to selectively make a blue sky even bluer, or make a field of grass a deeper green, without affecting other areas of the picture.

The advanced Curves controls provide similar options, and you are likely to choose one method or the other based on personal preference.

Vignette

It's surprising how much difference a simple vignette effect can make to a picture.

A vignette was originally caused by camera lenses darkening the edge of frame, but modern lenses rarely have this issue.

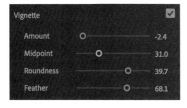

Instead, a vignette is commonly used to bring attention to the center of an image, and it can be highly effective, even when the adjustment is subtle.

The Lumetri Color panel in action

Because adjustments made using the Lumetri Color panel are added collectively as a regular Premiere Pro effect, you can also enable and disable the effect in the Effect Controls panel, or create an effect preset.

Let's try some prebuilt looks.

1 Open the sequence Jolie's Garden in the Sequences bin. This is a simple sequence with a series of clips that have a good range of color and contrast.

2 Position the playhead over the first clip in the sequence. The clip should highlight automatically in the Timeline panel.

3 Click the Creative section heading in the Lumetri Color panel to reveal its controls.

Fuji F125 Kodak 2393 (by Adobe) © ... 2016

4   Browse through several prebuilt looks by clicking the arrow on the right side of the preview display. When you see a look you like, click the preview image to apply it.

5   Try adjusting the Intensity slider to vary the amount of adjustment.

This is a good time to experiment with the other controls in the Lumetri Color panel. Some controls will make sense immediately, while others will take time to master. Use the clips in this sequence as a testing ground to learn about the Lumetri Color panel through experimentation; just drag all the controls from one extreme to the other to see the result. You'll learn about many of these controls in detail later in this lesson.

Understanding Lumetri Scopes essentials

You might have wondered why the Premiere Pro interface is so gray. There's a good reason: Vision is highly subjective. In fact, it's also highly relative.

If you see two colors next to each other, the way you see one is changed by the presence of the other. To prevent the Premiere Pro interface from influencing the way you perceive colors in your sequence, Adobe has made the interface almost entirely gray. If you've ever seen a professional color-grading suite, where artists provide the finishing touches to films and television programs, you've probably noticed that most of the room is gray. Colorists sometimes also have a large gray piece of card, or a section of a wall, that they can look at for a few moments to "reset" their vision before checking a shot.

The combination of your subjective vision and the variation that can occur in the way computer monitors and television monitors display color and brightness creates a need for an objective measurement.

Video scopes provide just that. And they're used throughout the media industry; learn them once, and you'll be able to use them everywhere.

1   Open the sequence Lady Walking.

2   Position the Timeline playhead so that it's over the clip in the sequence.

3   The Lumetri Scopes panel should be sharing the frame with the Source Monitor. Click to select the panel and make it active, or select it in the Window menu.

4   Open the Lumetri Scopes panel Settings menu 🔧 and choose Presets > Premiere 4 Scope YUV (float, no clamp).

You should see the lady walking in the street in your Program Monitor, along with the synchronized display in the Lumetri Scopes panel.

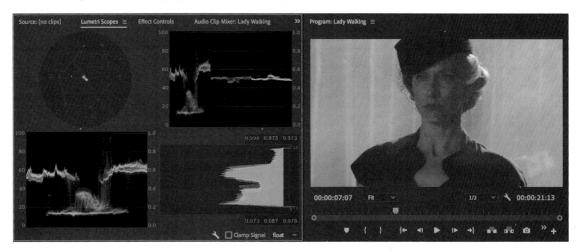

Working with the Lumetri Scopes panel

The Lumetri Scopes panel displays an array of industry-standard meters to get an objective view of your media.

The full complement of displays can be a little overwhelming at first, plus you'll have smaller graphs because they are all sharing one panel. You can turn individual items off and on by opening the Settings menu and choosing items on the list.

Also in the Settings menu, you can specify whether you are working to an ITU Rec. 2020 (UHD), ITU Rec. 709 (HD), or ITU Rec. 601 (SD) color space. If you're producing content for broadcast television, you will almost certainly be working to one of these standards. If not or if you're not sure, you will probably be happy with Rec. 709.

At the bottom right of the Lumetri Scopes panel, you can choose to display the scopes in 8 bit, float (which is 32-bit floating-point color), or even HDR.

The option you choose does not change the clip or the way effects are rendered but does change the way the information is displayed in the scopes. You'll want to choose an option that matches the color space you're working in.

HDR refers to High Dynamic Range, which has a much higher range between the darkest and brightest parts of the picture. Though HDR is beyond the scope of these lessons, it's an important new technology and one that will be increasingly relevant as new cameras and displays support it.

The Clamp Signal option constrains the scopes to standard legal levels for broadcast television. Again, this doesn't impact the image or the result of your effects—it's a matter of personal preference if you would like to limit the range of the scopes in this way to see the scales more clearly.

Let's simplify the view.

▶ **Tip:** You can also access the Lumetri Scopes Settings menu by right-clicking anywhere in the panel.

Use the Lumetri Scopes settings menu to click each of the selected items to deselect them and remove them from the display. When there's one item left, it'll be dimmed so you can't remove it.

Now let's take a look at two of the main components in the Lumetri Scopes panel.

Waveform

Right-click in the panel and choose Presets > Waveform RGB.

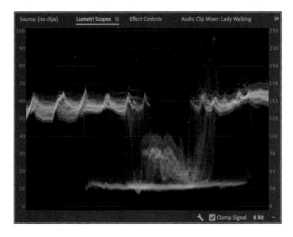

If you're new to waveforms, they can look a little strange, but they're actually simple. They show you the brightness and color saturation of your images.

Every pixel in the current frame is displayed in the waveform. The brighter the pixel, the higher it appears. The pixels have their correct horizontal position (that is, a pixel halfway across the screen will be displayed halfway across the waveform), but the vertical position is not based on the image at all.

Instead, the vertical position indicates brightness or color intensity; the brightness and color intensity waveforms are displayed together in this version of the waveform, using different colors.

- 0, at the bottom of the scale, represents no luminance at all and/or no color intensity.

- 100, at the top of the scale, represents a pixel that is fully bright. On the RGB scale, this value would be 255 (you can see this scale on the right side of the waveform display).

This all might sound rather technical, but in practice it's straightforward. There's a visible baseline that represents "no brightness" and a top level that represents "fully bright." The numbers on the edge of the graph might change depending on your settings, but the use is essentially always the same.

You can view the waveform in several ways. To access each type, open the Lumetri Scopes Settings menu and choose Waveform Type, followed by one of these options:

- **RGB:** Shows the Red, Green, and Blue pixels in their own colors.
- **Luma:** Shows the IRE value of pixels, from 0 to 100, against a scale of –20 to 120. This allows for precise analysis of bright spots and contrast ratio.
- **YC:** Shows the image luminance (brightness) in green and the chrominance (color intensity) in blue.
- **YC No Chroma:** Shows the luminance only, with no chrominance.

Why YC?

The letter *C*, for chrominance, makes simple sense, but the letter *Y*, for luminance, takes a little explaining. It comes from a way of measuring color information that uses x-, y-, and z-axes, where *Y* represents the luminance. The idea was originally to create a simple system for recording color, and the use of Y to represent brightness, or luminance, stuck.

Let's test this display a little.

1 Continue using the Lady Walking sequence. Set the Timeline playhead to 00:00:07:00 so you can see the lady against the smoky background.

2   Set the waveform display to YC No Chroma. This is a brightness-only waveform, with no color information, that shows a full range, with no limits set for broadcast television.

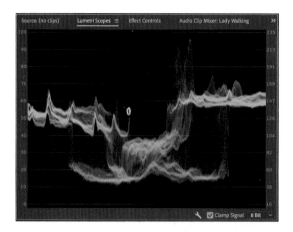

The smoky parts of the image have little contrast and are displayed as a relatively flat line in the waveform display. The lady's head and shoulders are darker than the smoky background. They're around the middle of the image, and they are clearly visible in the middle area of the waveform display.

3   Expand the Basic Correction section of the Lumetri Color panel.

▶ **Tip:** You can double-click any part of a slider control in the Lumetri Color panel to reset it.

4   Experiment with the Exposure, Contrast, Highlights, Shadows, Whites, and Blacks controls. As you adjust the controls, watch the waveform display to see the result.

If you make an adjustment to the image and then wait a few seconds, your eyes will adjust to the new appearance, and it will seem normal. Make another adjustment, and a few seconds later the new appearance seems normal too. Which is correct?

Ultimately, the answer is based on perceived quality. If you like what you see, it's right. However, the waveform display will give you objective information about how dark or bright pixels are or how much color is in the shot, which is useful when attempting to meet standards.

▶ **Tip:** It can sometimes seem as if the waveform display is showing an image. Remember, the vertical position of the pixels in your images is not used in a waveform display.

If you scrub through the sequence or play the sequence, you'll see the waveform display update live.

The waveform display is useful for showing how much contrast you have in your images (the difference between the bright and dark areas of the image) and for checking whether you are working on video that has "legal" levels (that is, the minimum and maximum brightness or color saturation permitted by a broadcaster). Broadcasters adopt their own standards for legal levels, so you will need to find out for each case where your work will be broadcast.

You can see right away that you do not have great contrast in this shot. There are some strong shadows, but few *highlights* in the upper part of the waveform display. Any time you see flat horizontal lines in the waveform display, it means there's no visible detail. In the following example, the shadows have been darkened so much, they're flattened at the bottom of the waveform.

The result is not necessarily bad and might be exactly the look you are seeking. It's just important to know when adjustments are so extreme that detail is being lost.

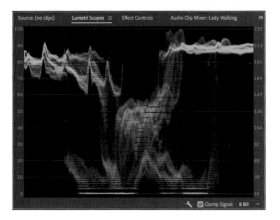 

You can reset the Lumetri Color panel at any time by clicking the Reset Effect button ⟳ at the upper-right corner of the panel.

YUV Vectorscope

Whereas the Luma waveform shows luminance in terms of the vertical position of pixels displayed, with brighter pixels displayed at the top and darker pixels displayed at the bottom, the vectorscope shows only color.

1 Open the sequence Skyline.

● **Note:** The HLS (Hue, Luminance, Saturation) vectorscope is sometimes used by film-grading artists in preference to the YUV vectorscope. It has no guiding overlay and is a little harder to read if you are not already familiar with it.

2 Open the Lumetri Scopes Settings menu and choose Vectorscope YUV; then open the Settings menu again and choose Waveform (YC No Chroma) to disable it.

Pixels in the image are displayed in the vectorscope. If a pixel appears in the center of the circle, it has no color saturation. The closer to the edge of the circle, the more color a pixel has.

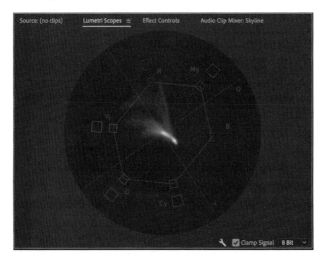

If you look closely at the vectorscope, you'll see a series of targets indicating primary colors.

- R = Red
- G = Green
- B = Blue

There are two boxes for each target. The smaller, inner box is at 75% saturation, the YUV color limit, while the larger, outer box is at 100% saturation, the RGB color limit. RGB color extends to a greater level of saturation than YUV. The thin line between the inner boxes shows the YUV color gamut (the range of YUV colors).

You'll also see a series of targets indicating secondary colors.

- Yl = Yellow
- Cy = Cyan
- Mg = Magenta

The closer a pixel is to one of these targets, the more of that color it has. Unlike the waveform display, which indicates the horizontal position of each pixel, no position information is indicated in the vectorscope.

It's clear enough to see what's happening in this shot of Seattle. There's a lot of blue, and there are a few spots of red and yellow. The small amount of red is indicated by the streak of peaks reaching out toward the R marking in the vectorscope.

About primary and secondary colors

Red, green, and blue are primary colors. It's common for display systems, including television screens and your computer monitor, to combine these three colors in varying relative amounts to produce all the colors you see.

There's a beautiful symmetry to the way a standard color wheel works, and a color wheel is essentially what the vectorscope displays.

Any two primary colors will combine to produce a secondary color. Secondary colors are the opposite of the remaining primary color.

For example, red and green (two of the primary colors) combine to produce yellow, which is the opposite of blue (the third primary color).

The vectorscope is helpful because it gives you objective information about the colors in your sequence. If there's a color cast, perhaps because the camera was not calibrated properly, it's often obvious in the vectorscope display. You can simply use one of the Lumetri Color panel controls to reduce the amount of the unwanted color or add more of the opposite color.

Some of the controls for color correction adjustments have the same color wheel design as the vectorscope, making it easy to see what you need to do.

Let's make an adjustment and observe the result in the vectorscope display.

1   Continue working with the Skyline sequence. Position the Timeline playhead at 00:00:01:00, where the colors are more vivid.

2   In the Lumetri Color panel, expand the Basic Correction section.

3   While watching the result in the vectorscope display, drag the Temperature slider from one extreme to the other.

The pixels displayed in the vectorscope move between the orange and blue areas of the display.

4   Reset the Temperature slider by double-clicking the slider control.

5   In the Lumetri Color panel, drag the Tint slider from one extreme to the other.

The pixels displayed in the vectorscope move between the green and magenta areas of the display.

6   Reset the Tint slider by double-clicking the slider control.

By making adjustments while checking the vectorscope, you can give an objective indication of the change you're making.

▶ **Tip:** You can jump to 00:00:01:00 by clicking the timecode in the Source Monitor, Program Monitor, or Timeline panel, and typing **1.** and then pressing Enter because each dot (.) adds one pair of zeros.

Additive and subtractive color

Computer screens and televisions use additive color, which means the colors are created by generating light in different colors and combining them to produce a precise mix. You produce white by combining equal amounts of red, green, and blue.

When you draw with color on paper, it is usually white paper, which reflects a full spectrum of colors. You subtract from the white of the paper by adding pigment. The pigment prevents parts of the light from reflecting. This is called *subtractive color*.

Additive color uses primary colors; subtractive color uses secondary colors. In a sense, they're opposite ends of the same color theory

RGB parade

Open the Lumetri Scopes Settings menu and choose Presets > Parade RGB.

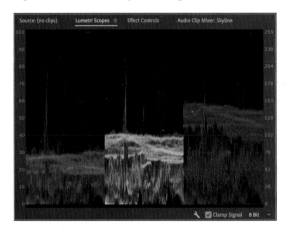

The RGB parade provides another form of waveform-style display. The difference is that the red, green, and blue levels are displayed separately. To fit all three colors in, each image is squeezed horizontally to one-third of the width of the display.

- RGB
  YUV
  RGB-White
  YUV-White

You can choose which kind of parade you see by clicking the Lumetri Scopes Settings menu or by right-clicking in the Lumetri Scopes panel and choosing Parade Type.

The three parts of the parade have similar patterns in them, particularly where there are white or gray pixels, because these parts will have equal amounts of red, green, and blue. The RGB parade is one of the most frequently used tools in color correction because it clearly shows the relationship between the primary color channels.

To see the dramatic impact color adjustments can have on the parade, go to the Basic Correction section of the Lumetri Color panel and try adjusting the White Balance Temperature and Tint controls. Be sure to reset them when you finish by double-clicking each control.

Using Comparison View

As mentioned earlier, there are usually two phases to color adjustment work.

- **Color correction:** Correcting for color cast or brightness issues and matching shots in the sequence to ensure they look like part of the same content were shot at the same time in the same location or that they match an in-house standard for final delivery.

- **Color grading:** Establishing a creative look for shots on a shot-by-shot, scene-by-scene, or sequence-wide basis.

When color correcting, it's helpful to compare one shot with another to achieve a match. This is especially helpful when the two shots come from different scenes, meaning some color variation is expected even if the overall tone should be similar.

You can drag your current sequence from the Project panel into the Source Monitor to use that monitor as a reference for side-by-side comparison, but there's an easier way: set the Program Monitor to Comparison view.

You can toggle between the regular playback view and Comparison View in the Program Monitor at any time. Let's take a look at the new controls.

- **Reference Frame:** The frame you are using as a reference or for automatic color matching.

- **Reference Position:** The timecode for the reference frame.

- **Playhead Position**: The timecode for the current frame.

- **Shot or Frame Comparison:** Toggle between using another frame as a reference, or the current state of the current frame. The latter option is useful when working on effects, as it allows a constant "before-and-after" view when working with effects so your eyes can't adjust to the finished version.

- **Side by Side:** View the two images separately, side by side.

- **Vertical Split:** View the two images as a single vertically split screen, with a divider you can drag to reposition.

- **Horizontal Split:** The same as the Vertical Split option but now with a horizontal divider.

- **Swap Sides:** Switch the left and right images.

- **Current frame:** The frame you're working on now.

1 Open the Jolie's Garden sequence, and position the Timeline playhead over the last clip in the sequence.

2 In the Lumetri Color panel, open the Color Wheels & Match section, and click the Comparison View button; or click the Comparison View button  in the Program Monitor.

3 Try changing the reference frame in one of these ways:

- Drag the mini playhead under the reference frame to a new position.

- Click the reference position timecode and enter a new time, or drag on the timecode to choose another time.

- Click the Go To Previous Edit or Go To Next Edit button on either side of the reference position timecode to jump between clips.

4 Try the split view options, and drag the divider between the two sides of the split.

Stay in Comparison View, ready for the next exercise.

Matching color

One of the most powerful and time-saving features of the Lumetri Color panel is the option to automatically match colors between two clips.

To use this feature, you'll switch to Comparison View in the Program Monitor, choose a reference frame and a current frame, and click the Apply Match button in the Color Wheels & Match section of the Lumetri Color panel.

The result will not always be perfect, and you may need to experiment with different reference and current frame selections to get a closer match, but it's often close enough for you to make final adjustments that are guided by the automated adjustment. If Premiere Pro gets you 80% of the way there, it's a huge time-saver.

Let's try it with our current sequence.

1 Continuing from the previous exercise: Set the reference frame to 00:01:00:00.

2 Set Timeline panel playhead to the start of the last clip in the sequence. You can use the Up and Down arrow keys to quickly jump between the clips in the sequence.

3 These are clips from different scenes in the same film. They don't need to have exactly the same colors, but it would be helpful if perhaps the skin tones matched better. Make sure the Face Detection option is selected in the Lumetri Color panel. This way, Premiere Pro will automatically detect faces in the shots and prioritize matching those tones.

4 Click the Apply Match button.

5 The difference is clear. Within a few moments, it's likely your eyes will adjust to the new appearance of the current frame. To help see the change more clearly, toggle the Color Wheels & Match check box off and on repeatedly.

6 Click the Comparison View button to switch back to the regular playback view in the Program Monitor.

The automated color matching offered by the Lumetri Color panel is not likely to produce an identical color match, partly because the perception of color is so subjective and contextual. However, all of the adjustments that were applied are editable, so you can finesse the result until it's perfect.

Exploring the color-oriented effects

<blockquote>**Tip:** You can always find an effect using the search box at the top of the Effects panel. Often, the best way to learn how to use an effect is to apply it to a clip that has a good range of colors, highlights, and shadows and then adjust all the settings to see the result.</blockquote>

As well as adjusting color using the Lumetri Color panel, there are a number of color-oriented effects worth familiarizing yourself with. You add, modify, and remove color correction effects in the same way that you manage the other effects in Premiere Pro. Just as with the other effects, you can use keyframes to modify the settings over time.

As you build familiarity with Premiere Pro, you may find yourself uncertain about which effect is best for a particular purpose; this is normal! There are often several ways of achieving the same outcome in Premiere Pro, and sometimes the choice comes down to which interface you prefer.

The following are a few effects you may want to try first.

Using coloring effects

<blockquote>**Tip:** While in the Color workspace, the Effects panel may not be easy to locate. You can always access any panel by choosing it from the Window menu.</blockquote>

Premiere Pro features several effects, all available in the Effects panel, for adjusting existing colors. The following two are for creating a black-and-white image and applying a tint and for simply turning a color clip into a black-and-white one.

Tint

Use the eyedroppers or color pickers to reduce any image to just two colors. Whatever you map to black and white replaces any other colors in the image.

Black & White

Convert any image to simple black and white. This is useful when combined with other effects that can add color.

Black-and-white images can often withstand much stronger contrast. Consider combining effects for the best results.

Leave Color

You can use the advanced HSL Secondary section of the Lumetri Color panel or the Hue Saturation curves to achieve a similar result, but this filter is sometimes faster.

Use the eyedropper or color pickers to select a color you want to keep. Adjust the Amount To Decolor setting to turn the saturation down on every other color.

Use the Tolerance and Edge Softness controls to produce a subtler effect.

Using the Video Limiter effect

In addition to creative effects, Premiere Pro's color correction repertoire includes effects used for professional video production.

When video is broadcast, there are specific limits that are permitted for maximum luminance, minimum luminance, and color saturation. Although it's possible to confine your video levels to the limits permitted using manual controls, it's easy to mix parts of your sequence that need adjustment.

In the Effects panel, the Video Limiter effect, found in Video Effect > Color Correction, automatically limits the levels of clips to ensure they meet the standards you set.

You'll need to check the limits applied by your broadcaster before adjusting the Clip Level setting with this effect. The levels will not be permitted to go above this.

Tip: While it's common to apply the Video Limiter effect to individual clips, you might also choose to apply it to the whole sequence by using it on an adjustment layer or by enabling it as an export setting (see Lesson 16, "Exporting Frames, Clips, and Sequences").

Then it's simply a question of choosing the Compression Before Clipping amount. Using this, rather than simply chopping off levels that go above the Clip Level setting, a gradual compression of the higher levels is applied to produce a more natural-looking result.

You can choose for this gradual compression to begin 3%, 5%, 10%, or 20% before the cutoff level.

If you turn on the Gamut warning, pixels that go above the Clip Level setting are highlighted in the Gamut Warning color. This is a useful option when reviewing your sequence, but be sure to deselect the Gamut Warning option before exporting your sequence, as the color highlight will be included in the exported file.

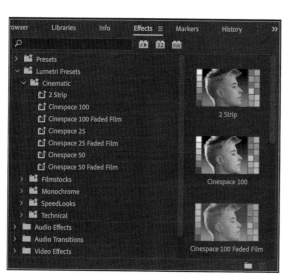

Using Lumetri Looks presets in the Effects panel

In addition to the manual controls available in the Lumetri Color panel, there are a number of Lumetri Look presets available in the Effects panel. These are a fantastic way to get started with advanced color adjustments, and as they are presets, you can modify the settings to achieve exactly the finish you want. If you resize the Effects panel, you can reveal previews of each of the built-in Lumetri Look preset effects.

You apply a Lumetri Look preset effect in the same way that you would apply any other effect available in the Effects panel.

Lumetri Look presets are actually Lumetri Color effects with settings already applied, including a Creative look in some cases.

You can modify the settings in the Effect Controls panel or in the Lumetri Color panel.

Fixing exposure problems

Let's look at some clips that have exposure issues and use some of the Lumetri Color panel controls to address them.

1   Make sure you are in the Color workspace, and reset it to the saved version if necessary.

2   Open the sequence Color Work.

3   In the Lumetri Scopes panel, right-click or open the Settings menu to choose Presets > Waveform RGB. This is just a quick way to close any other scopes and open the waveform display on its own.

4   Again, in the Lumetri Scopes panel, right-click or open the Settings menu to choose Waveform Type > YC No Chroma. This changes the display to a waveform that uses the standard broadcast television range, which is a useful reference for most video projects.

5   Position the Timeline playhead over the first clip in the sequence. It's the shot of the lady walking. You're going to add some contrast.

The environment is smoky; 100 IRE (displayed on the left on the waveform) means fully exposed, and 0 IRE means not exposed at all. No part of the image comes close to these levels. Your eye quickly adjusts to the image, and it'll soon appear fine. Let's see whether you can bring it to life a little.

6   In the Lumetri Color panel, click the Basic Correction heading to display that section.

7   Use the Exposure and Contrast controls to make adjustments to the shot while checking the waveform display to make sure the image doesn't become too dark or too light.

You'll get the best perceived results if you have a frame from a later part of the clip on-screen. Around 00:00:07:09 there's a section of sharp focus.

Try an Exposure setting of **0.6** and a Contrast setting of **60**.

Tip: If the Lumetri panel is active, you can use the Bypass Lumetri Color Effects keyboard shortcut. While pressing the key, all instances of the Lumetri Color effect are turned off. By default, this shortcut has no key associated with it. For information on assigning keyboard shortcuts, see Lesson 1, "Touring Adobe Premiere Pro CC."

8   Your eye is likely to adjust quickly to the new image. Use the check box to toggle the Basic Correction section off and on to compare the image before and after.

The subtle adjustment you made adds more depth to the image, giving it stronger highlights and shadows. As you toggle the effect off and on, you'll see the waveform changing in the Lumetri Scopes panel. You still don't have bright highlights in the image, but that's fine because the natural colors are mainly midtones.

Fixing underexposed images

Now let's work with an underexposed image.

1   Switch to the Effects workspace.

2   Position the Timeline playhead over the second clip in the Color Work sequence. When you first look at this clip, it might look OK. The highlights don't look strong, but there's a reasonable amount of detail throughout the image. The face, especially, is sharp and detailed.

Tip: Remember, you can open any panel by choosing it from the Window menu. The Lumetri Scopes panel, for example, isn't limited to the Color workspace.

3   Open the Lumetri Scopes panel so you can view this clip in the waveform. At the bottom of the waveform there are quite a few dark pixels, with some touching the 0 IRE line.

In this instance, it looks like the missing detail is in the shoulder of the suit, on the left. The problem with such dark pixels is that increasing the brightness will simply change the strong shadows into gray, and no detail will emerge.

4   In the Effects panel, locate the Brightness & Contrast effect. Apply the effect to the clip.

5 Drag the panel name for the Lumetri Scopes panel to move it into a new panel group between the Effect Controls panel and the Program Monitor so you can see all panels at once.

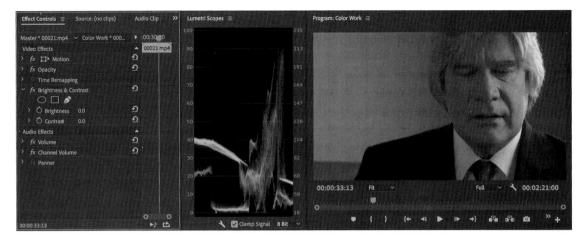

6 Use the Brightness control in the Effect Controls panel to increase the brightness. Rather than clicking the number and typing a new number, drag to the right so you can see the change happening incrementally.

As you drag, notice that the whole waveform moves up. This is fine for bringing out the highlights in the image, but the shadows remain a flat line. You're simply changing the black shadows to gray. If you drag the Brightness control all the way to 100, you'll see just how flat the image still is.

▷ **Tip:** The Brightness & Contrast effect offers a quick, easy fix, but it's easy to accidentally clip the black (dark) or white (bright) pixels, losing detail. The Lumetri Color panel Curves control keeps adjustments inside the 0 to 255 scale.

7 Remove the Brightness & Contrast effect.

8 Switch back to the Color workspace. Try to make an adjustment using the RGB Curves control in the Lumetri Color panel. Here's an example of an RGB Curves adjustment that would improve the image.

Experiment with the third clip in the sequence. This clip demonstrates that there are limits to what can be "fixed in post" (post-production)!

That doesn't mean it's unusable, but you'd probably have to apply some significant artistic effects to create a look that seemed intentional.

Fixing overexposed images

The next clip you'll work with is overexposed.

▶ **Tip:** Remember, you can reset Lumetri Color controls by double-clicking them. You can also delete the Lumetri Color effect in the Effect Controls panel to begin again, or you can click the Reset Effect button at the top of the panel.

1 Move the Timeline playhead to the fourth clip in the sequence. Notice that a lot of the pixels are burned out. Just as with the flat shadows in the second clip in the sequence, there's no detail in burned-out highlights. This means that lowering the brightness will simply make the character's skin and hair gray; no detail will emerge.

2 Notice that the shadows in this shot don't reach the bottom of the Waveform Monitor. The lack of properly dark shadows has a flattening effect on the image.

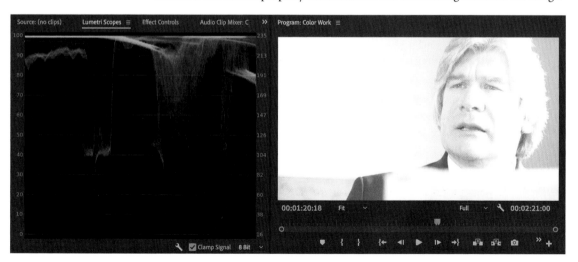

3 Try using the RGB Curves control in the Lumetri Color panel to improve the contrast range. This approach might produce acceptable results, although the clip definitely ends up looking processed.

When is color correction right?

Making adjustments to images is highly subjective. Though there are precise limits for image formats and broadcast technologies, whether an image should be light, dark, blue-tinted, or green is ultimately a subjective choice. The reference tools that Premiere Pro provides, such as the Lumetri Scopes panel, are a helpful guide, but only you can decide when the picture looks right.

If you're producing video for display on televisions, it's vital that you have a television screen connected to your Premiere Pro editing system to view your content. Television screens usually display color differently from computer monitors, and consumer screens sometimes have special color modes that change the appearance of video. For professional broadcast television, editors will usually have a carefully calibrated monitor that displays YUV color. The Display Color Management option will go a long way to showing the colors as they might be displayed on a TV, but nothing compares to a calibrated monitor.

The same rule applies if you are producing content for digital cinema projection, Ultra High Definition TV, or High Dynamic Range TV. The only way to know exactly how the picture will look is to view it using the destination medium. This means if your ultimate destination is a computer screen, perhaps as web video or part of a software interface, you are already looking at the perfect test monitor.

Fixing color balance

Your eyes adjust to compensate for changes in the color of light around you automatically. It's an extraordinary ability that allows you to see white as white, even if objectively it's orange, for example, because it's lit by tungsten light.

Cameras can automatically adjust their white balance to compensate for different lighting in the way that your eyes do. With the right calibration, white objects look white, whether you are recording indoors (under oranger tungsten light) or outdoors (in bluer daylight).

Sometimes automatic settings are hit or miss, so professional shooters often prefer to adjust white balance manually. If the white balance is set wrong, you can end up with some interesting results. The most common reason for a color balance problem in a clip is that the camera was not calibrated properly.

Balancing with the Lumetri color wheels

Let's try using the Lumetri Color panel color wheels to adjust the last shot in the sequence.

1 Switch to the Color workspace, and reset it if necessary.

2 Position the Timeline playhead over the last clip in the Color Work sequence.

3 In the Lumetri Color panel, expand the Basic Correction section, and click the Auto button to automatically adjust the levels.

The Tone controls change to reflect the new levels.

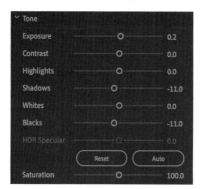

Premiere Pro has identified the darkest pixels and the brightest pixels and has balanced automatically.

The adjustment is tiny! Clearly, the problem is not with the range of contrast in the shot.

4 Set the Lumetri Scopes panel to display the Vectorscope YUV.

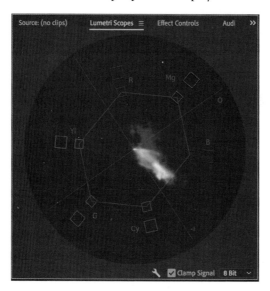

It's clear there's a reasonable range of colors in the shot, but there's a strong bias toward the blue. In fact, this scene has mixed lighting, with bluer daylight coming from the window and warmer tungsten light coming from the interior of the room.

5 In the Basic Correction section of the Lumetri Color panel, use the Temperature slider to push the colors toward the orange. You'll need to push the adjustment all the way to 100 to see a reasonable result because the color shift is so strong in the clip.

The result is pretty good, but perhaps it could be better.

The darker pixels in this shot are generally lit by the interior, warmer room light, while the lighter pixels are generally lit by the bluer daylight. This means different color wheels will interact with different areas of the picture in convincing and natural ways.

6 Expand the Color Wheels & Match section of the Lumetri Color panel. Try using the Shadows color wheel to pull the color toward the red, while using the Highlights color wheel to pull the color toward blue.

7 You've adjusted the color wheels to warm up the shadows and cool down the highlights. Experiment with the midtones to obtain the most natural result possible. Use the image as a guide.

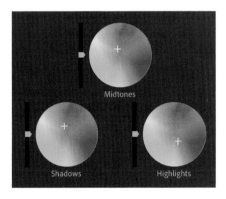

Experiment with the other controls in the Lumetri Color panel to see whether you can improve the result further.

Making a secondary color adjustment

The Lumetri Color panel allows you to make adjustments that are limited to a particular range of hues, a level of color saturation, or a level of brightness.

This is useful if you want to bring out the blue in a subject's eyes or give a flower a color boost.

Let's try it.

1   Open the sequence Yellow Flower and position the Timeline playhead over the first clip.

    This sequence has two shots with clearly distinguished areas of color.

2   Expand the HSL Secondary section of the Lumetri Color panel.

3   Click the eyedropper 🖊 to select it and then click the yellow petals of the flower to pick that color.

    You may get a more useful result by holding Command (macOS) or Ctrl (Windows) while clicking, as this captures a 5x5 pixel average sample.

    The color selection controls update based on the area of the petal you clicked.

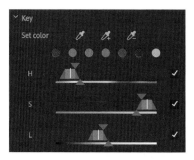

    When making a selection of this kind, it can be helpful to initially apply an extreme adjustment to the colors. This makes it easier to tell whether you have selected the right range of colors in the image.

4   Scroll down in the Lumetri Color panel and drag the Temperature and Tint controls to the far left to apply an extreme adjustment.

5   Drag the color range selection controls to expand the selection. Your initial selection probably selected only a few pixels, as there is quite a lot of variation in the yellow petals.

Each control sets the range of pixels you're selecting, based on one of three factors.

H: Hue

S: Saturation

L: Luminance

The upper triangles represent the hard-stop range of the selection. The lower triangles extend the selection with a softening that reduces hard edges.

6   Experiment with the Denoise and Blur options. These adjust the selection, rather than the image, helping to smooth the areas impacted by the effect.

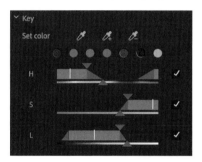

7   Once you're happy you have selected all the pixels in the petals of the flower, reset the Temperature and Tint controls, and make a subtler adjustment.

The adjustments you make will be limited to the pixels in your selection.

8   Once you have mastered this effect, experiment with the sky in the second clip in this sequence.

Making precise adjustments with curves

The Hue Saturation curves in the Curves section of the Lumetri Color panel offer precise controls for selecting and adjusting the hue and luminance of images.

Though there are several different controls, they all work essentially the same way. Each control focuses on a different type of selection and adjustment.

Click to add control points to the curve (it starts as a straight line, but curves are added when you apply adjustments). Use those control points to apply an adjustment according to the type.

The first part of the name of a curve indicates the horizontal axis, while the second part of the name indicates the vertical axis.

Let's take a look at each one.

- **Hue vs Sat:** Increase or decrease the saturation of pixels based on specific hues.

- **Hue vs Hue:** Change the hue of pixels based on their current hue.

- **Hue vs Luma:** Change the brightness (luma) of pixels based on their hue.

- **Luma vs Sat:** Change the color saturation of pixels based on their brightness (luma).

- **Sat vs Sat:** Change the color saturation of pixels based on their current level of saturation. This is particularly useful for reducing the impact of highly color saturated parts of an image while leaving the rest of the image untouched.

As with so many effects, the best way to learn what each of these controls can do is to try them on some clips and apply extreme adjustments.

Let's try these controls on some clips.

1   Open the sequence The Ancestor Simulation. Play the sequence to familiarize yourself with the shots. These images have muted colors with some specific regions with distinguishable colors, like the flowers on the table.

© Copyright Maxim Jago 2018

2   Expand the Curves section of the Lumetri Color panel, and then set the Timeline playhead over the first clip.

3   At the top right of each curve control, there's an eyedropper  that you use to automatically set a control point based on the part of the image you click and to add two control points (one on either side) to separate the adjustment you'll make from the rest of the curve.

Use the eyedropper for the Hue vs Sat curve to select the petals of the reddish flower closest to the camera on the table.

4   The selection is right at the edges of the hue graph. Drag the navigator at the bottom of the curve control to access the control points more easily.

5   Drag the middle control point up to increase the saturation for the flower.

6   Use the eyedropper for the Sat vs Sat curve to select the pale beige color of the sofa. This selects pixels that have little color saturation. Drag the left control point up, quite high in the graph, to bring some life to the sofa and similar pale areas of the image.

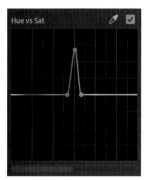 

Because you exclusively selected pixels that originally had little color saturation, other areas of the image with more saturation were unaffected. The result is a more natural-looking adjustment.

By combining multiple Lumetri Color effects with precise curve selections, you can make nuanced color adjustments to clips.

7   Experiment with the rest of the clips in this sequence. For example, for the sixth clip in the sequence, showing the castle with trees, try using the Hue vs Sat curve to increase the saturation of the green in the trees and then use the Hue vs Luma curve to darken the leaves. This adds more visual interest and contrast without making an adjustment to the whole clip.

Using special color effects

Several effects available in the Effects panel give you great creative control over the colors in your clips.

Using Gaussian Blur

While not technically a color adjustment effect, adding a tiny amount of blurring can soften the results of your adjustments, making an image look more natural. Premiere Pro has a number of blur effects. The most popular is Gaussian Blur, which has a natural-looking, smoothing effect on an image.

Using Stylize effects

The Stylize category of effects includes some dramatic options, some of which, like the Mosaic effect, you'll use for more functional applications in combination with an effect mask, such as hiding someone's face.

The Solarize effect gives vivid color adjustments that can be used to create stylized back plates for graphics or intro sequences.

Using Lumetri looks

The Lumetri Color panel includes a list of built-in looks you experimented with earlier, and as you have found, there are a number of Lumetri Look presets in the Effects panel to get you started.

These effects all make use of the Lumetri Color effect.

In addition to using the built-in Looks, the Lumetri effect allows you to browse to an existing .look or .lut file to apply nuanced, subtle color adjustments to your footage.

It's possible you will be given a LOOK or LUT file to use as a starting point for your color adjustments. It's increasingly common for cameras or location monitors to employ a color reference file of this kind. It helps to use the same reference when you are working on footage in post-production.

To apply an existing LOOK or LUT file, open the Input LUT menu in the Basic Correction section, at the top of the Lumetri Color panel, and choose Browse.

Creating a look

Once you've spent a little time with the color correction effects available in Premiere Pro, you should have a feel for the kinds of changes you can make and the impact those changes have on the overall look and feel of your footage.

You can use effect presets to create a look for your clips. You can also apply an effect to an adjustment layer to give your sequence, or part of a sequence, an overall look. Changes made using the Lumetri Color panel apply just as well when applied to an adjustment layer.

Try using an adjustment layer to apply a color adjustment to a scene.

1 Open the Theft Unexpected sequence.

2 In the Project panel, open the New Item menu 🗔 and choose Adjustment Layer. The settings automatically match the current sequence, so click OK.

> **Tip:** You may need to resize the Project panel to see the New Item menu.

3 Drag and drop the new adjustment layer onto the beginning of the Video 2 track in the sequence.

The default duration for adjustment layers is the same as the duration of still images. It's too short for this sequence.

4 Trim the adjustment layer until it stretches from the beginning to the end of the sequence.

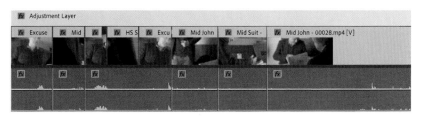

> ● **Note:** If you use adjustment layers in this way on a sequence that has graphics and titles, you may want to ensure that the adjustment layer is on a track between the graphics/titles and the video. Otherwise, you will adjust the appearance of your titles too.

5   In the Effects panel, browse to Lumetri Presets > SpeedLooks > Universal. Drag one of these SpeedLooks onto the adjustment layer. The look will apply to every clip in the sequence, and you can modify it using the controls in the Effect Controls panel or in the Lumetri Color panel.

▶ **Tip:** SpeedLooks available in the Effects panel are applied as regular effects, so it's easy to combine them—just apply another.

You can apply any standard visual effect this way and use multiple adjustment layers to apply different looks to different scenes.

The Lumetri Color panel controls will adjust the Lumetri Color effect selected at the top of the panel.

This is just a brief introduction to color adjustment, and there's an enormous amount more to explore. It's worth investing the time to familiarize yourself with the advanced controls in the Lumetri Color panel. There are a great many visual effects that can add nuance or a striking look to your footage. Experimentation and practice are key to developing your understanding in this important and creative aspect of post-production.

Review questions

1 How do you change the display in the Lumetri Scopes panel?

2 How do you access the Lumetri Scopes panel when not viewing the Color workspace?

3 Why should you use the vectorscope rather than depending on your eyes?

4 How can you apply a look to a sequence?

5 Why might you need to limit your luminance or color levels?

Review answers

1 Right-click in the panel or open the Settings menu and choose the display type you would like.

2 Choose the Lumetri Scopes panel, like all panels, from the Window menu.

3 The way you perceive color is highly subjective and relative. Depending on the colors you have just seen, you will see new colors differently. The vectorscope display gives you an objective reference.

4 You can use effect presets to apply the same color correction adjustments to multiple clips, or you can add an adjustment layer and apply the effects to that. Any clips on lower tracks covered by the adjustment layer will be affected.

5 If your sequence is intended for broadcast television, you'll need to ensure you meet the stringent requirements for maximum and minimum levels. The broadcaster you're working with will be able to tell you the required levels.

14 EXPLORING COMPOSITING TECHNIQUES

Lesson overview

In this lesson, you'll learn about the following:

- Using the alpha channel
- Using compositing techniques
- Working with opacity
- Working with a greenscreen
- Using mattes

 This lesson will take about 60 minutes to complete. Please log in to your account on peachpit.com to download the lesson files for this lesson, or go to the "Getting Started" section at the beginning of this book and follow the instructions under "Accessing the lesson files and Web Edition." Store the files on your computer in a convenient location.

Your Account page is also where you'll find any updates to the lesson files. Look on the Lesson & Update Files tab to access the most current content.

Anything that combines two images is compositing: blending, combining, layering, keying, masking, and cropping. Premiere Pro has powerful tools that enable you to combine layers of video, photos, graphics, and titles in your sequences. In this lesson, you'll learn about the key technologies that make compositing work and about approaches to preparing for compositing.

Starting the lesson

Until now, you have been mainly working with single, whole-frame images. You have created edits in which you have transitioned between one image and another or edited clips onto upper video tracks to have them appear in front of clips on lower video tracks.

In this lesson, you'll learn about ways to combine those layers of video. You'll still use clips on upper and lower tracks, but now they will become foreground and background elements in one combined composition.

This title…

…combines with this video…

…to produce this composite image.

The blend might come from cropping part of the foreground image or from *keying*—selecting a specific color to become transparent—but whatever the method, the way you edit clips onto a sequence is the same as ever.

Let's begin by learning about the important concept of *alpha*, which explains the way pixels are displayed, and then try several techniques.

1   Open Lesson 14.prproj in the Lesson 14 folder.

2   Save the project as **Lesson 14 Working.prproj**.

3   Switch to the Effects workspace by clicking Effects in the Workspaces panel or by choosing Window > Workspaces > Effects.

4   Reset the workspace by opening the Effects menu in the Workspaces panel and choosing Reset To Saved Layout, by choosing Window > Workspaces > Reset To Saved Layout, or by double-clicking the Effects workspace name in the Workspaces panel.

What is an alpha channel?

Cameras record the red, green, and blue parts of the light spectrum as separate color *channels*. Because each channel has a single color, they are commonly described as *monochrome*.

Adobe Premiere Pro CC uses these three monochromatic (single-color) channels to produce the corresponding primary color channels. They are combined using what's called *additive color* to create a complete RGB image (RGB stands for Red, Green, and Blue). You see the three channels combined as full-color video.

Finally, there is a fourth monochromatic channel: *alpha*. The fourth channel defines no colors at all. Instead, it defines *opacity*—how visible the pixel is. Several different words are used to describe this fourth channel, including *visibility*, *transparency*, *mixer*, and *opacity*. The name is not particularly important. What matters is that you can adjust the opacity of pixels independently of their colors because the alpha is separate from the color channels.

Just as you might use color correction to adjust the amount of red in a clip, you can use Opacity controls to adjust the amount of alpha. By default, the alpha channel, or opacity, of clips is 100%, or fully visible. On the 8-bit video scale of 0 to 255, this means it will be at 255. Not all media will include an alpha channel. Video cameras do not generally record an alpha channel, for example.

Clips that are animations or text or logo graphics will often have alpha channels to define which parts of an image are opaque or transparent.

You can set the Source Monitor and Program Monitor to display transparent pixels as a checkerboard instead of black, just as in Adobe Photoshop.

1 From the Graphics bin, open the clip Theft_Unexpected.png in the Source Monitor (be sure to open the PNG clip).

2 Open the Source Monitor Settings menu , and make sure Transparency Grid is not selected.

It looks as if the graphic has a black background, but those black pixels are actually displayed in place of transparency. Think of them as the background of the Source Monitor. If you were to export this as a file to a codec that does not support an alpha channel, the new file would have a black background.

3 Open the Source Monitor Settings menu and choose Transparency Grid.

Now you can clearly see which pixels are transparent. However, for some kinds of media, the transparency grid is an imperfect solution. In this case, for example, it can be a little difficult to see the edges of the text against the grid.

Theft Unexpected

4 Open the Source Monitor Settings menu and choose Transparency Grid again to disable it.

Media files that are created using a codec that does not support an alpha channel will always have a black background rather than transparent areas.

Making compositing part of your projects

Using compositing effects and controls can take your post-production work to a whole new level. Once you begin working with the compositing effects available in Premiere Pro, you'll find yourself discovering new ways of filming and new ways of structuring your edit to make it easier to blend images together.

A combination of preproduction planning, filming techniques, and dedicated effects will produce the most powerful results when compositing. You can combine still images of environments with complex, interesting patterns to produce extraordinary textured moods. Or you can cut out parts of an image that don't fit and replace them with something else.

Compositing is one of the most creative parts of nonlinear editing with Premiere Pro.

Shooting videos with compositing in mind

Much of the most effective compositing work begins when you are planning your production. Right at the start, you can think about how you can help Premiere Pro identify the parts of the image you'd like to be transparent, and there are a number of ways to do this. Consider chromakey, for example, a standard special effect used by major feature film productions to allow action to take place in environments that would otherwise be too dangerous or physically impossible—like the inside of a volcano!

The actors are actually standing in front of a screen that is solid green. Special-effects technology uses the green color to identify which pixels should be transparent. The video image of the actors is used as the foreground of a composition, with some visible pixels (the actors) and some transparent pixels (the green background).

This…

Next, it's just a question of putting the foreground video image in front of another background image. In an epic action feature film, it's the prebuilt set, a real-world location, or a composite created by visual effects artists; it could be anything.

Planning ahead makes a big difference to the quality of your compositing. For that greenscreen effect to work well, the background needs to be a consistent color. It also needs to be a color that does not appear anywhere on your subject. Green-colored jewelry, for example, might turn transparent when the Chromakey effect is applied.

…combined with this…

If you're shooting greenscreen footage, the way you film can make a big difference to the finished result. Try to match the lighting for your subject to the replacement background you intend to use.

Capture the greenscreen background with soft, evenly distributed light and try to avoid *spill*, where light reflected from the greenscreen bounces onto your subject. If this happens, you'll be in danger of *keying out*, or making transparent, parts of your subject because they will be the same green color as the background you are removing.

…becomes this.

Understanding essential terminology

In this lesson, you'll encounter some terms that might be new to you. Let's run through the important ones.

- **Alpha/alpha channel:** The fourth channel of information for each pixel. An alpha channel defines transparency for a pixel. It's a separate monochromatic channel, and it can be created entirely independently of the content of the image.

- **Key/keying:** The process of selectively making pixels transparent based on their color or brightness. The Chromakey effect uses color to generate transparency (that is, to change the alpha channel), and the LumaKey effect uses brightness.

- **Opacity:** The word used to describe the overall alpha channel value for clips in a sequence in Premiere Pro. The higher the value, the more opaque the clip is— the inverse of transparency. You can adjust the opacity for a clip over time using keyframes, just as you adjusted audio level in a previous lesson.

▶ **Tip:** For more information on blend modes in Adobe software, see *The Hidden Power of Blend Modes*, by Scott Valentine (Adobe Press).

- **Blend mode:** A technology originally seen in Adobe Photoshop. Rather than simply placing foreground images in front of background images, you can select one of several different blend modes that cause the foreground to interact with the background. You might, for example, choose to view only pixels that are brighter than the background or to apply only the color information from the foreground clip to the background. You used a blend mode in Lesson 12, "Adding Video Effects." Experimentation is a good way to learn about blend modes.

- **Greenscreen:** The common term that describes the process of filming a subject in front of a screen that is solid green and then using a special effect to selectively turn green pixels transparent. The clip is then combined with a background image. An old-style weather report is a good example of greenscreen.

- **Matte:** An image, shape, or video clip used to identify a region of your image that should be transparent or semitransparent. Premiere Pro allows multiple types of mattes, and you'll work with them in this lesson. You can use an image, another video clip, or a visual effect like Chromakey to generate a matte dynamically based on the color of the pixels.

When you made a secondary color adjustment in Lesson 13, "Improving Clips with Color Correction and Grading," Premiere Pro generated a matte that was applied to the color adjustment based on the selection you made.

Whereas secondary color adjustments apply a dynamically generated matte to an effect, limiting the pixels that are changed, the Chromakey effect applies the matte to the alpha channel, selectively making pixels transparent.

Working with the Opacity effect

You can adjust the overall opacity of a clip using keyframes on the Timeline panel or in the Effect Controls panel.

1. If it's not already open in the Timeline panel, open the sequence Desert Jacket. This sequence has a foreground image of a man in a jacket, with a background image of a desert.

2. Increase the height of the Video 2 track a little. You can do this by dragging the dividing line in the track header (at the far left of the Timeline panel) between Video 2 and Video 3. You can also hover the pointer over the Video 3 track header, hold Option (macOS) or Alt (Windows), and scroll your mouse wheel.

3. Open the Timeline panel Display Settings menu, and make sure Show Video Keyframes is enabled.

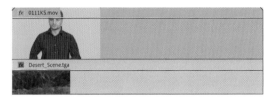

Now you can use the rubber band (the thin horizontal white line on clips) to adjust the settings and keyframe effects. There is only ever one rubber band per clip.

You can specify which control is adjusted with the rubber band by right-clicking the small fx badge *fx*, which changes color if an effect is applied to the clip or if a fixed effect is adjusted *fx*.

By default, the rubber band on visual clips controls Opacity. As you learned earlier, the default for audio clips is volume.

4. Try dragging the rubber band up and down using the Selection tool on the clip on Video 2. Try to set it to exactly 50%.

▶ **Tip:** When adjusting the rubber band, after you begin dragging, you can hold Command (macOS) or Ctrl (Windows) for fine control. Be careful not to press the modifier key before clicking or you'll add a keyframe instead.

When you use the Selection tool in this way, the rubber band is moved without additional keyframes being added.

Keyframing opacity

Keyframing opacity in the Timeline panel is almost the same as keyframing volume. You use the same tools and keyboard shortcuts, and the results are likely to be exactly what you expect: The higher the rubber band, the more visible a clip will be.

1 Open the Theft Unexpected sequence in the Sequences bin.

This sequence has a title in the foreground, on track Video 2. It's common to fade titles up and down at different times and with different durations. You can do so using a transition effect, just as you would add a transition to a video clip; or, for more control, you can use keyframes to adjust the opacity.

2 Make sure track Video 2 is expanded so you can see the rubber band for the foreground title, Theft_Unexpected.png.

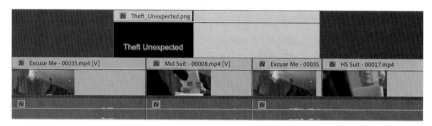

▶ **Tip:** It's often easier to add the keyframe markers to the rubber band first and then drag them to adjust them.

3 Command-click (macOS) or Ctrl-click (Windows) the rubber band for the title graphic four times to add four keyframes—two near the beginning and two near the end. Don't worry about the precise positions of the new keyframes.

▶ **Tip:** Once you've added a keyframe by Command-clicking (macOS) or Ctrl-clicking (Windows), you can release the key and start dragging with the mouse to set the keyframe position.

4 Adjust the keyframes so they represent a fade-up and a fade-down in the same way that you would adjust audio keyframes to adjust volume.

5 Play the sequence and watch the results of your keyframing.

You can also use the Effect Controls panel to add keyframes to the opacity for a clip. Like the audio volume keyframes controls, the Opacity setting has keyframing turned on by default in the Effect Controls panel. If you select the title clip in the Timeline panel, you'll see that the keyframes you just added are also displayed in the Effect Controls panel.

Combining tracks using a blend mode

Blend modes are special ways for foreground pixels (in clips on upper tracks) to combine with background pixels (in clips below them). Each blend mode applies a different calculation to combine the foreground red, green, blue, and alpha (RGBA) values with those of the background. Each pixel is calculated in combination with the pixel directly behind it.

The default blend mode is called Normal. In this mode, the foreground image has a uniform alpha channel value across the entire image. The more opacity the foreground image has, the more strongly you will see those pixels in front of the pixels in the background.

The best way to find out how blend modes work is to try them.

1   Replace the current title in the Theft Unexpected sequence with the more complex title Theft_Unexpected_Layered.psd in the Graphics bin.

   You can replace the existing title by dragging the new item onto it while holding Option (macOS) or Alt (Windows). Notice that replacing a clip this way retains the sequence clip keyframes you added.

2   Select the new title in the sequence and take a look at the Effect Controls panel.

3   In the Effect Controls panel, expand the Opacity controls, and browse through the Blend Mode options.

4   Right now, the blend mode is set to Normal. Try a few different options to see the results. Each blend mode calculates the relationship between the foreground layer pixels and the background pixels differently. See Premiere Pro Help for a description of the blend modes.

Tip: To quickly browse through the modes, hover the pointer over the Blend Mode menu, without clicking to open it, and scroll.

Try the Lighten blend mode. In this mode, a pixel is visible only if it is lighter than the pixel behind it.

5 Choose the Normal blend mode when you have finished experimenting.

Working with alpha-channel transparencies

Many types of media will already have varying alpha channel levels for pixels. A title graphic is an obvious example: Where text exists, pixels have 100% opacity, and where there is no text, pixels usually have 0% opacity. Elements such as drop shadows around text typically have a value somewhere in between. Keeping some transparency in a drop shadow helps it look a little more realistic.

Premiere Pro sees pixels with higher values in the alpha channel as being more visible. This is the most common way to interpret alpha channels, but occasionally you might come across media that is configured in the opposite way. You will immediately recognize the problem because you'll see a cutout in an otherwise black image. This is easy to address because, just as Premiere Pro can interpret the audio channels on a clip, it's also possible to choose a different interpretation of an alpha channel.

You can see the results using a title in the Theft Unexpected sequence.

1 Locate Theft_Unexpected_Layered.psd in the project panel.

2 Right-click the clip and choose Modify > Interpret Footage. In the lower half of the Modify Clip dialog box, you'll find the Alpha Channel interpretation options.

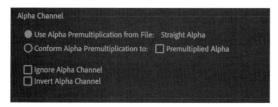

The Alpha Channel Premultiplication options relate to the way semitransparent areas are interpreted. If you find that soft semitransparent image areas are blocky or poorly rendered, try selecting Premultiplied Alpha and view the results.

3   Try selecting Ignore Alpha Channel; then try selecting Invert Alpha Channel. Observe the results in the Program Monitor (you will need to click OK before the display will update).

4   When you have finished experimenting, leave the Alpha Channel option set to Use Alpha Premultiplication From File.

- **Ignore Alpha Channel:** Treats all pixels as having 100% alpha. This can be useful if you don't intend to use a background clip in your sequence and would prefer black pixels.

- **Invert Alpha Channel:** Reverses the alpha channel for every pixel in the clip. This means that pixels that were fully opaque will become fully transparent, and pixels that were transparent will become opaque.

Note: Blend modes still apply when changing the interpretation of the alpha channel. If you invert the alpha channel and use a blend mode like Lighten, the black background won't be visible.

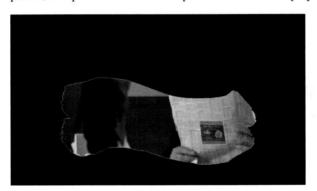

Color keying a greenscreen shot

When you change the opacity level of a clip using the rubber band or the Effect Controls panel, you adjust the alpha for every pixel in the image by the same amount. There are also ways to selectively adjust the alpha for pixels, based on their position on the screen, their brightness, or their color.

Chromakey effects adjust the opacity for a range of pixels based on their specific luminance, hue, and saturation values. The principle is quite simple: You select a color or range of colors, and the more similar a pixel is to the selection, the more transparent it becomes. The more closely a pixel matches the selection, the more its alpha channel value is lowered, until it becomes fully transparent.

Note: Highly compressed media files (such as H.264 4:2:0) will generally not give the same result as a RAW or lightly compressed file (such as ProRes 4:4:4:4) captured using a high-end camera.

Let's set up a chromakey composition.

1 Drag the clip Timekeeping.mov, in the Greenscreen bin, onto the New Item button ⬛ in the Project panel. This creates a sequence that matches the media perfectly. The clip will be added to the Video 1 track.

2 In the sequence, drag the Timekeeping.mov clip up to Video 2—this will be the foreground.

3 Drag the clip Seattle_Skyline_Still.tga from the Shots bin to track Video 1, under the Timekeeping.mov clip on the Timeline.

   Because this is a single-frame graphic, its default duration is too short.

4 Trim the Seattle_Skyline_Still.tga clip so that it's long enough to be a back-ground for the full duration of the foreground clip on Video 2.

5 In the Project panel, your sequence is still named after the Timekeeping.mov clip, and it's stored in the same Greenscreen bin. Rename the sequence Seattle Skyline, and drag it into the Sequences bin.

   This kind of on-the-fly organization is worth the extra effort, as it helps you stay in control of your project.

You now have foreground and background clips. All that remains is to make the green pixels transparent.

Preprocessing the footage

In a perfect world, every greenscreen clip you work with would have a flawless green background and nice, clean edges on your foreground elements. In reality, there are lots of reasons why you might be faced with less-than perfect material.

There are always potential problems caused by poor lighting when the video is created. However, there's a further problem caused by the way many video cameras store image information.

Because our eyes do not register color as accurately as they do brightness information, it's common for cameras to reduce the amount of color information stored. This saves storage space and is rarely immediately visible.

The approach varies from system to system. Sometimes color information is stored for every other pixel; other times it might be recorded for every other pixel on every second line. This type of file-size reduction is usually a good idea because otherwise the storage required would be *huge*. However, it can make keying more difficult because there simply isn't as much color detail.

If you find that your footage is not keying well, try the following:

- Consider applying a light blur effect before keying. This blends pixel detail, softening the edges and often giving a smoother-looking result. If the amount of blur is light, it should not dramatically reduce the quality of your image. You can simply apply a blur effect to the clip, adjust the settings, and then apply a chromakey effect on top. The chromakey effect will be applied after the blur because it appears next on the list in the Effect Controls panel.

- Consider color correcting your shot before you key it. If your shot lacks good contrast between your foreground and background, you can sometimes help the key by adjusting the picture first using the Lumetri Color panel.

Using the Ultra Key effect

Premiere Pro includes a powerful, fast, and intuitive chromakey effect called Ultra Key. The workflow is simple: Choose a color you want to become transparent and then adjust settings to suit. The Ultra Key effect, like every greenscreen keyer, dynamically generates a matte (defining which pixels should be transparent) based on the color selection. The matte is adjustable using the detailed settings of the Ultra Key effect.

1   Apply the Ultra Key effect to the Timekeeping.mov clip in the new Seattle Skyline sequence. You can find the effect easily by typing **Ultra** in the Effects panel search box.

2 In the Effect Controls panel, select the Key Color eyedropper (not the color swatch).

▶ **Tip:** If you hold Command (macOS) or Ctrl (Windows) when you click with the eyedropper, Premiere Pro takes a 5×5 pixel sample average, rather than a single-pixel selection. This often captures a better color for keying.

3 Holding the Command key (macOS) or Ctrl key (Windows), use the eyedropper to click a green area in the Program Monitor. This clip has a consistent green background, so it's not too important where you click. With other footage, you may need to experiment to find the right spot.

The Ultra Key effect identifies all pixels that have the green you selected and sets their alpha to 0%.

4 In the Effect Controls panel, change the Output setting for the Ultra Key effect to Alpha Channel. In this mode, the Ultra Key effect displays the alpha channel as a grayscale image, where dark pixels will be transparent and light pixels will be opaque.

It's a pretty good key, but there are a few areas of gray where the pixels will be partially transparent, which you don't want. Where there's naturally semitransparent detail, like hair or the soft edges of clothing, there should be some gray, and the right and left sides don't have any green, so none of those pixels can be keyed. You'll fix that later. Still, in the main areas of the alpha channel should be solid black or white.

5 In the Effect Controls panel, open the Setting menu for the Ultra Key effect and choose Aggressive. This cleans up the selection a little. Scrub through the shot to see whether it has clean black areas and white areas. If you see gray pixels in this view where there should not be, the result will be partially transparent parts in the picture.

6 Switch the Output setting back to Composite to see the result.

The Aggressive mode works better for this clip. The Default, Relaxed, and Aggressive modes modify the Matte Generation, Matte Cleanup, and Spill Suppression settings. You can also modify manually to get a better key with more challenging footage.

Here's an overview of the settings:

- **Matte Generation:** Once you've chosen your key color, the controls in the Matte Generation category change the way it's interpreted. You'll often get positive results with more challenging footage just by adjusting these settings.

- **Matte Cleanup:** Once your matte is defined, you can use these controls to adjust it:

  - Choke shrinks the matte, which is helpful if your key selection misses some edges. Be careful not to choke the matte too much because you'll begin to lose edge detail in the foreground image, often supplying a *digital haircut* in the vernacular of the visual-effects industry.

  - Soften applies a blur to the matte, which often improves the apparent "blending" of the foreground and background images for a more convincing composite.

  - Contrast increases the contrast of the alpha channel, making that black-and-white image a stronger black-and-white version and more clearly defining the key. You will often get cleaner keys by increasing the contrast. Mid Point is the level from which contrast is adjusted—a kind of anchor point for contrast. Adjust contrast around a different level for more subtle control.

- **Spill Suppression:** Spill Suppression compensates for color that bounces from the green background onto the subject. When this happens, the combination of the green background and the subject's own colors are usually different enough that it does not cause parts of the subject to be keyed transparent. However, it does not look good when the edges of your subject are green!

  Spill suppression automatically compensates by adding color to the foreground element edges that are positioned opposite, on a color wheel, to the key color. For example, magenta is added when greenscreen keying, or yellow is added when bluescreen keying. This neutralizes the color "spill" in the same way that you'd fix a color cast.

- **Color Correction:** The built-in Color Correction controls give you a quick and easy way to adjust the appearance of your foreground video to help it blend in with your background.

  Often, these three controls are enough to make a more natural match. Note that these adjustments are applied after the key, so you won't cause problems for your key by adjusting the colors with these controls. You can use any color adjustment tools in Premiere Pro, including the Lumetri Color panel.

> **Note:** In this example, you're using footage with a green background. It is also possible you'll have footage with a blue background for keying. The workflow is the same.

Masking clips

The Ultra Key effect generates a matte dynamically, based on the colors in your shot. You can also create your own custom matte or use another clip as the basis for a matte.

When you create your own matte, you'll use the mask feature applied to the Opacity settings for your clip. Let's create a matte to remove the edges from the Timekeeping.mov clip.

1 Return to the Seattle Skyline sequence.

   As you discovered earlier, the foreground clip has an actor standing in front of a greenscreen, but the screen does not reach the edge of the picture. It's common to shoot greenscreen footage this way, particularly when filming on location, where full studio facilities may not be available.

2 Disable the Ultra Key effect, without removing it, by clicking the Toggle Effect button *fx* in the Effect Controls panel. This allows you to clearly see the green areas of the picture again.

3 Still in the Effect Controls panel, expand the Opacity controls and click the Create 4-point Polygon Mask button ▦ just under that heading.

A mask is applied to the clip, making most of the image transparent.

4 Resize the mask so that it reveals the central area of the shot but hides the black edges. You will almost certainly need to reduce the Program Monitor zoom to 50% or 25% to see beyond the edges of the image.

As long as you have the mask selected in the Effect Controls panel, you can click directly in the Program Monitor to reposition the corner control points for the mask. Don't worry about precisely matching the edges of the frame. Instead, focus on selecting the areas in the picture the subject moves into.

▶ **Tip:** If you deselect the mask, the control points displayed in the Program Monitor will disappear. Select the mask in the Effect Controls panel to reactivate them.

▶ **Tip:** A rough mask of this kind, used to remove unwanted image elements, is often referred to as a *garbage matte*.

5 Set the Program Monitor zoom option to Fit.

6 Toggle the Ultra Key effect back on in the Effect Controls panel and deselect the clip to remove the visible mask handles.

This is particularly challenging footage because the original camera recording includes adjustments to the edges of the subject, and it uses a color compression system that reduces color fidelity. With patience and precise adjustments you can still achieve a reasonable effect.

Using mattes that use graphics or other clips

Adding a mask to the Opacity settings in the Effect Controls panel sets user-defined regions that should be visible or transparent. Premiere Pro can also use another clip as a reference for a matte.

The Track Matte Key effect uses the luminance information or alpha channel information from any clips on a track to define a transparency matte for a selected clip on another track. With a little planning and preparation, this simple effect can produce powerful results because you can use any clips as a reference and even apply effects to them, changing the resulting matte.

Using the Track Matte Key effect

Let's use the Track Matte Key effect to add a layered title to the Seattle Skyline sequence.

1   Select the Timekeeping.mov clip and delete it from the Video 2 track.

2   Edit the clip Laura_06.mp4, from the Shots bin, onto the Video 2 track, at the beginning of the sequence.

3   Drag the graphic clip SEATTLE from the Graphics bin onto the Timeline V3 track, directly above the Laura_06.mp4 clip.

4   Trim the SEATTLE graphic clip to match the duration of the Laura_06.mp4 clip.

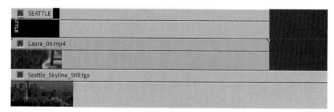

5   Find the Track Matte Key effect in the Effects panel, and apply it to the Laura_06.mp4 clip on the Video 2 track.

6   In the Effect Controls panel, choose Video 3 from the matte menu in the Track Matte Key controls.

7 Scrub through the sequence to see the result. The white text in the title clip on Video 3 is no longer visible. Instead, it's being used as a guide to define the visible and transparent regions of the clip on V3.

By default, the Track Matte Key effect uses the alpha channel from clips on the selected track to generate a key. If your reference clips don't use an alpha channel, change the Composite Using menu to Matte Luma, and the brightness of the reference clips will be used instead.

Tip: In this example, you're using a still image as a reference for the Track Matte Key effect. You can use any clip, though, including other video clips.

The Track Matte Key effect is an unusual effect because most other effects exclusively change the clip they are applied to. The Track Matte Key effect changes both the clip it's applied to *and* the clip used as a reference. In fact, it makes any clips on the selected reference track transparent.

The colors in the Laura_06.mp4 clip work well against the blue in the background clip, but they could be more vivid. You might want to experiment with color correction tools to make the red stronger and brighter so it's a more compelling composition.

You could also add a blur effect to the Laura_06.mp4 clip and change the playback speed to create a softer, slower-moving texture.

Review questions

1 What is the difference between the RGB channels and the alpha channel?

2 How do you apply a blend mode to a clip?

3 How do you keyframe clip opacity?

4 How do you change the way a media file's alpha channel is interpreted?

5 What does it mean to key a clip?

6 Are there any limits to the kinds of clips you can use as a reference for the Track Matte Key effect?

Review answers

1 RGB channels describe color information; the alpha channel describes opacity.

2 Choose a blend mode from the Blend Mode menu in the Opacity category in the Effect Controls panel.

3 You adjust clip opacity in the same way you adjust clip volume, in the Timeline panel or in the Effect Controls panel. To make an adjustment in the Timeline panel, make sure you're viewing the rubber band for the clip you want to adjust and then drag with the Selection tool. If you hold Command (macOS) or Ctrl (Windows) while clicking, you'll add keyframes. You can also work with keyframes using the Pen tool.

4 Right-click the file in the Project panel and choose Modify > Interpret Footage.

5 A key is usually a special effect where the color or brightness of pixels is used to define which part of the image should be transparent and which part should be visible.

6 You can use just about anything to create your key with the Track Matte Key effect, as long as it is positioned on a track above the clip you apply the effect to. You can apply special effects to the reference clip, and the results of those effects will be reflected in the matte. You can even use multiple clips because the setting is based on the track, rather than a particular clip.

15 CREATING GRAPHICS

Lesson overview

In this lesson, you'll learn about the following:

- Using the Essential Graphics panel
- Working with video typography
- Creating graphics
- Stylizing text
- Working with shapes and logos
- Making text roll and crawl
- Working with template graphics

 This lesson will take about 90 minutes to complete. Please log in to your account on peachpit.com to download the lesson files for this lesson, or go to the "Getting Started" section at the beginning of this book and follow the instructions under "Accessing the lesson files and Web Edition." Store the files on your computer in a convenient location.

Your Account page is also where you'll find any updates to the lesson files. Look on the Lesson & Update Files tab to access the most current content.

Although you will rely upon audio and video sources as the primary ingredients for building a sequence, you will often need to incorporate text into your project. Adobe Premiere Pro CC includes powerful title and graphic creation tools you can work with right in the Timeline panel; or you can use the Essential Graphics panel to create text and shapes.

Starting the lesson

Text is effective when you need to convey information quickly to your audience. For example, you can identify a speaker in your video by superimposing their name and title during the interview (often called a *lower-third*). You can also use text to identify sections of a longer video (often called *bumpers*) or to acknowledge the cast and crew (with credits).

Text, properly used, is clearer than a narrator and allows for information to be presented in the middle of dialogue. Text can be used to reinforce key information.

The Essential Graphics panel offers a range of text-editing and shape-creation tools that you can use to design graphics. You can use the fonts loaded on your computer (and those available via Adobe Fonts as part of your Creative Cloud membership).

You can also control opacity and color and insert graphic elements or logos created using other Adobe applications, such as Adobe Photoshop or Adobe Illustrator.

Let's try a few graphic and titling techniques.

1 Open Lesson 15.prproj in the Lesson 15 folder.

2 Save the project as **Lesson 15 Working.prproj**.

3 Switch to the Graphics workspace by clicking Graphics in the Workspaces panel or by choosing Window > Workspaces > Graphics.

4 Reset the workspace by opening the Graphics menu in the Workspaces panel and choosing Reset To Saved Layout, by choosing Window > Workspaces > Reset To Saved Layout, or by double-clicking the Graphics workspace name in the Workspaces panel.

The Graphics workspace reveals the Essential Graphics panel and positions the Tools panel next to the Program Monitor to make it easier to access the graphics tools you'll work with directly on the video preview.

Getting an overview of the Essential Graphics panel

The Essential Graphics panel has two sections.

- **Browse:** Allows you to browse a number of built-in or imported title templates, many of which include animation.

- **Edit:** Allows you to make changes to titles you have added to a sequence or created in a sequence.

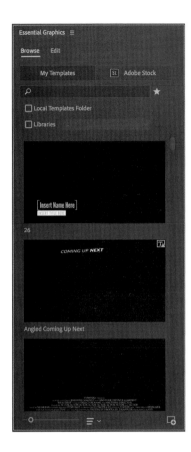

When browsing, you can look for templates you own in the My Templates area or switch to searching Adobe Stock. There are many free and paid templates available from Adobe Stock. For these lessons, we'll focus on templates available in My Templates.

In addition to starting with a template, you can use the Type tool , Pen tool , Rectangle tool [icon], or Ellipse tool [icon] to create a new graphic by clicking in the Program Monitor with no clips selected (if a title clip is selected, you'll add to that clip).

If you press and hold the Type tool, the Vertical Type tool is revealed, which allows you to type text in a column, instead of a row.

You can also use the Pen tool [icon] directly in the Program Monitor to create shapes to use as graphic elements in titles.

If you press and hold the Pen tool, the Rectangle tool and the Ellipse tool are revealed.

Once you have created new graphic and text elements, you can reposition and resize them using the Selection tool [icon].

All of this creative work is performed directly in the Program Monitor and in the Timeline panel.

Let's start with some preformatted text and modify it. This is a good way to get an overview of the powerful features of the Essential Graphics panel. Later in this lesson, you'll build a title from scratch.

1   If it's not open already, open the sequence 01 Clouds.

2   Position the playhead over the Cloudscape title on the V2 track and select it.

3   Switch to the Edit pane of the Essential Graphics panel.

Like the Effect Controls panel, the Edit pane of the Essential Graphics panel shows options for whichever clip is selected in the Timeline panel.

Also, just as with the Effect Controls panel, you can view the options for only one clip at a time.

Like the Lumetri Color panel, changes made in the Essential Graphics panel actually appear as effects in the Effect Controls panel, with the full range of settings available, including the options to create effect presets and to animate graphic elements with keyframes.

Notice there are two items listed at the top of the Essential Graphics panel: Cloudscape and Shape 02.

If you are familiar with Adobe Photoshop, you'll recognize these as layers. Each item in a graphic is displayed as a layer in the Essential Graphics panel.

Just like Timeline tracks, the layers at the top are in front of the layers at the bottom, and you can drag items up and down the list.

You'll also recognize the familiar eye button 👁 for making layers invisible or visible.

Below these layers you'll see the Responsive Design controls. These allow you to specify a section at the start and end of the graphic clip that should not be stretched if you change the duration of the clip in the sequence. This is important if there are animation keyframes for the start and end of the graphic.

4 Click to select the Shape 02 layer at the top of the Essential Graphics panel.

This displays standard alignment and appearance controls for Shape layers—in this case, the red band that goes across the screen.

Many of the options will be familiar to you from the Motion effect in the Effect Controls panel.

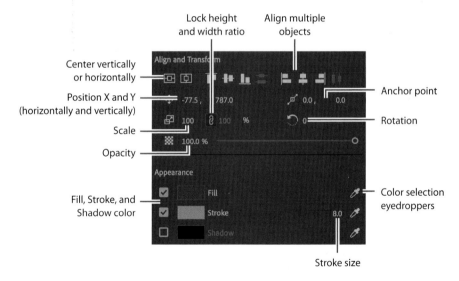

Items that are new to you are likely to be in the Appearance section, where you can specify a color for the shape fill, stroke (a colored line on the edges of a shape or text), and shadow (see "Text styles" later in this lesson for more information about these).

Perhaps these color swatches are already familiar to you. They work in an intuitive way.

5 Click the Fill color swatch.

A color picker appears that allows you to choose a precise color. There are a number of color systems to choose between, or you can move your pointer over a sample of the color you want and click to select it directly.

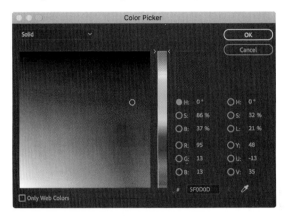

6 Click Cancel and then click the eyedropper  for the fill color on the right side of the Essential Graphics panel.

The eyedropper allows you to pick a color from anywhere in the image. In fact, you can pick colors from anywhere on your computer screen! This is particularly useful if you have a range of colors you always want to use, such as a logo or branding color.

7 Click the thin blue band of sky between the clouds. The shape fill changes color to match the sky.

8 Make sure you have selected the Selection tool in the Tools panel and that the Shape 02 layer is still selected in the Essential Graphics panel.

Notice the control handles visible on the shape in the Program Monitor. You can use the Selection tool to change the shape directly. For now, you're going to use the Selection tool to select another layer in the title.

To select a layer in the Program Monitor, you may need to first deselect the layer that's already selected. You can do this by clicking the background of the Program Monitor or by deselecting the title clip in the Timeline panel.

9 Use the Selection tool to click the word *Cloudscape* in the Program Monitor.

The same Align And Transform and Appearance controls are displayed in the Essential Graphics panel, but now there are additional controls that determine the appearance of the text.

> **Note:** You may have to expand the window or scroll to see all the Essential Graphics panel options.

> **Note:** When working with CJK fonts, Tsume adjusts the spacing around characters without adjusting the vertical or horizontal scaling of the characters.

> **Note:** With all the clicking and testing, it's easy to accidentally deselect layers. If there's no bounding box with handles around the text or shape, select it using the Selection tool.

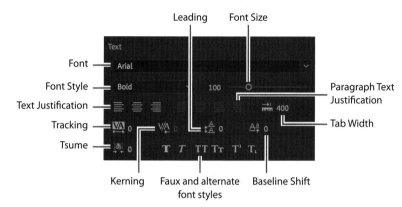

10 Try a few fonts and font styles to experiment with the controls. Anywhere you see blue numbers, you can drag with your mouse to update the setting. This is a quick way to find out what a control is for.

> **Tip:** If you're ever unsure about the purpose of a control, hover the pointer over an icon and a tooltip will tell you the name.

The specific fonts loaded on each system will vary, and your Adobe Creative Cloud membership includes access to many more fonts than you will have available to begin with.

To add more fonts, click the Add Fonts From Adobe button  (or choose Graphics > Add Fonts From Adobe Fonts on the main menu bar). This will open the Adobe Fonts website in your default internet browser, where you will find thousands of fonts to use.

> **Note:** Premiere Pro automatically saves your updated title in the project file. It does not show up as a separate file on your hard drive.

Mastering video typography essentials

Tip: If you'd like to learn more about typography, consider the book *Stop Stealing Sheep & Find Out How Type Works*, Third Edition (Adobe Press, 2013), by Erik Spiekermann.

When you design text for video, it's essential that you follow typography conventions. If text is composited over a moving video background with multiple colors, it can take some work to create a clear design.

Find a balance between legibility and style, making sure enough information is on the screen without crowding it. If there's too much text, it will quickly become hard to read, frustrating the viewer.

Choosing a font

Your computer probably has many fonts, which can make choosing a good font for video work difficult. To simplify the selection process, try using a triage mentality and consider these factors:

- **Readability:** Is the font easy to read at the size you're using? Are all the characters readable? If you look at it quickly and then close your eyes, what do you remember about the text block?

- **Style:** Using adjectives only, how would you describe the font you've chosen? Does the font convey the right emotion? Type is like a wardrobe or a haircut; picking the right font is essential to the overall success of the design.

- **Flexibility:** Does the font mix well with others? Does it come in various weights (such as bold, italic, and semibold) that make it easier to convey significance? Can you create a hierarchy of information that conveys different kinds of information, such as a name and title for a speaker's lower-third name graphic?

- **Language compatibility:** Does the font include all the characters required for the language you are using?

The answers to these guiding principles should help steer you toward better-designed titles. You may need to experiment to find the best font. Fortunately, you can easily modify an existing title or duplicate it and change the copy for a side-by-side comparison.

Choosing a color

Note: When creating text for use in a video, you will often find yourself placing it over a background that has many colors present. This will make it difficult to achieve proper contrast (which is essential to preserving legibility). To help in this case, you may need to add a stroke or shadow to get a contrasting edge. For more information about adding a stroke or shadow, see "Text styles" later in this lesson.

Although you can create a nearly infinite number of possible color combinations, choosing the right colors to use in a design can be surprisingly tricky. This is because only a few colors work well for text while remaining clear for the viewer. This task becomes even more difficult if you're editing your video for broadcast or if your design must match the style and branding of a series or product. The text may also need to work when placed over a busy moving background.

While it may feel a little conservative, the most common choices for text in video are black and white. If colors are used, they tend to be very light or very dark shades. The color you choose must provide suitable contrast from the background that the text is being placed over, which means you'll be making constant assessments about ideal colors, which often include factors such as branding requirements or a consistent color palette for your sequence.

Consider a positive example with clear light text over a dark background.

Note: The Adobe Color service helps you choose harmonious and appealing color combinations for your design projects. For more information, visit color.adobe.com.

And now here's a less positive example. The text is a similar color and tone to parts of the sky.

Adjusting the kerning

It's common to adjust the spacing between the letters in a title to improve the appearance of text and help match it to the design of the background. This process is called *kerning*. Taking the time to manually adjust text becomes more important the larger the font gets (because it makes improper kerning that much more visible). The goal is to improve the appearance and readability of your text while creating optical flow.

Note: A common place to start kerning is to adjust between an initial capital letter and the succeeding lowercase letters, particularly in the case of a letter with very little "base," such as *T*, which creates the illusion of excessive space along the baseline.

You can learn a lot about kerning by studying professionally designed materials such as posters and magazines. Kerning is applied letter by letter, allowing for creative use of spacing.

Try kerning an existing title.

1 Locate the title clip White Cloudscape in the Assets bin.

2 Edit the clip into the 01 Clouds sequence after the first title on the Video 2 track.

Make sure the title is positioned over the background video clip so you can use it as a reference for positioning.

3 Select the Type tool [T] and click to place the insertion point between the *D* and the *S* of the word *CLOUDSCAPE*. Note that the insertion point may be offset from the text in some graphics, particularly if the graphic is animated.

4 In the Edit pane of the Essential Graphics panel, in the Text section, set Kerning to **250**.

The kerning option is available only when a single letter is selected or when the I-bar is placed between two letters.

5 Repeat this process for the rest of the letters to the right.

6 Click the Horizontal Center button  in the Align And Transform section of the Essential Graphics panel to reposition the text. Then deselect the text by clicking an empty track in the Timeline panel.

7 Select the Selection tool.

● **Note:** After using a different tool, it's a good idea to return to the Selection tool to avoid accidentally adding new text or making unwanted changes to your sequence.

Setting the tracking

Another important text property is *tracking* (which is similar to kerning). This is the overall control of spacing between all the letters in a line of text. Tracking can be used to globally condense or expand a text selection.

It's often employed in the following scenarios:

- **Tighter tracking:** If a line of text is too long (such as a lengthy title for a speaker's lower-third), you may tighten it slightly to fit. This will keep the font size the same but fit more text into the available space.

- **Looser tracking:** A looser track can be useful when using all uppercase letters or a more complex font. It's used often for large titles or when text is used as a design or motion graphics element.

You can adjust tracking in the Text section of the Essential Graphics panel. Simply select a text layer and adjust the setting.

1 Drag the clip Cloudscape Tracking from the Assets bin onto the clip White Cloudscape in the 01 Clouds sequence to overwrite one clip with the other.

   If Snap is turned on in the Timeline panel, the new clip will snap to the beginning of the existing title in the sequence.

2 Make sure the clip is selected and use the Selection tool to select the text.

3 In the Edit pane of the Essential Graphics panel, experiment with the tracking control. As you increase the tracking, the letters expand to the right, away from the anchor point.

4 Set the tracking to **530**.

5 Click the Center Align Text button ▤ in the text section of the Essential Graphics panel, and then click Horizontal Center ▣ in the Align And Transform section to re-center the text.

It's not necessary to click the Center Align Text button to center the text, as the Horizontal Center button will achieve the same result. However, centering the text first will mean any additional lines of text will be properly aligned.

Tracking adjustments tend to look neater and more intentional than individual kerning adjustments.

Adjusting the leading

Kerning and tracking control the horizontal space between characters. *Leading* (pronounced "led-ing") controls the vertical space between lines of text. The name comes from the time when strips of lead were used on a printing press to create space between lines of text.

You adjust the leading in the Text section of the Essential Graphics panel Edit pane. Let's add another line of text.

1 Continue to work with the Cloudscape Tracking clip in the 01 Clouds sequence.

2 With the Cloudscape Tracking clip selected in the Timeline panel, use the Selection tool to double-click the CLOUDSCAPE text in the Program monitor. This highlights the text, ready for editing.

3 Press the Right arrow key to move the cursor to the end of the text.

4 Press Return (macOS) or Enter (Windows) to enter a second line of text. Type (all in caps) **A NEW LAND**.

5 Select the second line of text. Give the new text a font size of 48, set the tracking to 1000, and set the Leading ▦ to 40.

6 Click an empty track in the Timeline panel to deselect the graphic.

This increase in leading helps to separate the second line of text, but it's still difficult to read because of the background image.

7   Select the Cloudscape Tracking clip in the sequence, then select the text layer CLOUDSCAPE A NEW LAND at the top of the Essential Graphics panel (the text in the layer is condensed into a single layer name).

Now that the layer is selected, increase the leading to 140. This adds space between lines and improves readability.

8   Switch to the Selection tool, and click an empty track in the Timeline panel to deselect the clip.

In most cases, you'll find the default setting works well for leading. Adjusting leading can have a big impact on your title. Don't set the leading too tight; otherwise, descenders from the top line (such as the downward lines on *j*, *p*, *q*, and *g*) will cross ascenders from the lower line (like the upward lines on *b*, *d*, *k*, and *l*). This collision is likely to make the text more difficult to read, particularly against a moving background.

Setting the alignment

While you may be used to seeing text left-justified for things like a newspaper, there are no hard-and-fast rules for aligning video text. Generally, text used for a lower-third title is left- or right-justified.

alignment buttons

justification buttons

You'll often center text used in a rolling title sequence or segment bumper. In the Essential Graphics panel, there are buttons for aligning and justifying your text. The alignment buttons align selected point text to the left, center, or right relative to the origin point of the text. The buttons align paragraph type relative to the bounding box. Use the justification buttons to make paragraph text fill the width of its bounding box. The buttons set the justification for the final line of text: left, center, full, or right.

It's safe to experiment, and use the Undo option if necessary, so don't worry about memorizing which alignment option is which.

You may find the position of text in the frame changes when choosing a new alignment setting. If so, manually reposition the text or click the Vertical Center button ⊡ or Horizontal Center button ⊡ to bring the text back into the middle of the frame.

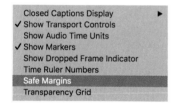

Setting the safe title margin

When creating titles, you may want to view guides to help you position text and graphic elements.

You can enable or disable these by opening the Settings menu in the Program Monitor and choosing Safe Margins.

By default, the outer box is 10 percent from the edge. The area inside this box is considered the *action safe area*. Things that fall outside this box may get cut off when the video signal is viewed on a television monitor. Be sure to place all critical elements that are meant to be seen (like a logo) in this region.

The inner box, is 20 percent from the edge by default. The area inside this box is called the *title safe area*. Just as this book has margins to keep the text from getting too close to the edge, it's a good idea to keep text inside the innermost safe margin. This will make it easier for your audience to read the information.

If text is outside the *title safe area*, there's a chance some letters may be missed on a miscalibrated screen.

Screen technology has improved over time, and it's now common to set the *action safe area* to 3.5% from the edge, and the *title safe area* to 5% from the edge.

You can change these settings by opening the Settings menu in the Source Monitor or Program Monitor and choosing Overlay Settings > Settings.

Creating Graphics

When you create a title, you'll need to make some choices about how the text is displayed. There are two approaches to creating text, each offering both horizontal and vertical text direction options.

- **Point text:** This approach builds a text bounding box as you type. The text runs on one line until you press Return (macOS) or Enter (Windows). Changing the shape and size of the box changes the Scale property in the Essential Graphics panel.

- **Paragraph (area) text:** You set the size and shape of the text box before entering text. Changing the box size later displays more or less text but does not change the size of the text.

When using the Type tool in the Program Monitor, you choose which type of text you are adding when you first click.

- Click and type to add point text.

- Drag to create a text box and then type to add paragraph text inside the box.

Most of the options in the Essential Graphics panel apply to both types of text.

Adding point text

Now that you have been introduced to some of the main factors when modifying and designing a graphic, let's build one from scratch, working with a new sequence.

You'll create a new title to help promote a tourist destination.

1 Open the sequence 02 Cliff.

2 Position the Timeline playhead at the beginning over the sequence and select the Type tool.

3 Click in the Program Monitor and type **The Dead Sea**.

A new graphic clip is added to the sequence in the Timeline panel on the next available video track. In this case, it's Video 2.

Note: If you have been experimenting with the Essential Graphics panel, your title may look different from the example shown. Whatever settings you used last will be applied to new titles you create.

4 If you clicked the white clouds in the background image before typing, it might be difficult to read the text.

Try changing the background video frame by dragging the Timeline playhead. Choose the background frame carefully when designing a title. Because video moves, you may find a title works at the start of a clip but not at the end.

5 Select the Selection tool. Handles appear on the text bounding box.

You won't be able to use a keyboard shortcut for the Selection tool because you're typing into a text bounding box.

Choose the following settings in the Essential Graphics pane:

Font: Arial Bold
Font size: 83
Tracking: 0
Kerning: 0
Fill color: White

Try to match the example given here.

6 Using the Selection tool, drag the corners and edges of the text bounding box. Notice that the Font Size, Width, and Height settings do not change. Instead, the Scale setting is adjusted.

By default, the height and width maintain the same relative scale. You can adjust the height and width separately by clicking Set Scale Lock .

Set the Scale back to 100%.

7 Hover the pointer just outside a corner of the text box until a curved pointer appears. This allows you to rotate the text box. Drag to rotate the bounding box off its horizontal orientation.

The anchor point is the point around which objects will rotate and the single point that's referenced by position controls. When you adjust position settings, the position applies specifically to the anchor point, which itself has a position on the object. For many items it's the exact center of the object (which makes sense, particularly when rotating).

Notice that the default location of this anchor point is the lower-left corner of the text (not the box around the text). When you rotate the text, it's not around the center but instead around that corner.

8 With the Selection tool still active, click the blue number for the rotation setting 🔄 45° in the Essential Graphics panel, type **45**, and press Enter to manually set the angle to 45 degrees.

9 Click anywhere in the bounding box and drag the text and its bounding box toward the upper-right corner of the frame.

10 Disable the Video 1 track output by clicking the Toggle Track Output button 👁 in the Timeline panel.

11 Open the Program Monitor Settings menu, and choose Transparency Grid to enable it.

Now you can see the graphic against a transparency checkerboard, but it's almost impossible to read!

12 With the text selected, go to the Appearance section of the Essential Graphics panel, and enable the Stroke option to add an outline to the letters. Set the color to black and set Stroke Width to 7.

Now it's easy to see the text, and you can be confident it will remain readable against a range of background colors. For more information about adding a stroke or a shadow to text, see "Text styles" later in this lesson.

Adding paragraph text

Although point text is flexible, you can take better control over layout with paragraph text. This option will automatically wrap the text as it reaches the edge of the paragraph text box.

Continue working with the same graphic clip.

1 Select the Type tool, and make sure the graphic clip is selected in the Timeline panel.

2 Drag in the Program Monitor to create a text box that fills the lower-left corner of the title-safe area.

3 Start typing. Start entering names of participants who will be attending the tour. Use the names here or add your own. Press Return (macOS) or Enter (Windows) after each name to start a new line.

▶ **Tip:** A good way to avoid spelling mistakes is to copy and paste text from an approved script or email that has already been reviewed by your client or producer.

Type at least one name with enough characters to go beyond the right edge of the text box. Unlike point text, area text remains within the confines of the bounding box you defined, and it wraps at the edges of the box onto the next line. If you add so much text that some won't fit in the text box, the extra letters won't be visible.

You may need to reduce the font size so you can see a few lines of text at once.

4 Use the Selection tool to change the size and shape of the bounding box to fit around the text a little better.

● **Note:** If a title clip is selected, clicking to add new text or a shape will add to the existing clip. If no clip is selected, a new clip will be created on the next available track.

As you resize the text box, the text stays the same size, adjusting its position in the text box.

There are now two layers in the Essential Graphics panel. Each text item is a separate layer, with its own controls.

Text styles

In addition to choosing settings like a font, position, and opacity, the Essential graphics panel also allows you to apply a stroke and shadow to text or shapes in a graphic.

Changing a title's appearance

In the Appearance section of the Essential Graphics panel, there are two main options for improving the readability of text.

- **Stroke:** A stroke is a thin edge added to text. It helps to keep text legible over moving video or a complex background.

- **Shadow:** A drop shadow is a common addition to video text because it makes the text easier to read. Be sure to adjust the softness of the shadow. Also, be sure to keep the angle of shadows identical for all titles in a project for consistency.

Just as with the text fill, you can give any color to strokes and shadows.

1 Enable the track output for Video 1.

2 Experiment with the options in the Essential Graphics panel to make the text more readable and add more color to the composition.

3 To set the color for point text in the upper right, select the text and use the Fill color eyedropper to select the orange rocks.

4 To set the color for the paragraph text in the lower left, select the text and use the Fill color eyedropper to select the pale blue sky around the clouds.

   Because the colors in the rocks and clouds vary, you may wish to use the eyedropper to select an approximate color, then click the Fill color swatch to manually adjust the selection.

   Try to match the appearance of the title in the following example.

Note: If you see an exclamation point next to the color you've chosen, Premiere Pro is warning you that a color is not broadcast-safe. This means it may cause problems when the video signal is put into a broadcast television environment. Click the exclamation point to automatically choose the closest color that is broadcast-safe.

Saving custom styles

If you create a look you like, you can save time by storing it as a style. A style describes the color and font characteristics for text. You can use a style to change the appearance of text with a single click; all the properties of the text update to match the preset.

Let's create a style from the text you modified in the previous exercise.

1   Continuing to work on the same title, use the Selection tool to select the paragraph text in the lower-left corner.

2   In the Essential Graphics panel, open the Master Styles menu, and choose Create Master Text Style.

3   Enter the name **Blue Bold Text** and click OK. The style is added to the Master Styles menu.

The new Master Style also appears in the Project panel.

4   Select the other text layer, and use the Master Styles menu to apply the Blue Bold Text style.

So far, you have worked with a title that was already created in a sequence, edited one from the Project panel, and created a new one.

In almost all cases, Premiere Pro requires that any item included in a sequence also exists in the Project panel. Graphics created in Premiere Pro are an exception to this rule.

Remember that Cloudscape Tracking title you edited into the 01 Clouds current sequence earlier? Open that sequence and edit a second instance of that title into the timeline on the Video 2 track. You may need to move the other version of the title out of the way to make space for the new copy.

The changes you made to the title have been applied to the master clip in the Project panel, and the new copy is identical to the one you worked on. That's because the title is a Master Graphic.

You can create a Master Clip item in your Project Panel from a graphic clip in your sequence. Any graphic clips made from that Master Graphic, including the one you upgraded it from, are duplicates of each other. Any changes made to the text, style, or contents in an instance of a Master Graphic get reflected in all other instances of the Master Graphic.

⬤ **Note:** Titles have a default duration set in the user preferences, just like other single-frame media.

You can convert any title to a Master Graphic by selecting it in the Timeline panel, going to the Graphics menu, and choosing Upgrade To Master Graphic.

A new graphic clip is added to the Project panel that you can easily share between sequences or multiple projects.

Creating a graphic or title in Adobe Photoshop CC

You can create titles or graphics for Premiere Pro in Adobe Photoshop. While Photoshop is known as the premier tool for modifying photos, it also has many capabilities for creating elegant titles or logo treatments. Photoshop offers several advanced options, advanced formatting (such as scientific notation), flexible layer styles, and even a spellchecker.

To create a new Photoshop document from inside Premiere Pro, follow these steps:

1 Choose File > New > Photoshop File.

2 The New Photoshop File dialog box appears, with settings based on your current sequence.

3 Click OK.

4 Choose a location to store your new PSD file, name it, and click Save.

5 Photoshop opens, ready for you to edit the file. Photoshop automatically displays safe action and safe title zones in the form of guides. These guides won't appear in the finished image.

6 Select the Horizontal Type tool by pressing T.

7 You can click to add point text or draw a text block for area text. As in Premiere Pro, using a text box in Photoshop allows you to precisely control the layout of text.

8 Enter some text you'd like to use.

9 Adjust the font, color, and point size to taste using the controls in the Options bar across the top of the screen.

10 Click the Commit button ☑ (in the Options bar) to commit the text layer.

11 To add a drop shadow, choose Layer > Layer Style > Drop Shadow. Adjust to taste.

> **Tip:** If you have disabled guides in the Photoshop View options, you can enable them by choosing View > Show > Guides.

When you're finished in Photoshop, you can save and close the file. It will already be in your Project panel in Premiere Pro.

If you'd like to edit the title in Photoshop, select it in the Project panel or Timeline and choose Edit > Edit In Adobe Photoshop. When you save changes in Photoshop, the title updates automatically in Premiere Pro.

Working with shapes and logos

When building titles, you'll likely need more than just words to build a complete graphic. Fortunately, Premiere Pro offers the ability to create vector shapes as graphic elements. Many of the title properties you worked with for text also apply to shapes. You can also import completed graphics (like a logo) to enhance your title.

Creating shapes

If you've created shapes in graphics-editing software such as Photoshop or Adobe Illustrator, you'll find creating geometric objects in Premiere Pro similar.

Select the Pen tool, and click multiple points in the Program Monitor to create a unique shape.

You can also use the Pen Tool submenu to select the Rectangle tool or Ellipse tool. Using either tool, drag in the Program Monitor to create a new shape.

Try these steps to draw shapes in Premiere Pro (this exercise is just for practice):

1 Open the sequence 03 Shapes.

2 Select the Pen tool, and click multiple points in the Program Monitor to create a shape. Each time you click, a new control point is added. Create something small and unique in the lower-left corner of the frame.

3 Complete the shape by clicking the first control point.

● **Note:** Remember, new shapes will have the same appearance you last selected in the Essential Graphics panel. You can easily change the settings.

4 Try changing the fill color, adding a stroke, and changing the stroke color while the shape is selected.

You will need to switch to the selection tool and select the shape as an object to see changes made to the stroke.

5 Create a new shape with the Pen tool. This time, instead of just clicking, drag each time you click.

Dragging when you click creates control points with Bezier handles; these are the same handles you experimented with when setting up keyframes. These handles give you precise control over the shape you have created.

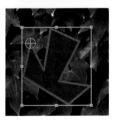

6 Press and hold the Pen tool in the Tools panel to give access to the Rectangle tool.

7 Use the Rectangle tool to create rectangles. Hold the Shift key as you drag to create squares.

8 Now press and hold the Rectangle tool in the Tools panel to select the Ellipse tool. Try drawing ellipses. The Shift key allows you to create perfect circles.

These kinds of random shapes may not win design awards, but they should give you an idea of the flexibility of these shape tools.

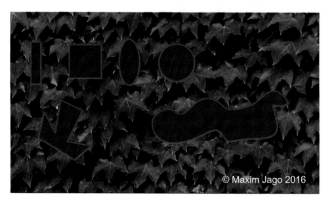
© Maxim Jago 2016

9 Press and hold the Ellipse tool in the Tools panel to select the Pen tool. The Pen tool allows you to adjust any existing shape. You can even click to add control points for more complex shapes. Try changing the existing shapes you have created.

10 Press Command+A (macOS) or Ctrl+A (Windows) and then press Forward Delete (macOS) or Delete (Windows) to make another clean slate.

▶ **Tip:** If the keyboard of your Mac doesn't have a Forward Delete key, press Fn-Delete.

You can also select layers in the Essential Graphics panel and delete them.

11 Experiment with the different shape options. Try overlapping them and using different colors, with different levels of opacity. The layer position for an object in the Essential Graphics panel sets which objects will appear in front, just as tracks do in the Timeline panel.

Adding a graphic

You can add image files to your title designs using common file formats, including vectors (.ai, .eps) and still images (.psd, .png, .jpeg).

Let's try this with an existing graphic.

1 Open the sequence 04 Logo.

This is a simple sequence with space in the graphic for a logo.

2   Select the "Add a logo" title clip in the sequence.

3   In the Essential Graphics panel, just below the layers area in the Edit pane, open the New Layer menu ![icon], and choose From File.

4   Browse to the file logo.ai in the Lessons/Assets/Graphics folder, and click Import.

5   With the Selection tool, drag the logo to position it where you want it in the title. Then adjust the size, opacity, rotation, or scale of the logo.

Making a graphic roll and crawl

You can make rolling text for opening and closing credits and crawling text for items such as headline bulletins. In fact, you can apply a roll or crawl to any graphic, not just to text.

Continued working with the 04 Logo sequence.

1   Use the Program Monitor Settings menu to deselect the transparency grid. For this exercise, you'll use the background of the Timeline to provide a black backdrop for a rolling end credit.

2 Position the Timeline panel playhead at the end of the sequence, just after the clip on the Video 1 track, so the Program Monitor displays a black screen.

Using the Type tool, click in the Program Monitor to add point text.

3 Type some text in the box that you would like to use as a credit roll, pressing Return (macOS) or Enter (Windows) after each line.

For the purposes of this exercise, don't worry about the precise words.

Type enough text to more than fill the screen vertically.

You'll find it difficult to add many lines of text without constantly repositioning it. It's often easier to have the text ready in a document so you can copy and paste it into Premiere Pro.

4 Use the Essential Graphics panel to format your text as desired.

5 Deselect the text layer (by clicking the background of the Program Monitor with the Selection tool).

This reveals the graphic properties in the Essential Graphics panel, including the option to create a title roll.

6 In the Essential Graphics panel, select the check box to add a Roll effect.

When you enable the Roll effect, a scroll bar appears in the Program Monitor. Now, when you play through the clip, it will roll on and off the screen.

You have the following options:

- **Start Offscreen:** This sets whether the credit begins off-screen and rolls in or whether it begins where you placed it in the Program Monitor.

- **End Offscreen:** This indicates whether the credits roll completely off the screen or end on the screen.

- **Preroll:** This sets the amount of time to delay before the first words appear on-screen.

- **Postroll:** This specifies the amount of time to play after the roll or crawl ends.

- **Ease In:** This specifies the number of frames at the beginning to gradually increase the speed of the roll or crawl from zero to full speed.

- **Ease Out:** This specifies the number of frames to slow down the speed of the roll or crawl at the end.

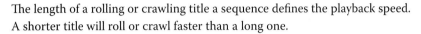

The length of a rolling or crawling title a sequence defines the playback speed. A shorter title will roll or crawl faster than a long one.

7   Play through your rolling title.

Working with template titles

The Browse pane of the Essential Graphics panel includes many prebuilt template graphics you can add to your sequences and modify to suit your projects. Many of the presets include motion, so they are referred to as Motion Graphics templates.

Motion Graphics templates can be created in Premiere Pro or Adobe After Effects, and there are differences in the templates each application creates:

- Motion Graphics templates created in Premiere Pro produce graphics that are completely editable.

- Motion Graphics templates created in After Effects can include more advanced design and complex animation. They also have restricted controls, set by the original designer to give flexibility while retaining the original core design.

The templates are divided into categories. Drag a template directly into any sequence to add it.

Some templates may have a yellow font warning symbol ⬚. This indicates that the template uses a font not currently installed on your system.

If you use one of these templates, the Resolve Fonts dialog box will appear.

If a missing font is available from the Adobe Fonts service, the option to automatically download the font will be available in this dialog box.

Select the box for the missing font, and click Sync Fonts, and it will be automatically installed, ready for use in this title.

Creating a custom template graphic

You can add your own custom graphics to the Browse pane of the Essential Graphics panel. Simply select a graphic clip in a sequence, open the Graphics menu on the main menu bar, and choose Export As Motion Graphics Template.

Choose a name for the new template graphic and choose a location from the Destination menu. You can add keywords to make the template easier to locate when searching by entering each keyword and pressing Return/Enter.

When you're happy with the settings, click OK.

If you chose a local drive location, you can import the file on any computer by choosing Graphics > Install Motion Graphics Template or by clicking the button in the lower-right corner of the Essential Graphics panel Browse pane.

This makes it easy to share your custom template titles or store them in a collection for future use.

Introducing captions

There are two kinds of captions you might encounter when producing video for television broadcast and beyond: closed and open.

Closed captions are embedded in the video stream and can be enabled or disabled by the viewer. Open captions are always on-screen.

Premiere Pro allows you to work with either kind of caption in the same way. In fact, you can even convert one kind of caption file to another.

Closed caption files have a more limited range of colors and design features than open captions. This is because they are actually generated and displayed by the viewer's TV, set-top box, or online viewing software, so controls are in place before you begin.

The following workflow describes working with closed captions, but open captions work the same way, as you'll see in "Using open captions" later in this lesson.

Using closed captions

Video content can be enjoyed by more people when it is accessible. It's a requirement for most broadcast television stations to add closed-captioning information that can be decoded by television sets. Visible captions are inserted into a video file and travel through supported formats to specific playback devices.

Adding closed-captioning information is relatively easy as long as you have captions that have been properly prepared. Caption files are often generated with software tools and there are multiple competing systems available.

Here's how to add captions to an existing sequence:

1   Keeping the current project open, choose File > Open Project. Browse to the Lesson 15 folder, and open Lesson 15_02.prproj.

2   Save the project as **15_02 Working.prproj**.

> /MEDIA/Lessons/Lesson 15/Lesson 15_02 Working.prproj

3   If it's not displayed in the Timeline panel already, open the sequence NFCC_PSA.

4   Choose File > Import, and navigate to the Lessons/Assets/Closed Captions folder. Import the file NFCC_PSA.scc (.scc, .mcc, .xml, and .stl formats are supported).

The caption file is added to the bin as if it were a video clip, with a frame rate and duration.

5   Edit the closed captions clip to a track above all the clips in your sequence. In this case, use the V2 track.

6   Open the Settings menu ![icon] in the Program Monitor and choose Closed Captions Display > Enable.

There are different caption types for different television systems. Within each type there are multiple possible streams. For example, one stream might be English language, while another might be French.

By default, the Program Monitor is configured to display Teletext captions, which are the wrong type for this caption file, so nothing will be displayed.

Open the Program Monitor Settings menu again and choose Closed Captions Display > Settings. Choose CEA-608 from the Standard menu for this caption file and click OK.

7   Play the sequence to see the captions.

8   After selecting the caption file in the sequence, you can adjust the captions using the Captions panel (Window > Captions). You can adjust the content, timing, and formatting of captions using the panel's controls.

This public service announcement was produced by RHED Pixel and is provided courtesy of the National Foundation for Credit Counseling.

You can also change the timing by dragging the handles for each caption in the sequence.

Creating new captions

You can create your own closed captions right within Premiere Pro.

1 Choose File > New > Captions. The New Captions dialog box opens.

2 The default settings are based on your current sequence.

3 The Timebase will automatically match your current sequence. Use the Standard menu to choose the type of caption that will be created.

- CEA-608 (also known as Line 21) is the most commonly used standard for analog broadcast.

- CEA-708 is for digital broadcast.

- Teletext is sometimes used in PAL countries.

- Open Subtitling creates regular subtitles that are automatically visible (they don't need to be enabled by the viewer).

- Australian is the Australian OP4T2 closed captioning standard, particular to Australian broadcast television networks.

- Open Captions are always visible and give the maximum flexibility for appearance (popular for social media videos).

For this clip, choose CEA-708.

4 The default option of Service 1 from the Stream menu sets this as the first stream of closed captions. Click OK. The closed caption clip is added to the Project panel.

5 Remove the existing closed caption clip on the Video 2 track by selecting it and pressing Delete (macOS) or Backspace (Windows).

6 Edit the new closed-caption clip onto the Video 2 track. It will be too short for the sequence (by default it's three seconds long). Drag the end of the caption to trim it to the duration you need (usually the full length of the sequence). Next, select the closed-caption clip in the sequence and go to the Captions panel (Window > Captions).

7 Click the Program Monitor Settings menu and choose Closed Captions Display > Settings. In the Standard menu, choose CEA-708 to match the new captions, and click OK.

8 In the Captions panel, click where you see the words *Type Caption Text Here* to edit the caption contents. Enter text that matches the dialogue and/or narration being spoken and then click the + (plus) button at the bottom of the Captions panel to add another caption.

9 Adjust the In and Out durations for each caption in the Captions panel or directly on the Timeline.

10 Use the formatting controls at the top of the Captions panel to adjust the appearance of each caption. The options for these standard closed captions are quite limited (by design). For more information about this, see the next section, "Using open captions."

If the total caption duration increases, you may need to trim the sequence clip longer to display all of its contents.

Using open captions

You can create, import, adjust, and export open captions in the same way that you would work with closed captions.

The difference is that open captions are always visible, so in many ways they function like graphic clips.

The benefit of working with open captions is that the timing is set in the caption file, or caption clip in Premiere Pro, saving you significant time synchronizing the text with the spoken words.

Another similarity with regular graphics is the broader range of appearance options than you'll find with closed captions.

The reason for the limited range of colors and fonts when working with closed captions is that they're actually displayed by the television set or software player. To be certain of the layout and appearance, universal standards have been set.

No such limitations exist for open captions.

You can modify the caption type by right-clicking a caption's clip in the Project panel and choosing Modify > Captions to open the Modify Clip dialog box.

In the Target Stream Format section, you can specify the stream type for this caption clip by choosing Open Captions from the Standard menu.

Because of the additional options available for open captions, you can convert a closed-caption clip to an open caption type, but not the other way around.

Review questions

1   What are the differences between point text and paragraph (or area) text?

2   Why display the title-safe zone?

3   How do you use the Rectangle tool to make a perfect square?

4   How do you apply a stroke or drop shadow?

Review answers

1   You create point text by clicking in the Program Monitor with the Type tool. Its text box expands as you type. When you drag in the Program Monitor with the Type tool, you define a bounding box, and the characters remain within its confines. Changing the box's shape displays more or fewer characters.

2   Some TV sets cut off the edges of the picture. The amount lost varies from set to set. Keeping your text within the title-safe margin ensures that viewers will see all your title. This is less of a problem with newer flat-screen TVs and isn't important for online video, but it's still a good idea to use the title-safe zone to frame your titles.

3   To create a perfect square, hold down the Shift key as you draw using the Rectangle tool. You can create a perfect circle with the Ellipse tool in the same way.

4   To apply a stroke or drop shadow, select the text or object to edit, and enable the Stroke (Outer or Inner) or Shadow options in the Essential Graphics panel.

16 EXPORTING FRAMES, CLIPS, AND SEQUENCES

Lesson overview

In this lesson, you'll learn about the following:

- Choosing the right export options

- Exporting single frames

- Creating movie, image sequence, and audio files

- Using Adobe Media Encoder

- Uploading to social media and Adobe Stock

- Working with edit decision lists

This lesson will take about 90 minutes to complete. Please log in to your account on peachpit.com to download the lesson files for this lesson, or go to the "Getting Started" section at the beginning of this book and follow the instructions under "Accessing the lesson files and Web Edition." Store the files on your computer in a convenient location.

Your Account page is also where you'll find any updates to the lesson files. Look on the Lesson & Update Files tab to access the most current content.

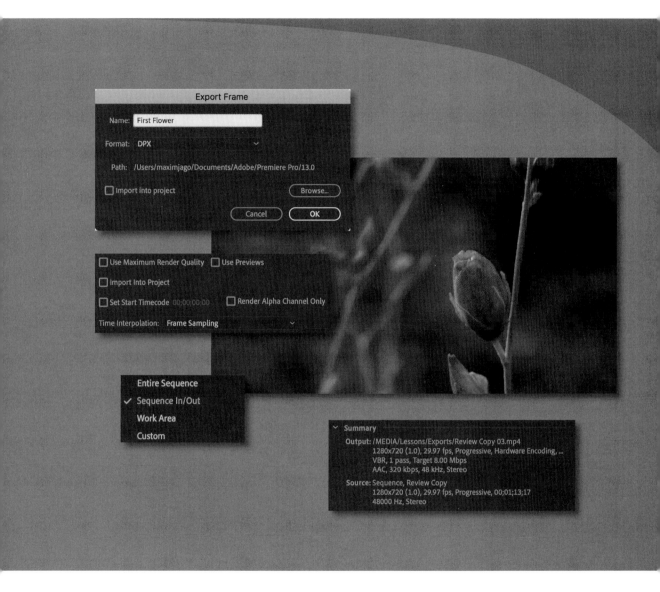

One of the best things about editing video is the feeling you have when you can finally share it with your audience. Adobe Premiere Pro CC offers a wide range of export options. Exporting your project is the final step in the video production process. Adobe Media Encoder offers multiple high-level output formats. Within those formats you have dozens of options and can also export in batches.

Starting the lesson

The most common form of media distribution is via digital files. To create these files, you can use Adobe Media Encoder CC. Adobe Media Encoder is a stand-alone application that handles file exports in batches, so you can export in several formats simultaneously and process in the background while you work in other applications, including Premiere Pro and Adobe After Effects.

Understanding the export options

Whether you've completed a project or you just want to share an in-progress review, you have a number of export options.

- You can export to a file for posting online or create a Digital Cinema Package (DCP) file for theatrical distribution.

- You can export a single frame or a series of frames.

- You can choose audio-only, video-only, or full audio/video output.

- Exported clips or stills can be reimported into the project automatically for easy reuse.

- You can play directly to videotape.

   ● **Note:** Premiere Pro can export clips selected in the Project panel, as well as sequences or ranges within sequences or the Source panel. The content that's selected when you choose File > Export is what Premiere Pro will export.

Beyond choosing an export format, you can set several other parameters.

- You can choose to create files in a similar format and at the same visual quality and data rate as your original media, or you can compress them to a smaller size to make distribution easier.

- You can transcode your media from one format to another to make it easier to exchange with creative collaborators.

- You can customize the frame size, frame rate, data rate, or audio and video compression choices if an existing preset doesn't fit your needs.

- You can apply a color lookup table (LUT) to assign a look; set overlay timecode and other clip text information; add an image overlay; or upload a file directly to social media accounts, an FTP server, or Adobe Stock.

- You can add timecode, name, and image overlays, and apply a video limiter or apply audio normalization, all at the time of exporting the file.

Exporting single frames

While an edit is in progress, you may want to export a still frame to send to a team member or client for review. You might also want to export an image to use as the thumbnail of your video file when you post it to the Internet.

When you export a frame from the Source Monitor, Premiere Pro creates a still image that matches the resolution of the source video file.

When you export a frame from the Program Monitor, Premiere Pro creates a still image that matches the resolution of the sequence.

Let's give it a try.

Note: The music in this project is titled "Tell Somebody," by Alex featuring Admiral-Bob. Licensed under Creative Commons Attribution 3.0.

1   Open Lesson 16.prproj from the Lessons/Lesson 16 folder.

2   Save the project as **Lesson 16 Working.prproj**.

3   Open the sequence Review Copy. Position the Timeline playhead on a frame you want to export.

4   In the Program Monitor, click the Export Frame button ![camera icon] on the lower right.

If you don't see the button, it may be because you've customized the Program Monitor buttons. You might also need to resize the panel. You can also select the Program Monitor or the Timeline panel and press Shift+E (macOS) or Shift+Ctrl+E (Windows) to export a frame.

5   In the Export Frame dialog box, enter a filename.

6   Use the Format menu to choose a still-image format.

   • JPEG, PNG, GIF, and BMP (Windows only) are universally readable. JPEG and PNG files are commonly used in website design.

   • TIFF, Targa, and PNG are suitable for print and animation workflows.

   • DPX is often used for digital cinema or color-grading workflows.

   • OpenEXR is used to store high dynamic range picture information.

Note: If your video format uses non-square pixels, the resulting image file will appear to have a different aspect ratio. This is because still image formats have square pixels. You can use Photoshop to resize the image horizontally and restore the original aspect ratio.

7   Click the Browse button to choose a location to save the new still image. Create a folder named Exports in the Lessons folder, select it, and click Choose.

   Note: In Windows, you can export to the BMP, DPX, GIF, JPEG, OpenEXR, PNG, TGA, and TIFF formats. On a Mac, you can export to the DPX, JPEG, OpenEXR, PNG, TGA, and TIFF formats.

8   Select the Import Into Project option to add the new still image into your current project, and click OK.

Exporting a master copy

Creating a master copy allows you to make a pristine digital copy of your edited project that can be archived for future use. A master copy is a self-contained, fully rendered digital file output of your sequence at the highest resolution and best quality possible. Once it's created, you can use a file of this kind as a separate source to produce other compressed output formats without opening the original project in Premiere Pro.

Choosing the source range

On the lower left of the Export Settings dialog box you'll find the Source Range controls, which you'll use to define the portion of the source clip or sequence to export. You can export the entire sequence, a range defined by setting an In point and an Out point in the sequence, or a custom range set in this dialog box.

You can apply new In and Out points by using the small triangular handles and navigator directly above the menu, by positioning the playhead in this dialog box and clicking the Set In point and Set Out buttons, or by pressing I and O.

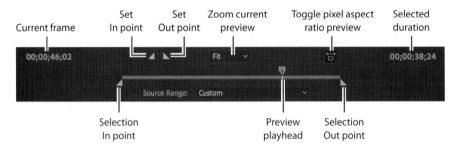

By default, if In and Out points have already been applied, they are used to define the export range.

Matching sequence settings

Ideally, the frame size, frame rate, and codec of a master file will closely match the sequence it's based on. Premiere Pro makes this easy by offering a Match Sequence Settings option when you export.

1 Continue working with the Review Copy sequence.

2 With the sequence selected in the Project panel or open in the Timeline panel, with that panel active, choose File > Export > Media. The Export Settings dialog box opens.

3   You'll learn more about this dialog box later. For now, select the Match
    Sequence Settings check box.

> **Note:** In some cases, the Match Sequence Settings option cannot write an exact match of
> the original camera media. For example, XDCAM EX will write to a high-quality MPEG2 file. In
> most cases, the file written will have an identical format and closely match the data rate of the
> original sources.

☑ Match Sequence Settings

4   The blue text showing the output name is actually a button that opens a Save
    As dialog box. You'll find the same type of text-as-a-button in Adobe Media
    Encoder. Click the output name now.

Output Name: Review Copy.mxf

5   Choose a target location (such as the Exports folder you created earlier), name
    the file **Review Copy 01**, and click Save.

6   Review the Summary information to check that the output format matches the
    sequence settings. In this case, you should be using DNxHD media (as MXF
    files) at 29.97fps. The Summary information is a quick, easy reference that helps
    you avoid minor errors that can have big consequences. If the Source and Out-
    put Summary settings match, it minimizes conversion, which helps maintain
    the quality of the final output.

When exporting a sequence, the sequence itself is the source in the Export dialog box—not the clips inside the sequence, which will have already been conformed to the sequence settings.

```
⌄  Summary
   Output: /MEDIA/Lessons/Exports/Review Copy 01.mxf
           1280x720 (1.0), 29.97 fps, Progressive, 00;01;13;17
           48000 Hz, Stereo, 16 bit

   Source: Sequence, Review Copy
           1280x720 (1.0), 29.97 fps, Progressive, 00;01;13;17
           48000 Hz, Stereo
```

7 Click the Export button to create a media file based on the sequence. Note that DNxHD media files can be viewed and edited in Premiere Pro but cannot (usually) be previewed in macOS or Windows.

Choosing another codec

When you export to a new media file, you can choose the codec that's used. Some camera capture formats (such as the popular H.264 .MP4 files commonly produced by DSLR cameras) are already heavily compressed. Using a higher-quality mastering codec can help to preserve quality.

Note: The settings displayed change depending on the format you choose. Most of the critical options are accessed in the Video and Audio tabs.

Choose your format and presets first, then pick the output, and finally decide whether you'd like to export audio, video, or both.

1 With the same sequence selected, choose File > Export > Media or press Command+M (macOS) or Ctrl+M (Windows).

2 In the Export Settings dialog box, open the Format menu, and choose Quick-Time. In the Preset menu, choose GoPro CineForm YUV 10-bit.

This is a rather specific-sounding preset, but it is just that—a preset, which automatically chooses options from other menus in this dialog box that you can change if you need to.

Note: On the Video tab, you'll also find the option Render At Maximum Depth. When working without GPU acceleration, this can improve the visual quality of your output by using greater precision to generate colors. However, this option can add to the render time.

3 Click the output name (the blue text), and give the file a new name, **Review Copy 02**. Navigate to the same destination you used in the previous exercise and click Save.

Below the Export Settings area is a tabbed group of important settings. Here's an overview of those tabs:

• **Effects:** You can add a number of useful effects and overlays as you output your media (see these options in the next section).

• **Video:** The Video tab allows you to set the frame size, frame rate, field order, and profile. The settings available are based on the preset you chose.

• **Audio:** The Audio tab allows you to adjust the bit rate of the audio and, for some formats, the codec. The default settings are based on the preset you chose.

- **Multiplexer:** These settings specify whether the video and audio will be combined or delivered as separate files. These controls also let you determine whether the file will be optimized for compatibility with a specific device.

- **Captions:** If your sequence has captions, you can specify whether they are ignored, "burned in" (added to the visuals permanently), or exported as a separate file (referred to as a *sidecar* file).

- **Publish:** This tab lets you enter the details of several social media services for your file to be delivered to. You'll learn more about this later in this lesson.

4   Click to select the Video tab near the bottom of the window.

5   In the Video Codec section of the dialog box, choose one of the available video codecs.

Try the GoPro CineForm codec. This produces a high-quality (but reasonably sized) file. Make sure the frame size and frame rate match your source settings. You might need to scroll down or resize the panel to see all the settings.

Note: GoPro CineForm is a professional codec that is supported natively by Adobe Creative Cloud applications. Like all codecs, it will play back only in media applications that support it.

6   Click the Match Source button in the Basic Video Settings area.

Below the Match Source button is a series of output format settings. If the setting is selected, the setting will automatically match the source.

7   Click to select the Audio tab. In the Basic Audio Settings section, make sure 48000 Hz is chosen from the Sample Rate menu and choose 16-bit from the Sample Size menu. Just below that, in the Audio Channel Configuration area, choose Stereo from the Output Channels menu.

8 Click the Export button at the bottom of the dialog box to export the sequence and transcode it to a new media file. Files encoded with the GoPro CineForm codec cannot usually be previewed in macOS or Windows. Import the file into Premiere Pro, to preview and edit it.

The most popular delivery format and codec is an MPEG4 (.mp4) file, using the H.264 codec. If you choose H.264 in the Format menu, you'll find presets for YouTube and Vimeo.

Cropping the source image

Moving to the left side of the Export Settings dialog box, you will find the Source and Output tabs.

Click the Source tab to bring it to the front. The Source tab gives access to cropping controls.

1 Click the Crop The Output Video button  to enable the controls.

You can enter specific settings (in pixels) at the top of the dialog box or drag the handles in the Source preview to crop the image.

2 The Crop Proportions menu has several options to restrict the settings to a particular aspect ratio. Choose 4:3 from the Crop Proportions menu. Now, if you make changes to the crop settings they will be locked to a 4:3 aspect ratio.

3 Click the Output tab to bring it to the front.

The Output tab shows a preview of the video to be encoded. The Source Scaling menu let you choose the way a mismatch between the source aspect ratio and the output settings.

4 Try each of the options in the Source Scaling menu to see the results. The option Change Output Size To Match Source is not available for all export formats. It achieves the same result as clicking the Match Source button on the Video tab in the Export settings.

5 Leave the Source Scaling menu set to Scale To Fit. Switch to the Source tab and click the Crop The Output Video button to disable cropping. Switch back to the Output tab to make sure the image fills the screen.

After making changes on the Source tab or choosing a new output frame size, it's always a good idea to check the Output tab to spot errors such as unwanted letter-boxing or distortion caused by the irregularly shaped pixels used in some video formats.

Working with Adobe Media Encoder CC

Adobe Media Encoder CC is a stand-alone application that can be run independently of or be launched from Premiere Pro. One advantage of using Media Encoder is that you can send an encoding job directly from Premiere Pro and then continue working on your edit as the encoding is processed. If your client asks to see your work before you finish editing, Media Encoder can produce the file in the background without interrupting your flow.

By default, Media Encoder pauses encoding when you play video in Premiere Pro to maximize playback performance. You can change this in the Premiere Pro Playback preferences.

Choosing a file format for export

It can be a challenge to know how to deliver your finished work. Ultimately, choosing delivery formats is a process of planning backward; find out how the file will be presented, and it's usually straightforward to identify the best file type for the purpose. Often, clients will have a delivery specification you must follow, making it easy to select the right options for encoding.

Premiere Pro and Adobe Media Encoder can export to many formats.

● **Note:** If working with a professional mastering format (such as MXF OP1a, DNxHD MXF OP1a, or QuickTime), you can export up to 32 channels of audio where the format allows. The original sequence must be configured to use a multichannel master track with the corresponding number of tracks.

Configuring the export

To export from Premiere Pro to Adobe Media Encoder, you'll need to queue the export. The first step is to use the Export Settings dialog box to make choices about the file you're going to export.

1 Continue working with the Review Copy sequence. Either select the sequence in the Project panel or have it open in the Timeline panel, with that panel active.

2 Choose File > Export > Media, or press Command+M (macOS) or Ctrl+M (Windows).

   It's best to work through the Export Settings dialog box from the top down, starting with the Export Settings area.

Using the formats

Adobe Media Encoder supports many formats. Knowing which setting to use can seem a little overwhelming. Let's take a look at some common scenarios and review which formats are typically used. There are few absolutes, but these should get you close to the correct output. It's a good idea to test your output on a short section of your video before producing a full-length finished file.

- **Encoding for uploading to user-generated video sites:** The H.264 format includes presets for YouTube and Vimeo in widescreen, SD, HD, and 4K. Use these presets as a starting point.

- **Encoding for devices:** Use the H.264 format for current devices (Apple iOS devices, Apple TV, Kindle, Nook, Android, and TiVo), as well as for some generic 3GPP presets; use MPEG4 for older MPEG4-based devices. Be sure to check the manufacturer's specifications on its website.

- **Producing a DCP for theatrical distribution:** Choose the Wraptor DCP and then pick 24 or 25 frames per second. If your sequence is 30 frames per second, choose 24 frames per second for output to a DCP. Settings are limited to ensure compatibility with standard cinema projection systems.

In general, the Premiere Pro presets are proven and will work for your intended purpose. Avoid adjusting settings when using presets designed for devices or optical discs, because changes that seem subtle might make the files unplayable; hardware players have stringent media requirements.

Most Premiere Pro presets are conservative and will deliver good results with the default settings, so you probably won't improve the quality by making adjustments.

3   Choose H.264 from the Format menu. This is a popular choice for files you'll upload to online video websites.

4   In the Preset menu, choose Vimeo 720p HD.

These settings match the frame size and frame rate of the sequence. The codec and data rate match the requirements for the Vimeo.com website.

5   Click the output name (the blue text) and give the file a new name, **Review Copy 03**. Save it to the same destination you selected in the previous exercise.

6   Check the Summary information text to verify your choices.

Export effects

You have the option to apply several effects, add information overlays, and make automated adjustments to the output file.

Here's an overview:

- **Lumetri Look/LUT:** Choose from a list of built-in Lumetri looks or browse to your own, allowing you to quickly apply a nuanced adjustment to the appearance of your output file.

- **SDR Conform:** If your sequence is high dynamic range, you can produce a standard dynamic range version.

- **Image Overlay:** Add a graphic, like a company logo or network "bug," and position it on-screen. The graphic will be incorporated into the image.

- **Name Overlay:** Add a text overlay to the image. This is particularly useful as a simple watermark to protect your content or as a way of marking different versions.

- **Timecode Overlay:** Display timecode for your finished video file, making it easy for viewers without specialized editing software to note reference times for commenting purposes.

- **Time Tuner:** Specify a new duration or playback speed, up to + /−10%, achieved by applying subtle adjustments to periods of low action where the soundtrack is silent. Results vary depending on the media you are working with, so test different speeds to compare the end result. A continuous music soundtrack is likely to interfere with the results.

- **Video Limiter:** While it's usually best to get your video levels right in the sequence, you can apply a limiter here too, just in case.

- **Loudness Normalization:** Use the Loudness scale to normalize audio levels in your output file. As with video levels, it's best to get this right in the sequence, but it can be a helpful extra security to know your levels will be limited during export.

Queuing the export

When you're ready to create your media file, you have a few more options to consider. These are found in the lower-right portion of the Export Settings dialog box.

- **Use Maximum Render Quality:** Consider enabling this setting when scaling from larger image sizes to smaller image sizes. This option requires more RAM and can slow down the output. This option is usually not needed except when working without GPU acceleration (in software-only mode), when scaling the image down and seeking the highest quality possible.

- **Use Previews:** When you render effects, preview files are produced that look like your original footage combined with the effects. If you enable this option, the preview files will be used as the source for the new export. This can save a significant amount of time that would otherwise be spent rendering the effects again. The result might be lower quality, depending on the sequence preview files format (see Lesson 2, "Setting Up a Project").

- **Import Into Project:** This option automatically imports the newly created media file into your current project so you can check it or use it as source footage.

- **Set Start Timecode:** This allows you to specify a new file start timecode. This is particularly useful if you are working in a broadcast environment where a specific timecode start may be a delivery requirement.

- **Render Alpha Channel Only:** Some post-production workflows require a separate grayscale file representing the alpha channel (the channel that defines opacity). This option produces just that file.

- **Time Interpolation:** If your exported file will have a different frame rate than your sequence, this menu lets you specify the way the frame-rate change is rendered. The options are the same as those that apply when changing clip play-back speed in a sequence.

- **Metadata:** Click this button to open the Metadata Export panel. You can specify a wide range of settings, including information about copyright, creator, and rights management. You can even embed useful information such as markers, script, and speech transcription data for advanced delivery options. In some cases, you may prefer to set the Metadata Export Options setting to None, removing all metadata.

- **Queue:** Click the Queue button to send the file to Adobe Media Encoder, which will open automatically, allowing you to continue working in Premiere Pro while the export takes place.

- **Export:** Select this option to export directly from the Export Settings dialog box rather than sending the file to the Adobe Media Encoder queue. This is a simpler workflow and usually a faster export, but you won't be able to edit in Premiere Pro until the export is complete.

Click the Queue button to send the file to Adobe Media Encoder, which starts up automatically.

Media Encoder will not begin encoding automatically. To begin encoding, click the Start Queue button ▶ in the upper-right corner.

Looking at additional options in Adobe Media Encoder

Using Adobe Media Encoder brings a number of benefits. Although it involves a few extra steps beyond simply clicking the Export button in the Export Settings panel of Premiere Pro, the extra options are worth it.

Here are some of the most useful features you'll find in Adobe Media Encoder:

- **Add files for encoding:** You can add files to Adobe Media Encoder by choosing File > Add Source. You can even drag and drop files into it from Finder (macOS) or Windows Explorer (Windows). There's a Media Browser panel too, which you can use to locate select items, just as you would in Premiere Pro.

- **Import Premiere Pro sequences directly:** You can choose File > Add Premiere Pro Sequence to select a Premiere Pro project file and choose sequences to encode (without ever launching Premiere Pro).

- **Render After Effects compositions directly:** You can import and encode compositions from Adobe After Effects by choosing File > Add After Effects Composition. Once again, you don't need to open Adobe After Effects.

- **Use a watch folder:** If you'd like to automate some encoding tasks, you can create watch folders by choosing File > Add Watch Folder and then assigning a preset to that watch folder. Watch folders exist in Finder (macOS) or Windows Explorer (Windows) like any other folder. If Adobe Media Encoder is running, media files placed into the folder are automatically encoded to the format specified in the preset.

> **Note:** Adobe Media Encoder does not have to be used from Premiere Pro. You can launch Adobe Media Encoder on its own and browse Premiere Pro projects to choose items to transcode directly.

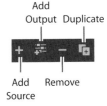

- **Modify a queue:** You can add, duplicate, or remove any encoding tasks using buttons at the top of the list.

- **Start encoding:** You can set the queue to start automatically in the Media Encoder preferences. Alternatively, click the Start Queue button  to start encoding. Files in the queue are encoded one after another. You can add files to the queue after encoding has begun. You can even add files to the queue directly from Premiere Pro while encoding is taking place.

- **Modify settings:** Once the encoding tasks are loaded into the queue, changing settings is easy; click the item's Format or Preset entry (in blue text), and the Export Settings dialog box appears.

When encoding has completed, you can quit Media Encoder.

Uploading to social media

Return to Premiere Pro, make sure the Timeline panel is active, and choose File > Export > Media to display the Export Settings dialog box.

Click the Publish tab to bring it to the front.

The Publish settings allow you to upload exported videos to your Creative Cloud Files folder, Adobe Stock, Adobe Behance, Facebook, an FTP server (FTP is a standard way to transmit files to a remote file server), Twitter, Vimeo, and YouTube when the encoding is complete.

Each platform will have its own delivery standards, though in many cases you can choose a high-quality master file and let the platform do the work of producing more highly compressed alternative versions from that file. Adobe Stock, for example, supports a range of video formats and codecs. If you produce a UHD (3840 x 2160) file, the rest can be handled by the server.

Social media platforms are increasingly important media distribution outlets, and Adobe is closely involved in developing new technologies and workflows to make it easier to share your creative work and maximize audience engagement. Click Cancel to close the Export Settings dialog box.

Exchanging with other editing applications

Collaboration is often essential in video post-production. Premiere Pro can both read and write project files and footage files that are compatible with many of the top editing and color-grading tools on the market. This makes it straightforward to share creative work, even if you and your collaborators are using different editing systems.

Premiere Pro supports EDLs, OMF, AAF, ALE, and XML import and export.

If you're collaborating with an Avid Media Composer editor, you can use AAF as an intermediary, allowing the exchange of clip information, edited sequences, and a limited number of effects.

If you're collaborating with an Apple Final Cut Pro editor, you can use XML as an intermediary in a similar way.

It's easy to export an AAF or XML file from Premiere Pro. Just select a sequence you want to export and either choose File > Export > AAF or choose File > Export > Final Cut Pro XML.

For more information about best practices when sharing creative work between applications, see the online help.

Exporting to OMF

Open Media Framework (OMF) is an industry standard file type for exchanging audio information between systems (typically for audio mixing). When you export an OMF file, the typical method is to create a single file that contains all the audio files included in a sequence, arranged as clips on audio tracks. When the OMF file is opened by a compatible application, the clips will appear on tracks, timed and edited, just as they do in the Premiere Pro sequence.

Here's how to create an OMF file:

1 With a sequence selected, choose File > Export > OMF.

2 In the OMF Export Settings dialog box, enter a name for the file in the OMF Title field.

3 Check that the Sample Rate and Bits Per Sample settings match your footage; 48000 Hz and 16 bits are the most common settings.

4 From the Files menu, choose one of the following:

- **Embed Audio:** This option exports an OMF file that contains the project metadata and all the audio files for the selected sequence.

- **Separate Audio:** This option separates all audio files, including stereo audio, into new multiple mono audio files, which are exported into a folder called omfiMediaFiles. This is a popular standard for audio engineers who are using advanced audio mixing workflows.

5 If you're using the Separate Audio option, choose between the AIFF and Broadcast Wave formats. Both are high quality, but check with the system you need to exchange with. AIFF files tend to be the most compatible.

6 Using the Render menu, choose either Copy Complete Audio Files or Trim Audio Files (to reduce the file size). You can specify that handles (extra frames) be added to give you some flexibility when modifying the clips.

7 Click OK to generate the OMF file.

8 Choose a destination, and click Save. You can target your lesson folder for now.

When the export is complete, the OMF Export Information dialog box appears. It displays information about the export and reports any errors that were encountered. Click OK to close the dialog box.

⬤ **Note:** All OMF files have 2GB file limit—if you're working on a long sequence, you may need to separate it into two or more sections and export them separately.

Working with edit decision lists

An edit decision list (EDL) is a simple text document with a list of instructions for automating editing tasks. The formatting follows standards that allow the EDL to be read by a number of different systems.

It's rare for an EDL to be requested. Still, you can export a sequence to the most commonly used type, CMX3600.

To create a CMX3600 EDL, select a sequence in the Project panel or open it in the Timeline panel, and choose File > Export > EDL.

The requirements for EDLs are usually particular, so be sure to request the EDL specifications before creating one. Thankfully, EDL files are usually small, so if you are unsure of the settings you should choose, you can quickly produce several alternative versions to see which works best.

Final practice

Congratulations! You have now learned enough about Adobe Premiere Pro to import media; organize projects; create sequences; add, modify, and remove effects; mix audio; work with graphics and titles; and output to share your work with the world.

Now that you have completed this book, you may want to practice a little. To make this easier, the media files for a few productions have been combined in a single project file so you can explore the techniques you have learned.

These media files can be used only for personal practice and are not licensed for any form of distribution, including YouTube or any other online distribution, so please *do not upload* any of the clips or the results of any editing work you do with them. They are not for sharing with the public; they are just for you to practice with privately.

The Final Practice.prproj project file, in the MEDIA folder, contains original clips for a few productions.

- **360 Media:** A short excerpt from an introduction to a 360 Video feature film. Use this media to experiment with the playback controls for 360 Video.

- **Andrea Sweeney NYC:** This is a short road-movie diary piece. Use the voice-over as a guide to practice combining 4K and HD footage in a single timeline. Experiment with panning and scanning in the 4K footage if you choose to use HD sequence settings.

- **Bike Race Multi-Camera:** This is simple multicamera footage. Experiment with live editing on a multicamera project.

- **Boston Snow:** This is a mixture of shots of Boston Common filmed in three resolutions. Use this media to experiment with Scale To Frame Size, Set To Frame Size, and keyframe controls to scale shots. Try using the Warp Stabilizer effect to lock one of the high-resolution clips and then scale up the clip and create a pan from one side to the other.

- **City Views:** This is a series of shots from the air and on land. Use these to experiment with image stabilization, color adjustment, and visual effects.

- **Desert:** Use the diverse colors to try color correction tools and combine the footage with music to produce a montage.

- **Jolie's Garden:** This consists of atmospheric tableaux shot at 96fps, set to play back at 24fps, filmed for a new feature film social media marketing campaign. Use these clips to experiment with the Lumetri Color panel looks and speed change effects.

- **Laura in the Snow:** This is a spec commercial shot at 96fps, set to play back at 24fps. Use this footage to practice color correction and grading adjustments. Experiment with ramping slow motion and masking both the video and the effects you apply.

- **Music:** Use these music clips to practice creating an audio mix and editing visuals to music.

- **Music Video Multi-Camera:** This is a music video shoot. Practice multi-camera editing skills with this media. For more information, see Lesson 18, "Multicamera Editing," which is integrated into ebook and Web Edition versions of this book. Purchasers of the print edition can download Lesson 18 from peachpit.com along with the lesson files. See "Getting Started" in the opening pages of this book for instructions.

- **She:** This is a series of stylized, mostly slow-motion clips that will be useful for experimenting with speed changes and visual effects.

- **TAS:** This is footage from a short film, *The Ancestor Simulation*. Use this footage to try color grading and, as the footage is in two aspect ratios, mixing and matching the shots.

- **Theft Unexpected:** This is footage from an award-winning short film directed and edited by the author. Use this footage to experiment with trimming, and practice adjusting timing in simple dialogue to achieve different comic and dramatic results.

Review questions

1 What's an easy way to export digital video if you want to create a self-contained file that closely matches the original quality of your sequence preview settings?

2 What Internet-ready export options are available in Adobe Media Encoder?

3 What encoding format should you use when exporting to most mobile devices?

4 Must you wait for Adobe Media Encoder to finish processing its queue before working on a new Premiere Pro project?

Review answers

1 Use the Match Sequence Settings option in the Export dialog box.

2 This varies by platform, but both macOS and Windows include H.264.

3 H.264 is the encoding format used when exporting to most mobile devices.

4 No. Adobe Media Encoder is a stand-alone application. You can work in other applications or even start a new Premiere Pro project while the render queue is processed.

GLOSSARY

Throughout this book, several terms will be used that relate to video and audio technology and to nonlinear post-production in particular. You may already be familiar with some of these terms, but there are several that may be new to you if you are learning to edit for the first time.

The following terms will make more sense as you explore the lessons in this book. Still, you may find it useful to bookmark this page and return to the list from time to time to make sure you are clear about the language used in the exercises.

- **Aspect ratio:** This describes the shape of an image. 1:1 is square. Most video is 16:9. Regardless of the size of the screen or the resolution of an image, the frame will have a particular aspect ratio.

- **Bin:** Bins look and work very much like a folder in the Finder (macOS) or Explorer (Windows). However, they exist only inside the Premiere Pro project file you are working on and contain only *clips*.

- **Clip:** This is a link (or shortcut) to a media file (which might be video, a graphic, audio, or any other kind of media). Clips look and behave as if they were the thing they link to, with information that relates to the media file, such as image size and frame rate (fps).

- **Codec:** This is short for *coder/decoder*. This is a way to store information (like video and audio) as a smaller file. Like shorthand writing, this takes less space but requires more effort to write and, later, to read. Most video is recorded using a codec to reduce the file size, with the exception of camera systems that record data as raw media with no processing applied.

- **Compression:** This is usually used in one of two ways: 1) a way to reduce the size of video and audio files by storing the information using a *codec*, which normally produces a file that is smaller than the original uncompressed file; 2) a way to reduce the difference between the loudest and quietest parts of sound. This allows the overall sound level to seem louder.

- **Cut:** In a sequence, a cut is the moment one clip ends and another begins. The term comes from celluloid film editing, where the film is literally cut. A cut is technically a form of *transition* and is the most common kind.

- **Effect:** This is a way to modify the appearance of images or the quality of sound. Effects are used to change the shape of an image, to make visuals brighter or darker, to animate the position of images on the screen, to make audio louder or quieter, or to apply any number of other adjustments.

- **Export:** When your clips are combined in a *sequence*, you will then export to share the creative work with the world in the form of a new media file. When you export, you choose the format, codec, and settings for the file that will be created.

- **Footage:** Originally a film term used to indicate recording duration because film is measured in feet, this now refers to any original video material and is usually described in hours and minutes.

- **Format:** Sometimes this refers to a file type (.avi, .mov, etc.), but more commonly it refers to the specific frame size (image size), frame shape, pixel shape, and sometimes frames per second.

- **Frame:** This means one whole image. Video is made up of a series of frames that play fast enough to appear to be a continuous image. The number of frames playing per second is called the *frame rate* and is often measured in frames per second (fps).

- **Import:** When you bring a media file into a Premiere Pro project, nothing is really moved into the project file. Instead, shortcuts are created that contain information about the media, and it's those shortcuts that you combine when editing.

- **Media:** This is your original content. This could be video files, graphics, photos, animation, music, voice-over, or audio special effects (like a sword clash or explosion).

- **Metadata:** Metadata is information about information. There are many forms of metadata, but they always include information about something. For example, metadata associated with a video file might include the camera system used to record it or the name of the camera operator.

- **Pixel:** This is a single dot, or point of light. Pixels have color settings (sometimes called *values*) that are often (but not always) measured as a combination of red, green, and blue color.

- **Project:** This is the container for all of your clips and sequences. A project is stored as a file that stores all your creative work.

- **Sequence:** This is a series of clips, combined in a particular order, often in multiple layers. Most of the creative work you will perform in Premiere Pro will be on sequences and on the clips in sequences.

- **Timecode:** This is a system for defining a particular moment in time in a piece of recorded media in terms of hours, minutes, seconds, and frames. Professional video recording systems always record timecode for every frame, and this is the primary system used to record time when working in a nonlinear editing system.

- **Transition:** In a sequence, when one clip ends and another begins, the transition between the two is most commonly a *cut*. However, there are many transition effects available to add visual interest or enhance storytelling. A dip to black, for example, usually tells the viewer some time has passed.

INDEX

audio channels
  choosing, 95–97
  explanation of, 96, 244
  interpretation tips, 97
  setting number of, 243
Audio Clip Mixer, 15, 242, 263–265
audio effects, 270, 282–289, 291–293, 299
  Loudness Radar effect, 291–293
  Notch effect, 287–289
  Parametric Equalizer effect, 283–287
  See also video effects
Audio Gain dialog box, 255
Audio Master setting, 46
audio meters, 244–245
audio noise reduction, 274, 275, 276–278, 289–291
Audio Plug-in Manager, 287
Audio Track Mixer, 242, 291–292
Audio workspace, 241–243
Audition, Adobe, 8, 9, 257–258, 289–291
Auto Bezier interpolation, 228, 319
Auto Gain option, 279
Auto Save feature, 20, 38–39
Avid Media Composer, 443

B

background noise removal, 289–291
backups, file, 20–21
Balance control, 265
Basic 3D effect, 234–235
Bass effect, 270
bevel effects, 231–233
Bezier interpolation, 228, 319
bins, 5, 80–88
  creating new, 80–81
  customizing, 86–88
  filtering content in, 77–78
  managing media in, 81
  metadata displayed for, 86–88
  opening multiple, 88

origin of term, 78
Project panel and, 64, 82
renaming clips in, 85–86
Search bin creation, 84
view options for, 82–84
See also Project panel
bit depth, 45
Black & White effect, 303, 355
blend modes, 378
  alpha channels and, 383
  combining tracks using, 381–382
  tip for browsing through, 382
  video effects and, 307
Brightness & Contrast effect, 313, 359
broadcast-safe colors, 413
bumpers, 396
Button Editor, 94, 119, 241, 287, 426

C

captions, 423–426
  closed, 423–426
  creating new, 425–426
  open, 426
Captions panel, 424, 425–426
capture format setting, 35–36
capturing media
  from DV and HDV cameras, 36
  from third-party hardware, 36
  from videotape, 69
Center Align Text button, 406
chain icon, 189, 190
Change Clip Speed option, 184
channels
  alpha, 375–376, 378
  audio, 95–97, 243, 244
chapter marker, 142
Character Animator, 8
chromakey effects, 383–388
Cinespace 100 effect, 311
Clamp Signal option, 344
Clarity options, 280–281
clip markers, 145
Clip Name effect, 326

Clip Speed/Duration dialog box, 189–190
clipboard, 155
clips
  closing, 90
  conforming, 41, 113
  deleting, 74, 157
  disabling, 157–158
  dragging, 133, 135, 153
  finding, 76–80
  handles of, 165–166
  importing, 61
  label colors for, 84–85
  linking and unlinking, 152
  loading, 105
  locating on drives, 82
  markers added to, 145
  masking, 388–391
  master, 310–313
  media files vs., 52, 86
  merging, 97–98
  moving, 152–155
  nudging, 153–154
  organizing, 74–88
  origin of term, 4, 28
  playback speed of, 89, 184, 186–192
  playing, 89–92
  previewing, 60–61
  rearranging, 154–155
  removing, 155–157
  renaming, 85–86
  replacing, 192–194
  repositioning, 219–221
  resizing, 224–227
  rotating, 222–223
  selecting, 106–108, 149–151, 180
  splitting, 151–152
  subclips created from, 109–110
  volume adjustments, 261–265
closed captions, 423–426
CMX3600 EDLs, 444
codecs, 43, 434–436
collaboration, 443
color balance. *See* white balance

The fastest, easiest, most comprehensive way to learn
Adobe Creative Cloud

Classroom in a Book®, the best-selling series of hands-on software training books, helps you learn the features of Adobe software quickly and easily.

The **Classroom in a Book** series offers what no other book or training program does—an official training series from Adobe Systems, developed with the support of Adobe product experts.

**To see a complete list of our Classroom in a Book titles covering the 2019 release of Adobe Creative Cloud go to:
www.adobepress.com/cc2019**

Adobe Photoshop CC Classroom in a Book (2019 release)
ISBN: 9780135261781

Adobe Illustrator CC Classroom in a Book (2019 release)
ISBN: 9780135262160

Adobe InDesign CC Classroom in a Book (2019 release)
ISBN: 9780135262153

Adobe Dreamweaver CC Classroom in a Book (2019 release)
ISBN: 9780135262146

Adobe Premiere Pro CC Classroom in a Book (2019 release)
ISBN: 9780135298893

Adobe Dimension CC Classroom in a Book (2019 release)
ISBN: 9780134863542

Adobe Audition CC Classroom in a Book, Second edition
ISBN: 9780135228326

Adobe After Effects CC Classroom in a Book (2019 release)
ISBN: 9780135298640

Adobe Animate CC Classroom in a Book (2019 release)
ISBN: 9780135298886

Adobe Lightroom CC Classroom in a Book (2019 release)
ISBN: 9780135298657

Adobe Photoshop Elements Classroom in a Book (2019 release)
ISBN: 9780135298657

Adobe**Press**